Chapter 338 - Birth

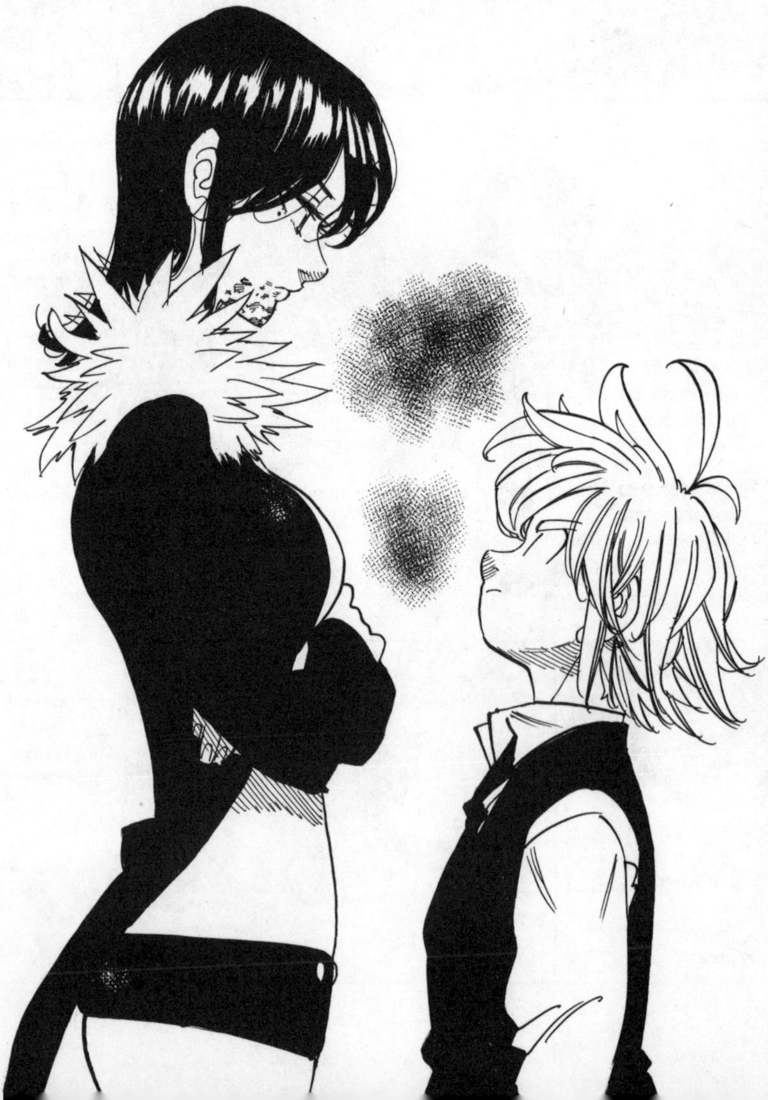

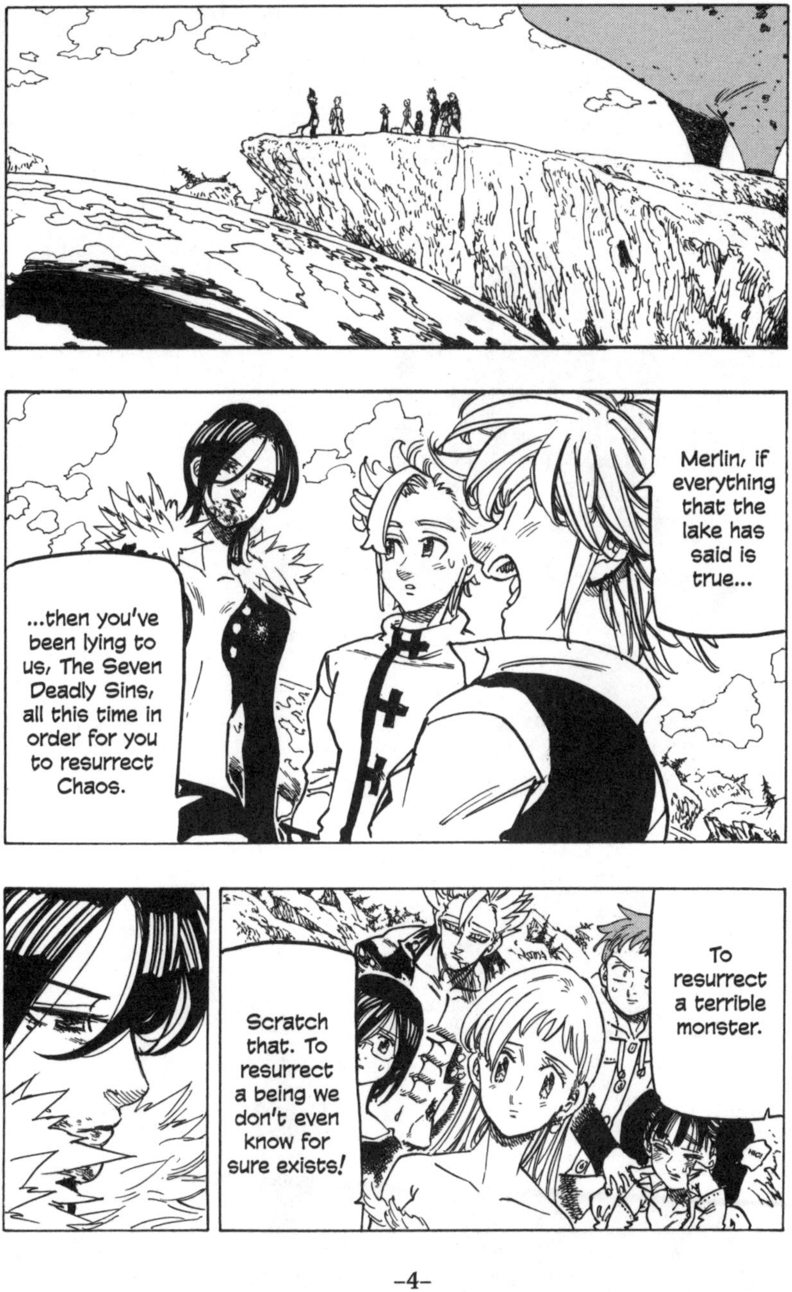
Merlin, if everything that the lake has said is true...
...then you've been lying to us, The Seven Deadly Sins, all this time in order for you to resurrect Chaos.
To resurrect a terrible monster.
HIC!
Scratch that. To resurrect a being we don't even know for sure exists!

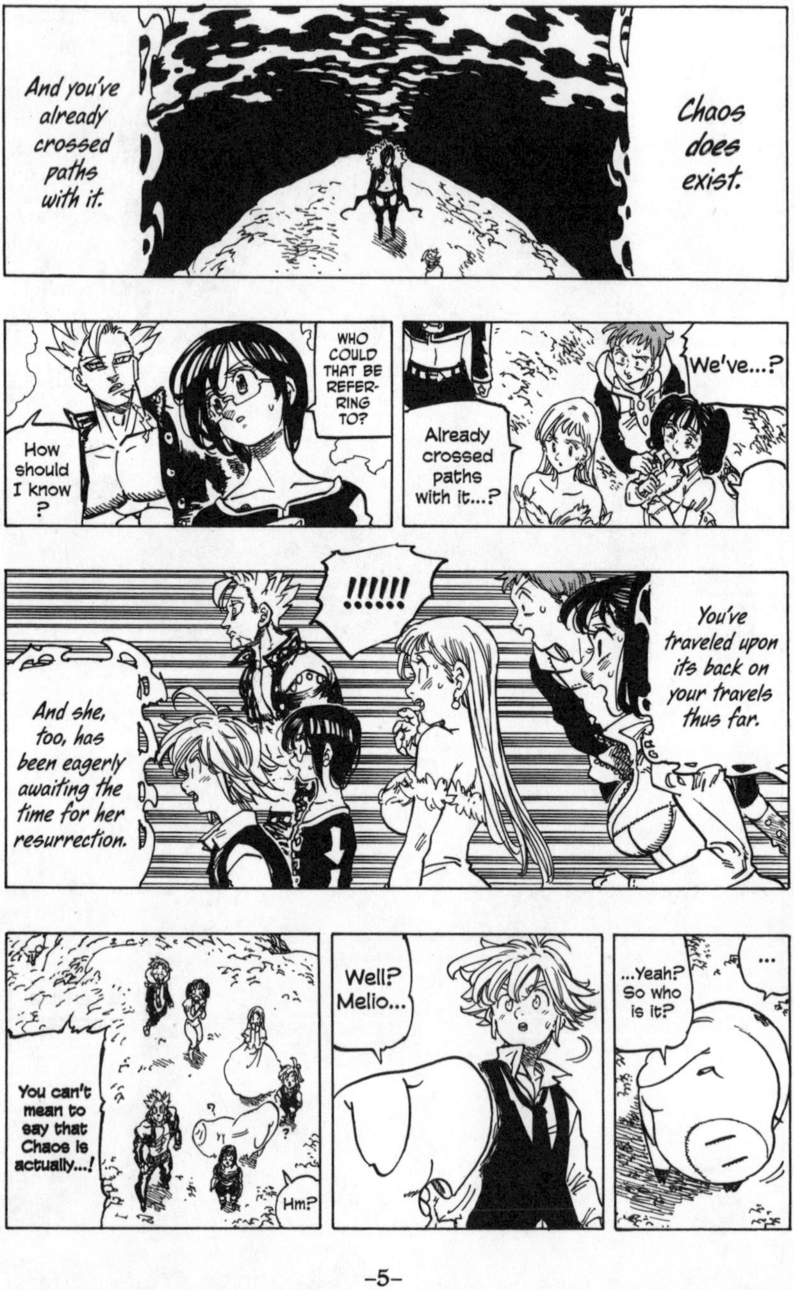
Chaos does exist.
And you've already crossed paths with it.
We've...?
Already crossed paths with it...?
WHO COULD THAT BE REFERRING TO?
How should I know?
You've traveled upon its back on your travels thus far.
!!!!!!
And she, too, has been eagerly awaiting the time for her resurrection.
...
...Yeah? So who is it?
Well? Melio...
You can't mean to say that Chaos is actually...!
Hm?

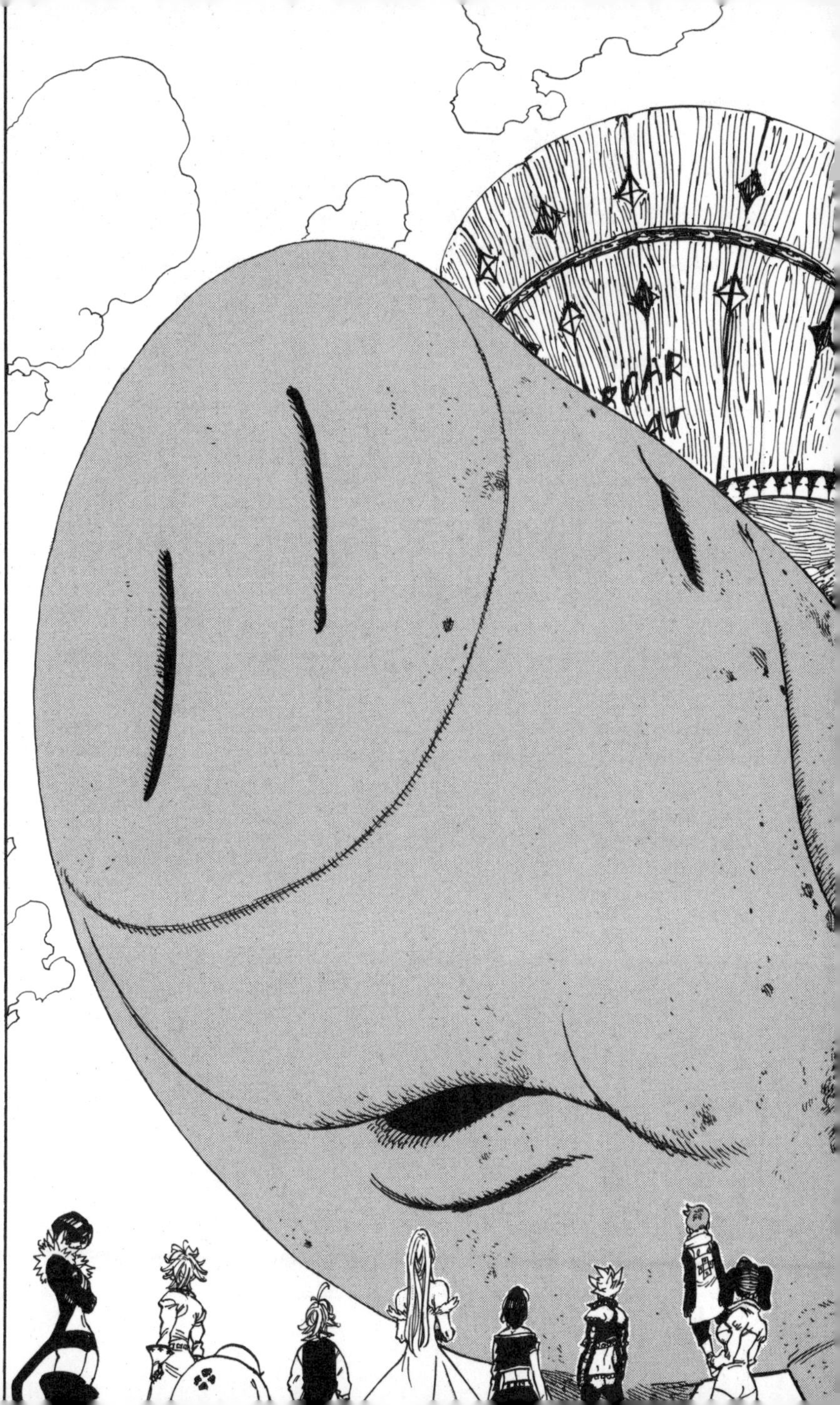
BOAR

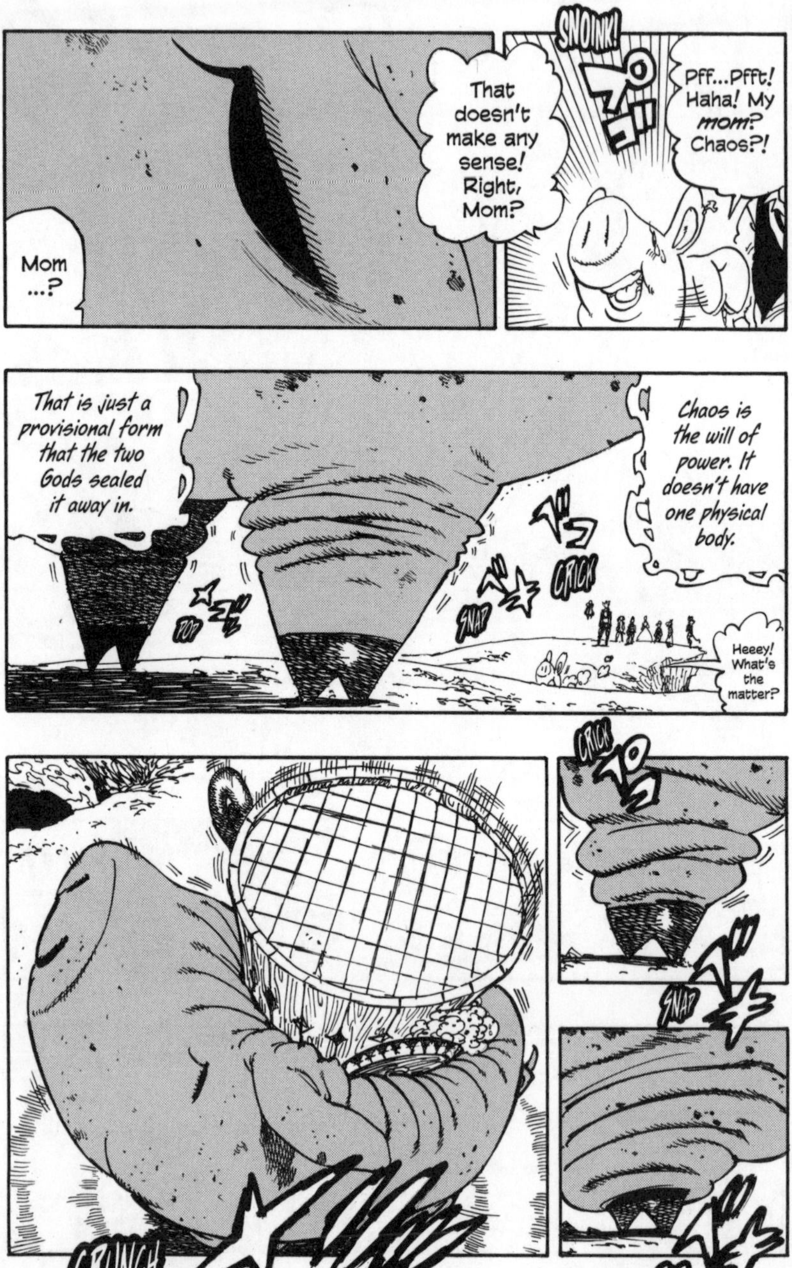
SNOINK!
Pff...Pfft! Haha! My *mom*? Chaos?!
That doesn't make any sense! Right, Mom?
Mom ...?
Chaos is the will of power. It doesn't have one physical body.
CRICK
SNAP
Heeey! What's the matter?
That is just a provisional form that the two Gods sealed it away in.
POP
CRICK
SNAP
POP
CRUNCH

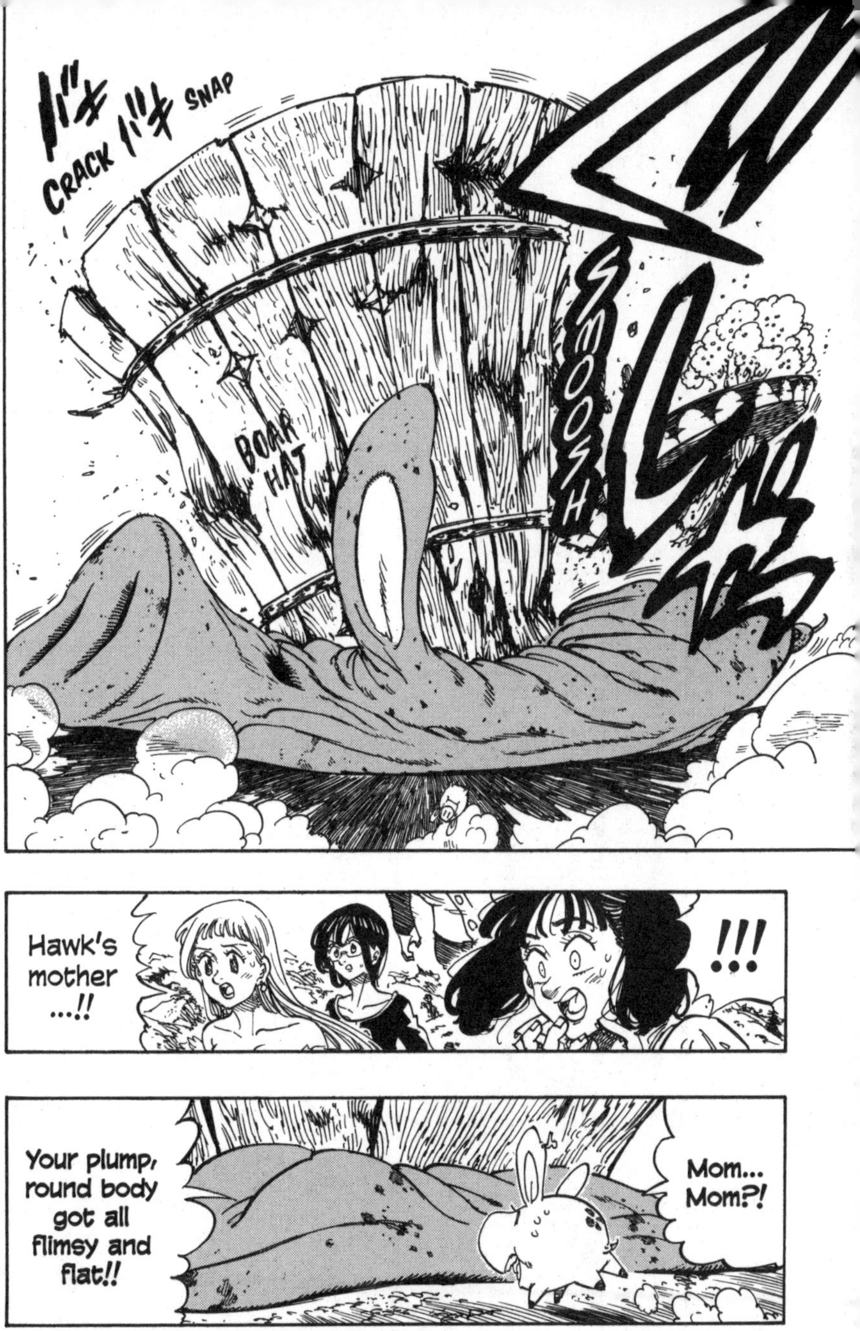
SWOOSH
バキ
CRACK
バキ
SNAP
BOAR HAT
!!!
Hawk's mother ...!!
Mom... Mom?!
Your plump, round body got all flimsy and flat!!

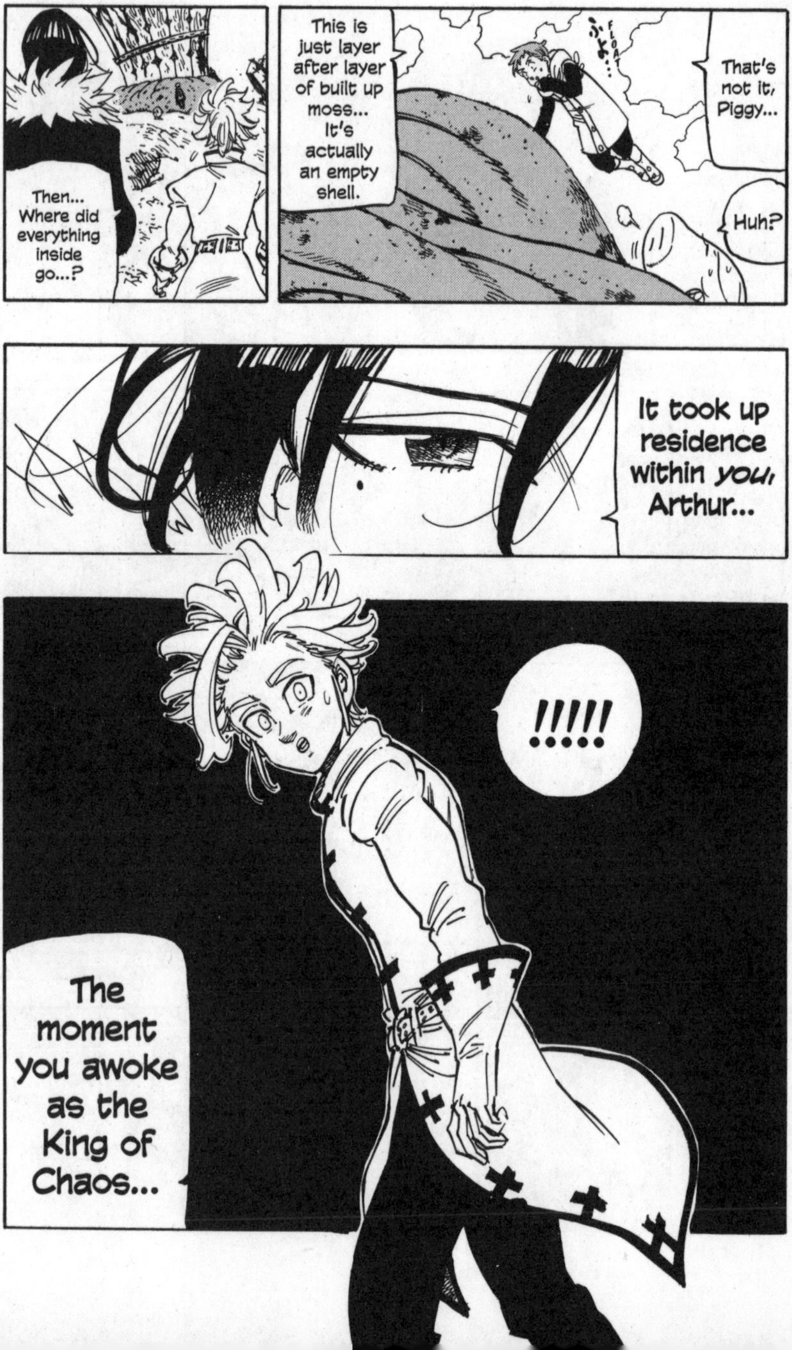

That's not it, Piggy...
Huh?
ふよ… FLOAT
This is just layer after layer of built up moss... It's actually an empty shell.
Then... Where did everything inside go...?
It took up residence within *you*, Arthur...
!!!!!
The moment you awoke as the King of Chaos...

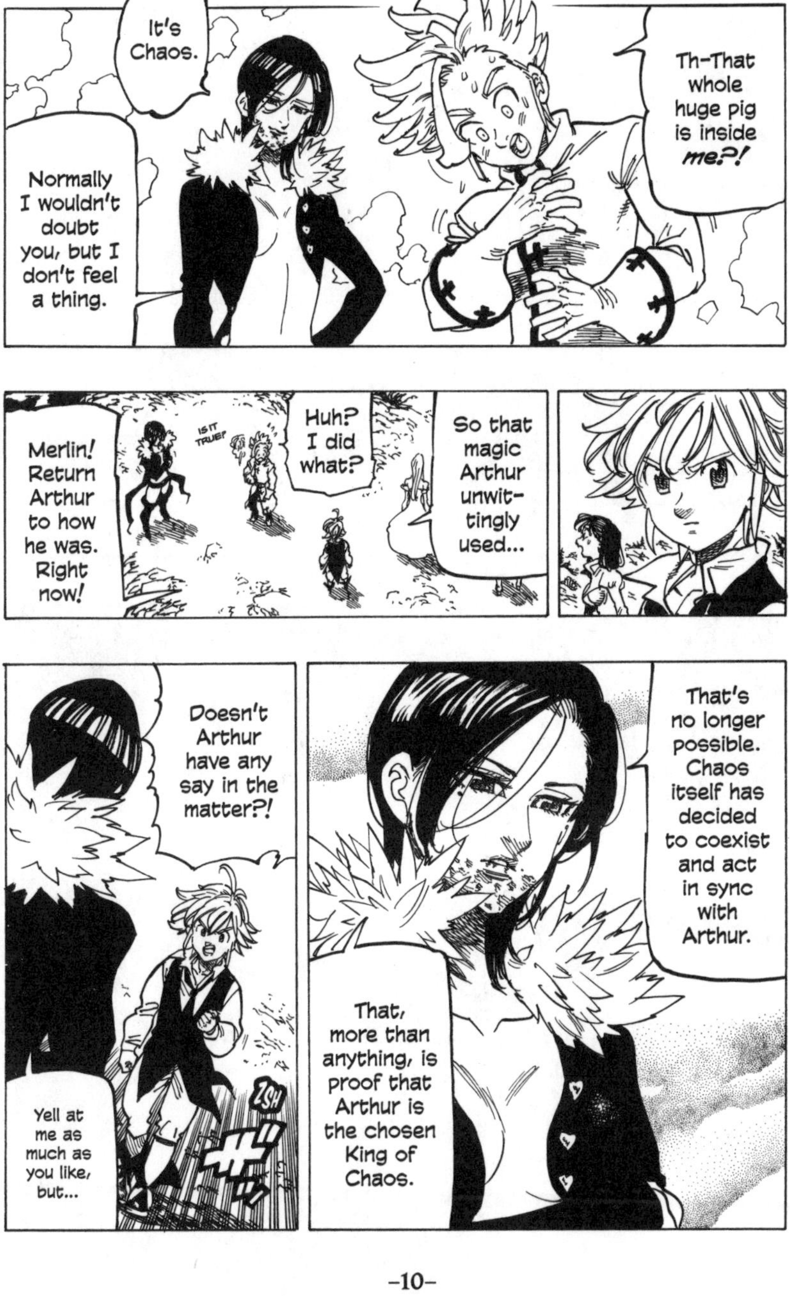
Th-That whole huge pig is inside *me?!*
It's Chaos.
Normally I wouldn't doubt you, but I don't feel a thing.
So that magic Arthur unwittingly used...
Huh? I did what?
IS IT TRUE?
Merlin! Return Arthur to how he was. Right now!
That's no longer possible. Chaos itself has decided to coexist and act in sync with Arthur.
That, more than anything, is proof that Arthur is the chosen King of Chaos.
Doesn't Arthur have any say in the matter?!
ZSH
Yell at me as much as you like, but...

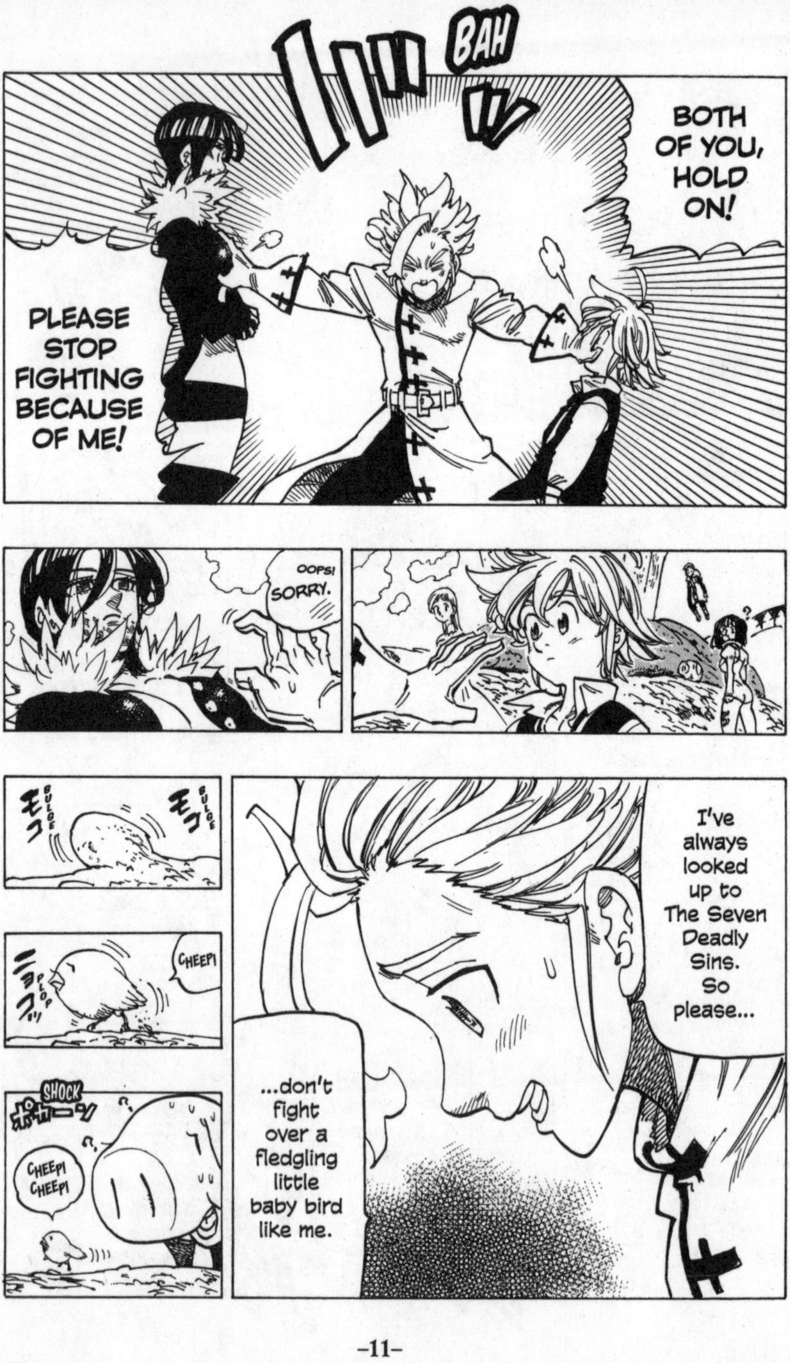

BAH
BOTH OF YOU, HOLD ON!
PLEASE STOP FIGHTING BECAUSE OF ME!
OOPS! SORRY.
I've always looked up to The Seven Deadly Sins. So please...
...don't fight over a fledgling little baby bird like me.
BULGE
BULGE
CHEEP!
PLOP
SHOCK
CHEEP! CHEEP!

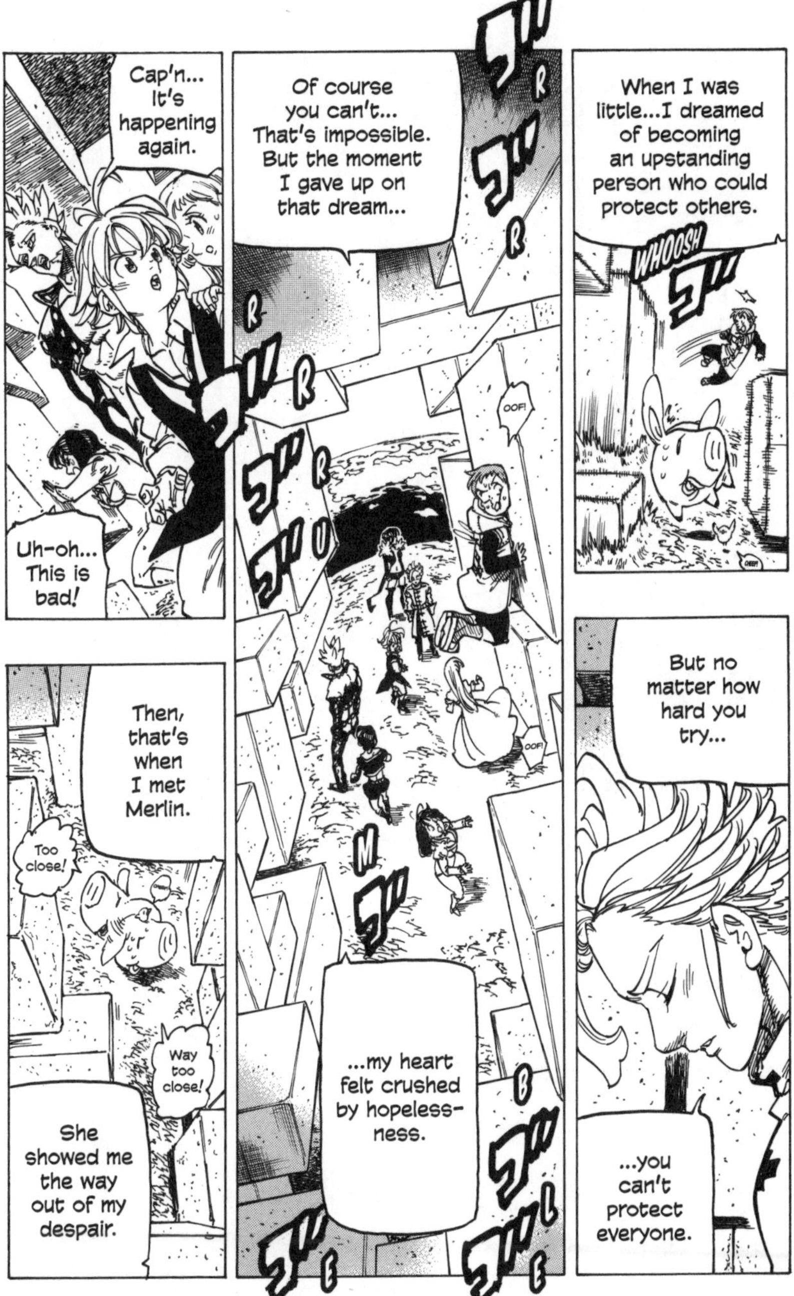
When I was little...I dreamed of becoming an upstanding person who could protect others.
WHOOSH
But no matter how hard you try...
...you can't protect everyone.
Of course you can't... That's impossible. But the moment I gave up on that dream...
OOF!
OOF!
...my heart felt crushed by hopeless-ness.
Cap'n... It's happening again.
Uh-oh... This is bad!
Then, that's when I met Merlin.
Too close!
Way too close!
She showed me the way out of my despair.

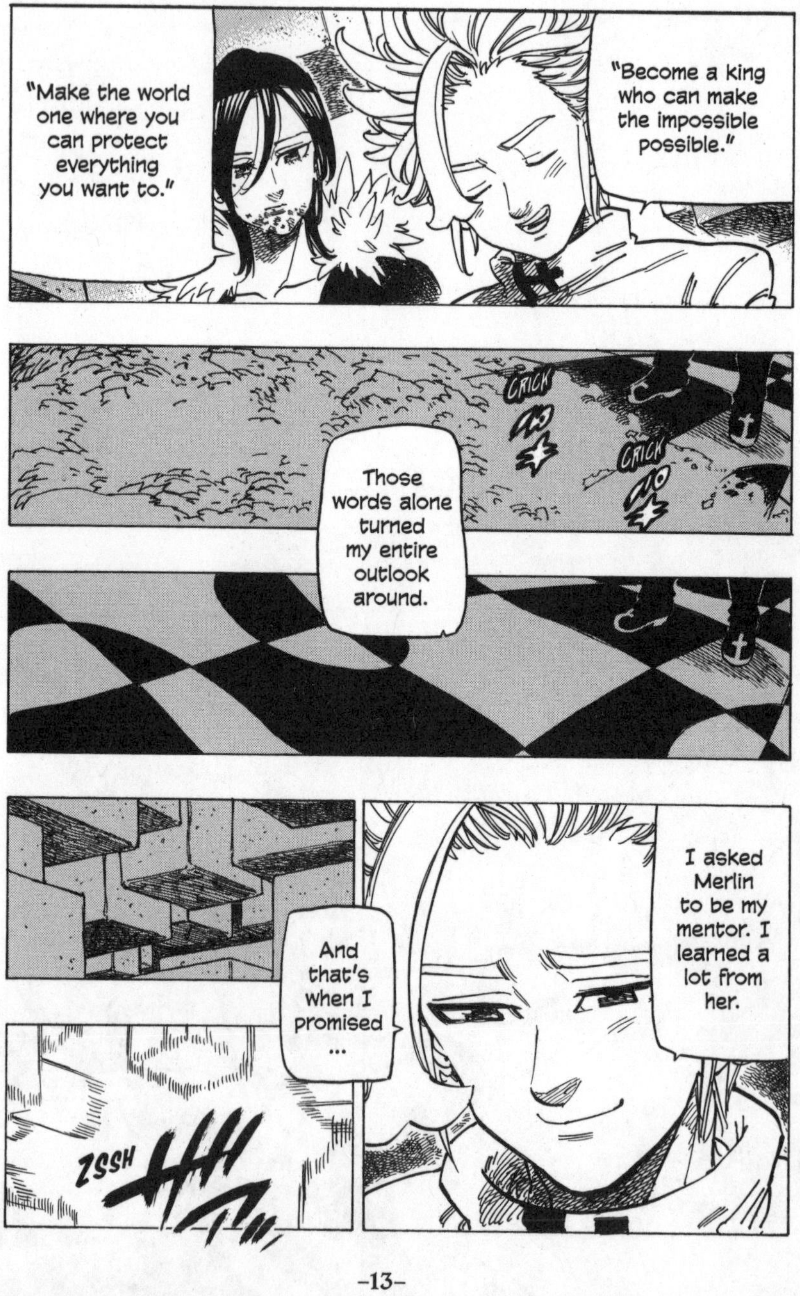
"Become a king who can make the impossible possible."
"Make the world one where you can protect everything you want to."
CRICK
CRICK
Those words alone turned my entire outlook around.
I asked Merlin to be my mentor. I learned a lot from her.
And that's when I promised ...

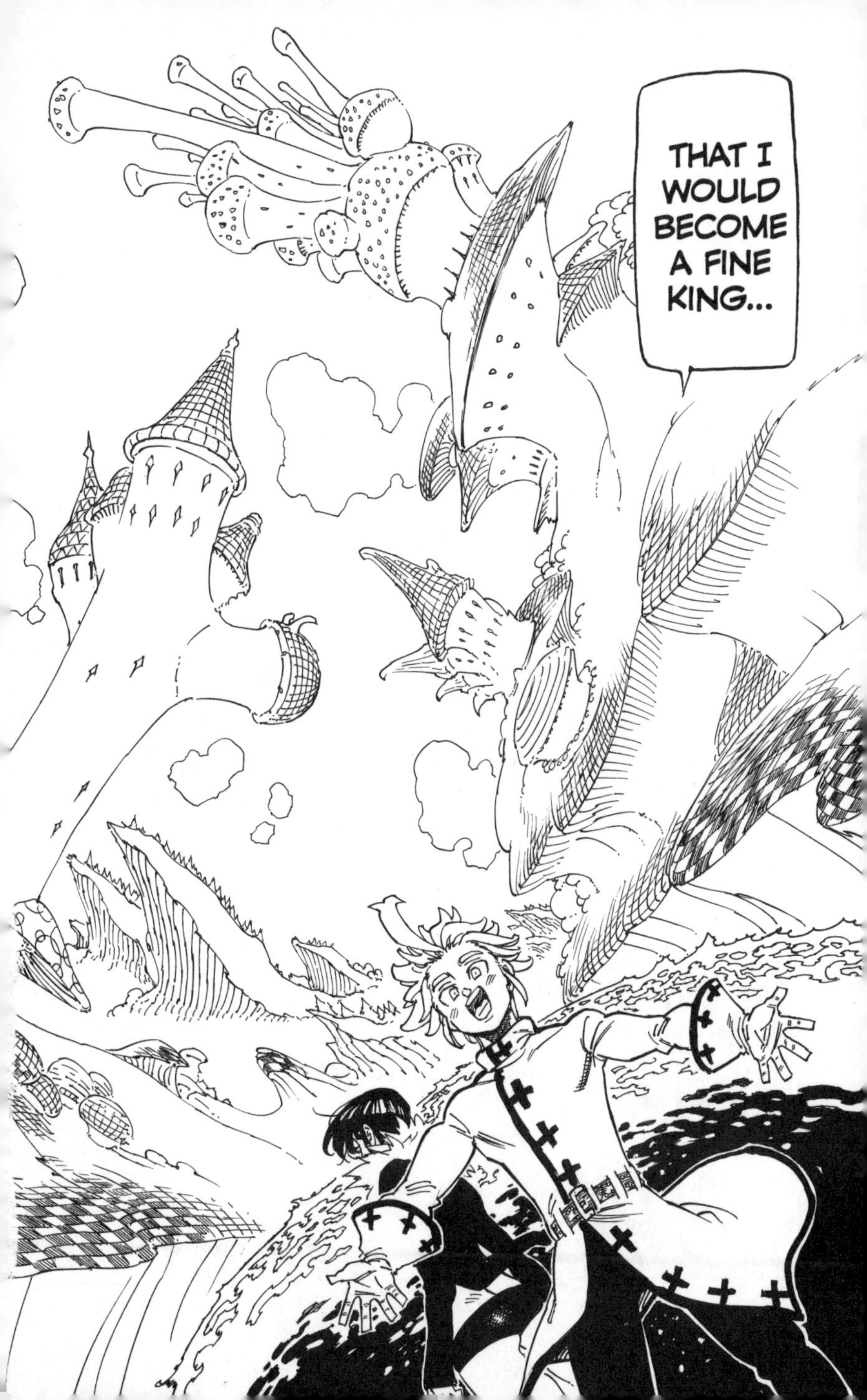
THAT I WOULD BECOME A FINE KING...

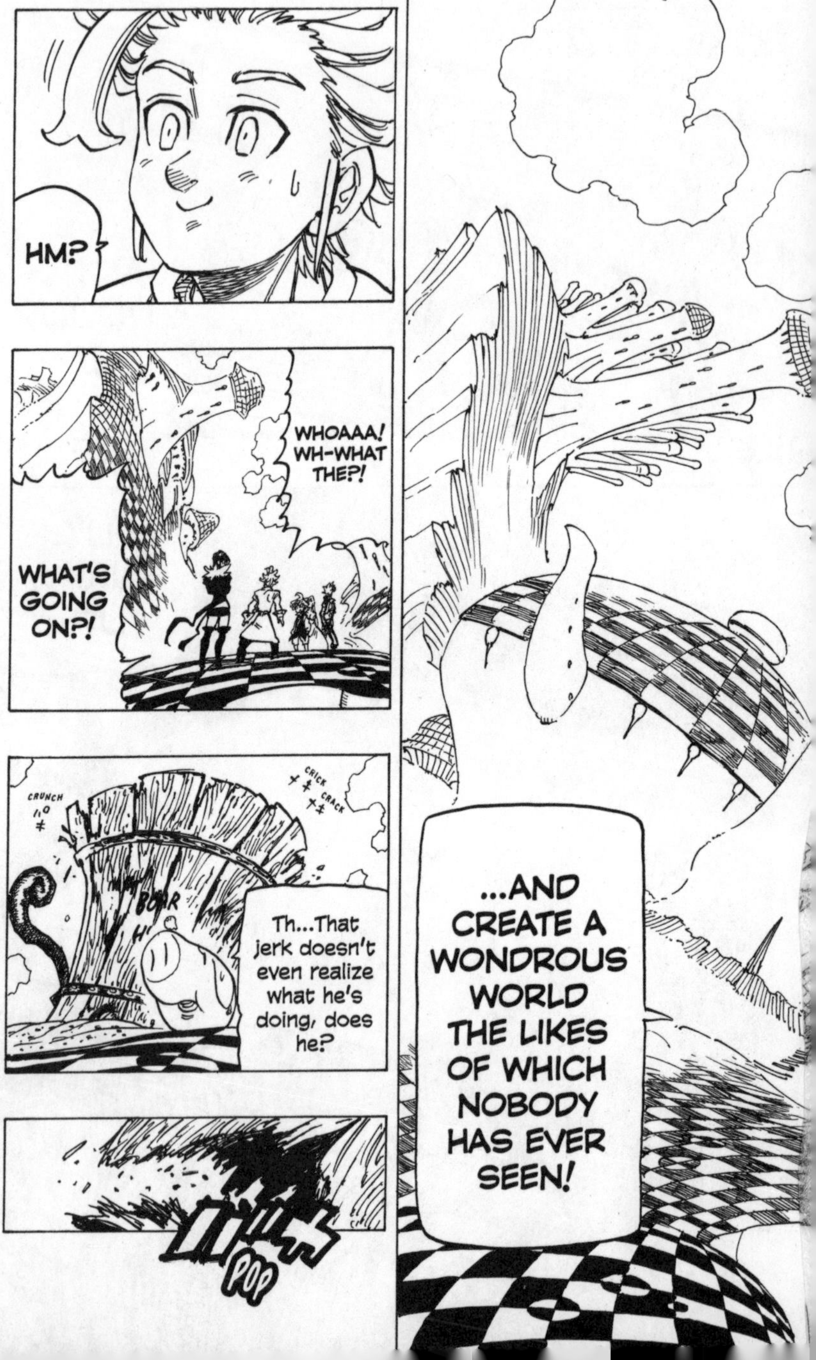
...AND CREATE A WONDROUS WORLD THE LIKES OF WHICH NOBODY HAS EVER SEEN!
HM?
WHOAAA! WH-WHAT THE?!
WHAT'S GOING ON?!
CRICK
CRACK
CRUNCH
Th...That jerk doesn't even realize what he's doing, does he?
POP

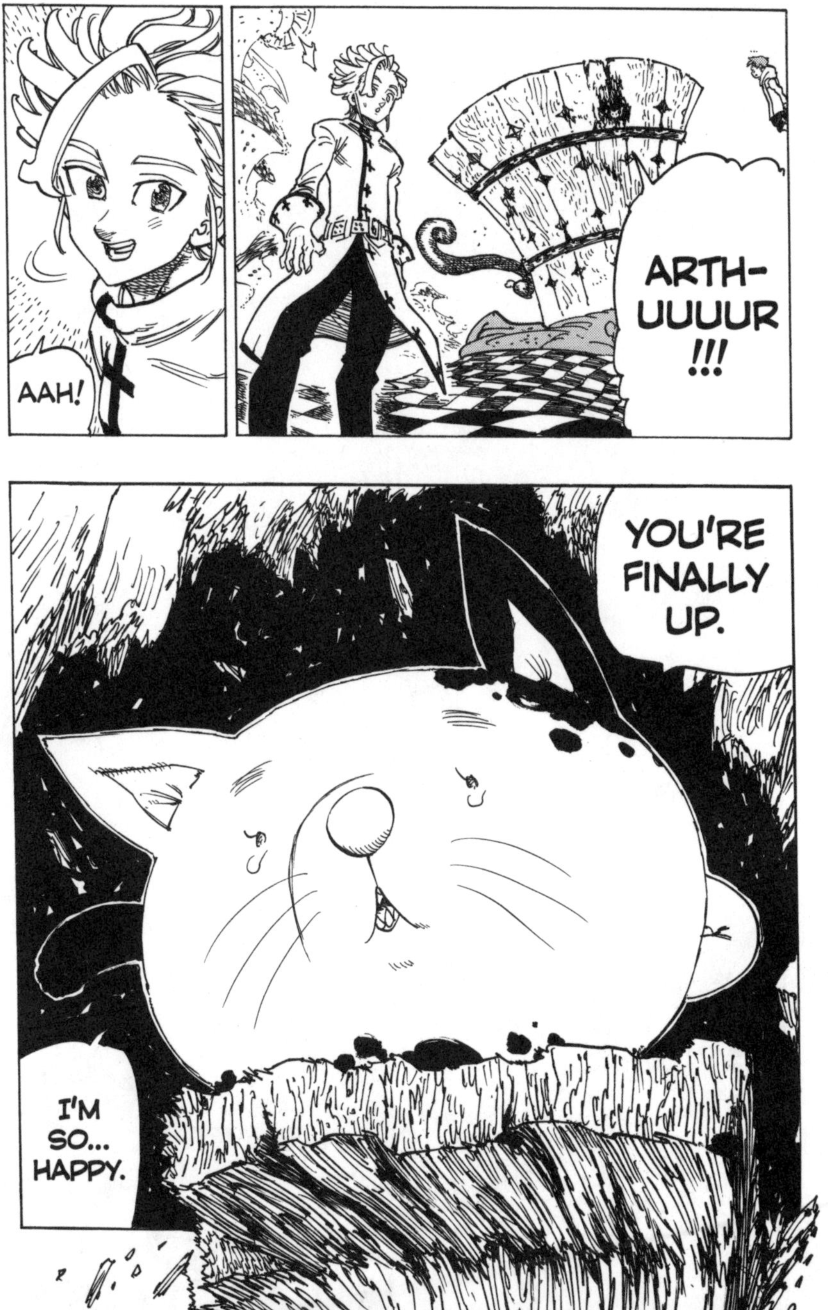
ARTH-UUUUR!!!
AAH!
YOU'RE FINALLY UP.
I'M SO... HAPPY.

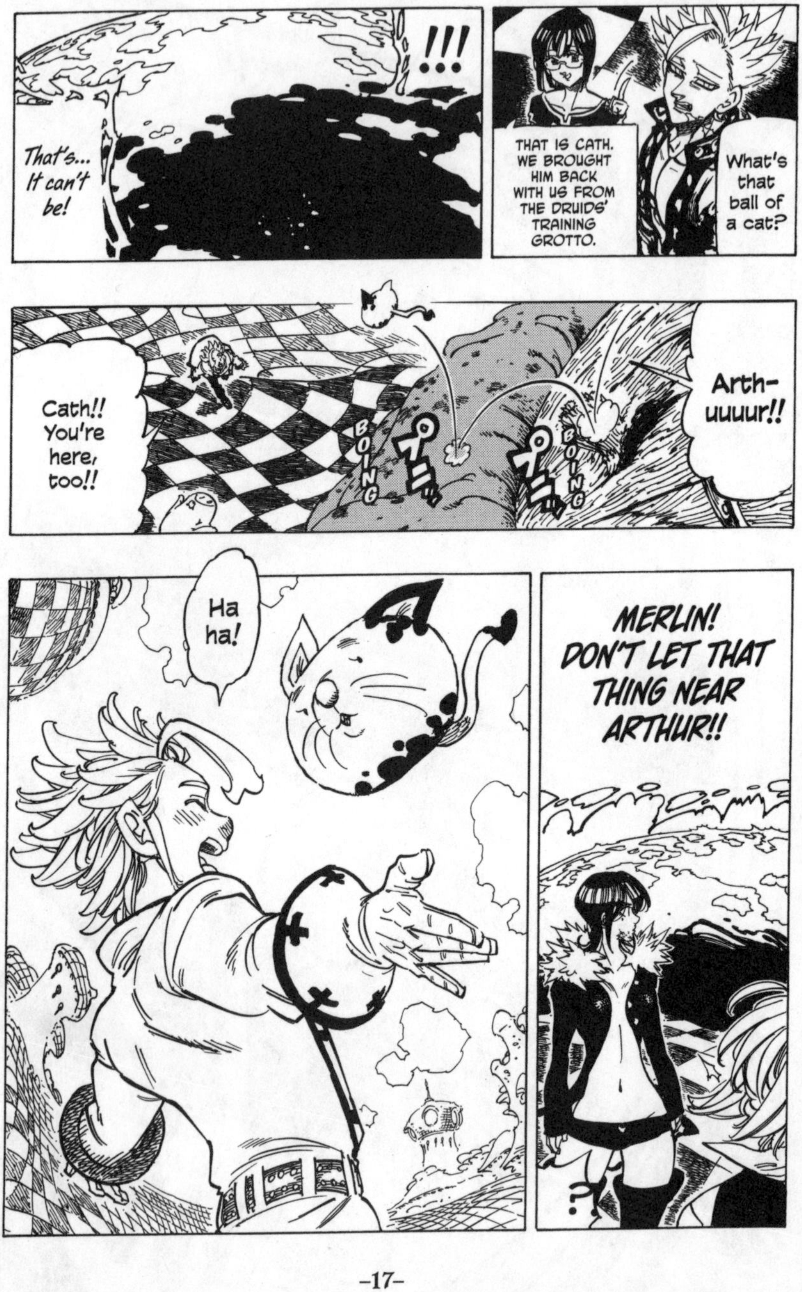
What's that ball of a cat?
THAT IS CATH. WE BROUGHT HIM BACK WITH US FROM THE DRUIDS' TRAINING GROTTO.
!!!
That's... It can't be!
Arth-uuuur!!
BOING
BOING
Cath!! You're here, too!!
MERLIN! DON'T LET THAT THING NEAR ARTHUR!!
?
Ha ha!

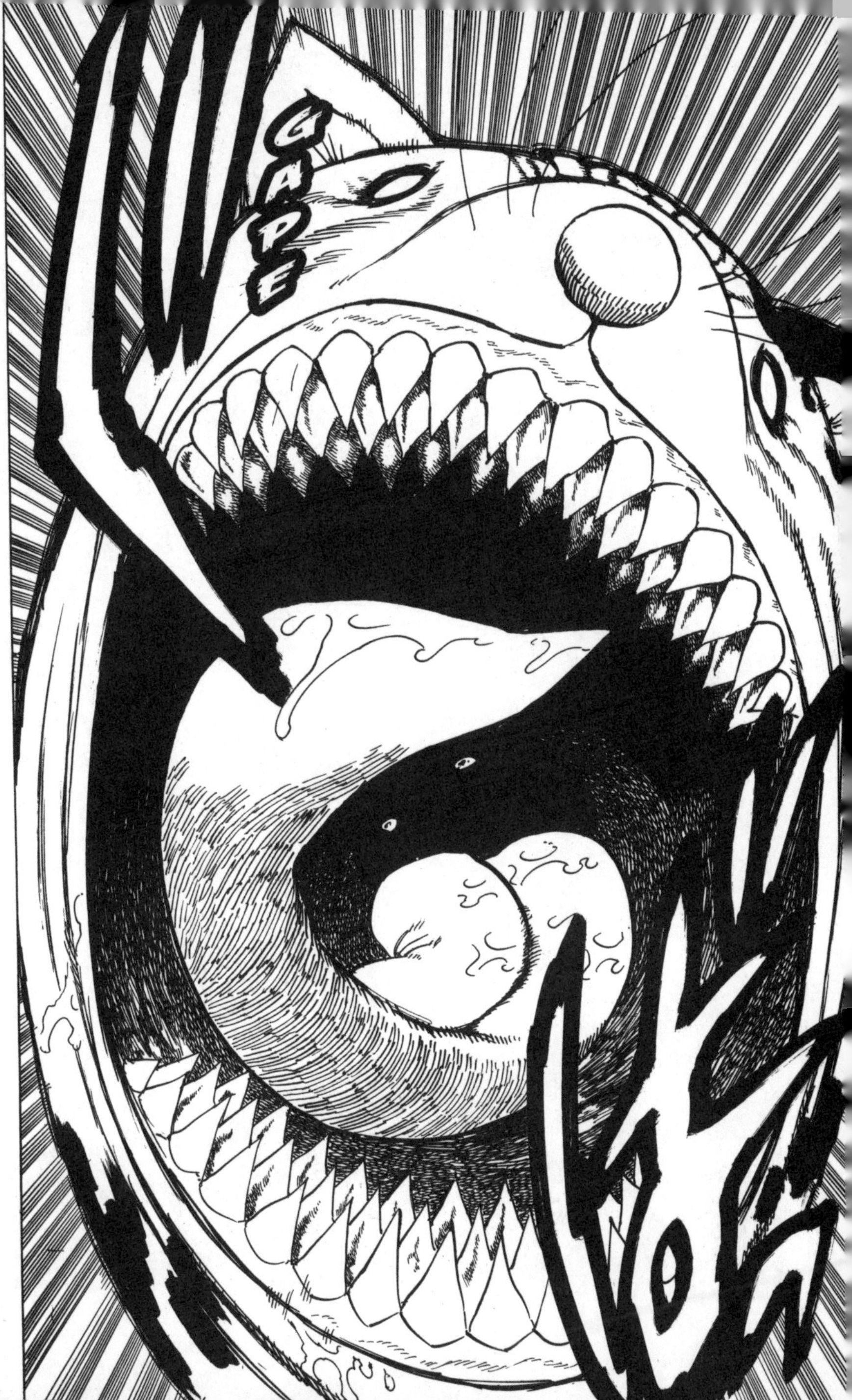
GAPE

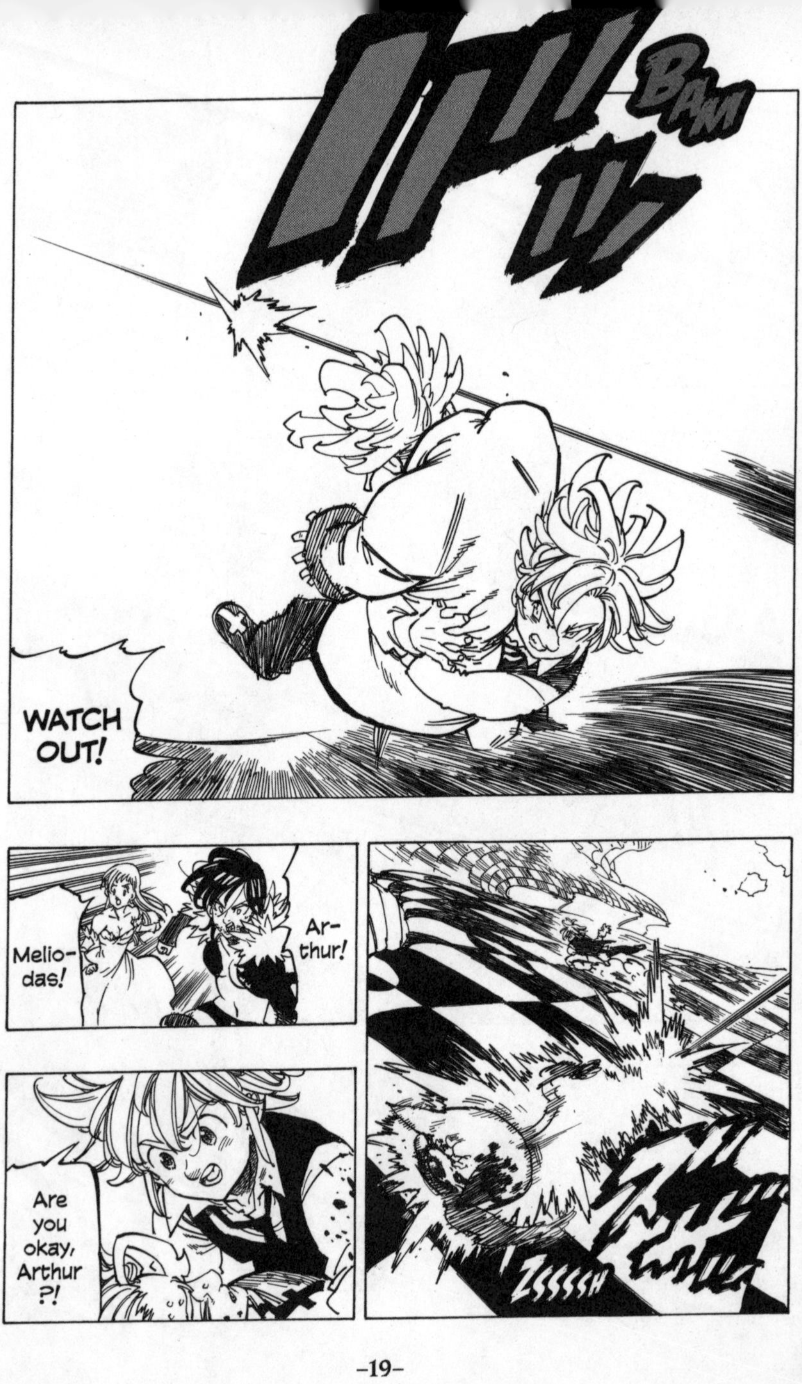
BAM
WATCH OUT!
ZSSSSH
Ar-thur!
Melio-das!
Are you okay, Arthur?!

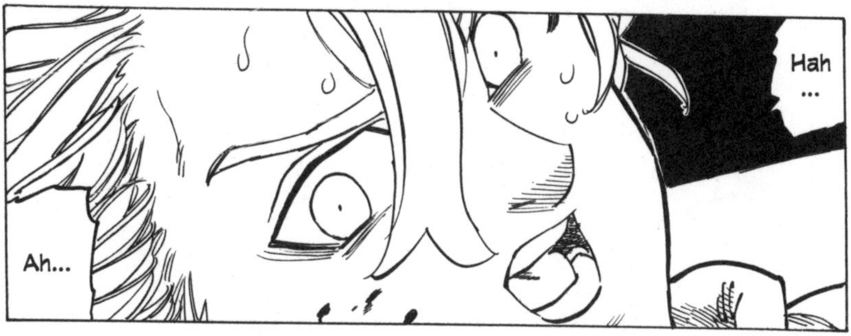
Hah
...
Ah...

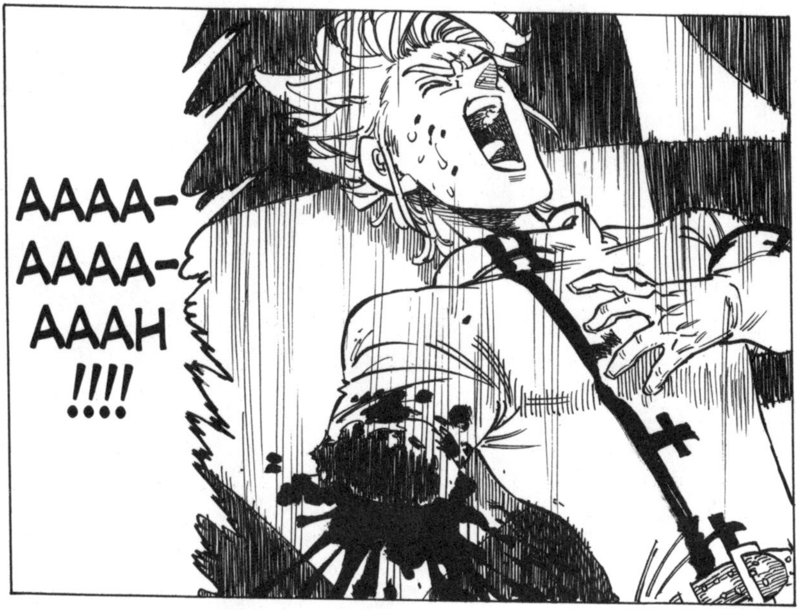
AAAA-
AAAA-
AAAH
!!!!

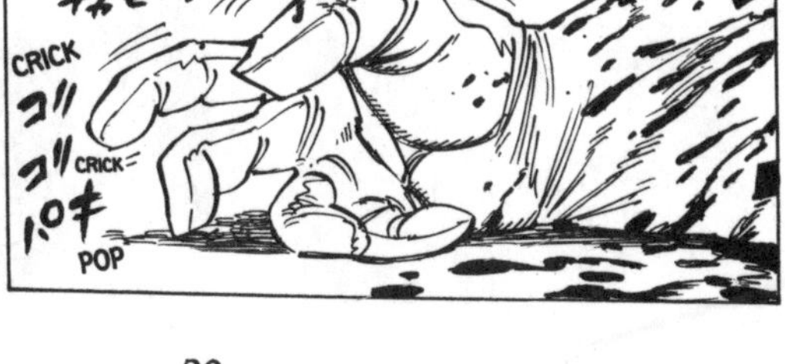
CHEW
CHEW
CRICK
CRICK
POP

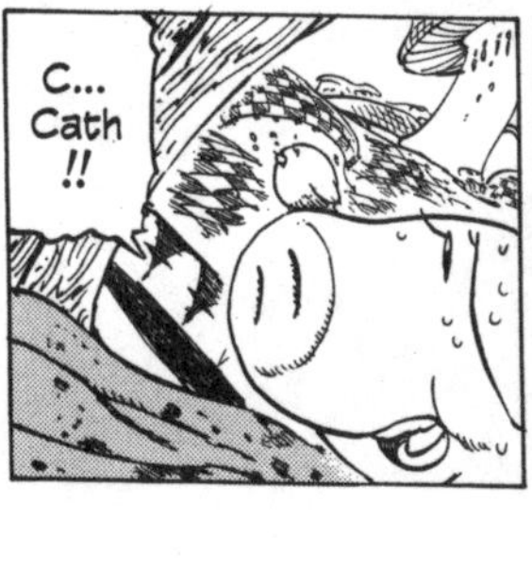
C...
Cath
!!

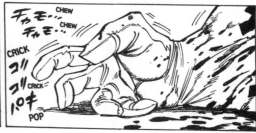

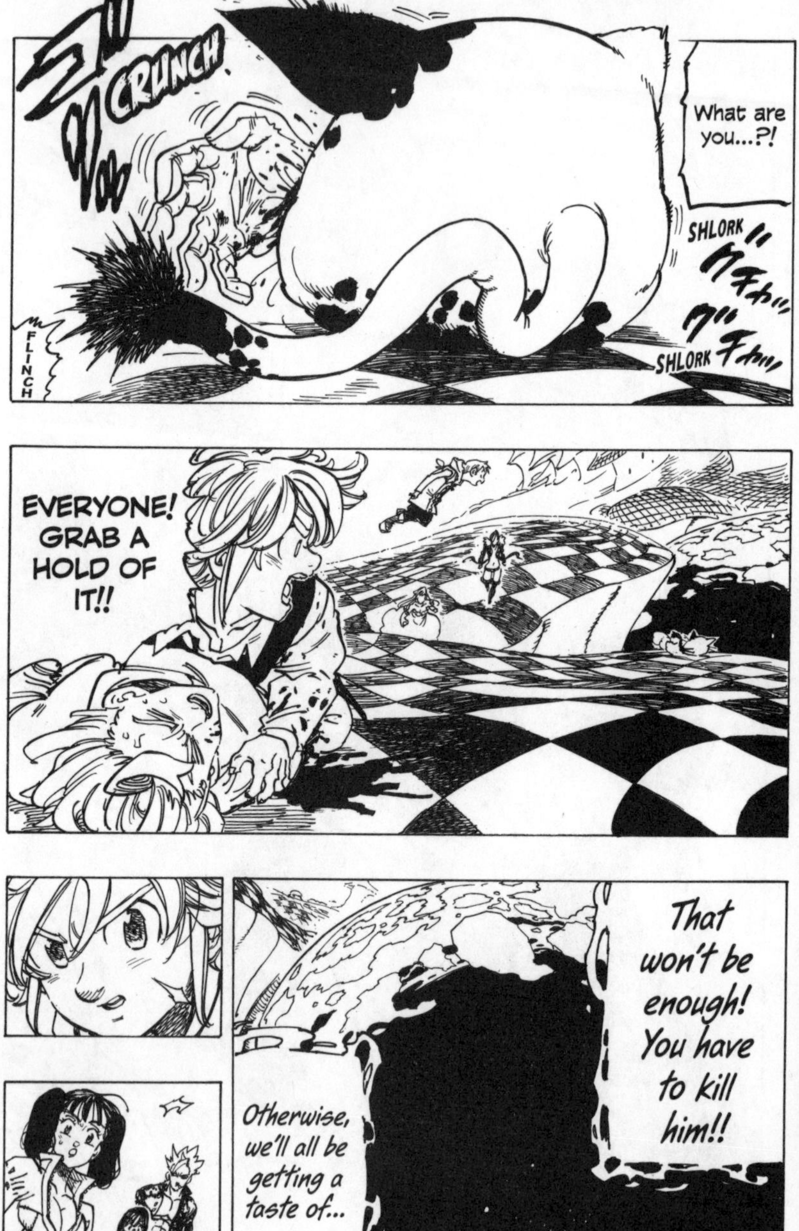
What are you...?!
SHLORK
SHLORK
CRUNCH
FLINCH
EVERYONE! GRAB A HOLD OF IT!!
That won't be enough! You have to kill him!!
Otherwise, we'll all be getting a taste of...

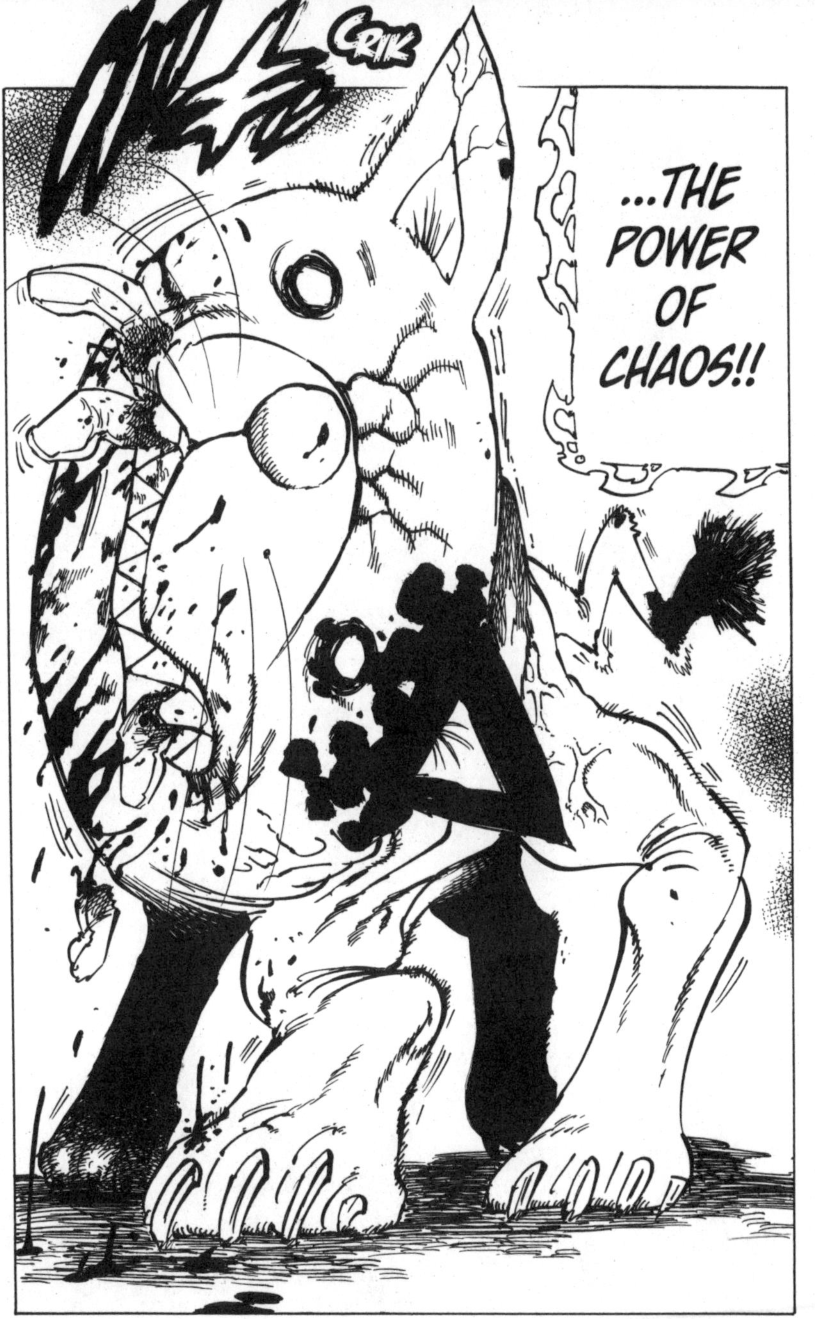
CRIK
...THE POWER OF CHAOS!!

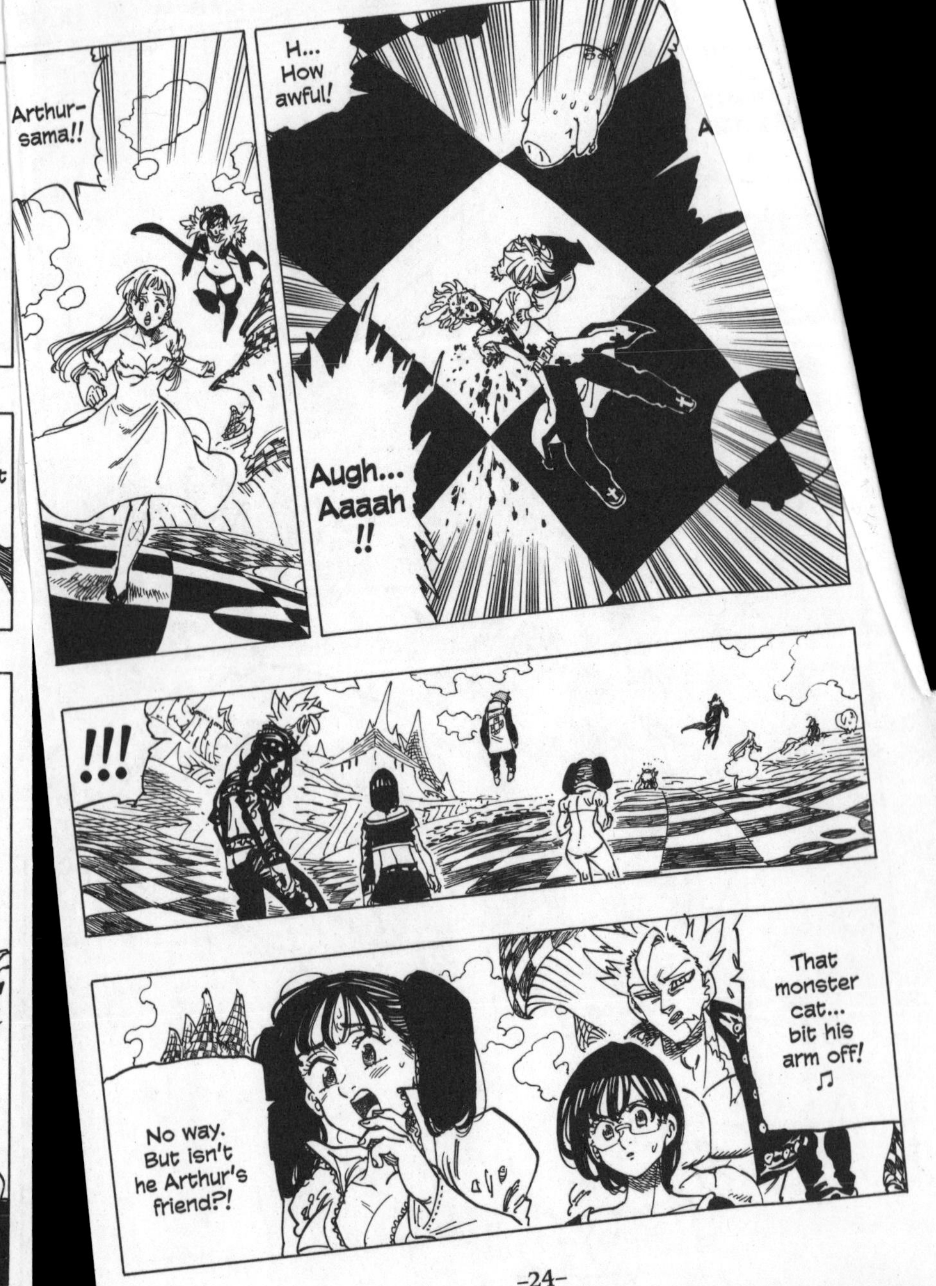
H... How awful!
Augh... Aaaah!!
Arthur-sama!!
!!!
That monster cat... bit his arm off! ♫
No way. But isn't he Arthur's friend?!

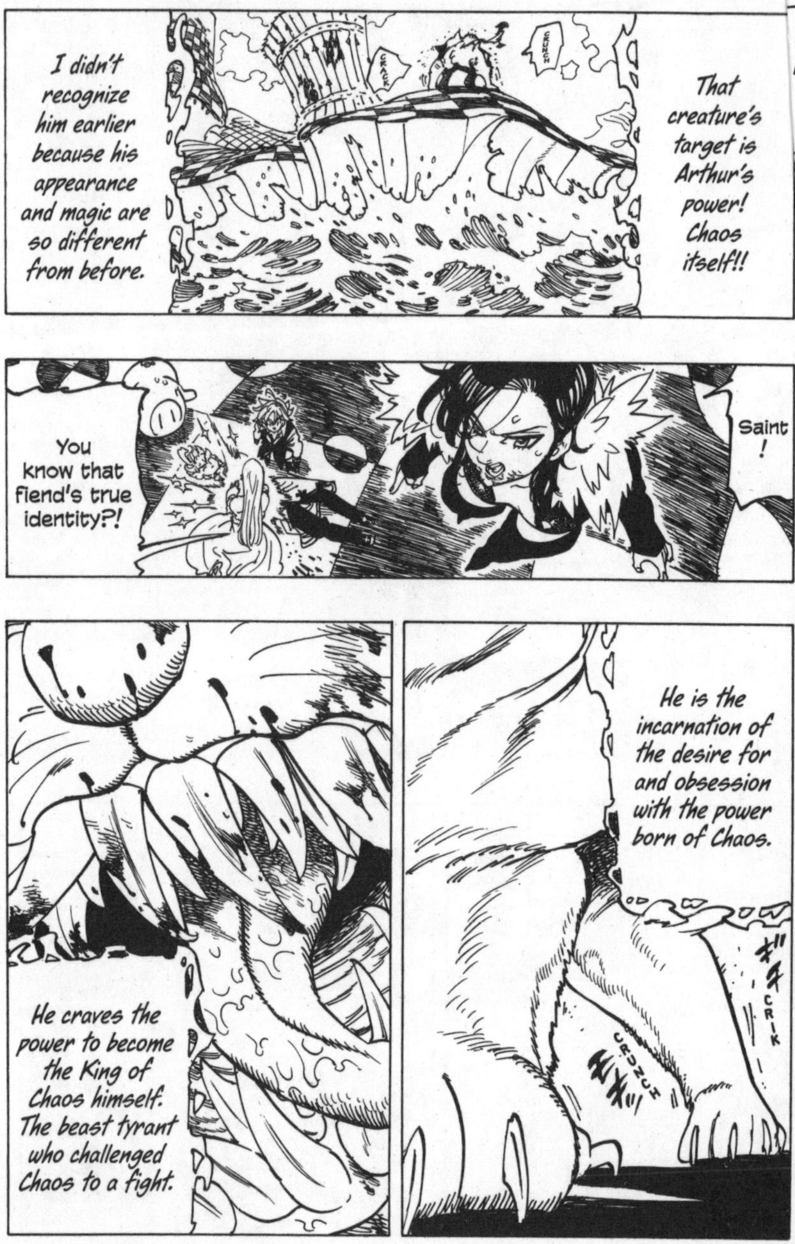
That creature's target is Arthur's power! Chaos itself!!
CRUNCH
CRACK
I didn't recognize him earlier because his appearance and magic are so different from before.
Saint!
You know that fiend's true identity?!
He is the incarnation of the desire for and obsession with the power born of Chaos.
CRIK
CRUNCH
He craves the power to become the King of Chaos himself. The beast tyrant who challenged Chaos to a fight.

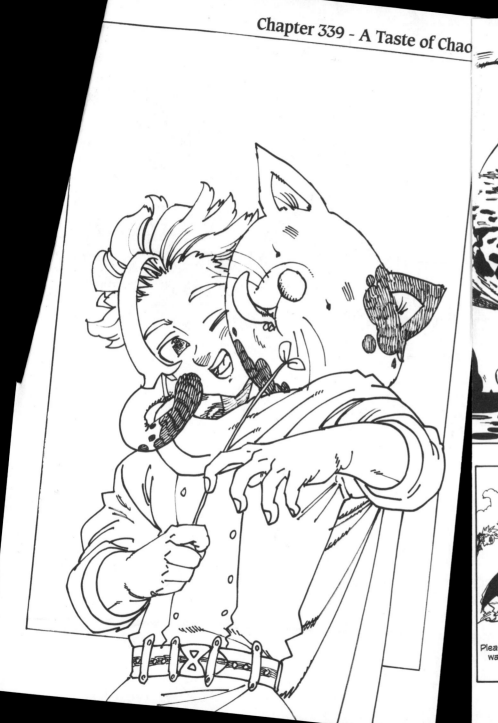

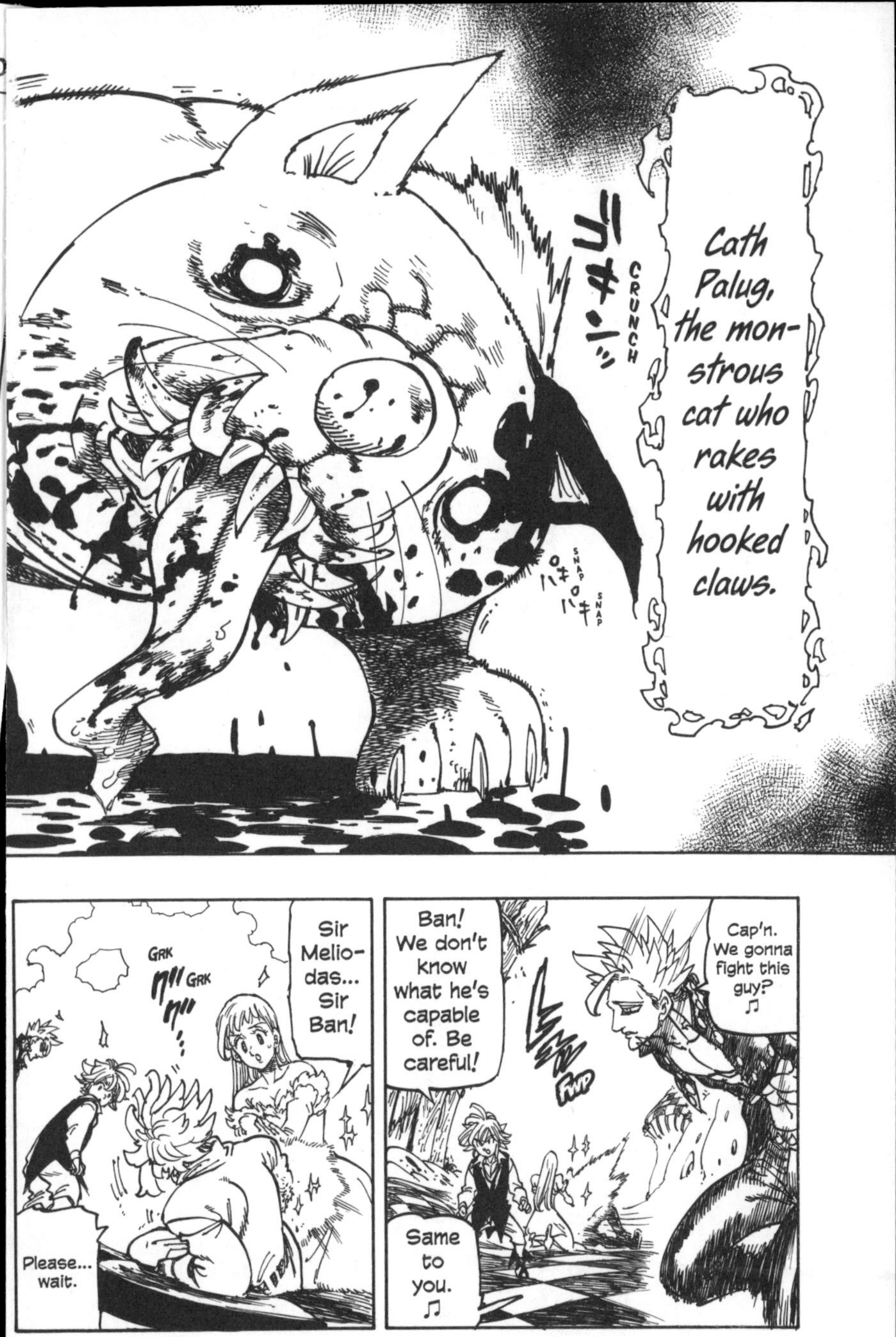
CRUNCH
Cath Palug, the mon-strous cat who rakes with hooked claws.
SNAP
SNAP
Cap'n. We gonna fight this guy? ♫
Ban! We don't know what he's capable of. Be careful!
FWUP
Same to you. ♫
Sir Melio-das... Sir Ban!
GRK
GRK
Please... wait.

Chapter 339 - A Taste of Chao

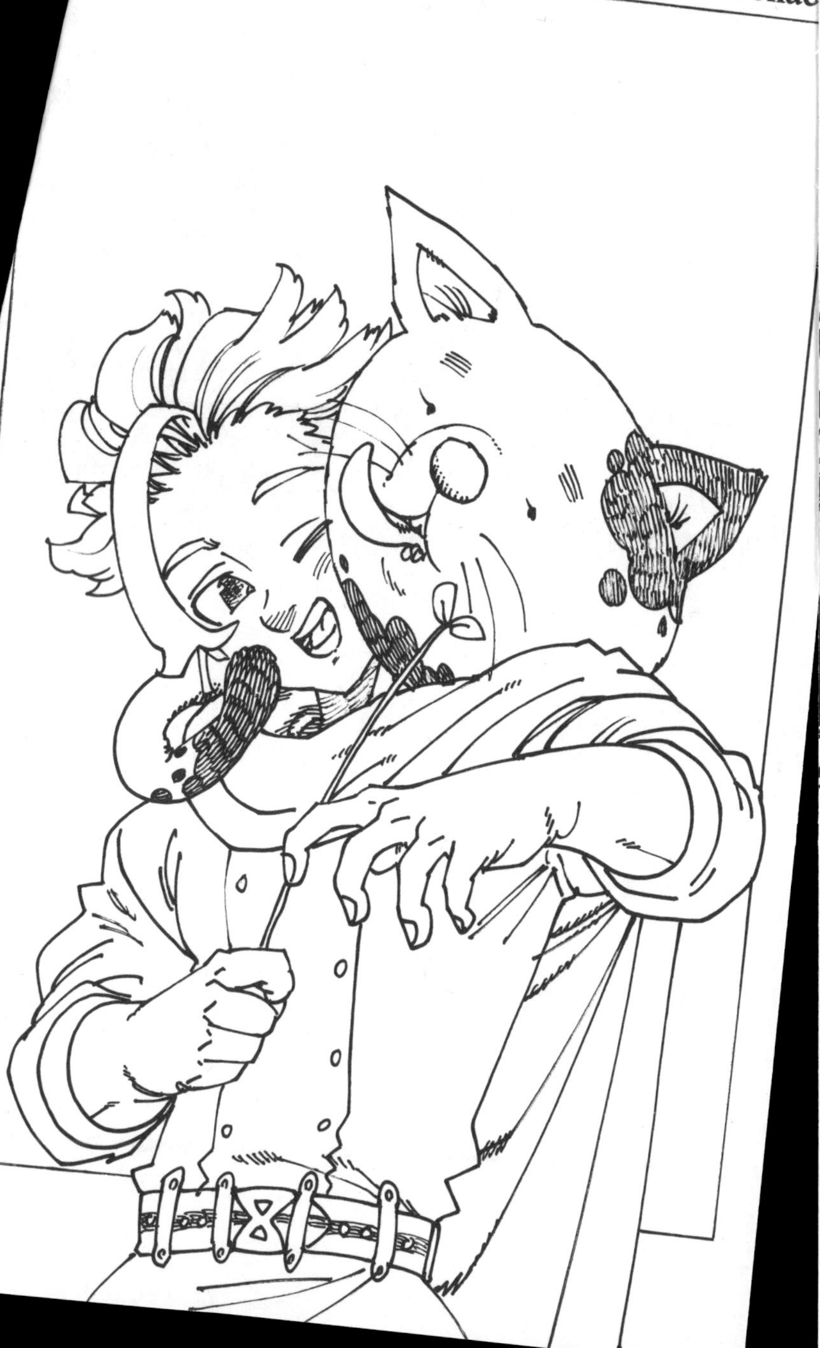

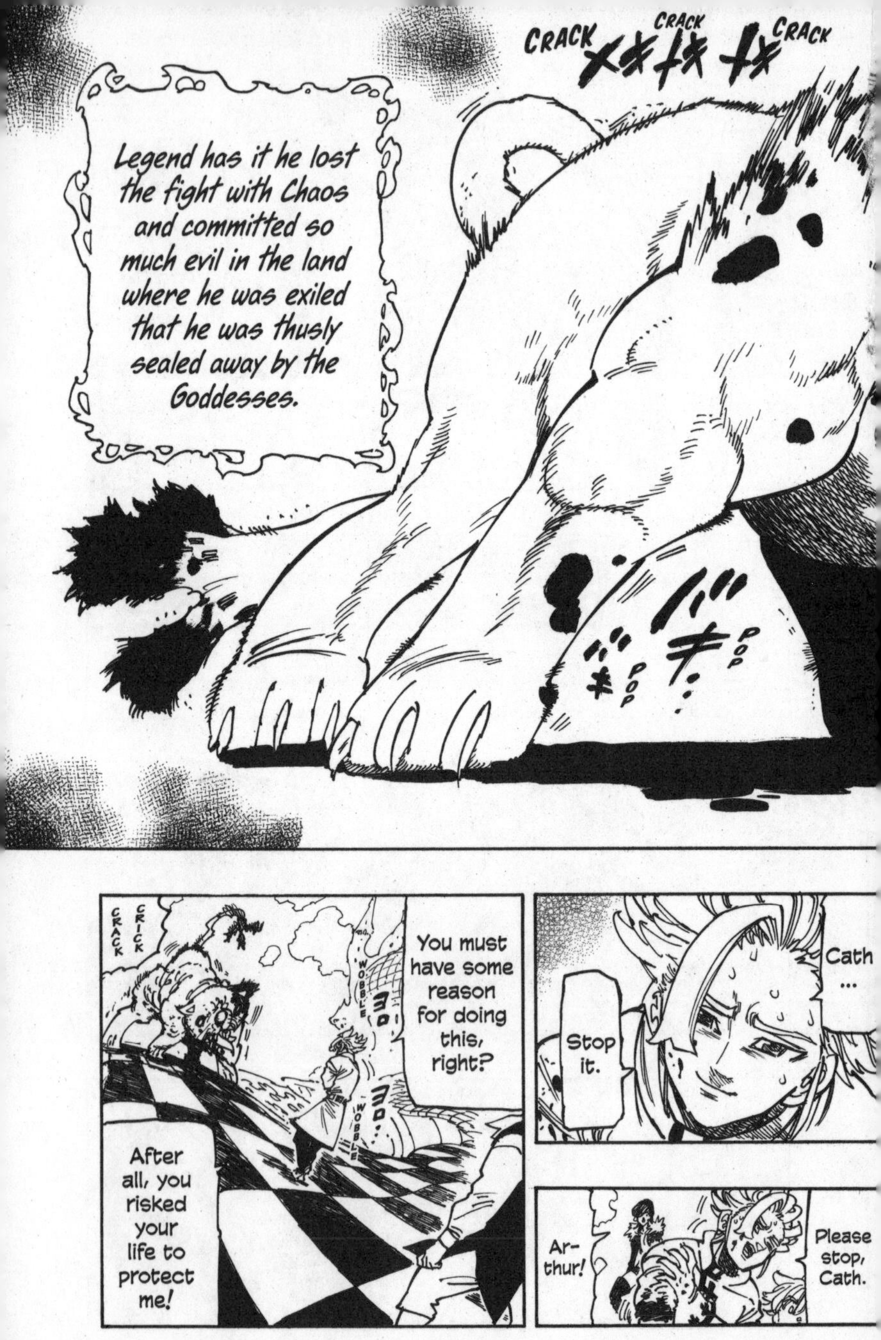
CRACK
CRACK
CRACK
Legend has it he lost the fight with Chaos and committed so much evil in the land where he was exiled that he was thusly sealed away by the Goddesses.
POP
POP
Cath...
Stop it.
Please stop, Cath.
Ar-thur!
CRACK
CRICK
WOBBLE
You must have some reason for doing this, right?
WOBBLE
After all, you risked your life to protect me!

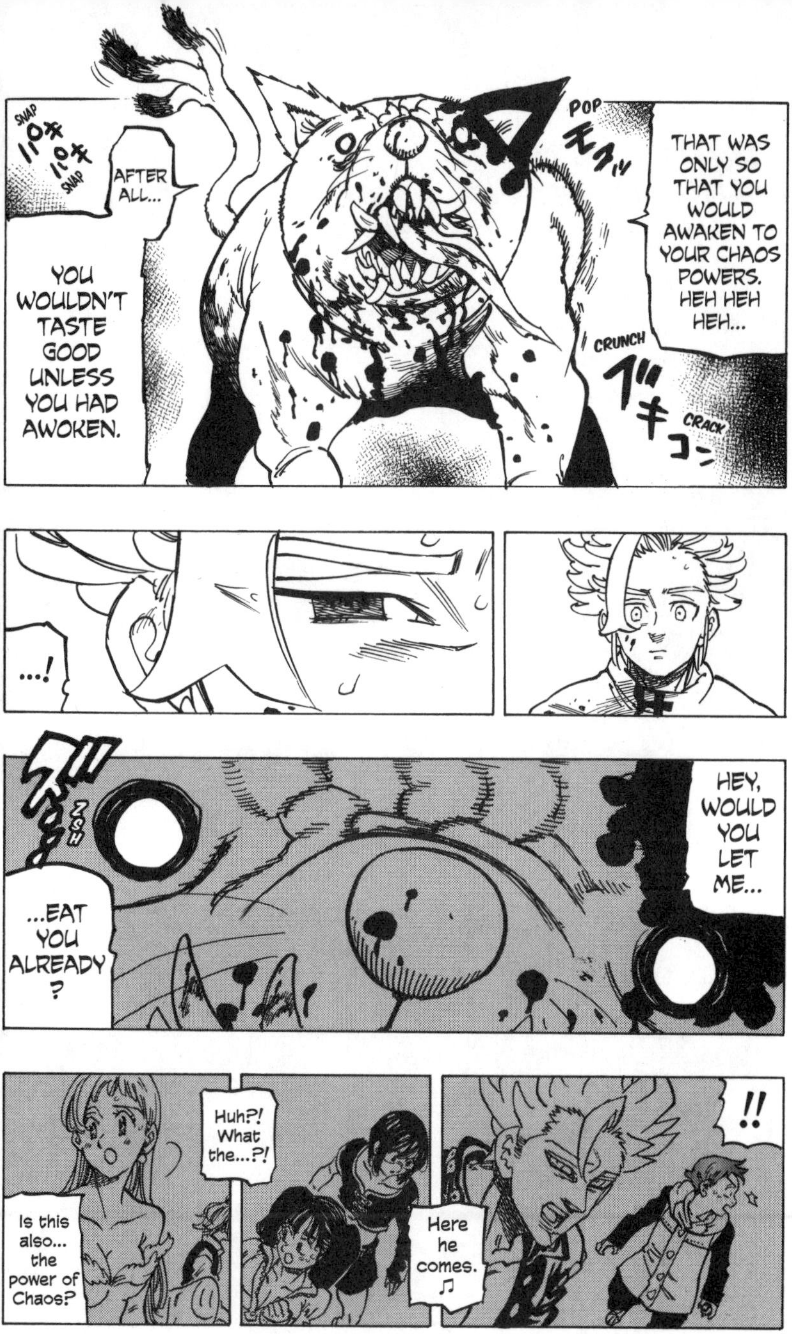
POP
THAT WAS ONLY SO THAT YOU WOULD AWAKEN TO YOUR CHAOS POWERS. HEH HEH HEH...
SNAP
SNAP
AFTER ALL...
YOU WOULDN'T TASTE GOOD UNLESS YOU HAD AWOKEN.
CRUNCH
CRACK
...!
HEY, WOULD YOU LET ME...
ZSH
...EAT YOU ALREADY?
!!
Huh?! What the...?!
Here he comes. ♫
Is this also... the power of Chaos?

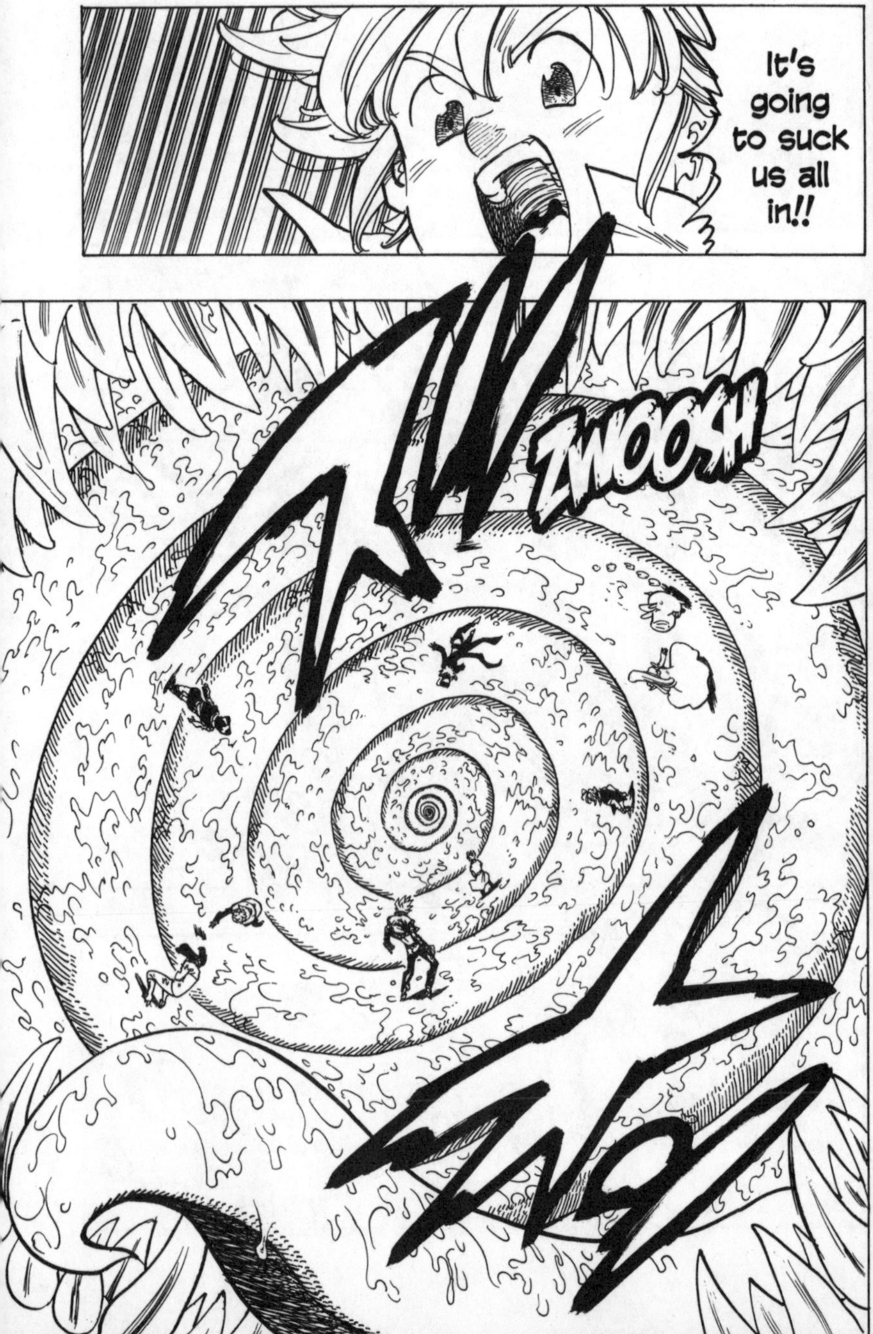
It's going to suck us all in!!
ZWOOSH

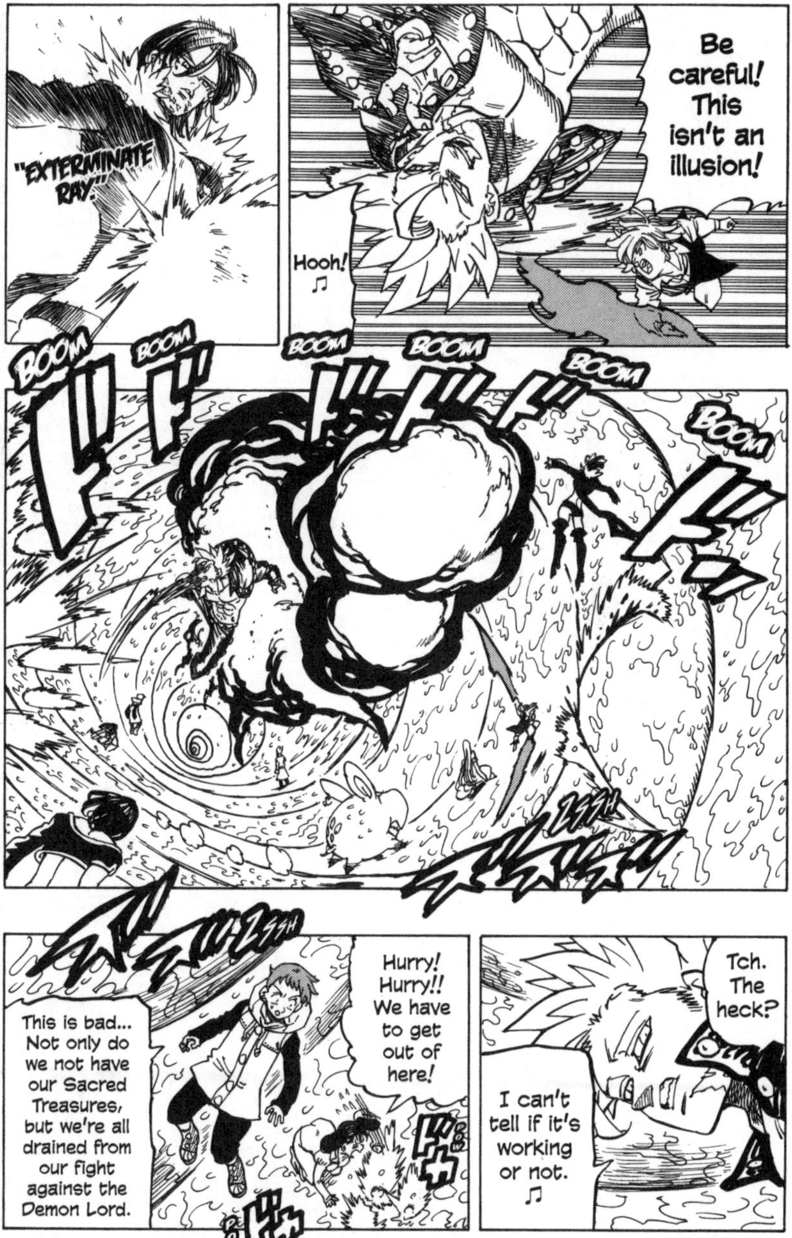
Be careful! This isn't an illusion!
Hooh! ♫
"EXTERMINATE RAY."
BOOM
BOOM
BOOM
BOOM
BOOM
BOOM
ZSSH
ZZZSSH
Tch. The heck?
I can't tell if it's working or not. ♫
Hurry! Hurry!! We have to get out of here!
This is bad... Not only do we not have our Sacred Treasures, but we're all drained from our fight against the Demon Lord.
POW
POW

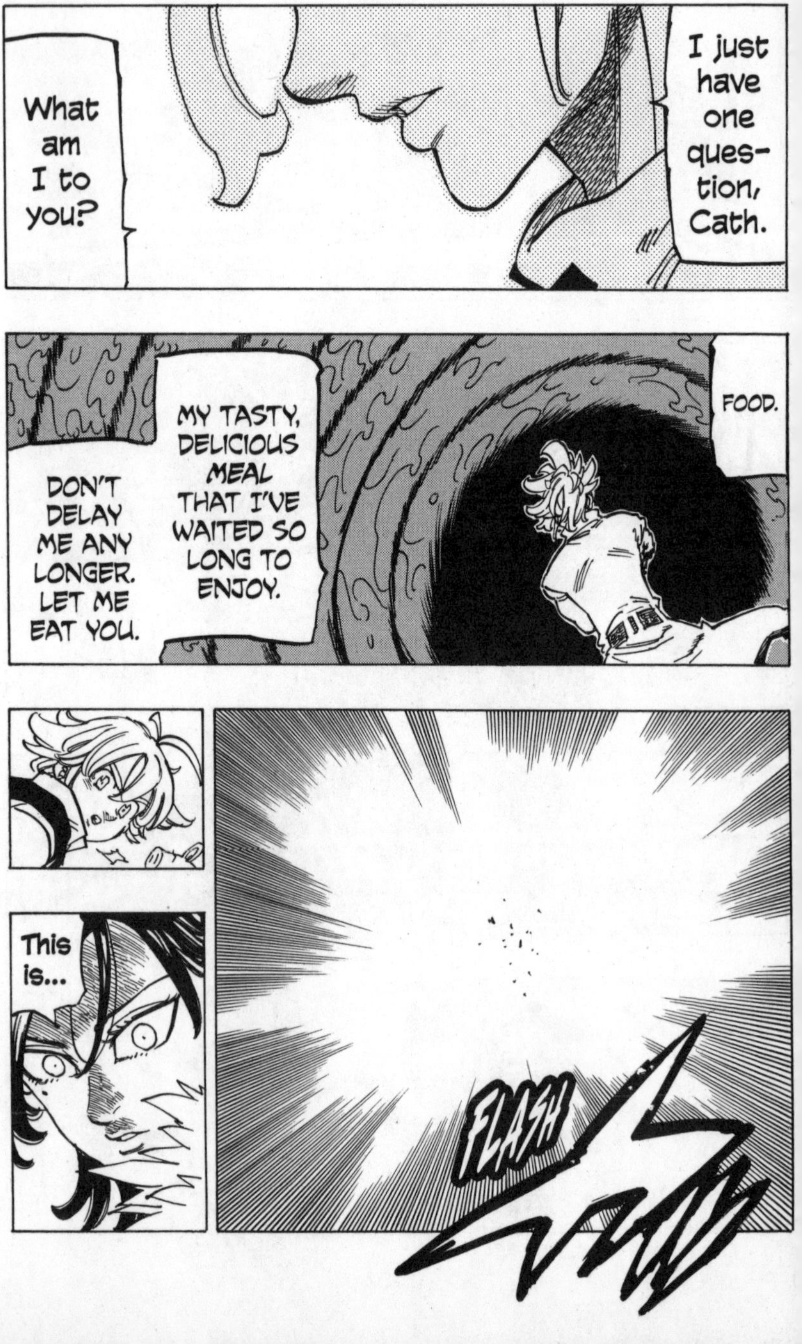
I just have one question, Cath.
What am I to you?
FOOD.
MY TASTY, DELICIOUS *MEAL* THAT I'VE WAITED SO LONG TO ENJOY.
DON'T DELAY ME ANY LONGER. LET ME EAT YOU.
FLASH
This is...

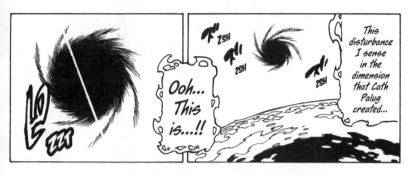

Ooh... This is....!!

This disturbance I sense in the dimension that Cath Palug created...

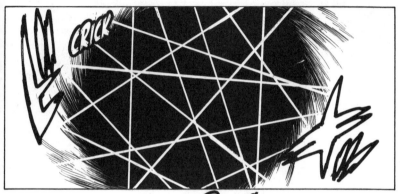

CRICK

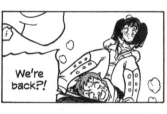

We're back?!

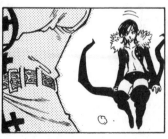

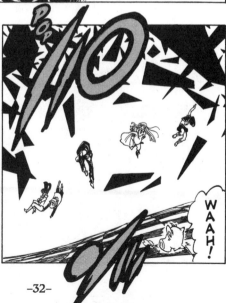

POP

WAAH!

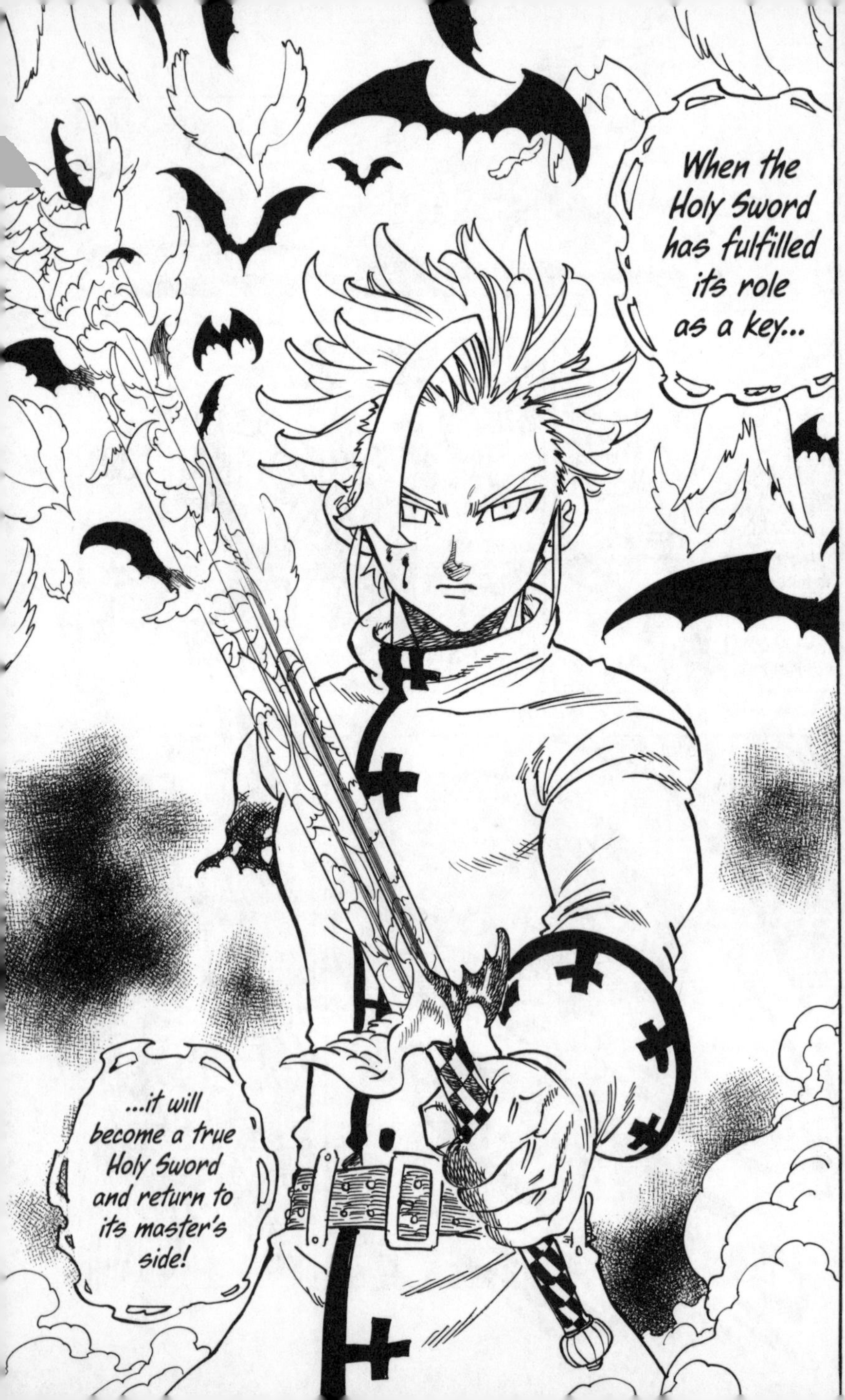
When the Holy Sword has fulfilled its role as a key...
...it will become a true Holy Sword and return to its master's side!

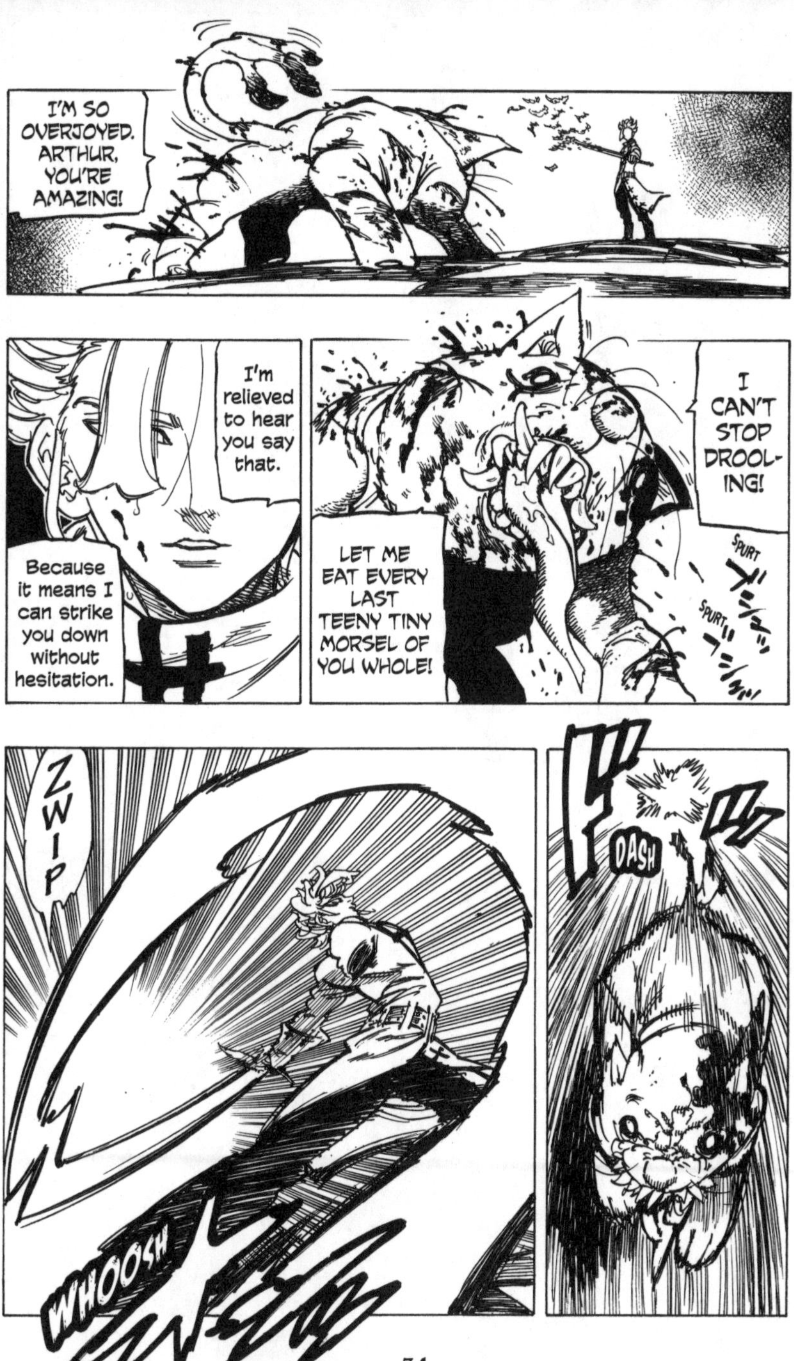
I'M SO OVERJOYED. ARTHUR, YOU'RE AMAZING!
I CAN'T STOP DROOL-ING!
LET ME EAT EVERY LAST TEENY TINY MORSEL OF YOU WHOLE!
SPURT
SPURT
I'm relieved to hear you say that.
Because it means I can strike you down without hesitation.
DASH
ZWIP
WHOOSH

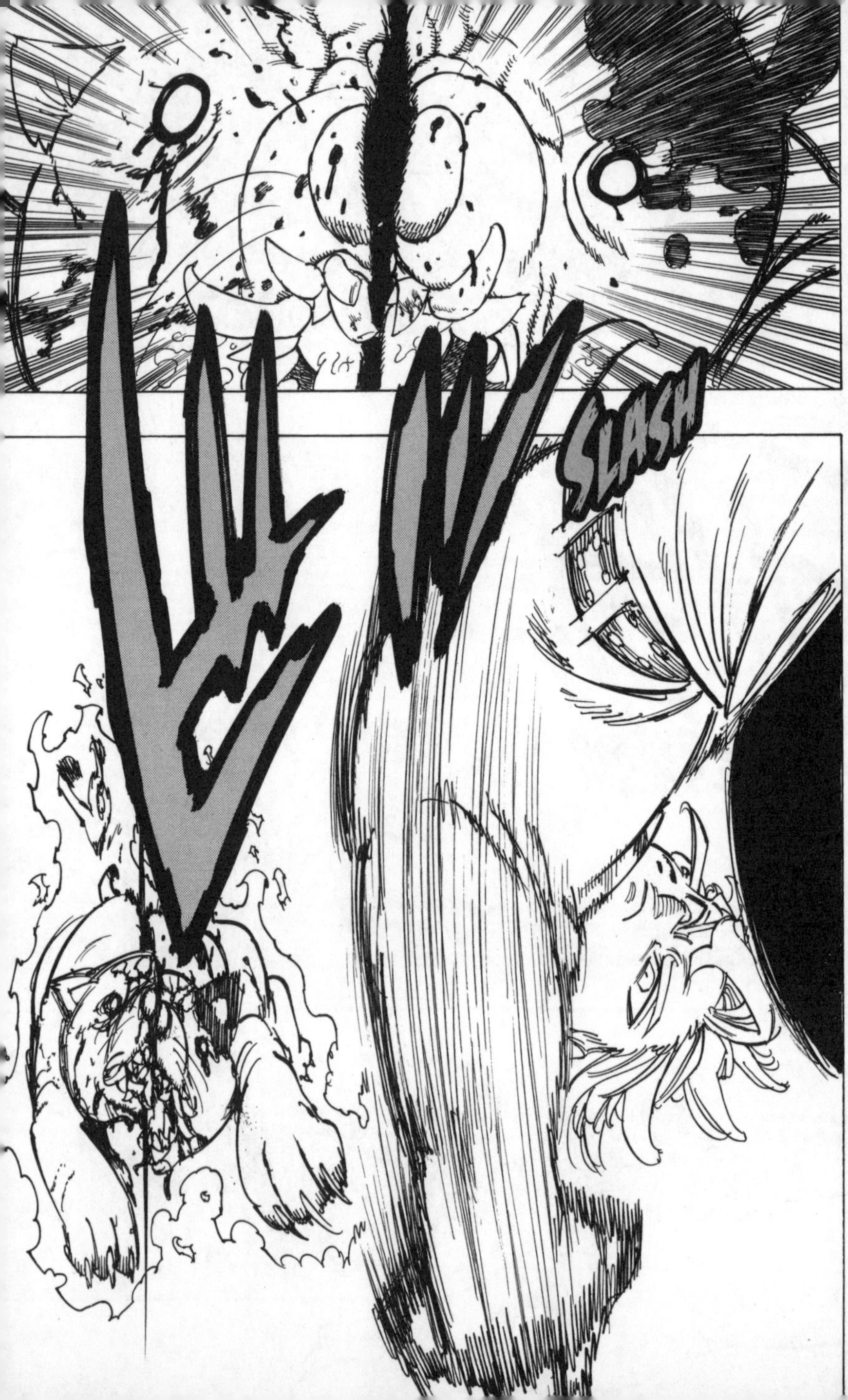
SLASH

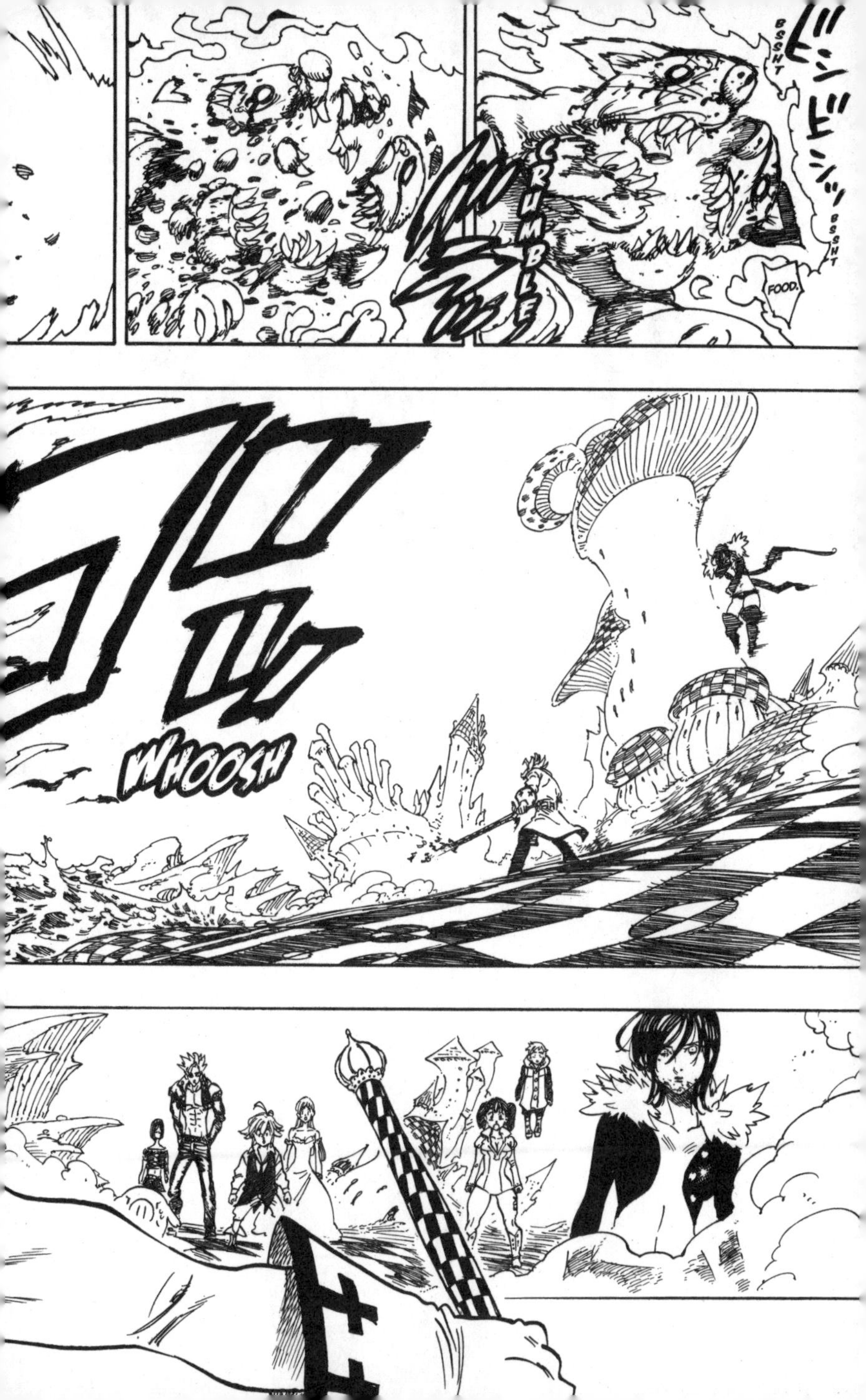
ビシビシッ
BSSHT
BSSHT
FOOD.
CRUMBLE
WHOOSH

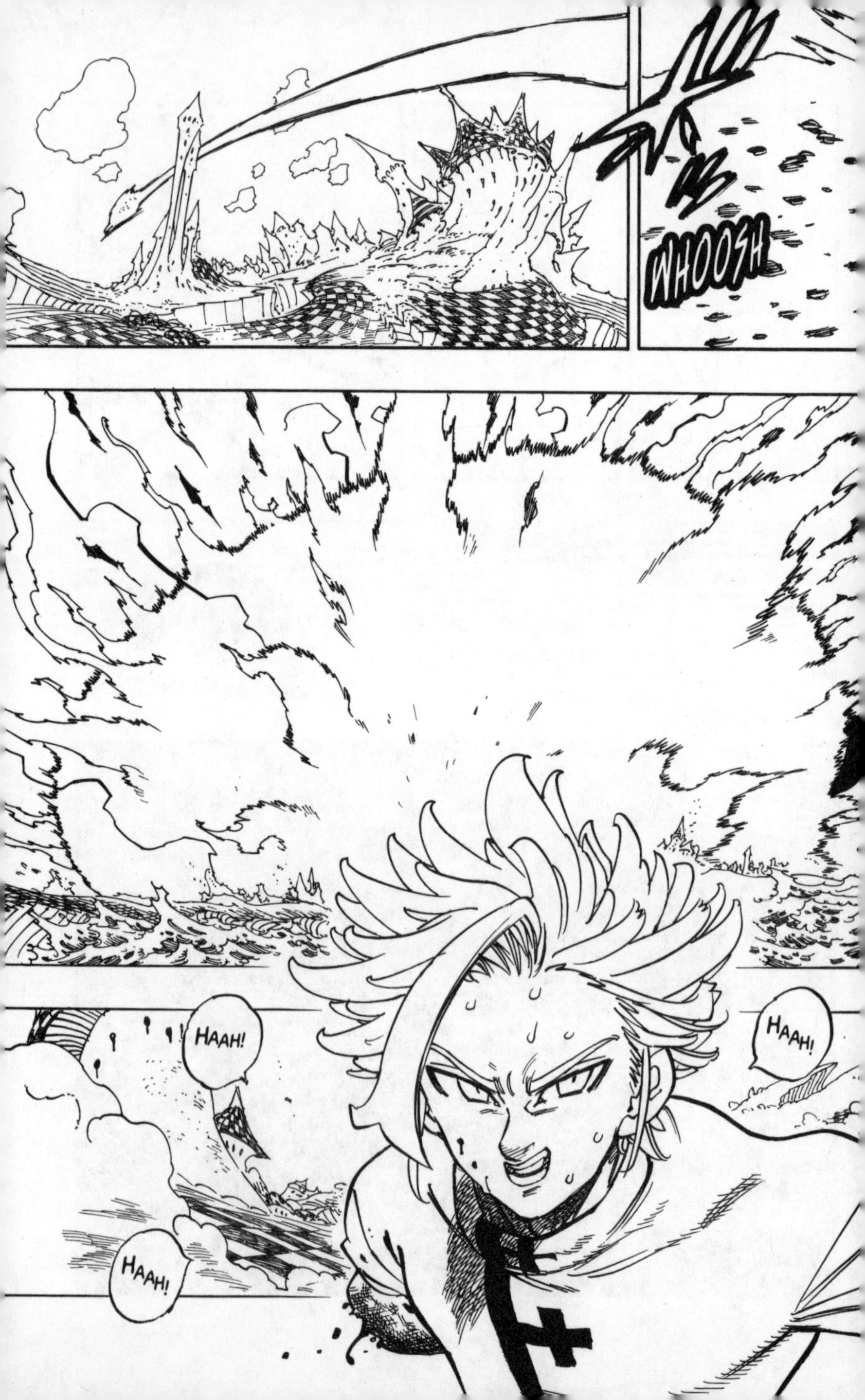
WHOOSH
HAAH!
HAAH!
HAAH!

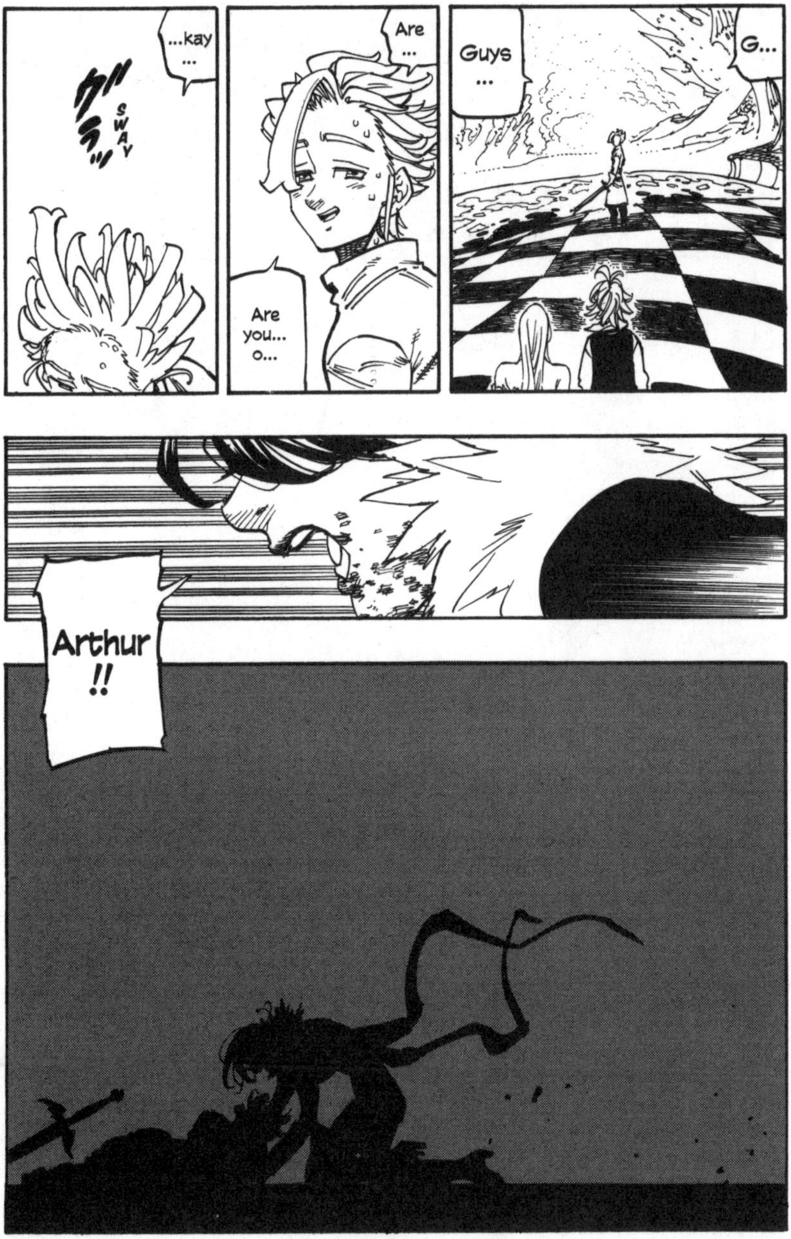
G...
Guys...
Are...
Are you... o...
...kay...
SWAY
Arthur!!

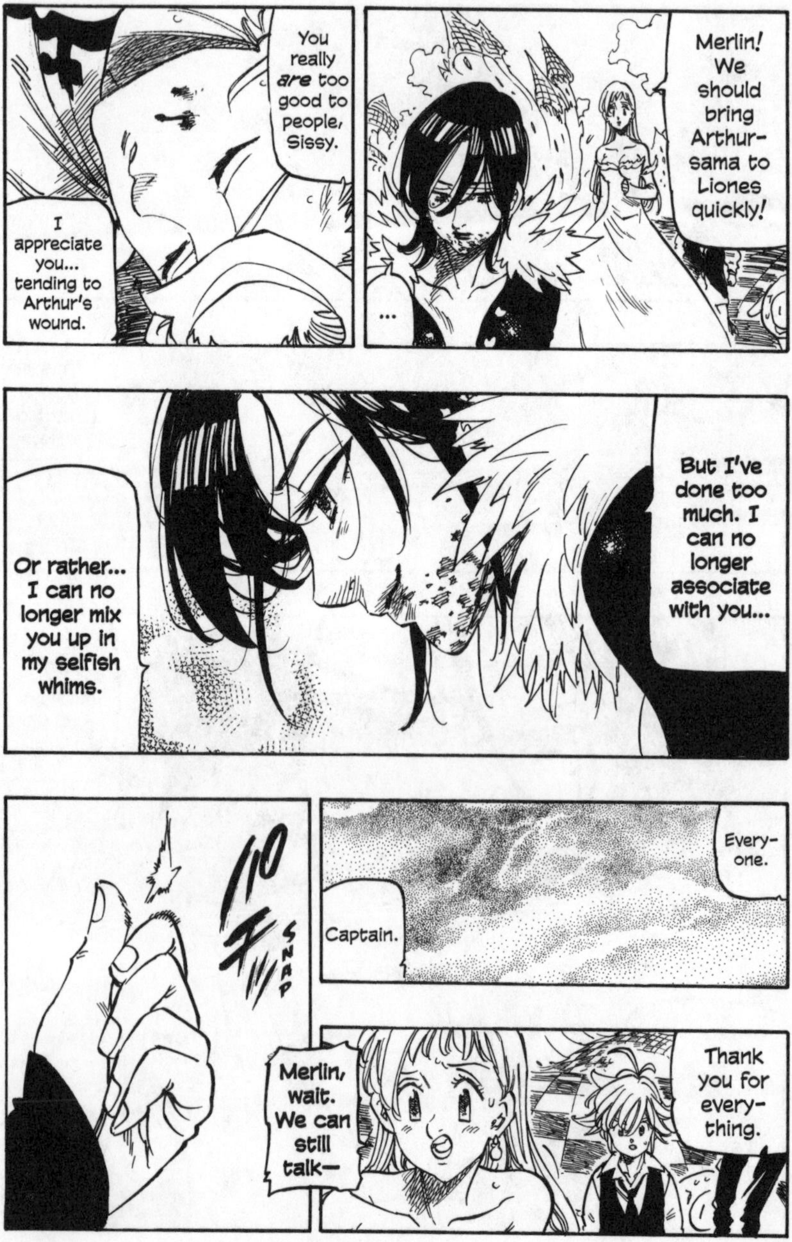
Merlin! We should bring Arthur-sama to Liones quickly!
...
You really are too good to people, Sissy.
I appreciate you... tending to Arthur's wound.
But I've done too much. I can no longer associate with you...
Or rather... I can no longer mix you up in my selfish whims.
Every-one.
Captain.
Thank you for every-thing.
Merlin, wait. We can still talk—
SNAP

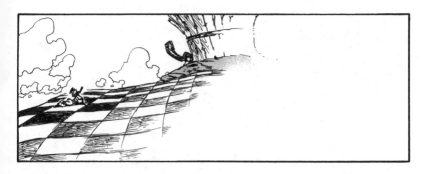

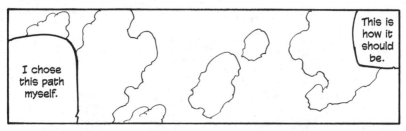

This is how it should be.

I chose this path myself.

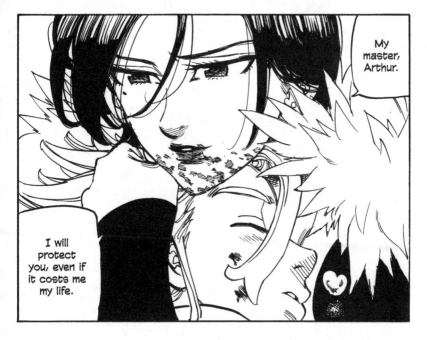

My master, Arthur.

I will protect you, even if it costs me my life.

The Seven Deadly Sins

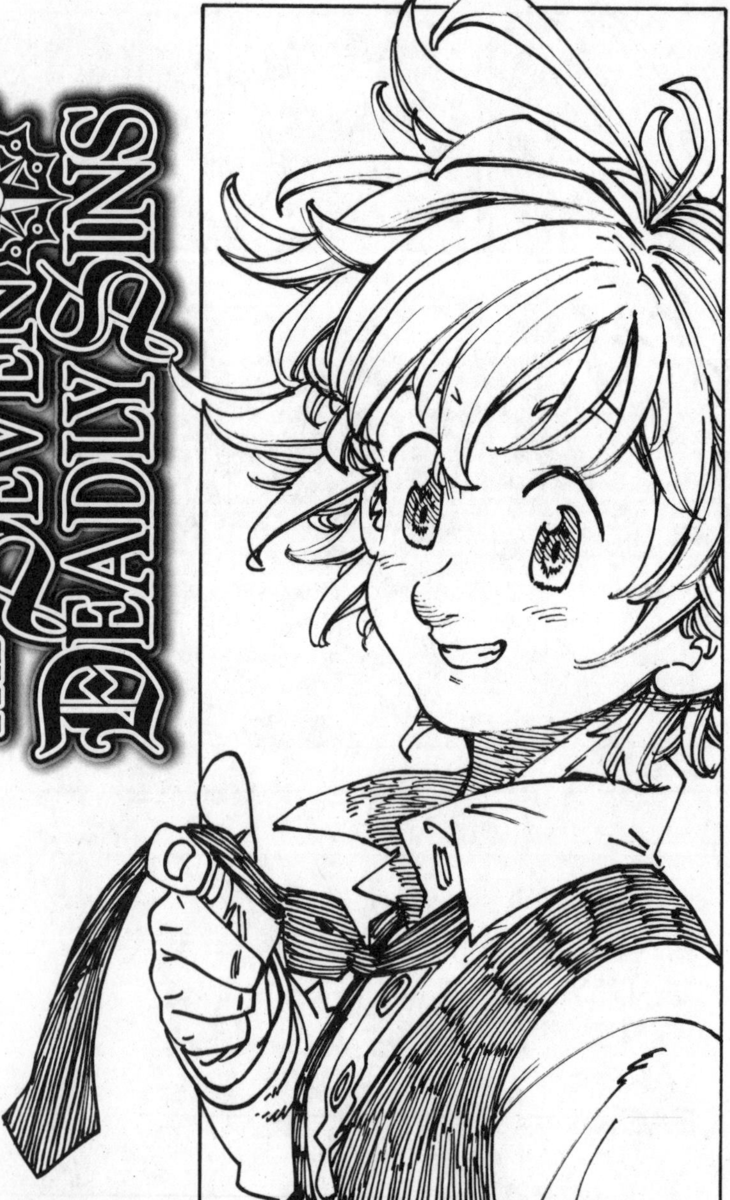

Chapter 340 - I Miss You

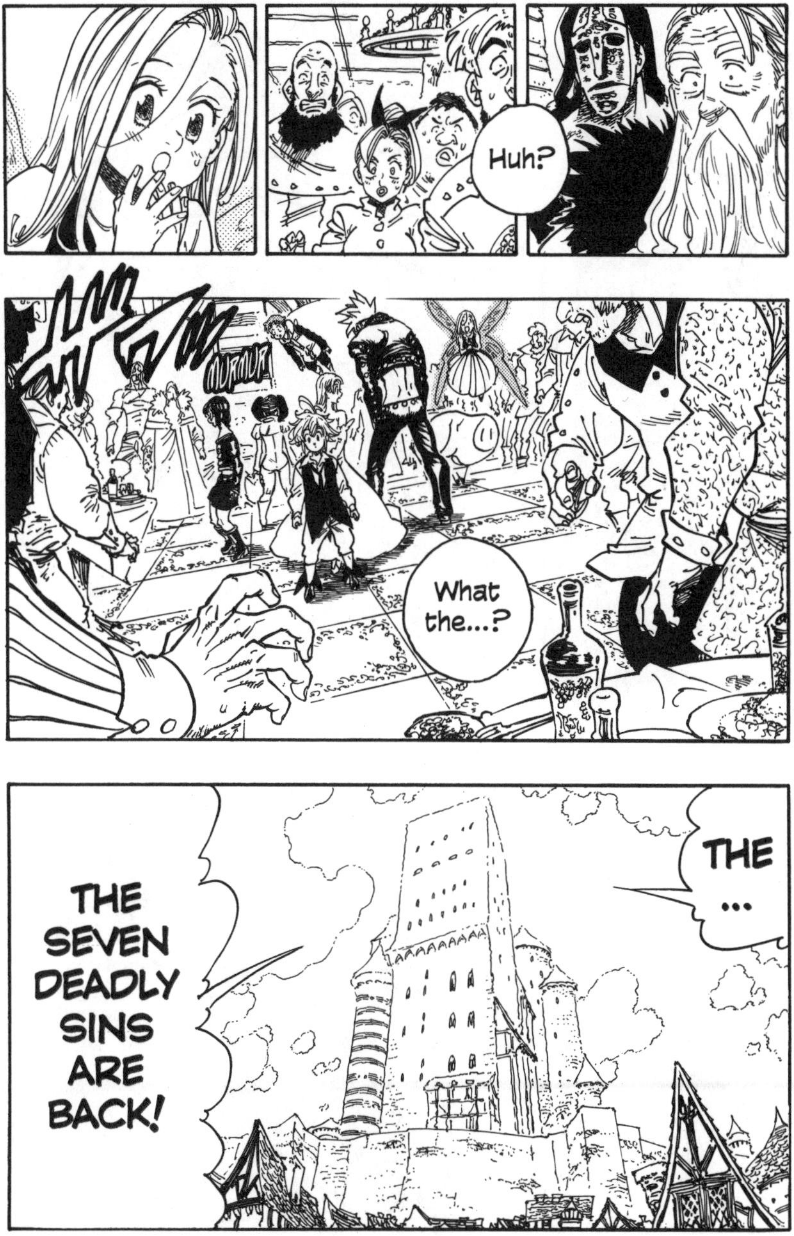
Huh?
MURMUR
What the...?
THE ...
THE SEVEN DEADLY SINS ARE BACK!

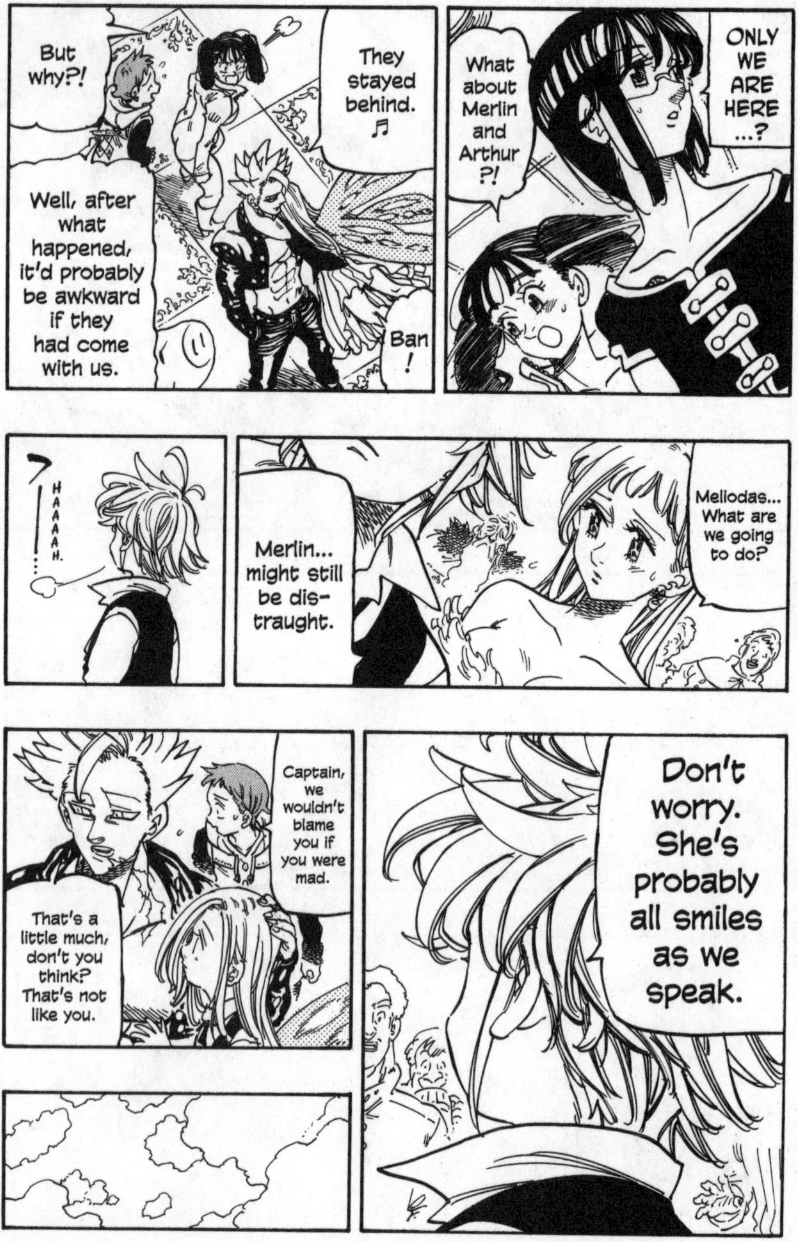
ONLY WE ARE HERE ...?
What about Merlin and Arthur ?!
They stayed behind. ♫
But why?!
Well, after what happened, it'd probably be awkward if they had come with us.
Ban!
Meliodas... What are we going to do?
Merlin... might still be distraught.
HAAAAH...
Don't worry. She's probably all smiles as we speak.
Captain, we wouldn't blame you if you were mad.
That's a little much, don't you think? That's not like you.

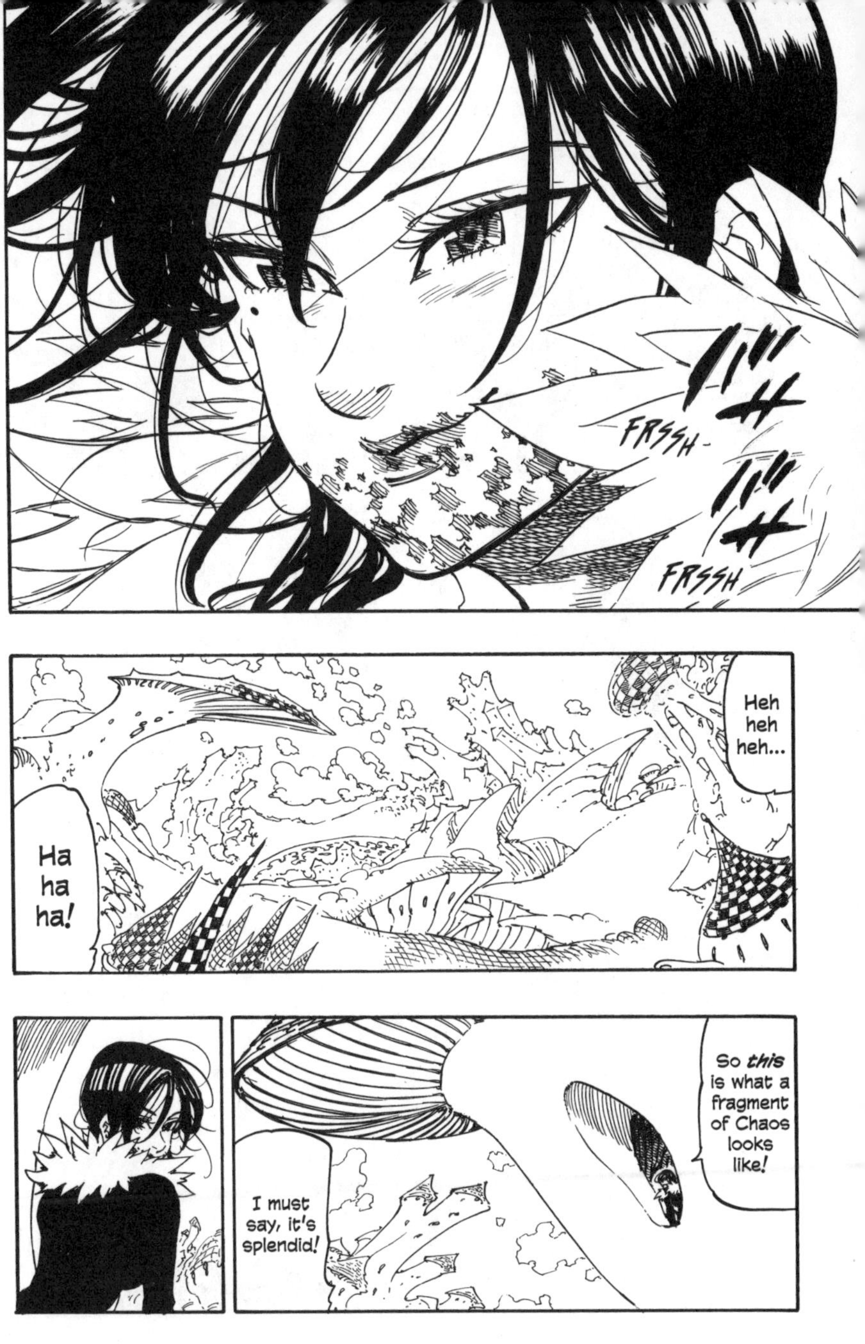
FRSSH
FRSSH
Heh heh heh...
Ha ha ha!
So *this* is what a fragment of Chaos looks like!
I must say, it's splendid!

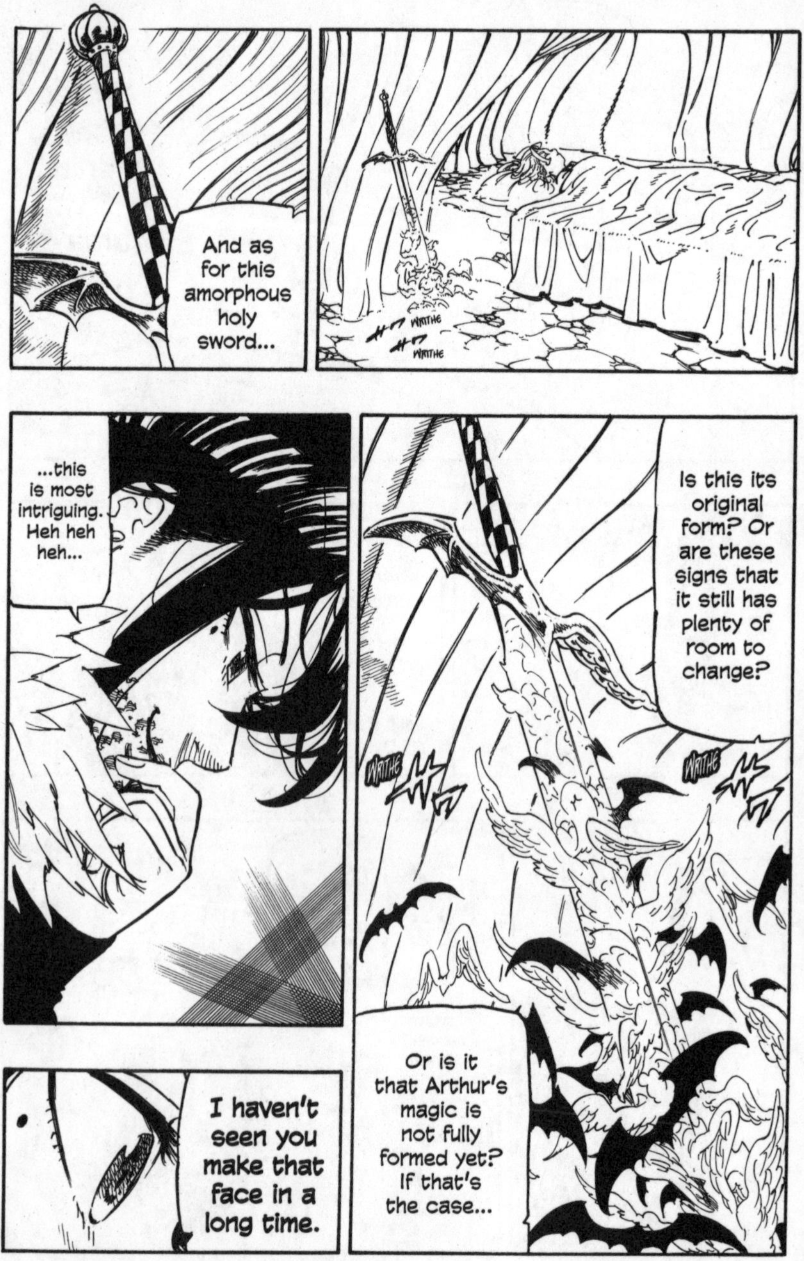
WRITHE
WRITHE
And as for this amorphous holy sword...
Is this its original form? Or are these signs that it still has plenty of room to change?
WRITHE
WRITHE
Or is it that Arthur's magic is not fully formed yet? If that's the case...
...this is most intriguing. Heh heh heh...
I haven't seen you make that face in a long time.

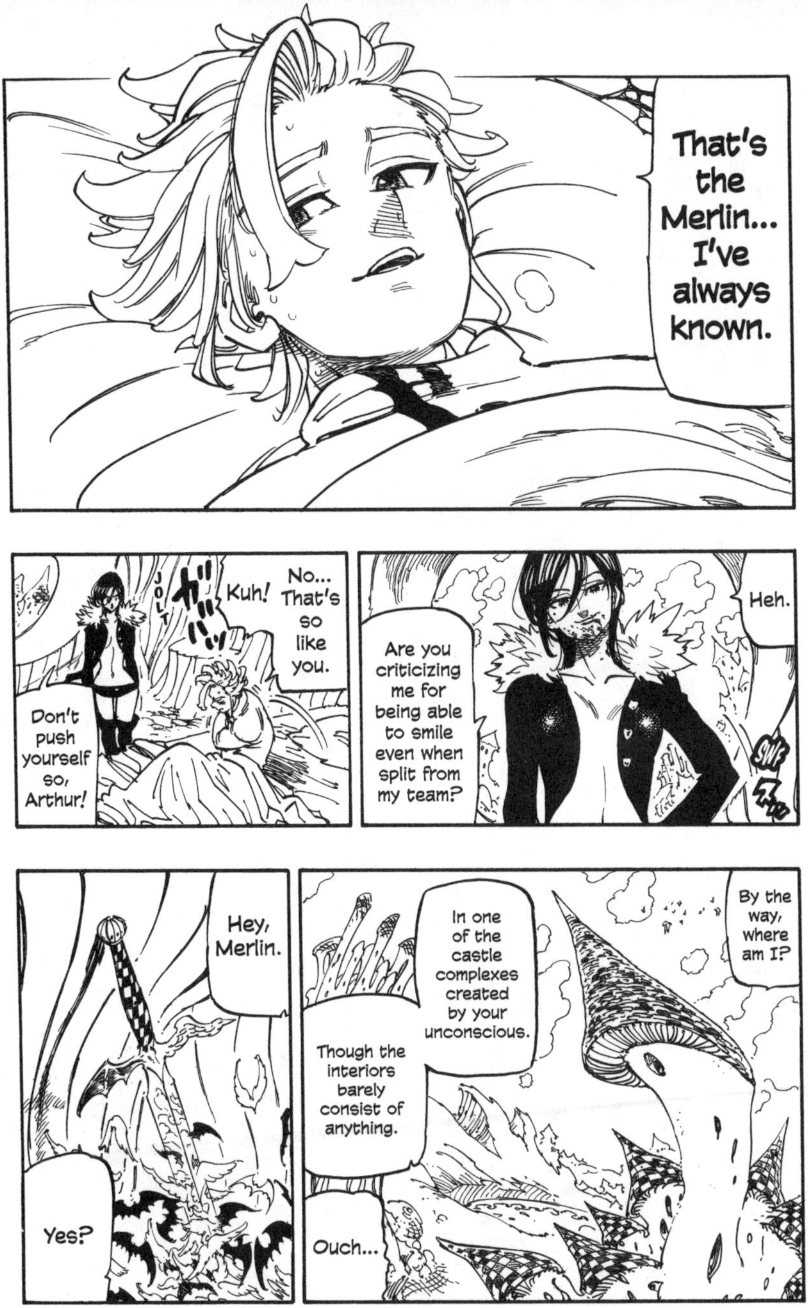
That's the Merlin... I've always known.
Heh.
Are you criticizing me for being able to smile even when split from my team?
SWF
No... That's so like you.
Kuh!
JOLT
Don't push yourself so, Arthur!
By the way, where am I?
In one of the castle complexes created by your unconscious.
Though the interiors barely consist of anything.
Ouch...
Hey, Merlin.
Yes?

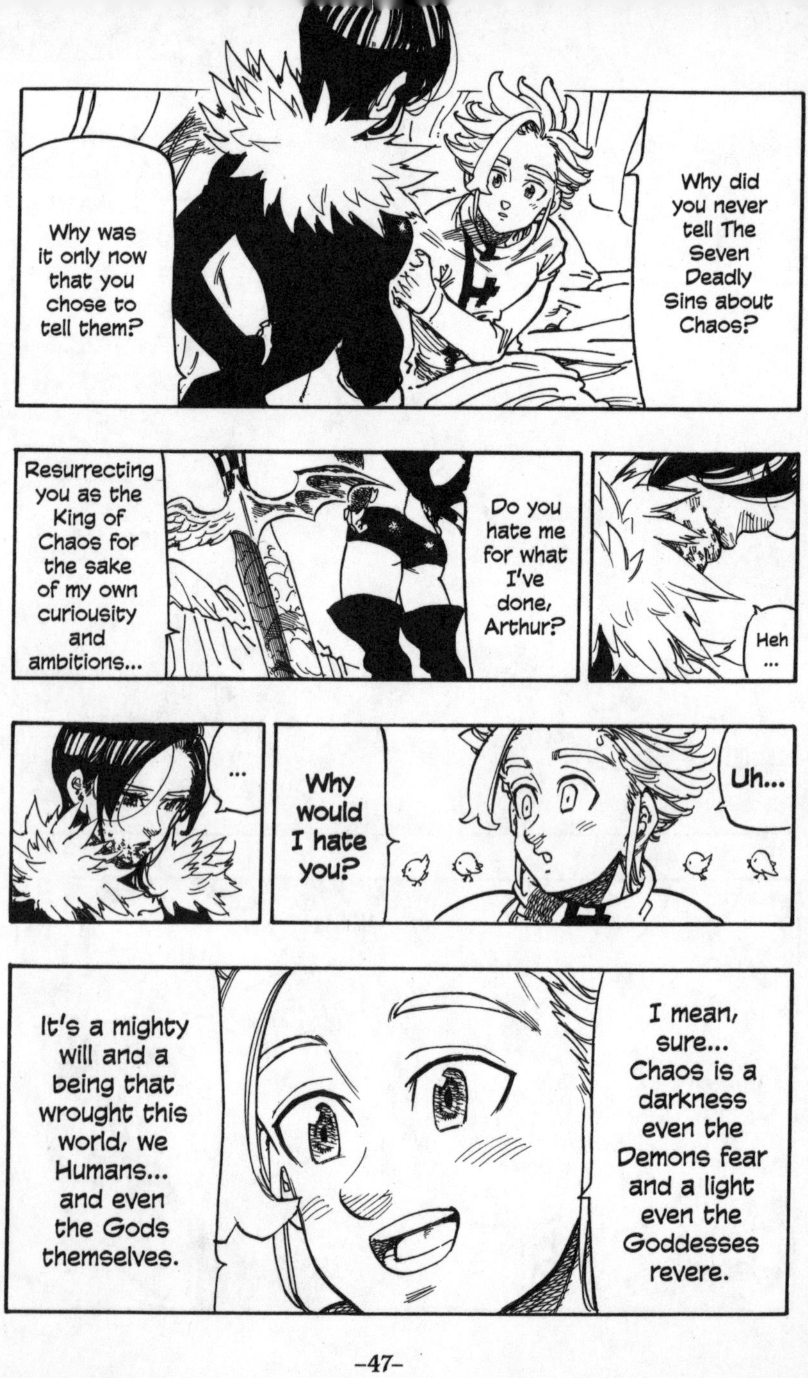
Why did you never tell The Seven Deadly Sins about Chaos?
Why was it only now that you chose to tell them?
Heh ...
Resurrecting you as the King of Chaos for the sake of my own curiousity and ambitions...
Do you hate me for what I've done, Arthur?
Uh...
Why would I hate you?
...
I mean, sure... Chaos is a darkness even the Demons fear and a light even the Goddesses revere.
It's a mighty will and a being that wrought this world, we Humans... and even the Gods themselves.

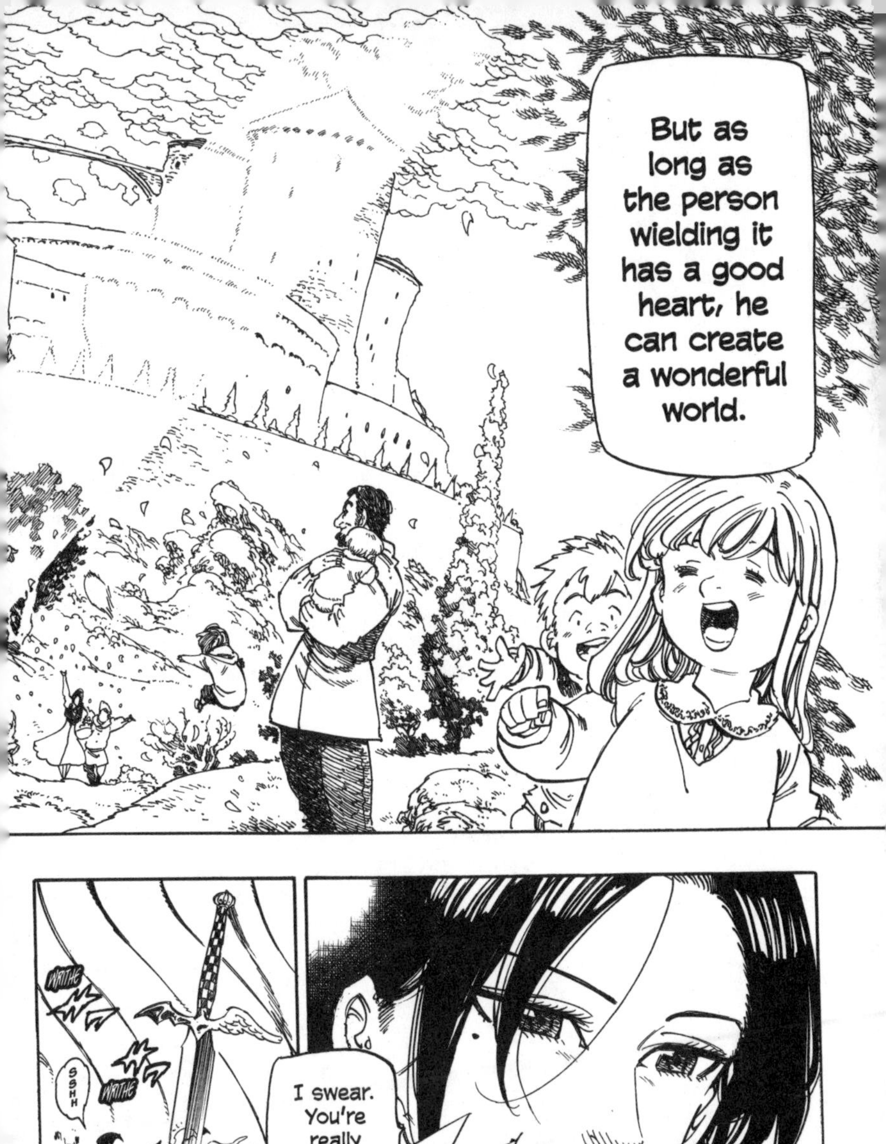
But as long as the person wielding it has a good heart, he can create a wonderful world.
I swear. You're really something else.
WRITHE
SSHH
WRITHE

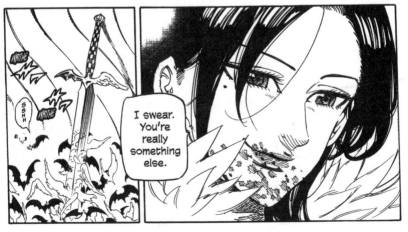

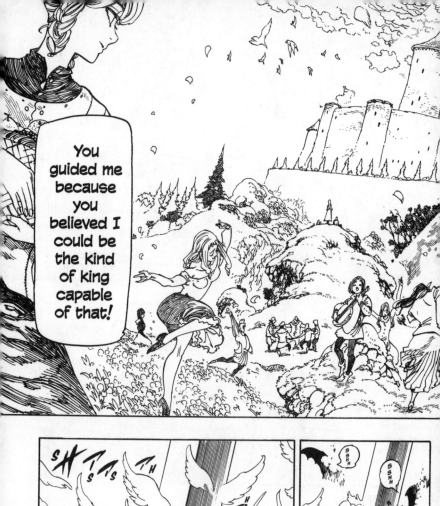

You guided me because you believed I could be the kind of king capable of that!

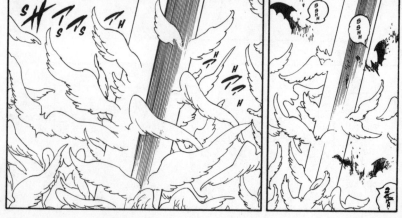

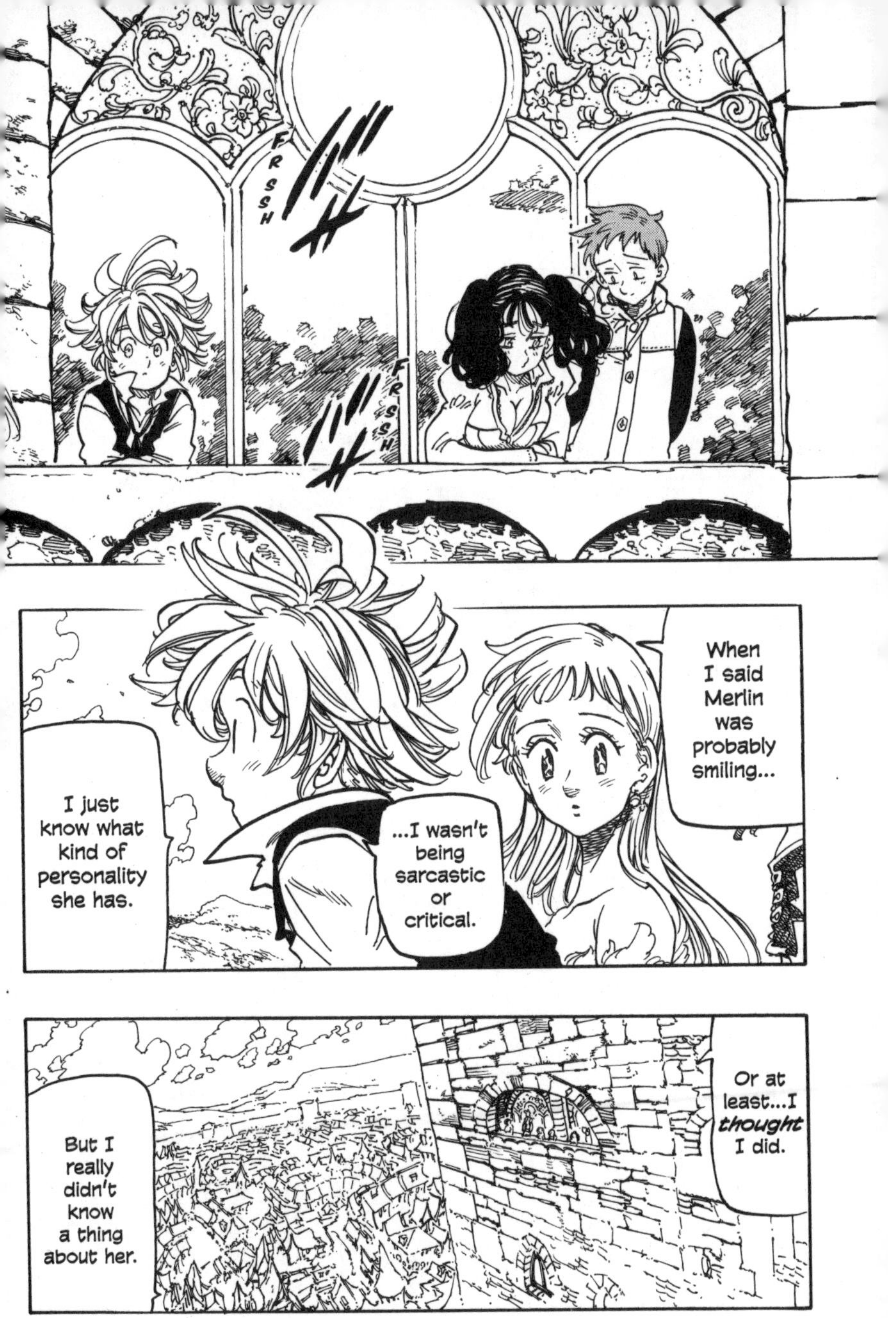
FRSSH
FRSSH
When I said Merlin was probably smiling...
...I wasn't being sarcastic or critical.
I just know what kind of personality she has.
Or at least...I *thought* I did.
But I really didn't know a thing about her.

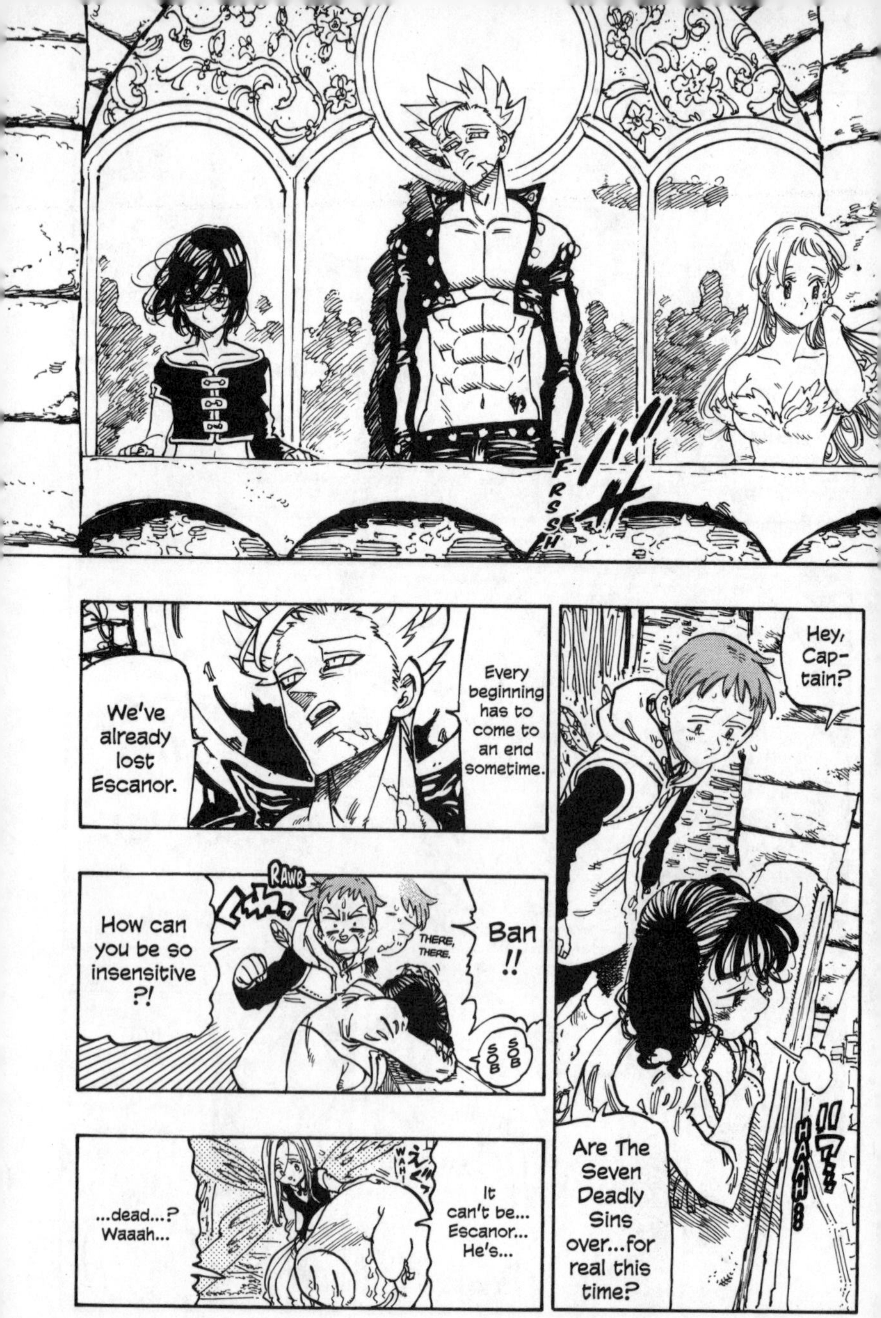
FRSSH
Hey, Captain?
Are The Seven Deadly Sins over...for real this time?
Every beginning has to come to an end sometime.
We've already lost Escanor.
Ban!!
RAWR
THERE, THERE.
SOB SOB
How can you be so insensitive?!
WAH!
It can't be... Escanor... He's...
...dead...? Waaah...

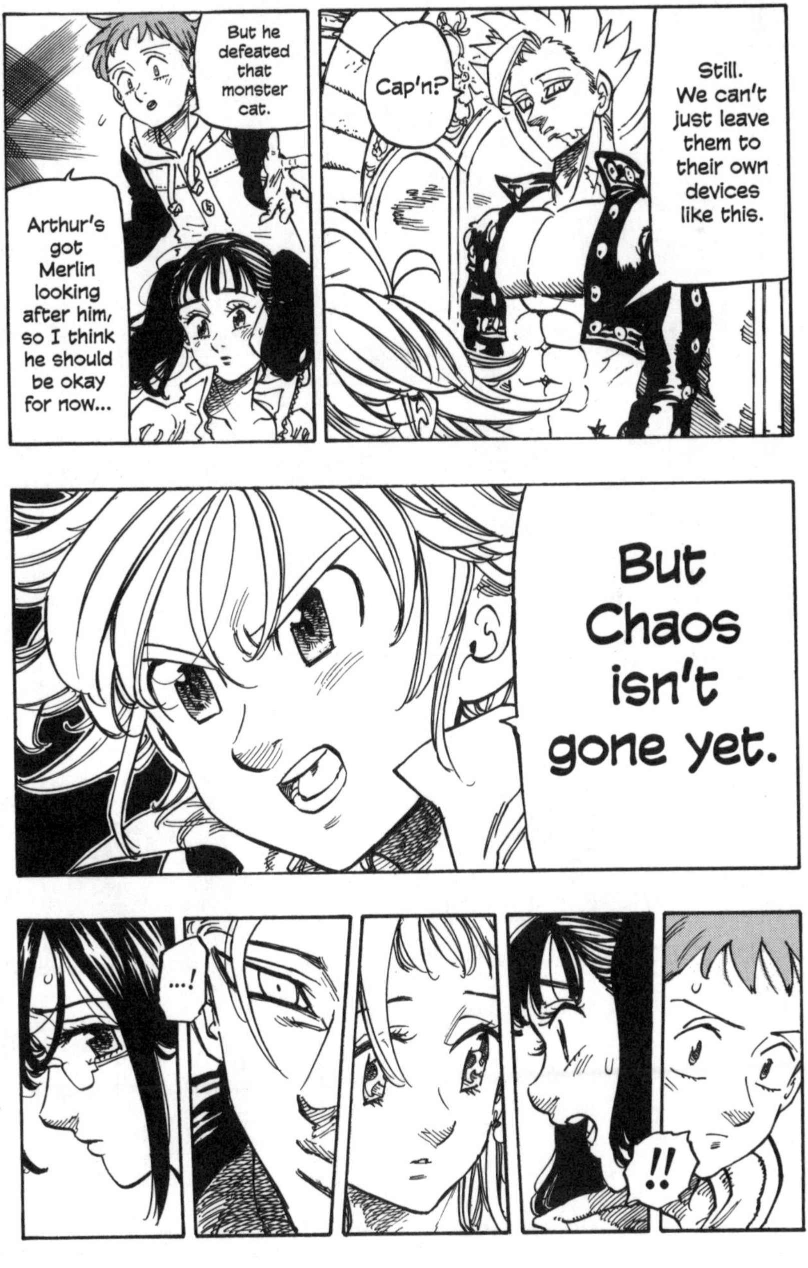
Still. We can't just leave them to their own devices like this.
Cap'n?
But he defeated that monster cat.
Arthur's got Merlin looking after him, so I think he should be okay for now...
But Chaos isn't gone yet.
!!
...!

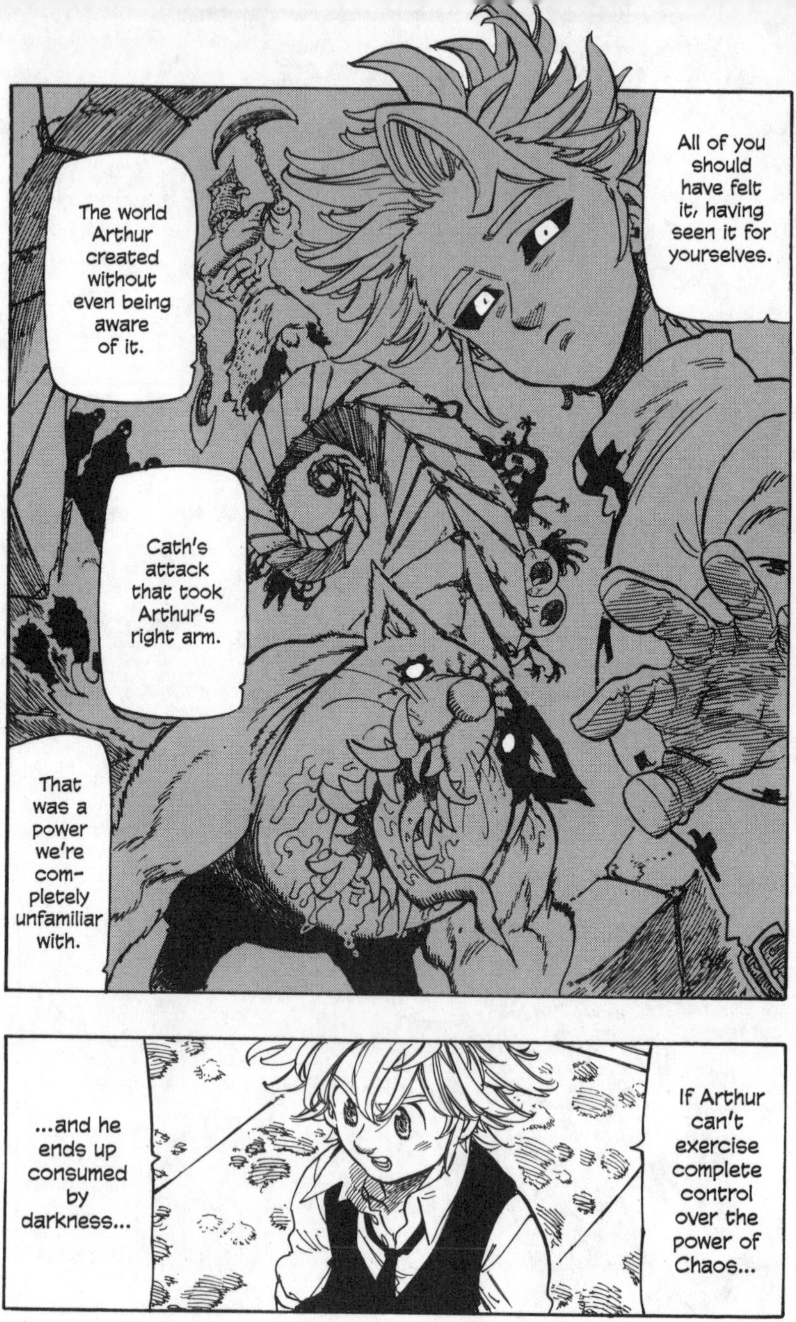
All of you should have felt it, having seen it for yourselves.
The world Arthur created without even being aware of it.
Cath's attack that took Arthur's right arm.
That was a power we're com-pletely unfamiliar with.
If Arthur can't exercise complete control over the power of Chaos...
...and he ends up consumed by darkness...

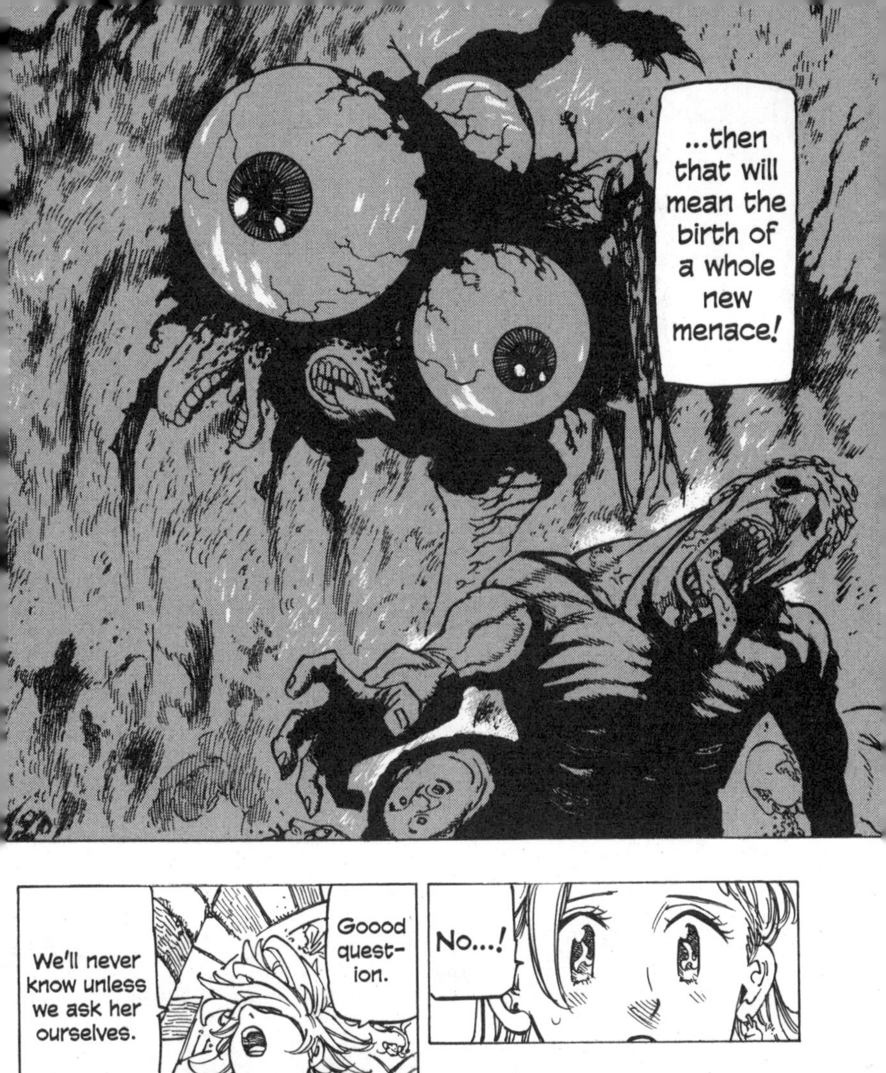
...then that will mean the birth of a whole new menace!
No...!
Why did Merlin stay quiet about Chaos all this time?
Why did she only tell us about it now?
Goood question.
We'll never know unless we ask her ourselves.

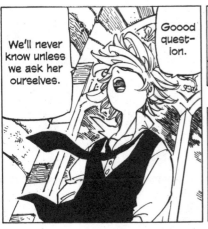

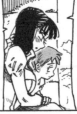

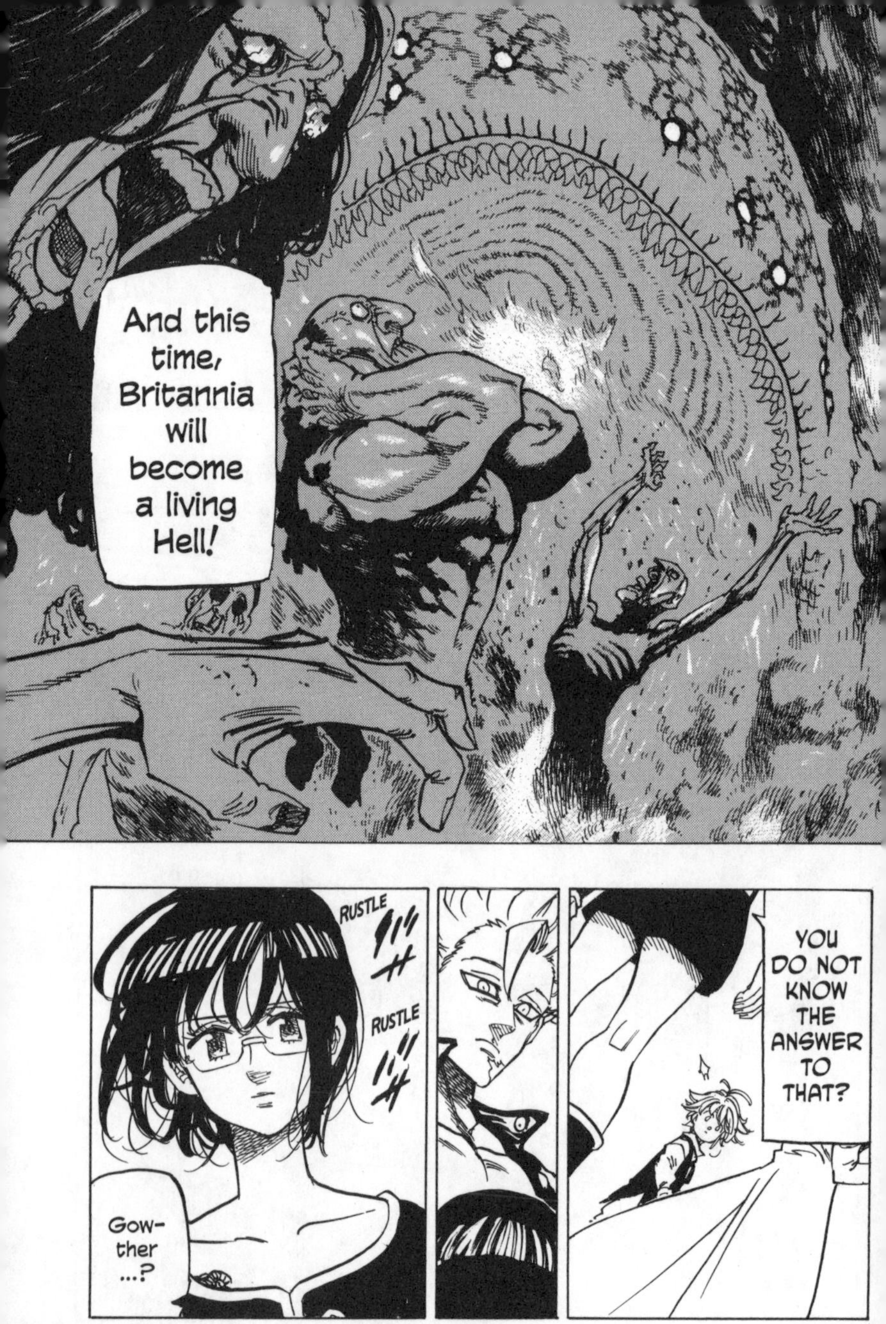
And this time, Britannia will become a living Hell!
YOU DO NOT KNOW THE ANSWER TO THAT?
RUSTLE
RUSTLE
Gow-ther ...?

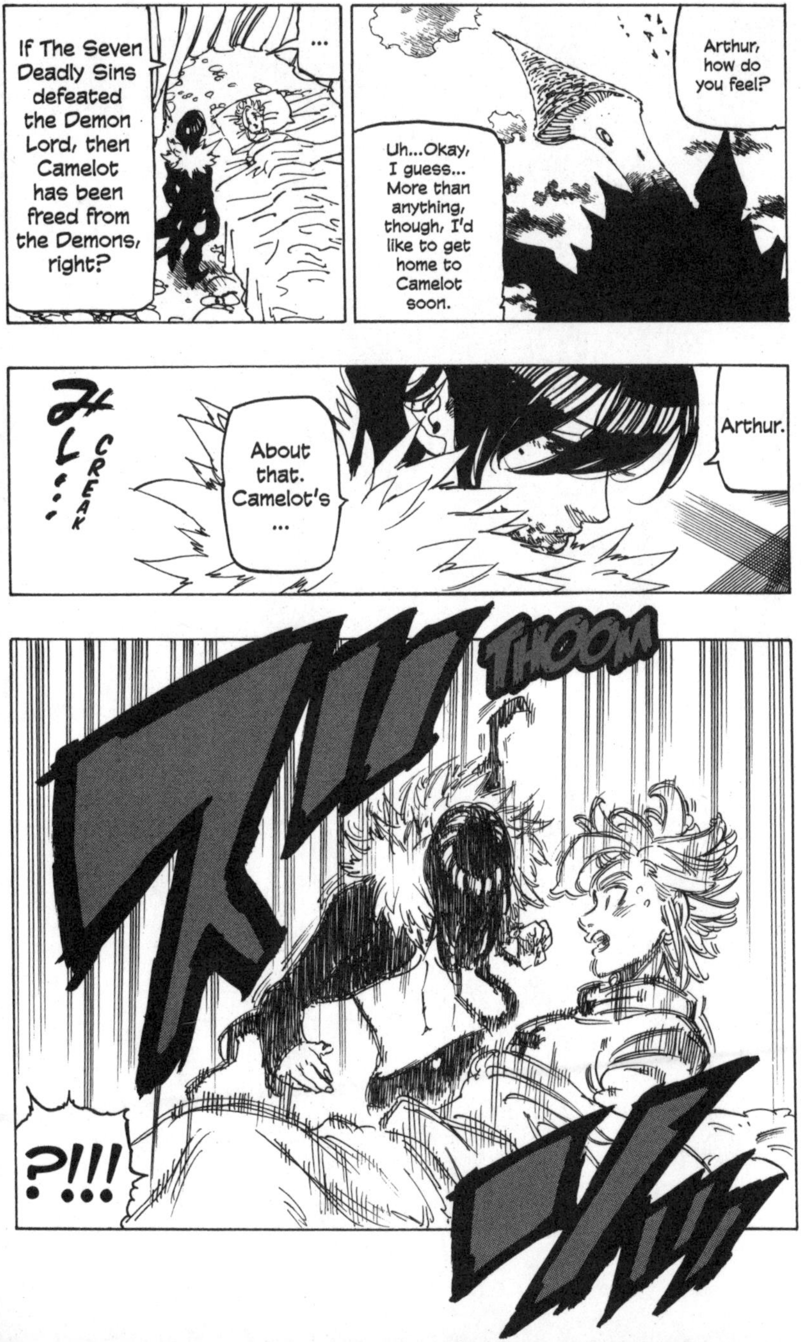
Arthur, how do you feel?
Uh...Okay, I guess... More than anything, though, I'd like to get home to Camelot soon.
...
If The Seven Deadly Sins defeated the Demon Lord, then Camelot has been freed from the Demons, right?
Arthur.
About that. Camelot's ...
CREAK
THOOM
?!!!

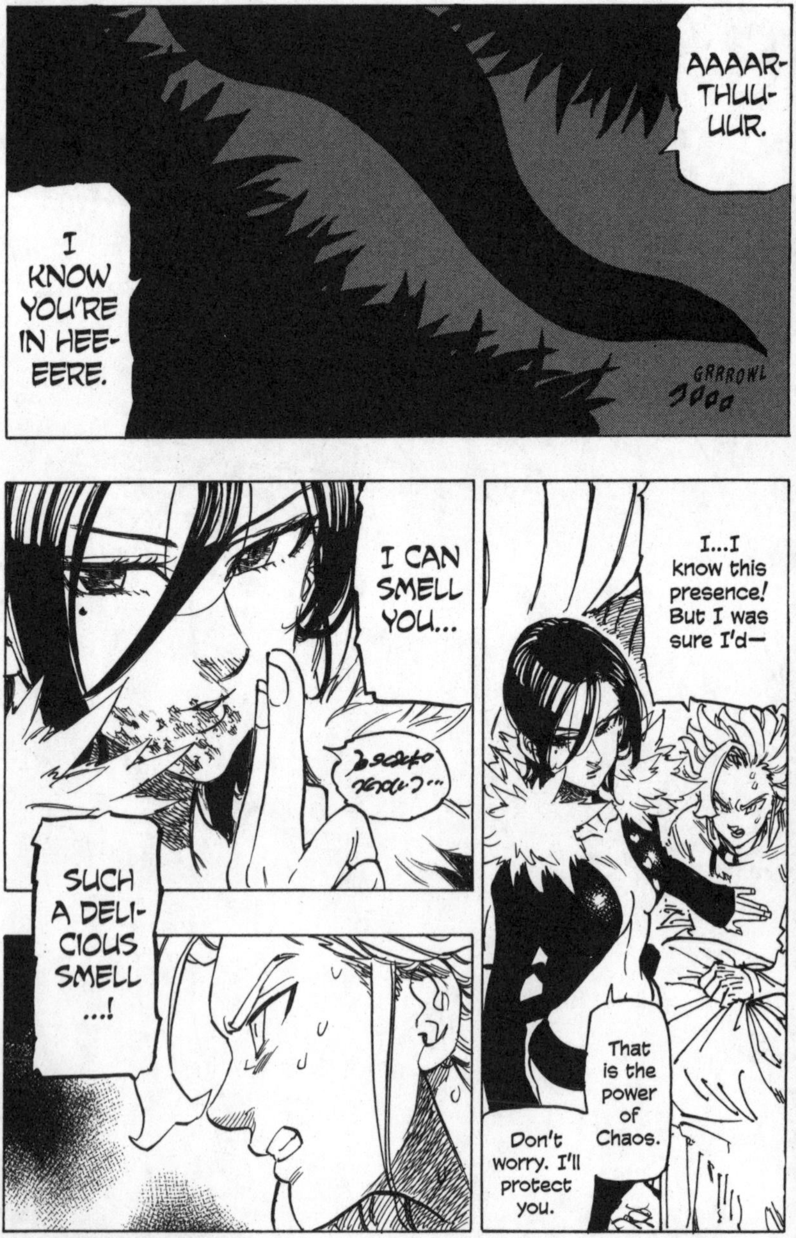
AAAAR-THUU-UUR.
I KNOW YOU'RE IN HEE-EERE.
GRRROWL
I...I know this presence! But I was sure I'd—
That is the power of Chaos.
Don't worry. I'll protect you.
I CAN SMELL YOU...
SUCH A DELICIOUS SMELL ...!

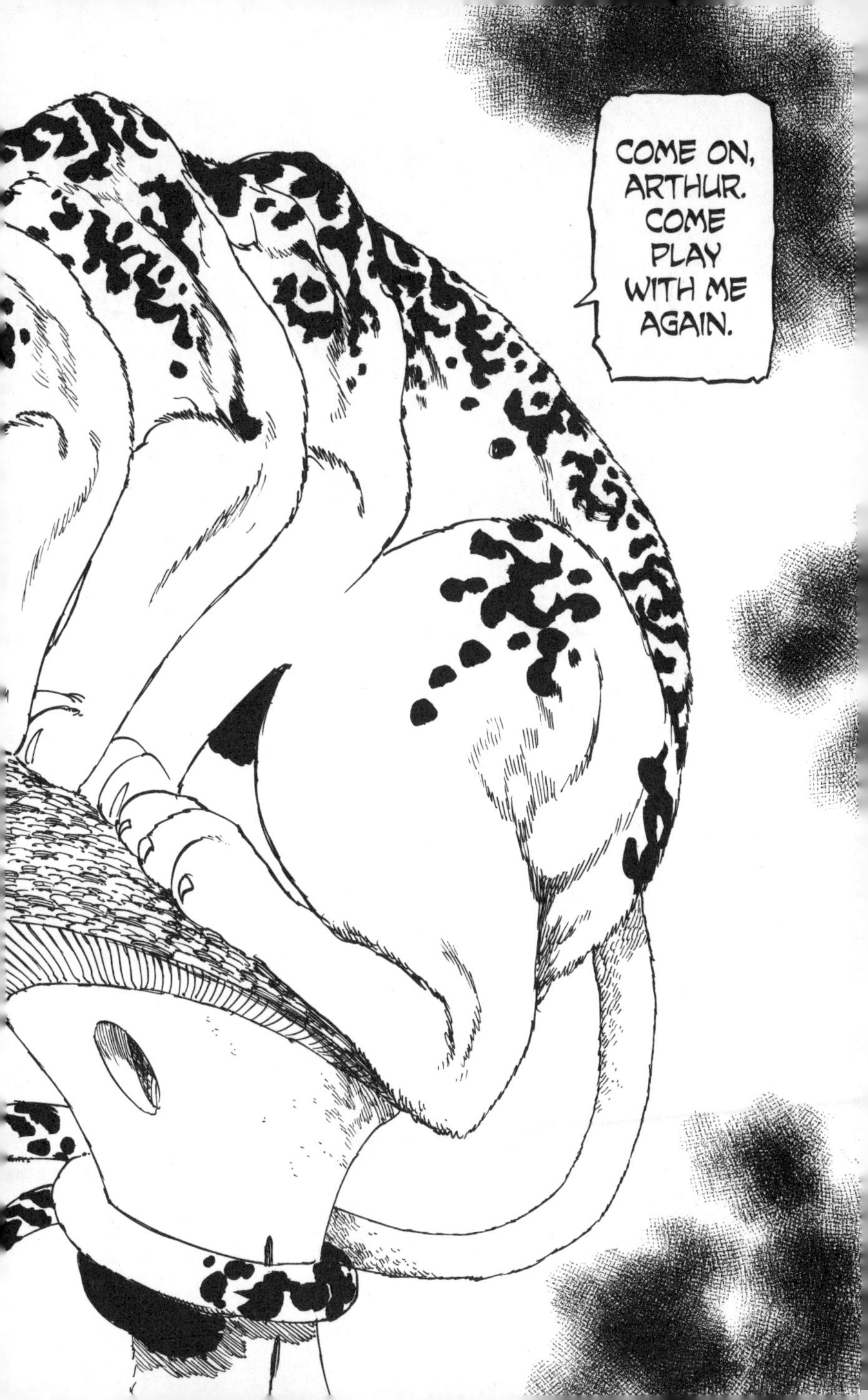
COME ON, ARTHUR. COME PLAY WITH ME AGAIN.

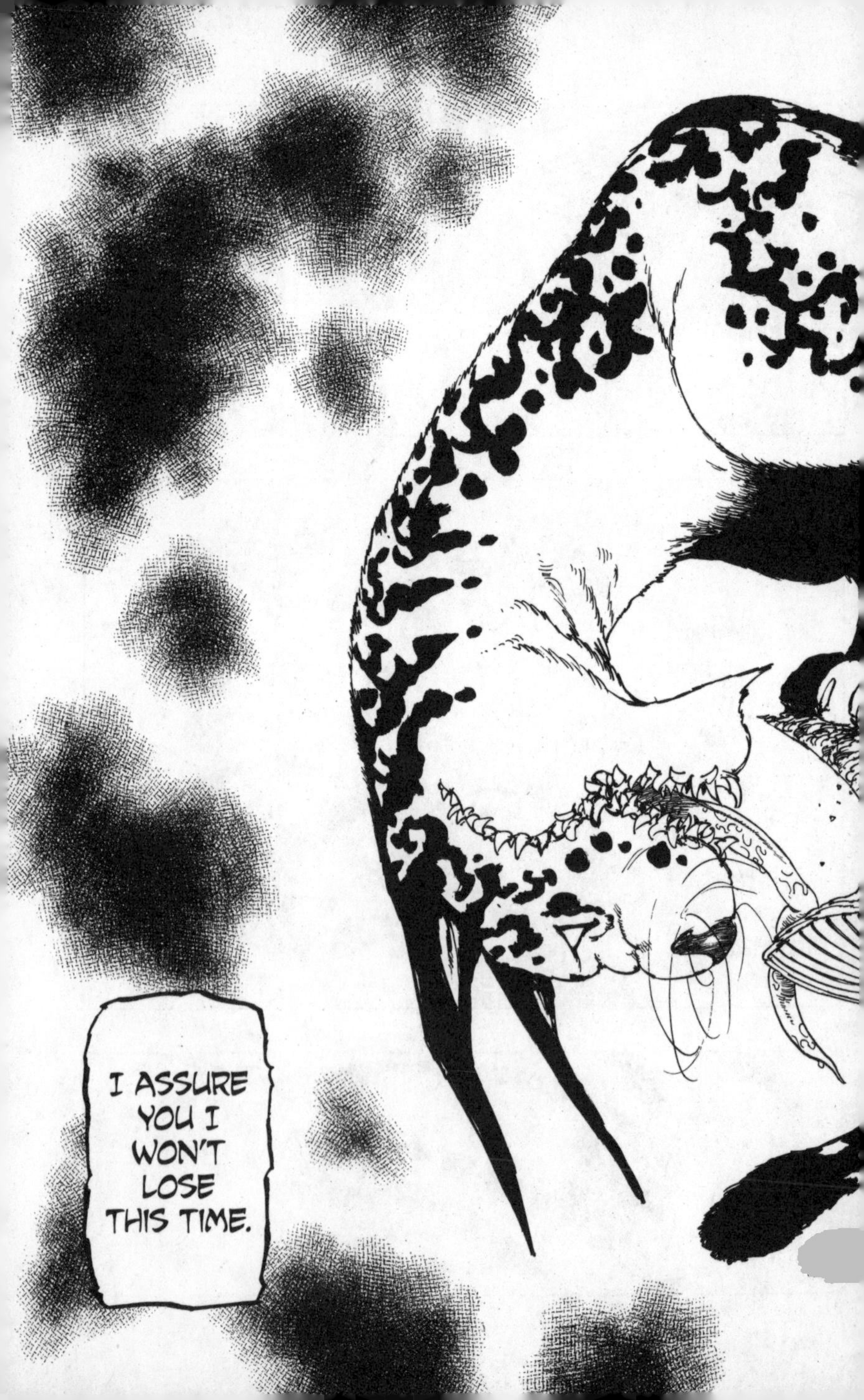
I ASSURE YOU I WON'T LOSE THIS TIME.

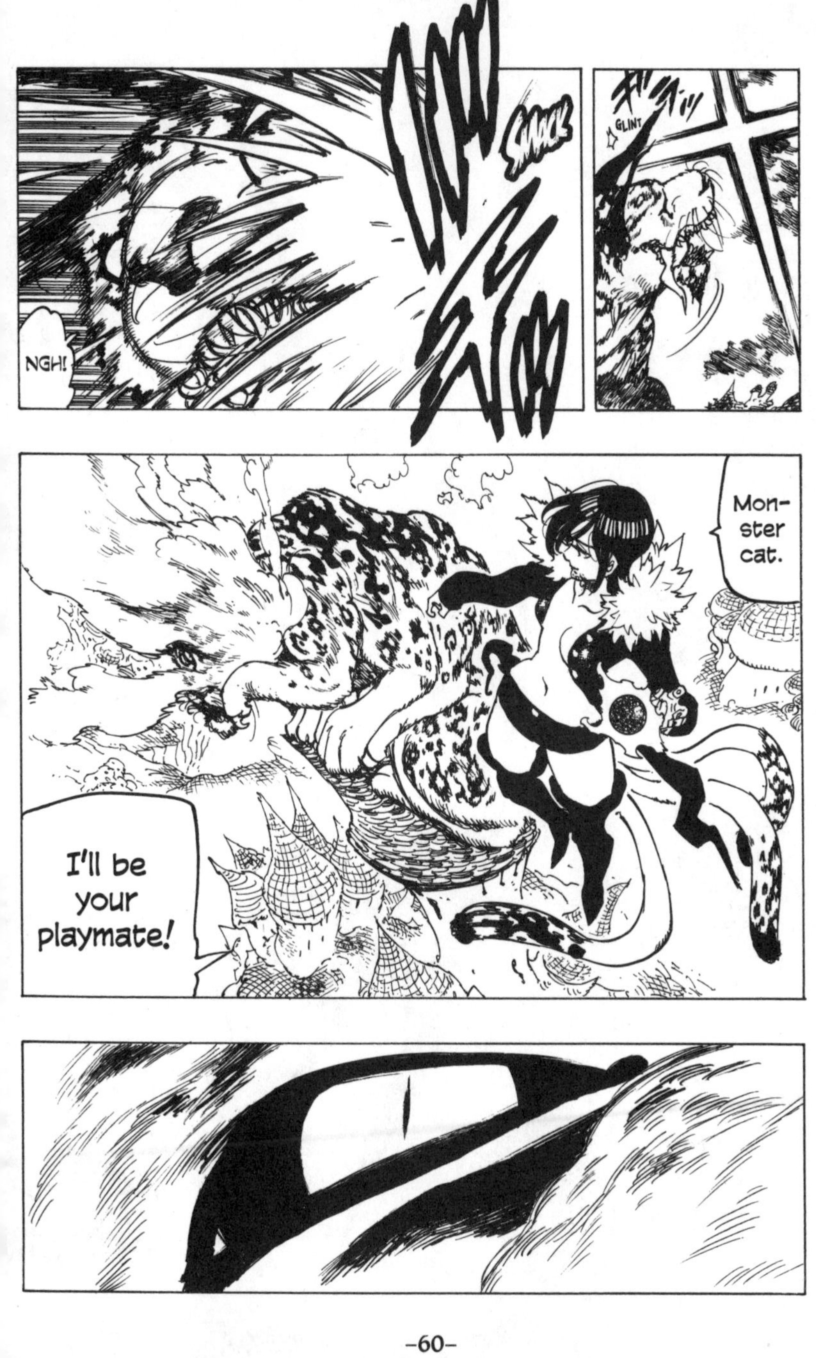
GLINT
SMACK
NGH!
Monster cat.
I'll be your playmate!

Chapter 341 - Cath Palug

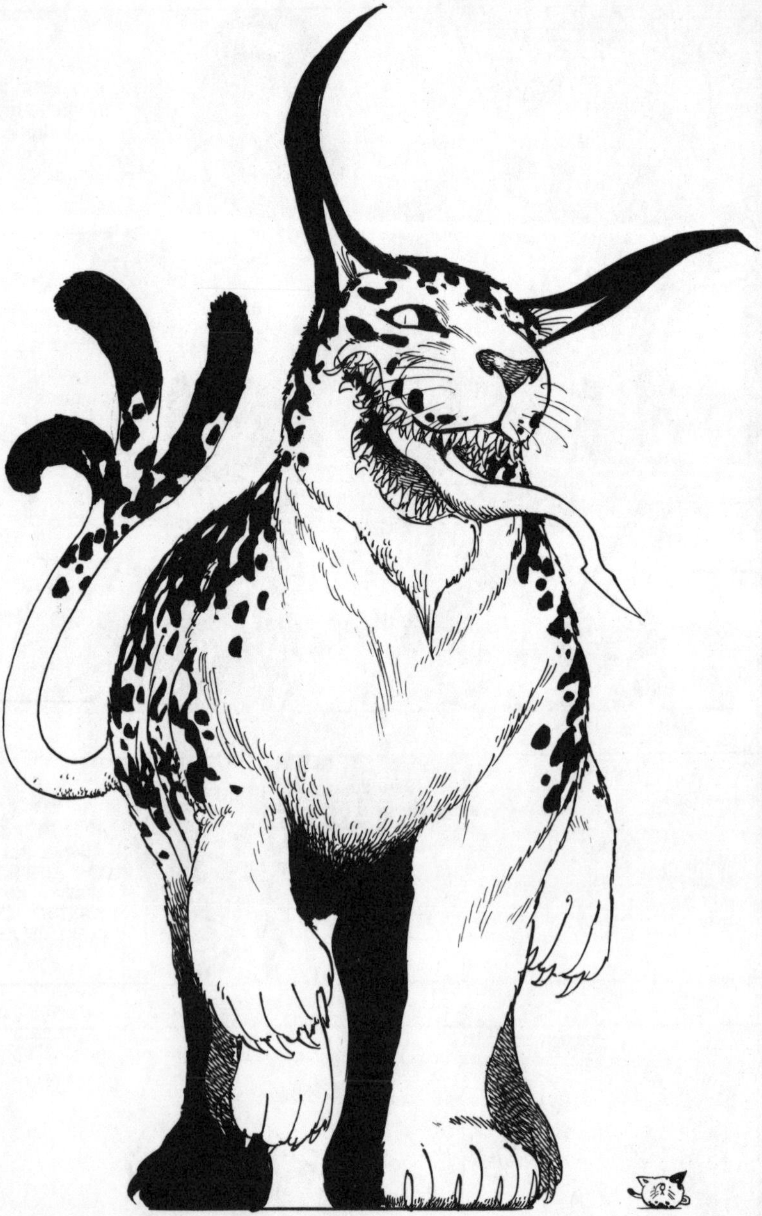

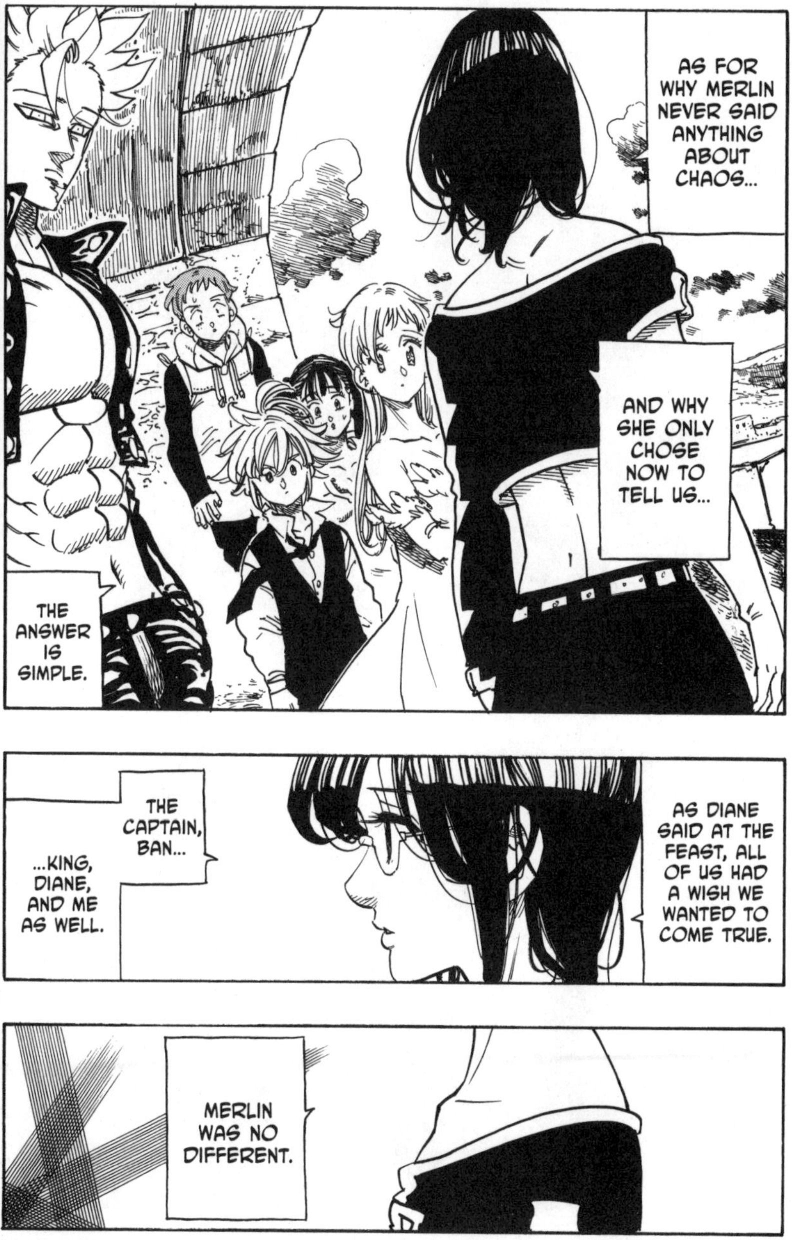
AS FOR WHY MERLIN NEVER SAID ANYTHING ABOUT CHAOS...
AND WHY SHE ONLY CHOSE NOW TO TELL US...
THE ANSWER IS SIMPLE.
AS DIANE SAID AT THE FEAST, ALL OF US HAD A WISH WE WANTED TO COME TRUE.
THE CAPTAIN, BAN...
...KING, DIANE, AND ME AS WELL.
MERLIN WAS NO DIFFERENT.

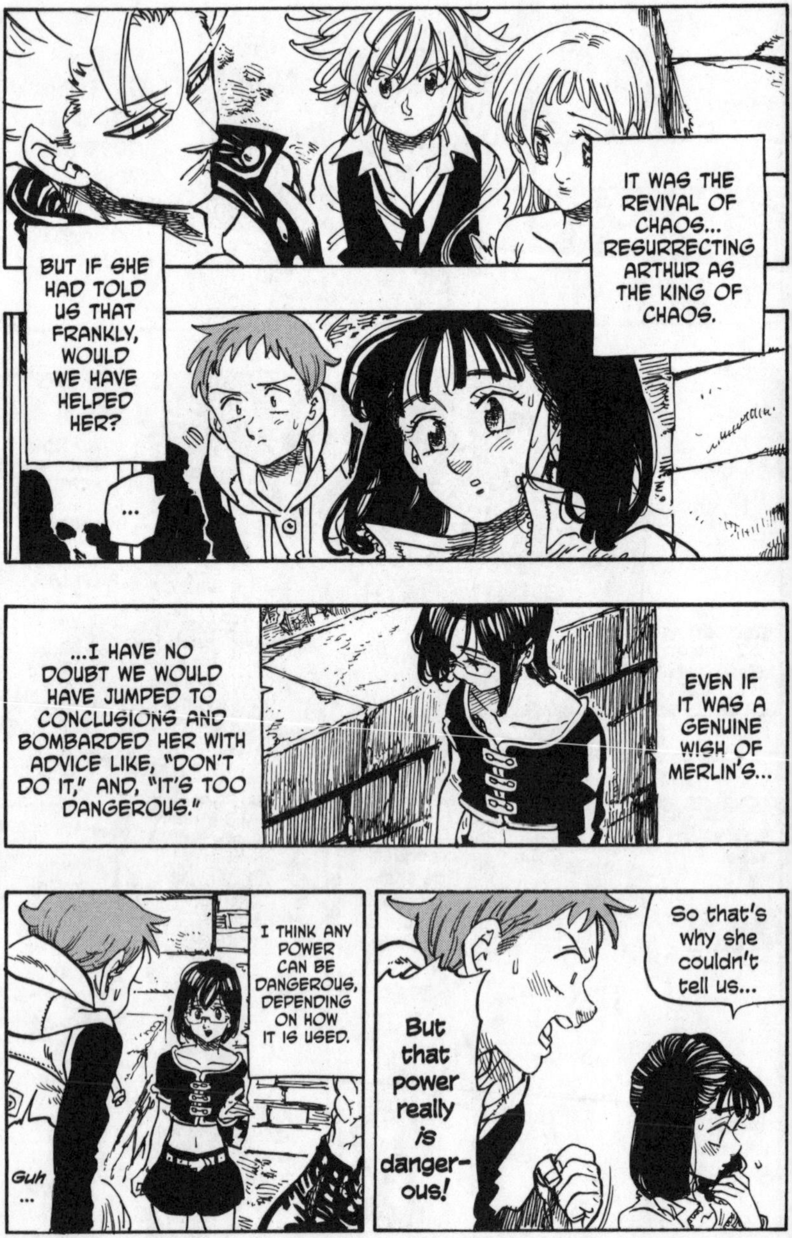
IT WAS THE REVIVAL OF CHAOS... RESURRECTING ARTHUR AS THE KING OF CHAOS.
BUT IF SHE HAD TOLD US THAT FRANKLY, WOULD WE HAVE HELPED HER?
...
EVEN IF IT WAS A GENUINE WISH OF MERLIN'S...
...I HAVE NO DOUBT WE WOULD HAVE JUMPED TO CONCLUSIONS AND BOMBARDED HER WITH ADVICE LIKE, "DON'T DO IT," AND, "IT'S TOO DANGEROUS."
So that's why she couldn't tell us...
But that power really *is* danger-ous!
I THINK ANY POWER CAN BE DANGEROUS, DEPENDING ON HOW IT IS USED.
Guh ...

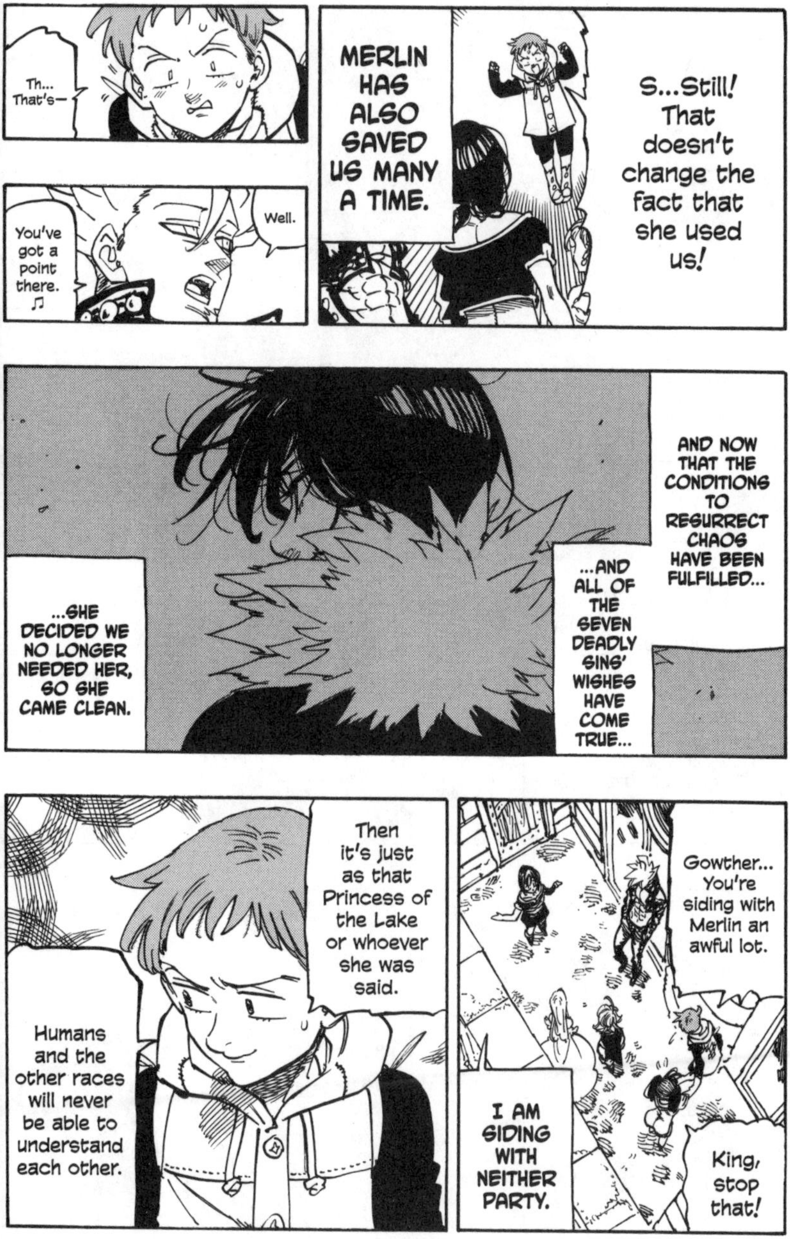
S...Still! That doesn't change the fact that she used us!
MERLIN HAS ALSO SAVED US MANY A TIME.
Th... That's—
Well.
You've got a point there. ♫
AND NOW THAT THE CONDITIONS TO RESURRECT CHAOS HAVE BEEN FULFILLED...
...AND ALL OF THE SEVEN DEADLY SINS' WISHES HAVE COME TRUE...
...SHE DECIDED WE NO LONGER NEEDED HER, SO SHE CAME CLEAN.
Gowther... You're siding with Merlin an awful lot.
I AM SIDING WITH NEITHER PARTY.
King, stop that!
Then it's just as that Princess of the Lake or whoever she was said.
Humans and the other races will never be able to understand each other.

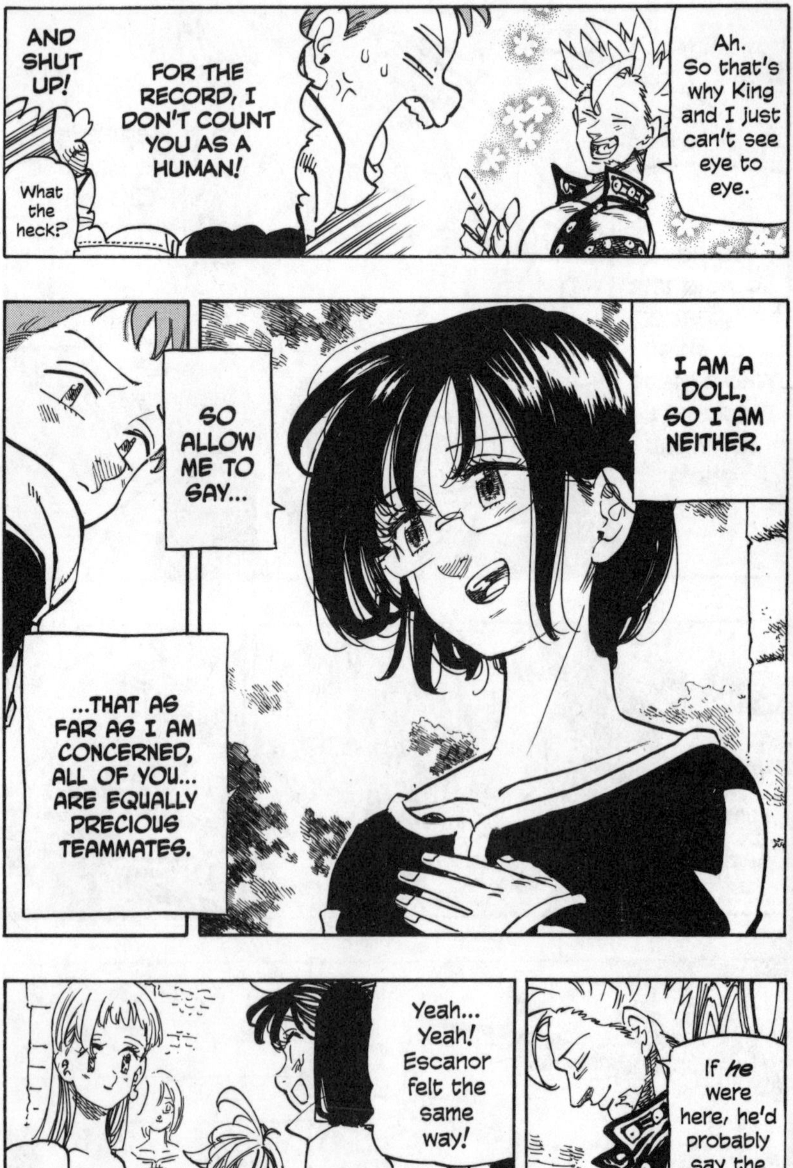
Ah. So that's why King and I just can't see eye to eye.
FOR THE RECORD, I DON'T COUNT YOU AS A HUMAN!
AND SHUT UP!
What the heck?
I AM A DOLL, SO I AM NEITHER.
SO ALLOW ME TO SAY...
...THAT AS FAR AS I AM CONCERNED, ALL OF YOU... ARE EQUALLY PRECIOUS TEAMMATES.
If *he* were here, he'd probably say the same thing. ♫
Yeah... Yeah! Escanor felt the same way!
He did.

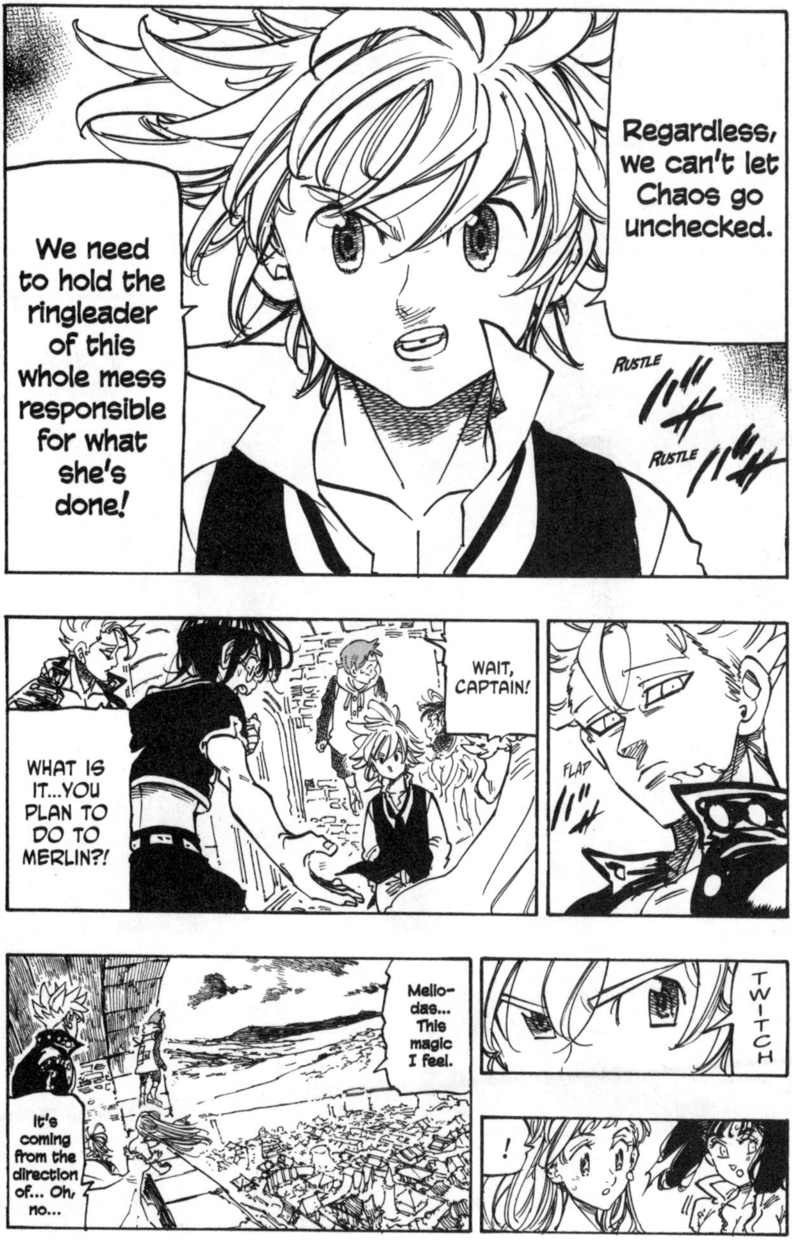
Regardless, we can't let Chaos go unchecked.
We need to hold the ringleader of this whole mess responsible for what she's done!
RUSTLE
RUSTLE
FLAP
WAIT, CAPTAIN!
WHAT IS IT...YOU PLAN TO DO TO MERLIN?!
TWITCH
!
Mello-das... This magic I feel.
It's coming from the direction of... Oh, no...

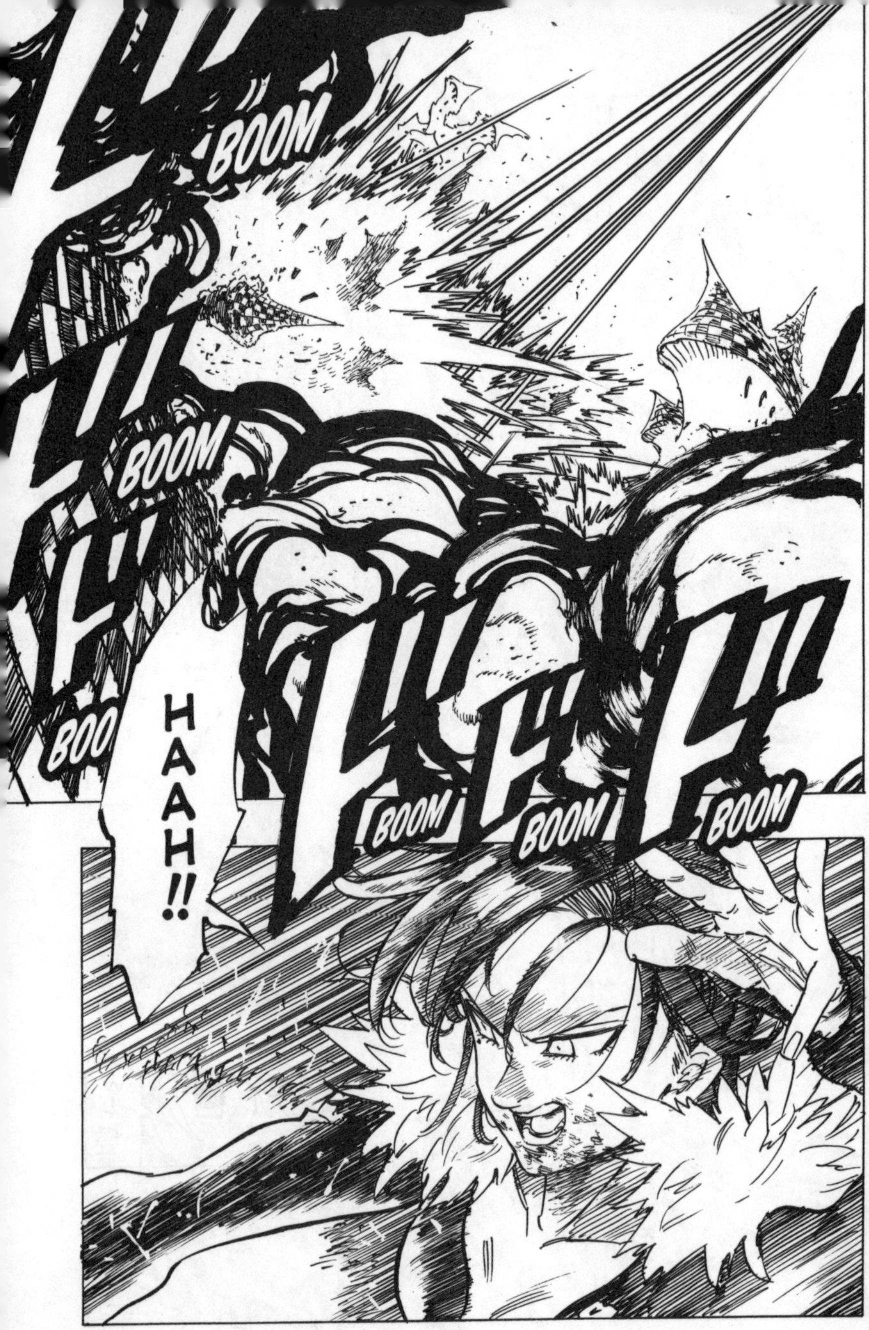
BOOM
BOOM
BOO
BOOM
BOOM
BOOM
HAAH!!

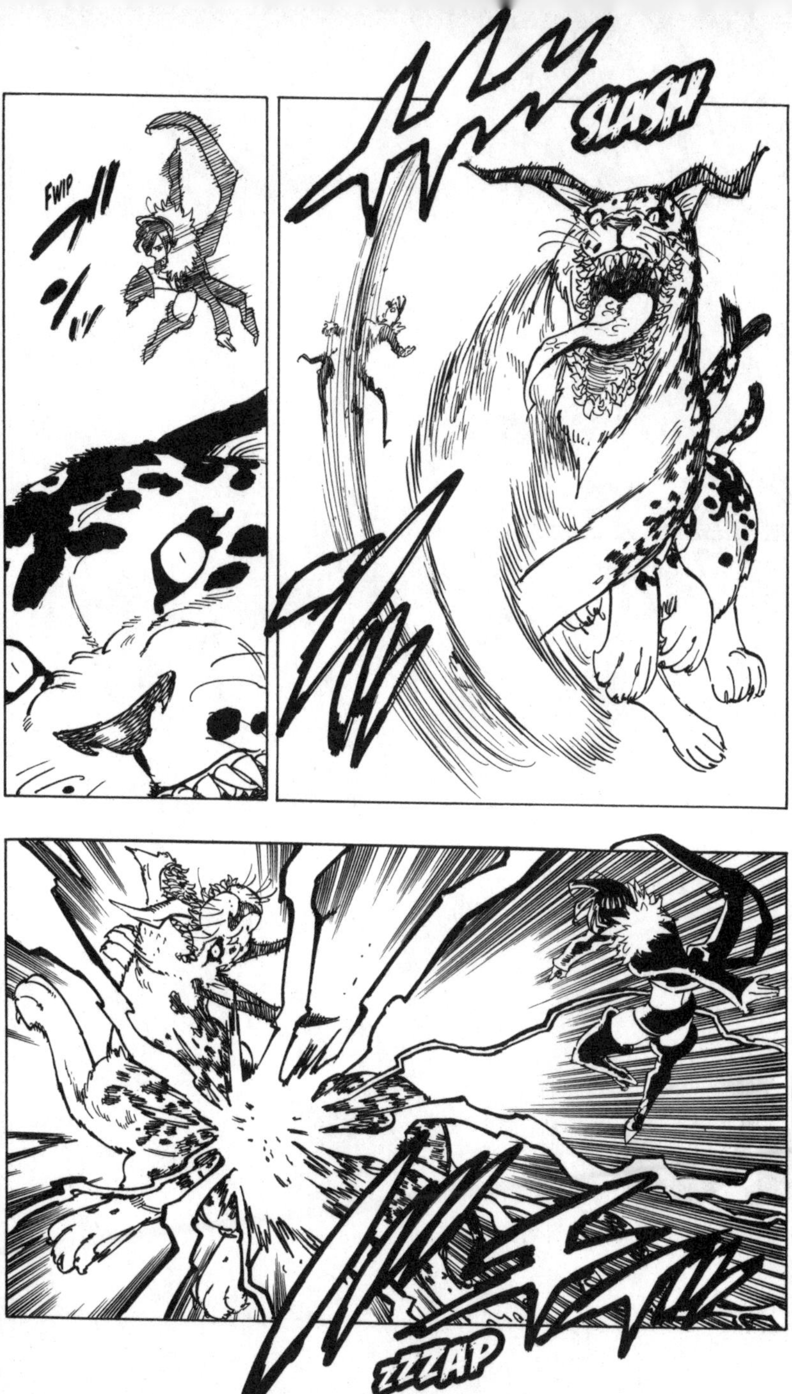
SLASH
FWIP
ZZZAP

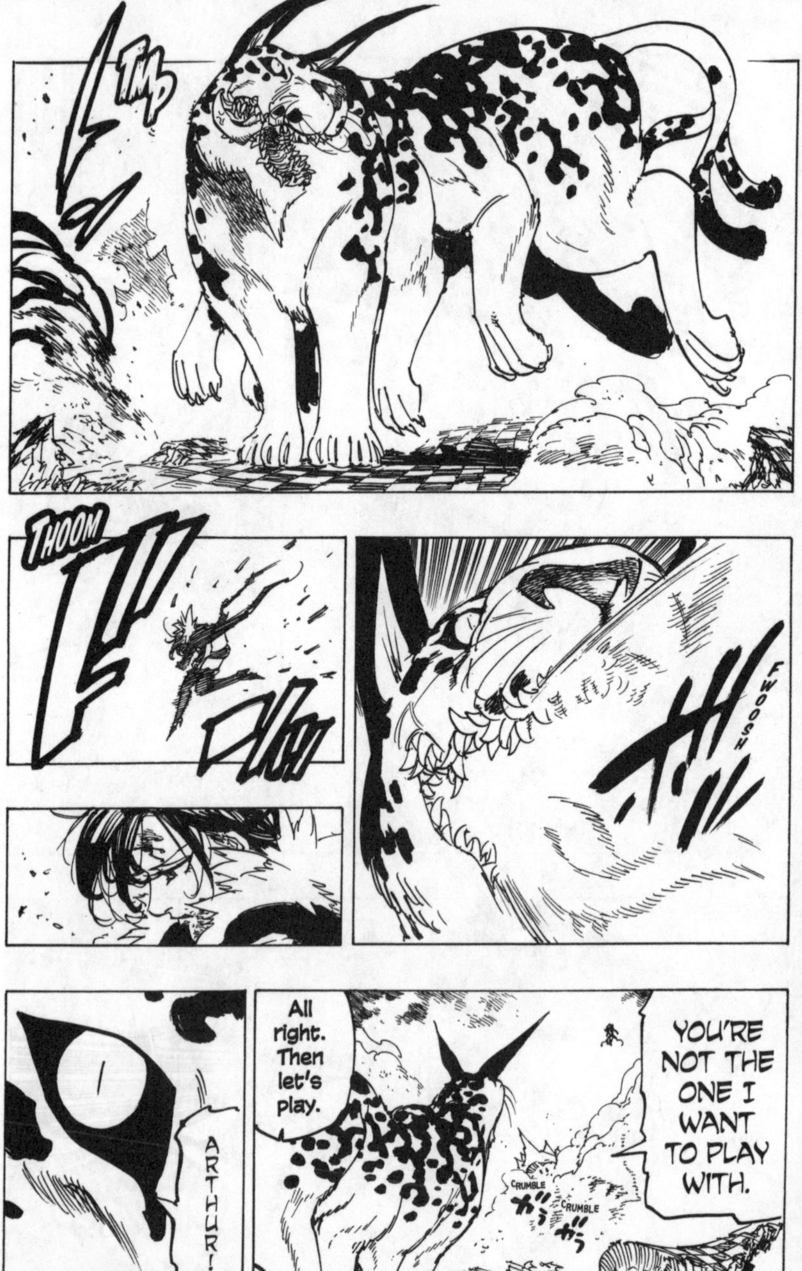
TMP
FWOOSH
THOOM
YOU'RE NOT THE ONE I WANT TO PLAY WITH.
CRUMBLE
CRUMBLE
All right. Then let's play.
ARTHUR!

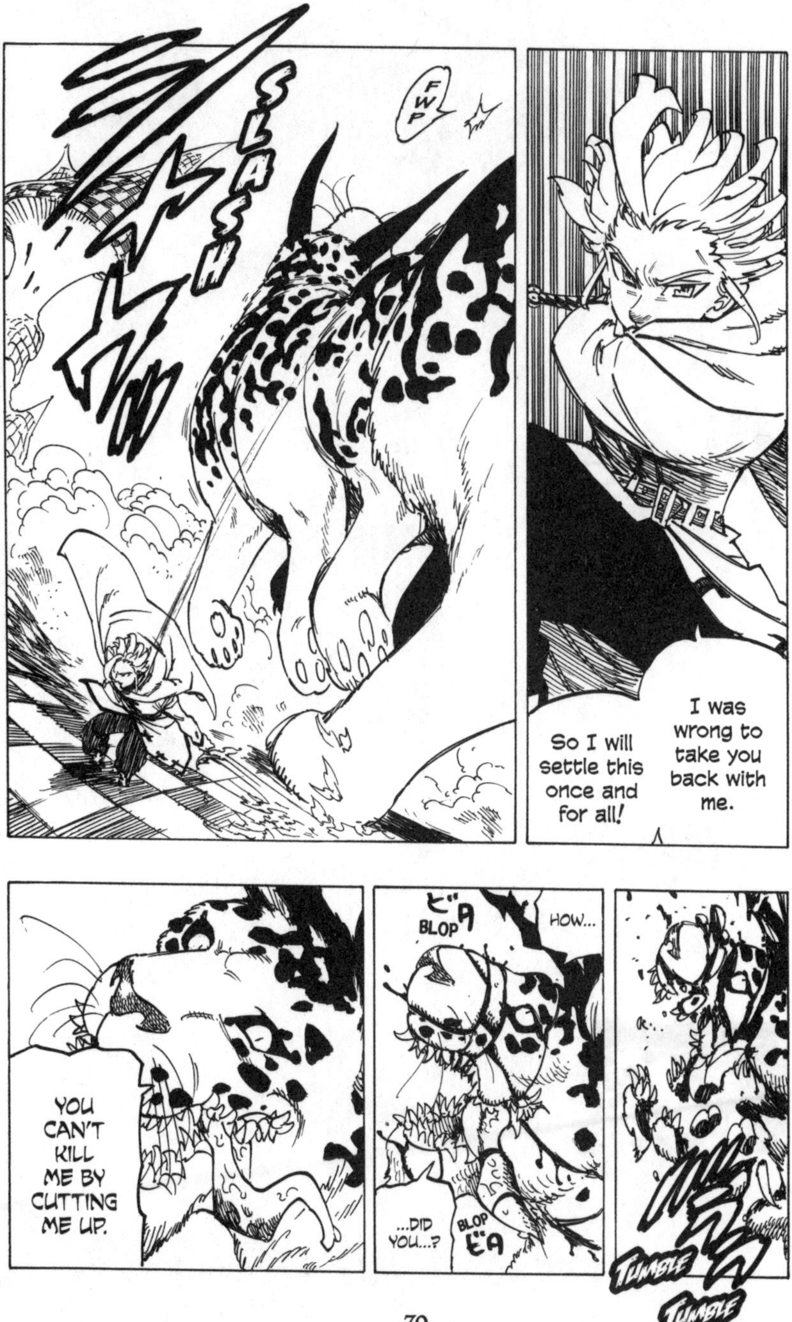
I was wrong to take you back with me.
So I will settle this once and for all!
FWP
SLASH
TUMBLE
TUMBLE
ビタ
BLOP
HOW...
...DID YOU...?
BLOP
ビタ
YOU CAN'T KILL ME BY CUTTING ME UP.

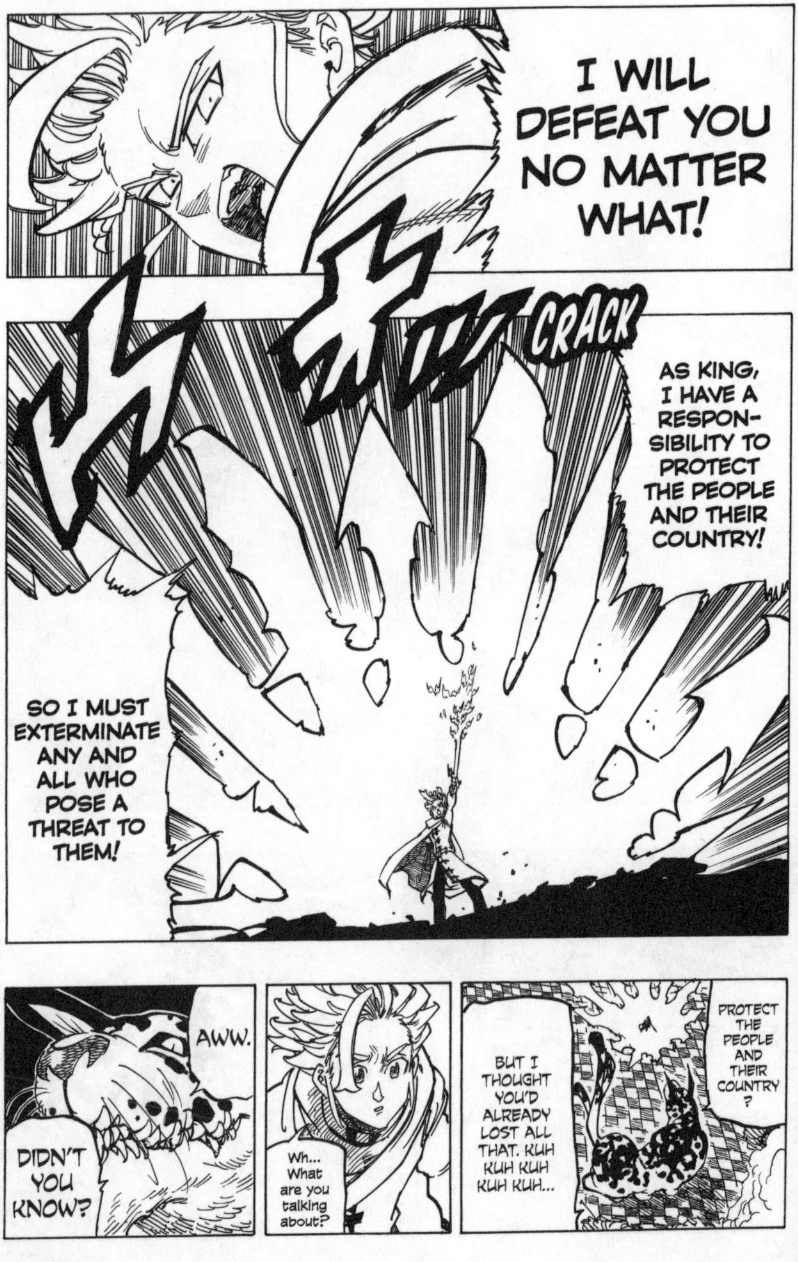
I WILL DEFEAT YOU NO MATTER WHAT!
CRACK
AS KING, I HAVE A RESPON-SIBILITY TO PROTECT THE PEOPLE AND THEIR COUNTRY!
SO I MUST EXTERMINATE ANY AND ALL WHO POSE A THREAT TO THEM!
PROTECT THE PEOPLE AND THEIR COUNTRY?
BUT I THOUGHT YOU'D ALREADY LOST ALL THAT. KUH KUH KUH KUH KUH...
Wh... What are you talking about?
AWW.
DIDN'T YOU KNOW?

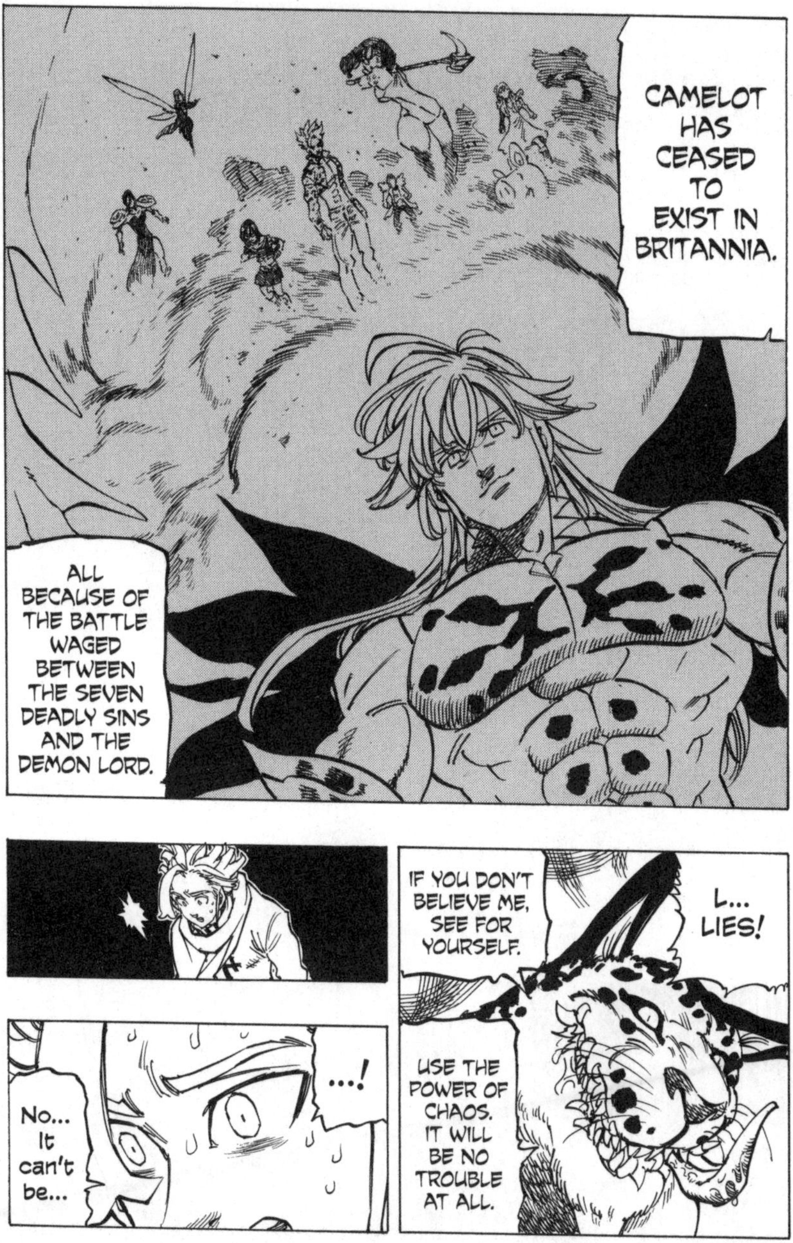
CAMELOT HAS CEASED TO EXIST IN BRITANNIA.
ALL BECAUSE OF THE BATTLE WAGED BETWEEN THE SEVEN DEADLY SINS AND THE DEMON LORD.
L... LIES!
IF YOU DON'T BELIEVE ME, SEE FOR YOURSELF.
USE THE POWER OF CHAOS. IT WILL BE NO TROUBLE AT ALL.
...!
No... It can't be...

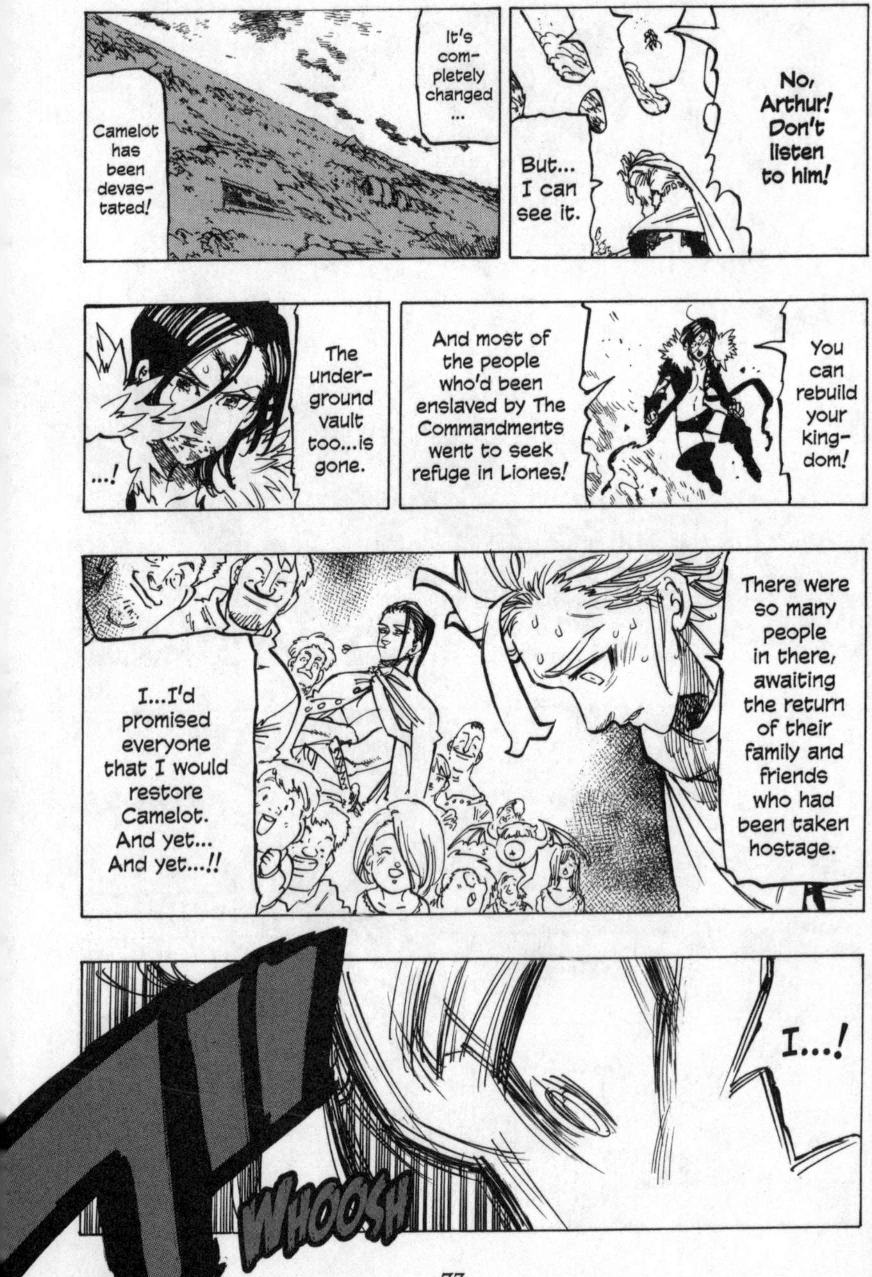

No, Arthur! Don't listen to him!
But... I can see it.
It's completely changed...
Camelot has been devastated!
You can rebuild your kingdom!
And most of the people who'd been enslaved by The Commandments went to seek refuge in Liones!
The underground vault too...is gone.
...!
There were so many people in there, awaiting the return of their family and friends who had been taken hostage.
I...I'd promised everyone that I would restore Camelot. And yet... And yet...!!
I...!
WHOOSH

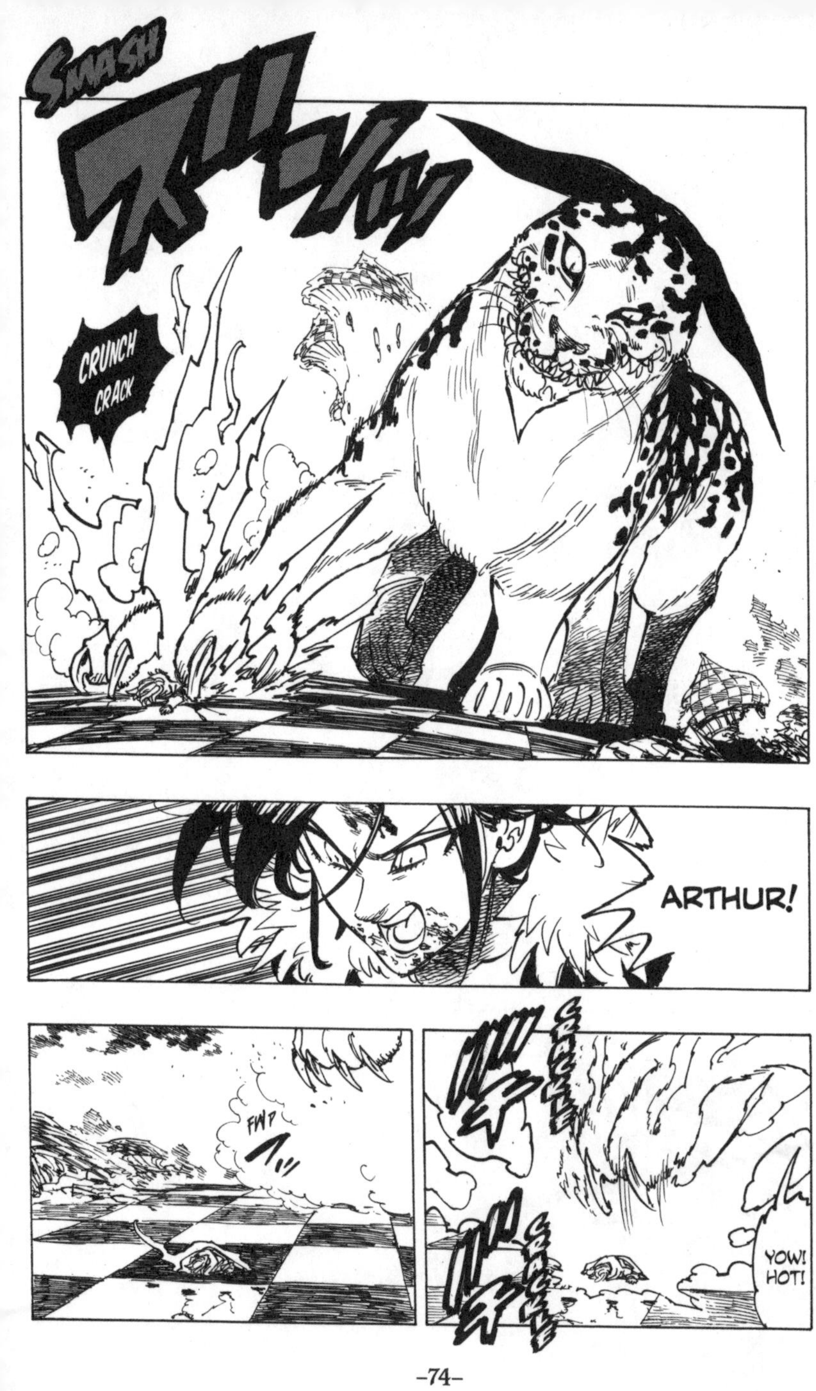
SMASH
CRUNCH
CRACK
ARTHUR!
CRACKLE
CRACKLE
YOW! HOT!
FWP

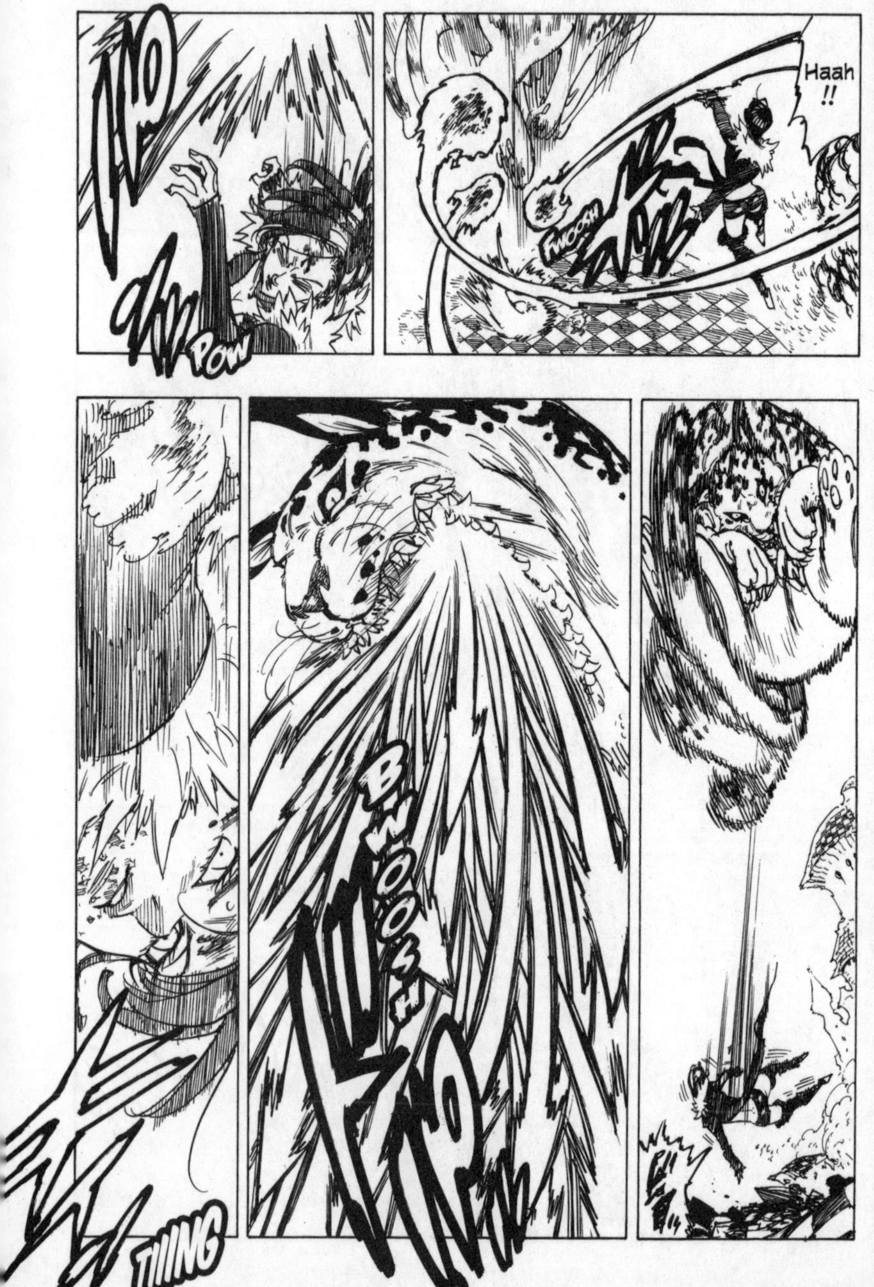
Haah !!
FWOOSH
POW
BWOOOSH
TIIIING

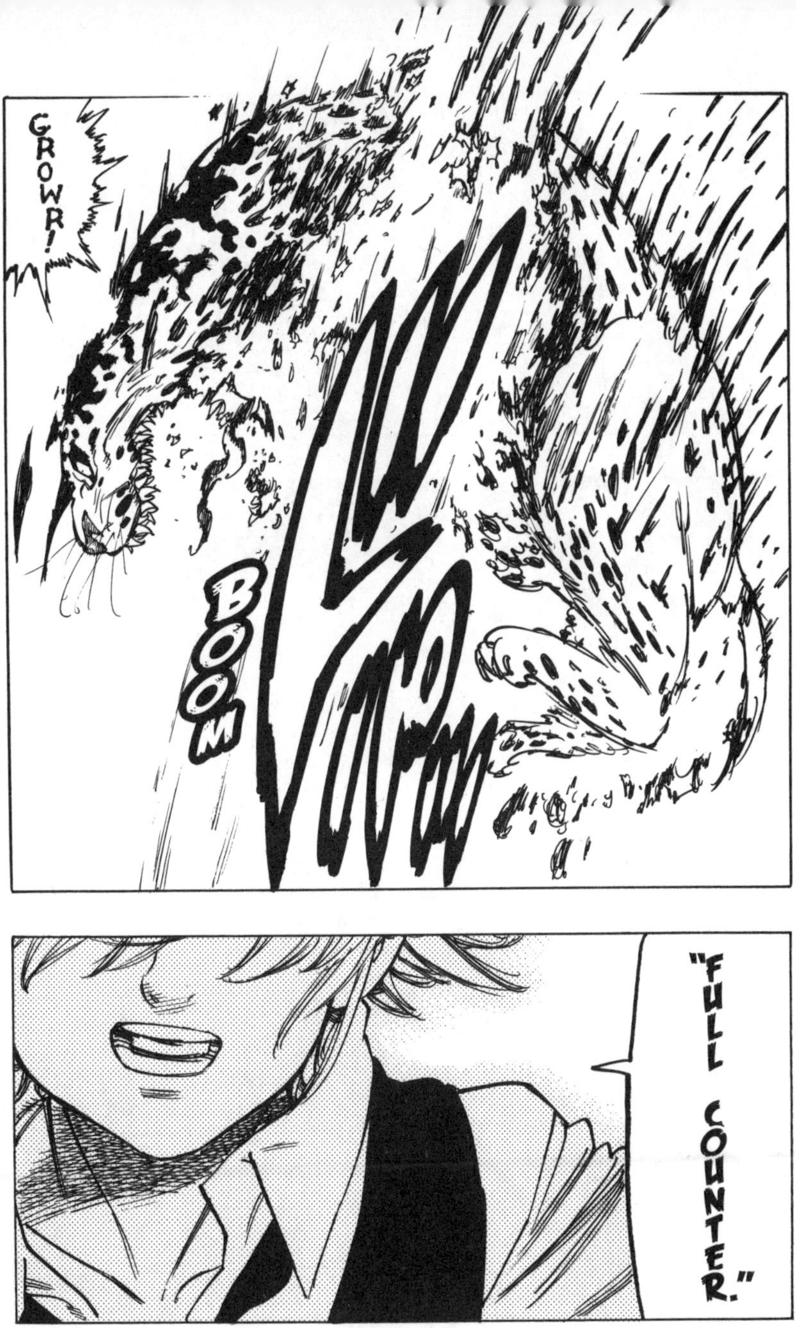
GROWR!
BOOOM
"FULL COUNTER."

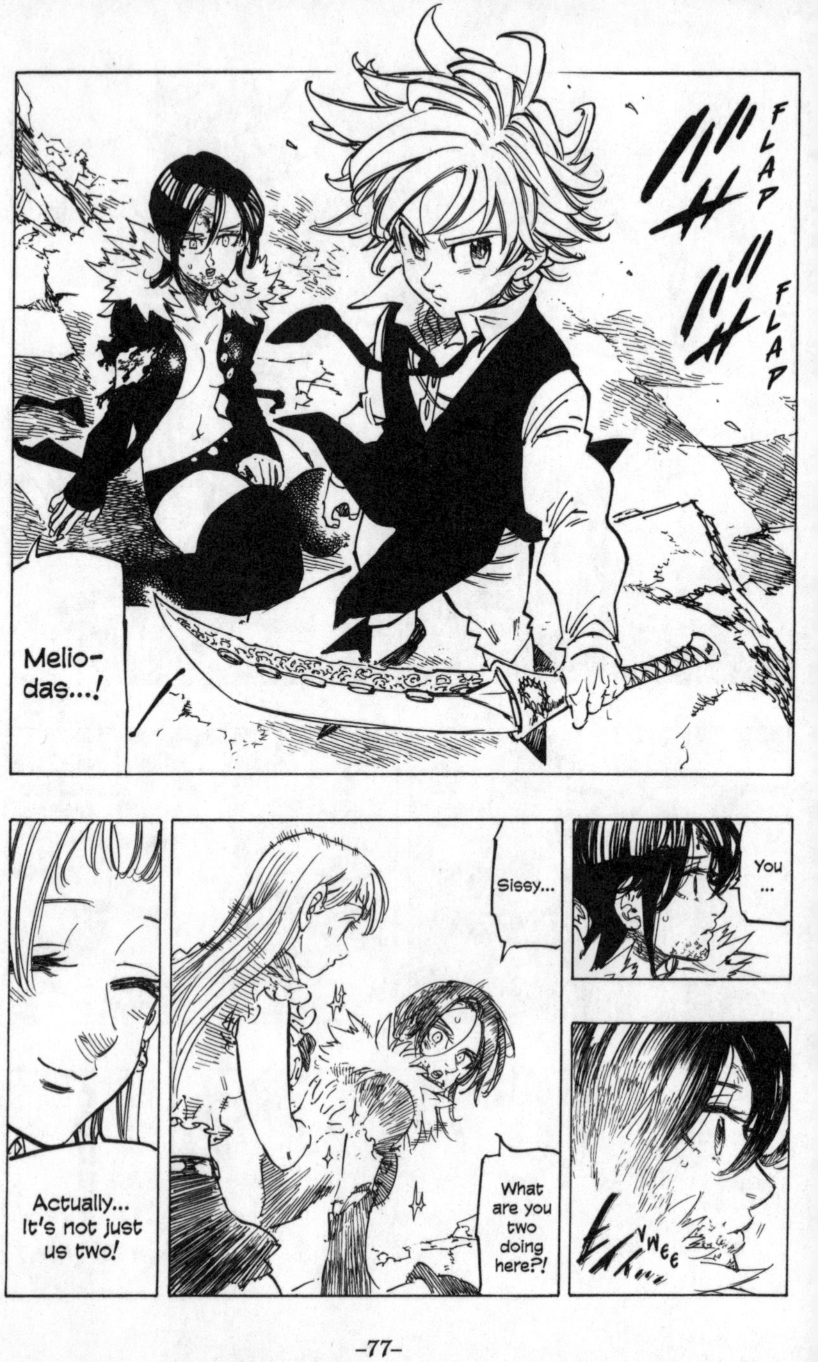
FLAP FLAP
Melio-das...!
You ...
VWEE
Sissy...
What are you two doing here?!
Actually... It's not just us two!

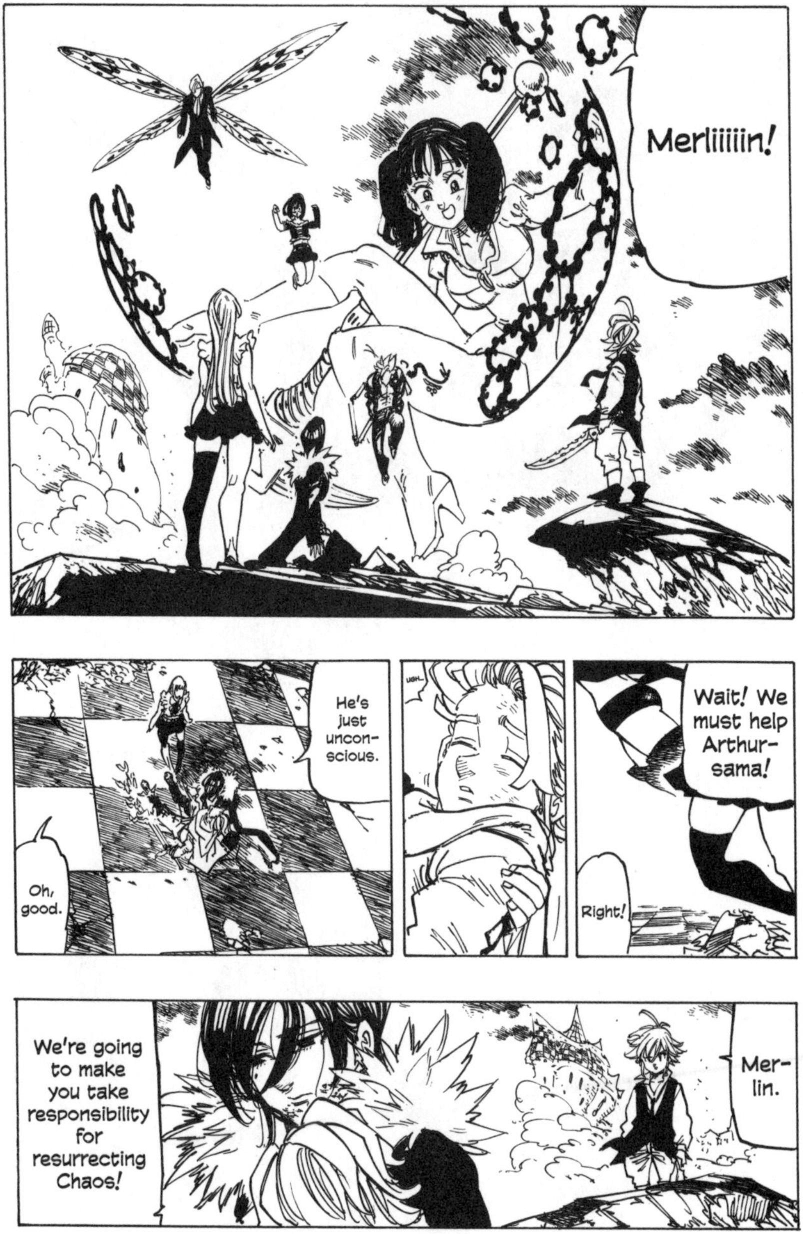
Merliiiiin!
Wait! We must help Arthur-sama!
Right!
UGH...
He's just unconscious.
Oh, good.
Merlin.
We're going to make you take responsibility for resurrecting Chaos!

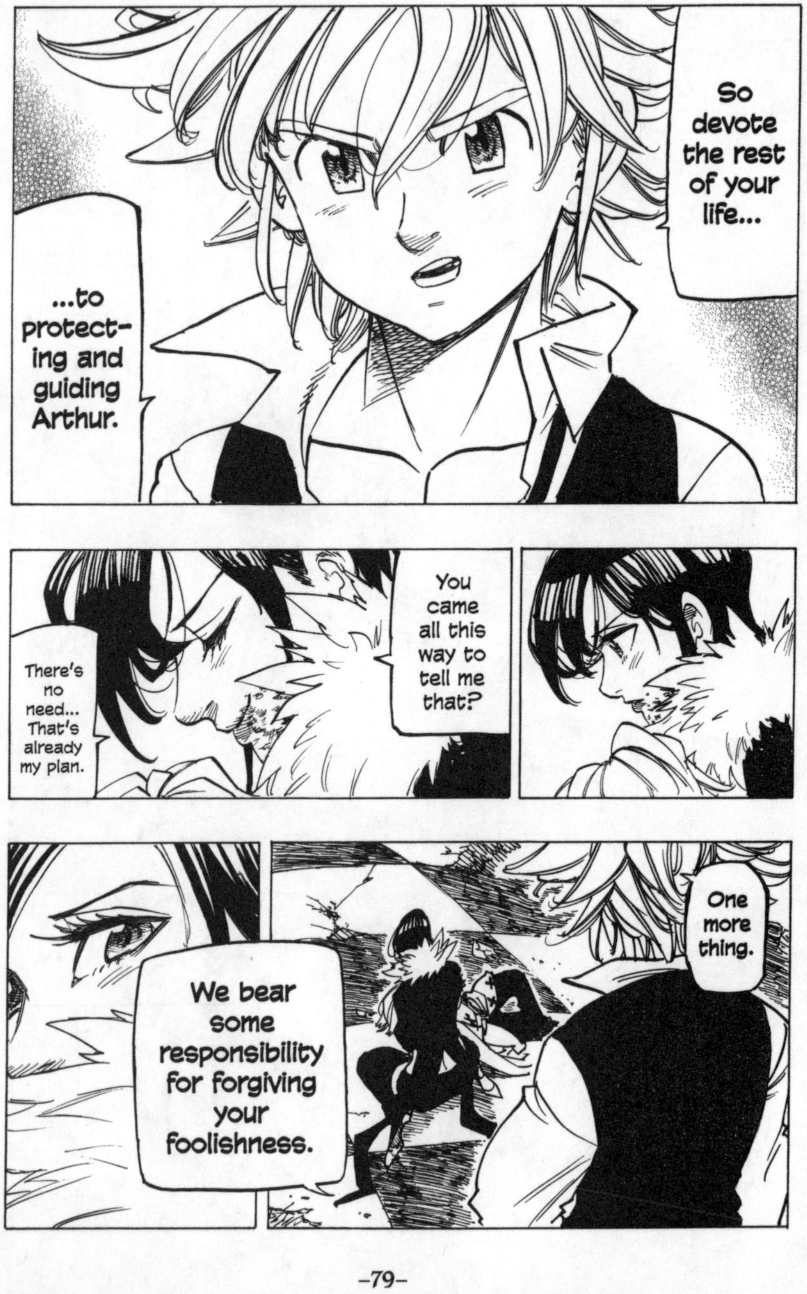
So devote the rest of your life...
...to protecting and guiding Arthur.
You came all this way to tell me that?
There's no need... That's already my plan.
One more thing.
We bear some responsibility for forgiving your foolishness.

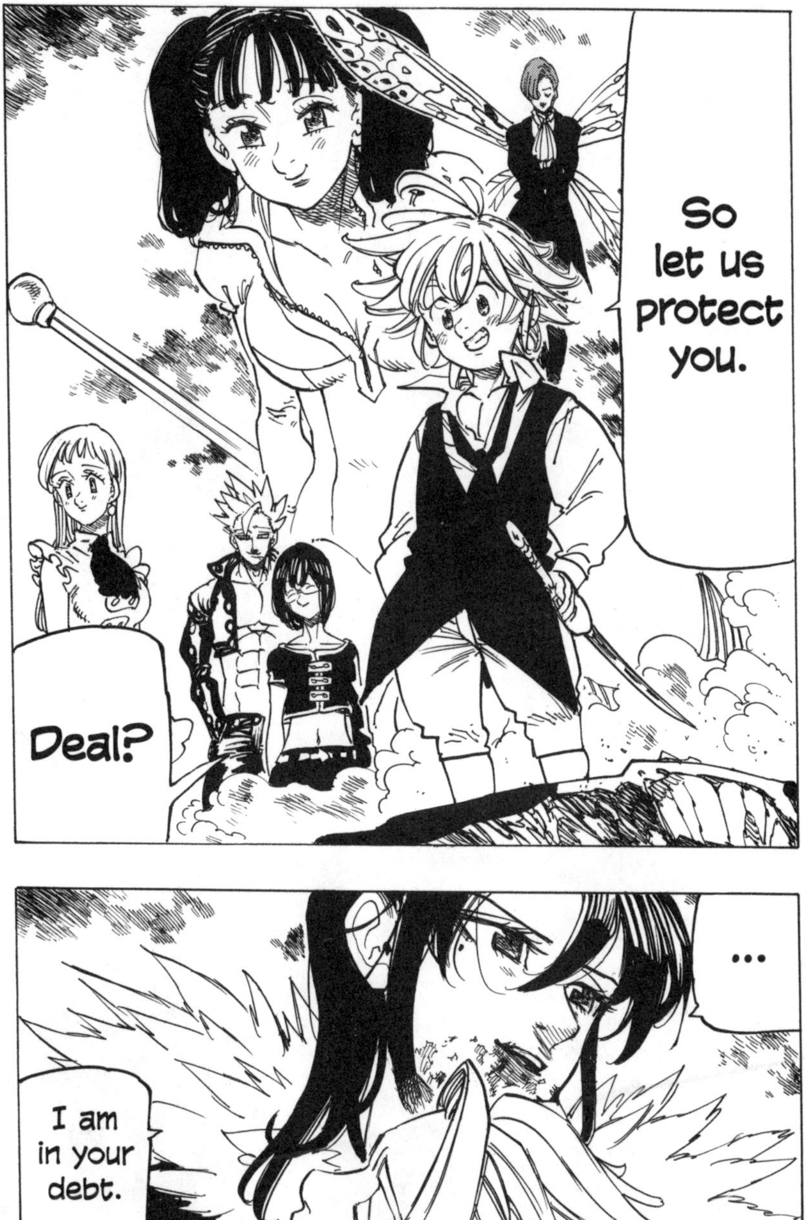
So let us protect you.
Deal?
...
I am in your debt.

Chapter 342 - Victory Cry

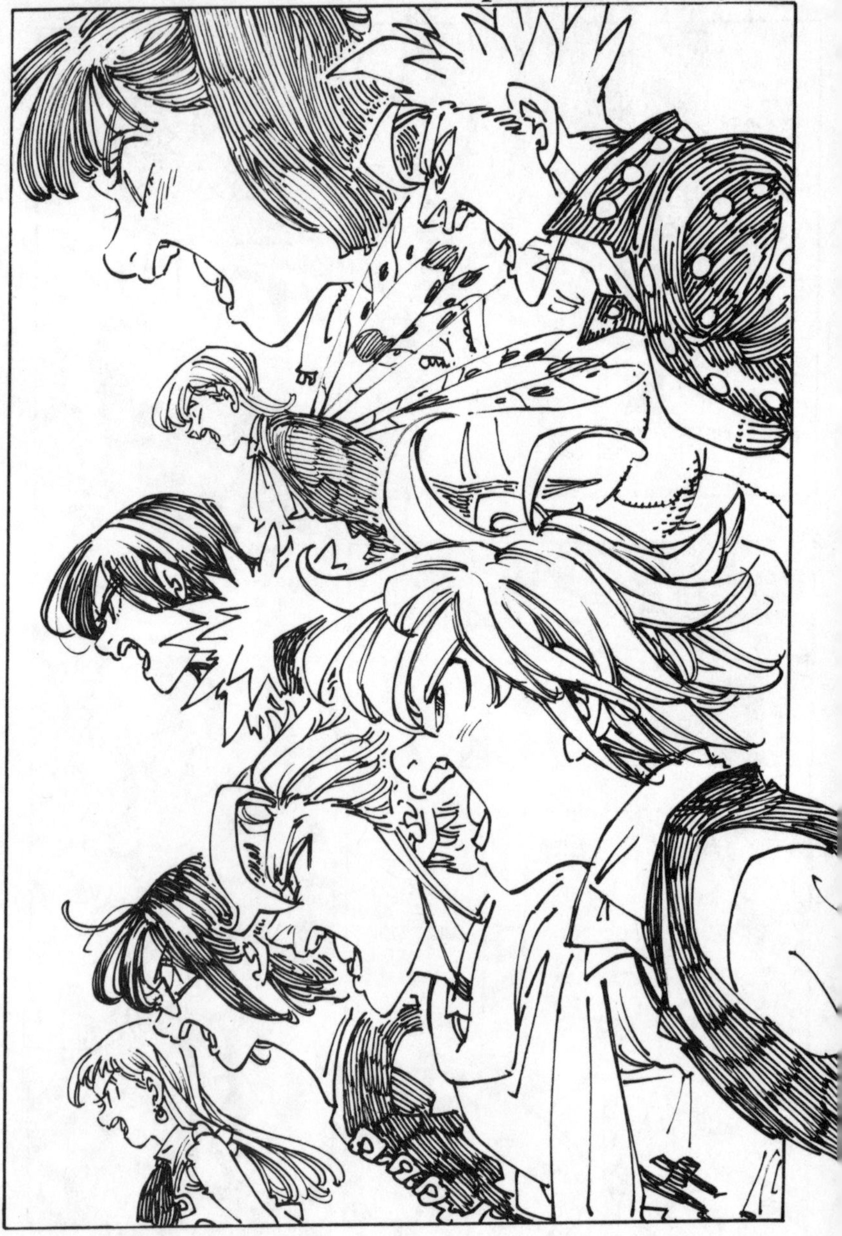

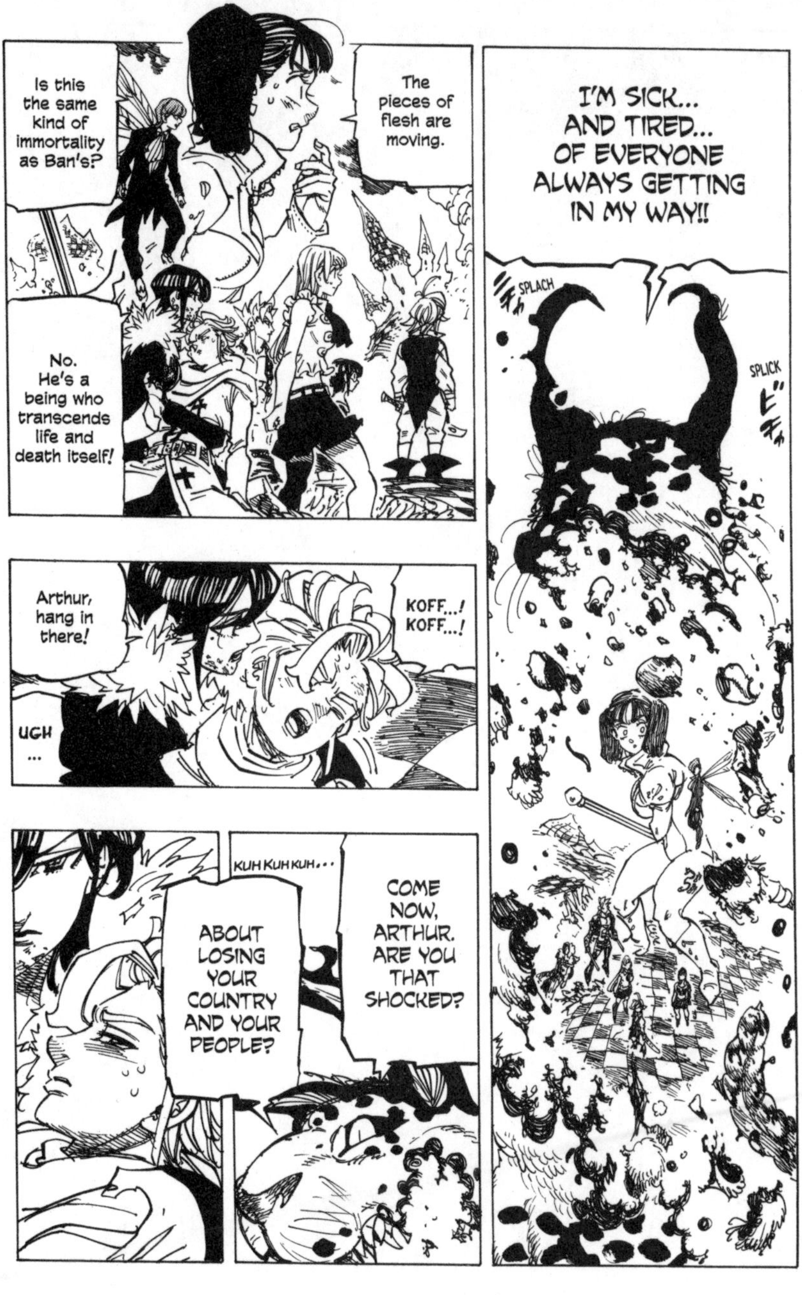
I'M SICK... AND TIRED... OF EVERYONE ALWAYS GETTING IN MY WAY!!
SPLACH
SPLICK
The pieces of flesh are moving.
Is this the same kind of immortality as Ban's?
No. He's a being who transcends life and death itself!
KOFF...! KOFF...!
Arthur, hang in there!
UGH ...
KUH KUH KUH...
COME NOW, ARTHUR. ARE YOU THAT SHOCKED?
ABOUT LOSING YOUR COUNTRY AND YOUR PEOPLE?

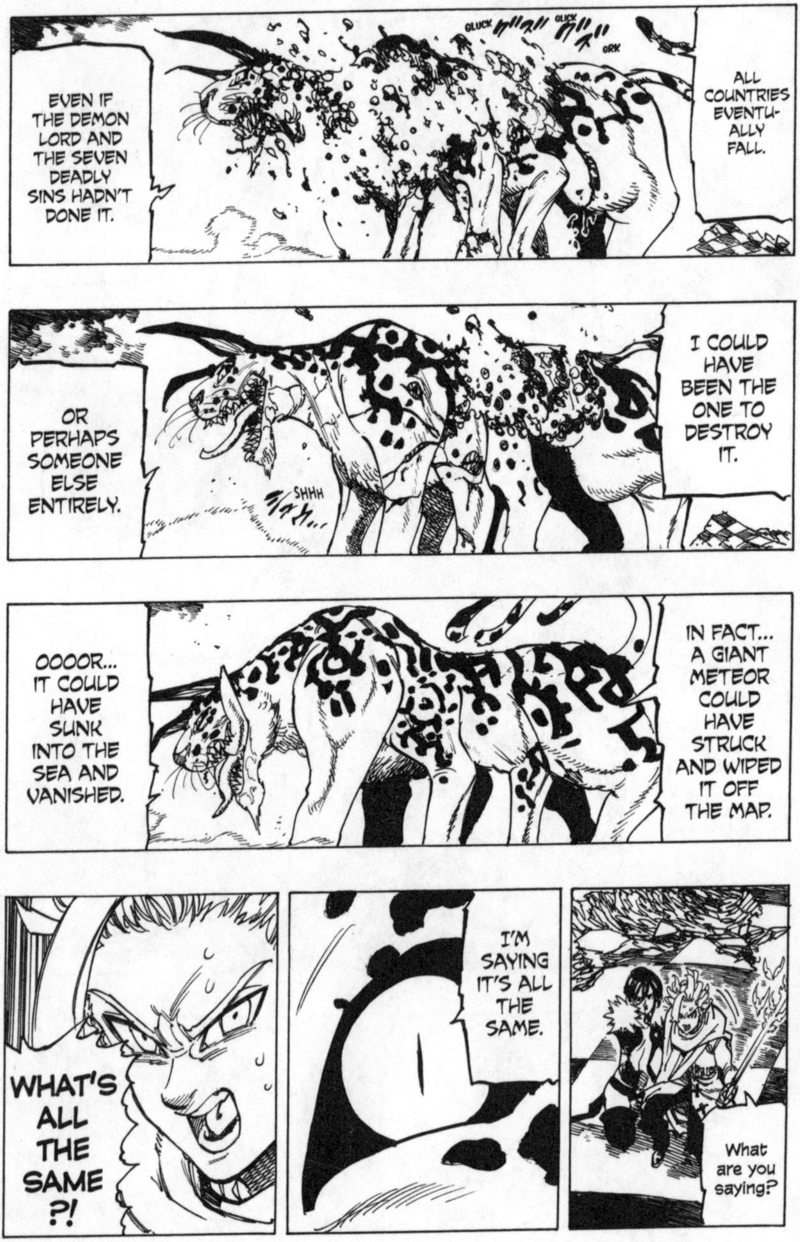
ALL COUNTRIES EVENTU-ALLY FALL.
GLICK
GRK
GLUCK
EVEN IF THE DEMON LORD AND THE SEVEN DEADLY SINS HADN'T DONE IT.
I COULD HAVE BEEN THE ONE TO DESTROY IT.
SHHH
OR PERHAPS SOMEONE ELSE ENTIRELY.
IN FACT... A GIANT METEOR COULD HAVE STRUCK AND WIPED IT OFF THE MAP.
OOOOR... IT COULD HAVE SUNK INTO THE SEA AND VANISHED.
What are you saying?
I'M SAYING IT'S ALL THE SAME.
WHAT'S ALL THE SAME?!

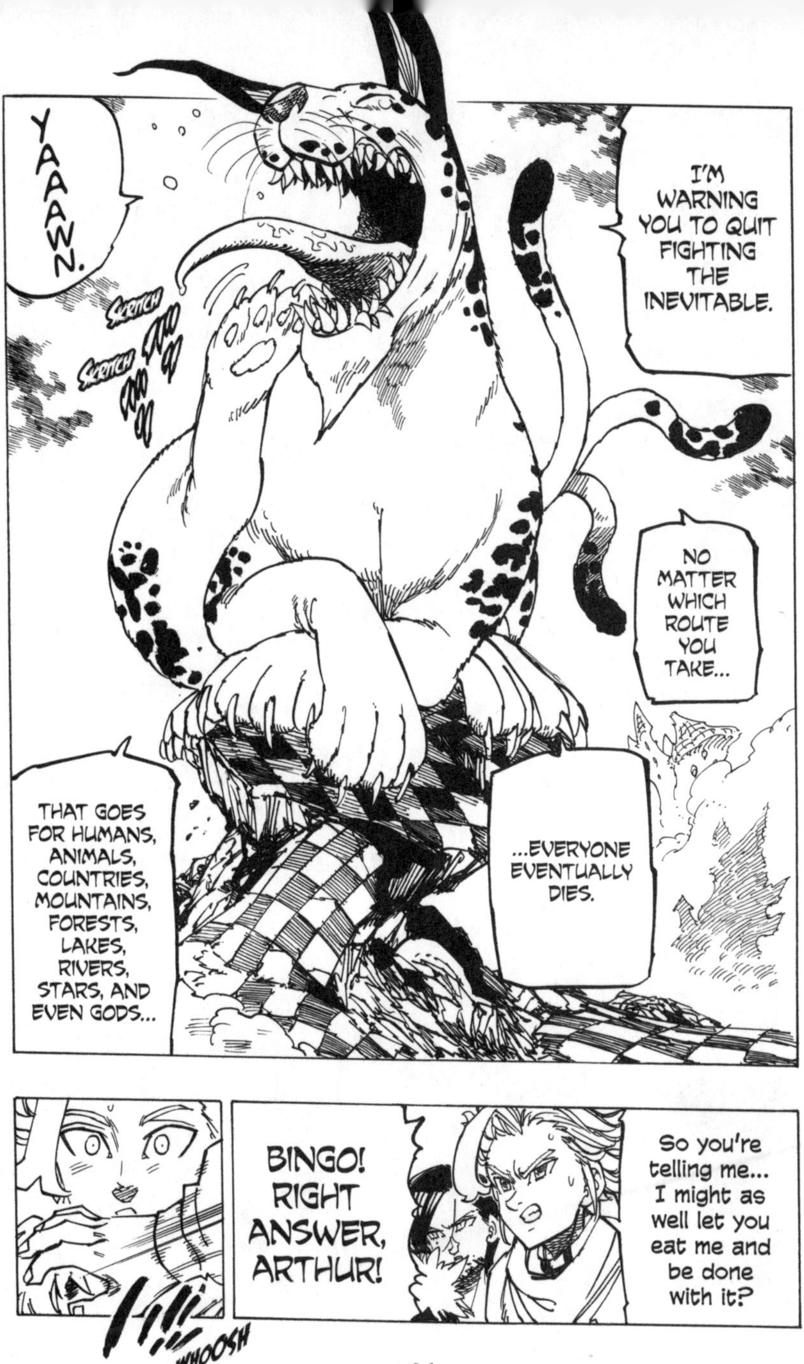
I'M WARNING YOU TO QUIT FIGHTING THE INEVITABLE.
YAAAAWN.
SCRITCH
SCRITCH
NO MATTER WHICH ROUTE YOU TAKE...
...EVERYONE EVENTUALLY DIES.
THAT GOES FOR HUMANS, ANIMALS, COUNTRIES, MOUNTAINS, FORESTS, LAKES, RIVERS, STARS, AND EVEN GODS...
So you're telling me... I might as well let you eat me and be done with it?
BINGO! RIGHT ANSWER, ARTHUR!
WHOOSH

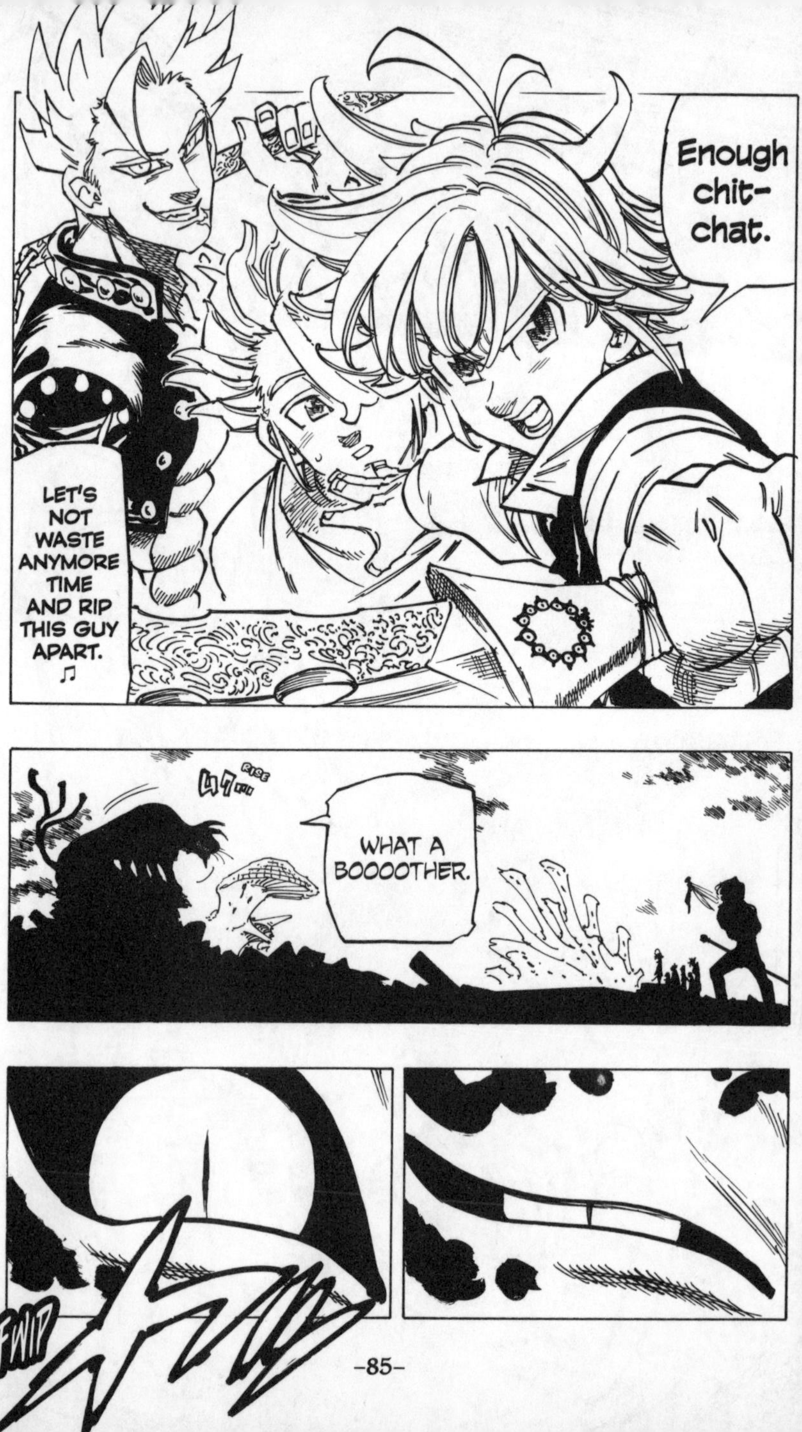
Enough chit-chat.
LET'S NOT WASTE ANYMORE TIME AND RIP THIS GUY APART. ♫
WHAT A BOOOOTHER.
RISE
FWIP

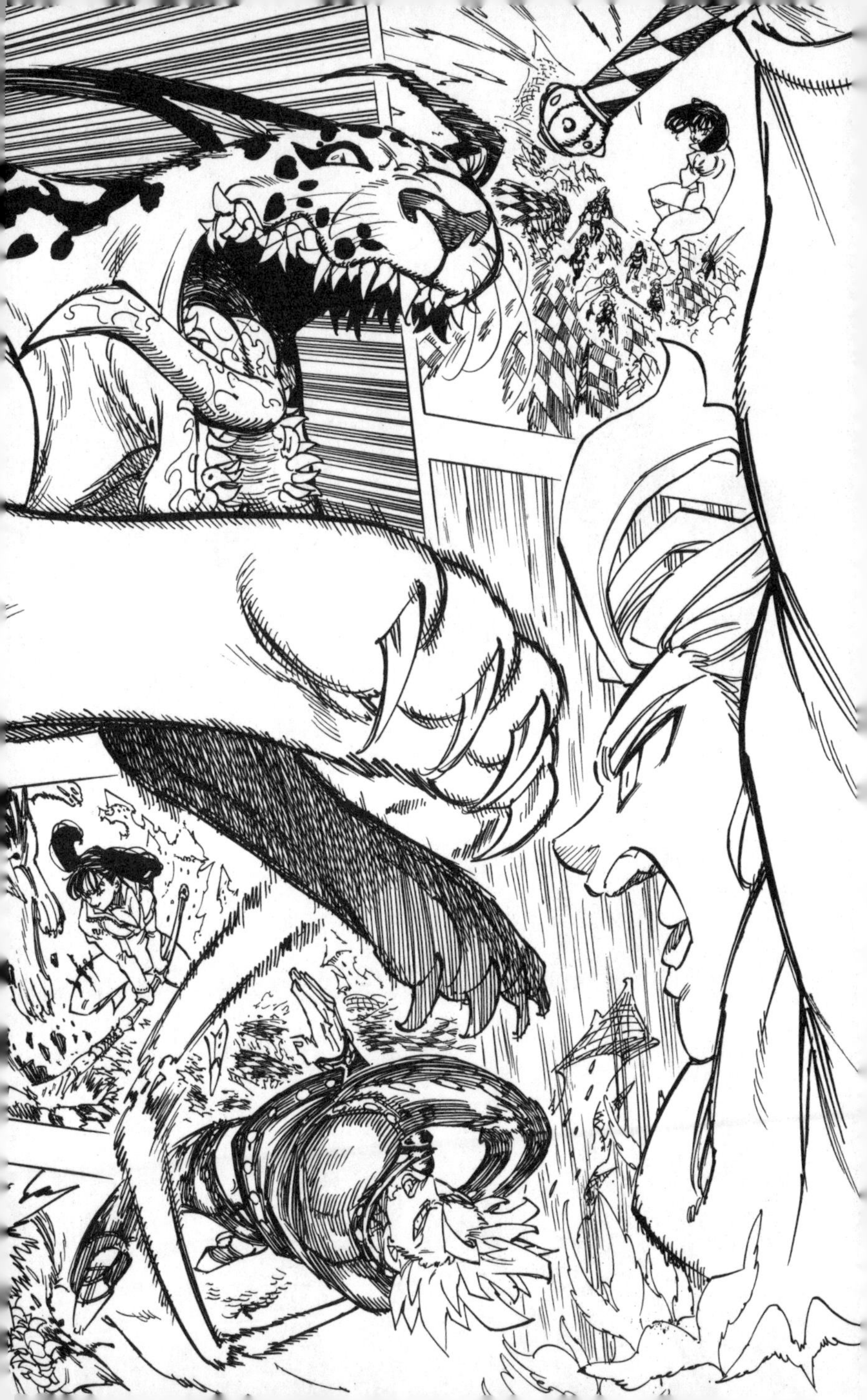

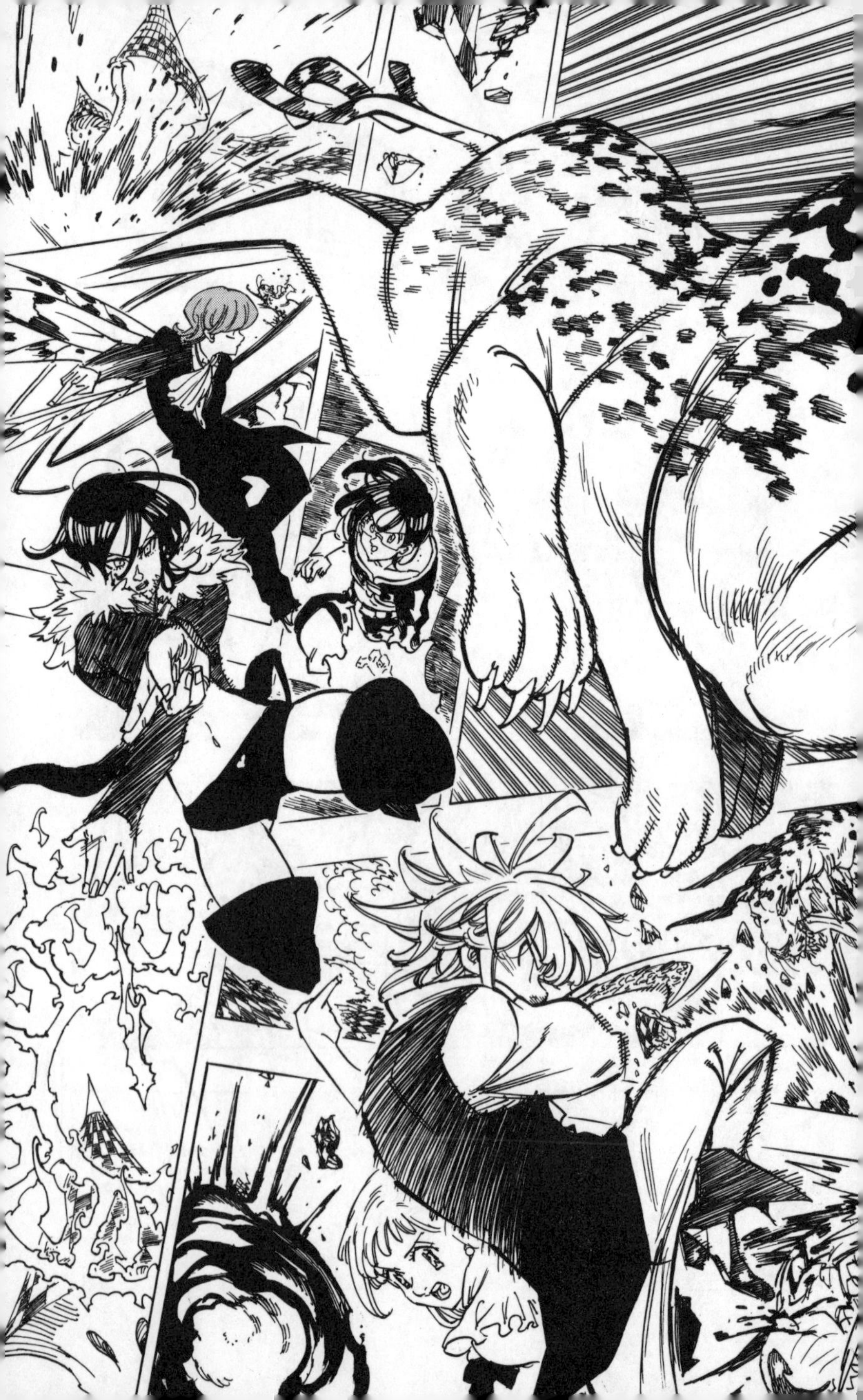

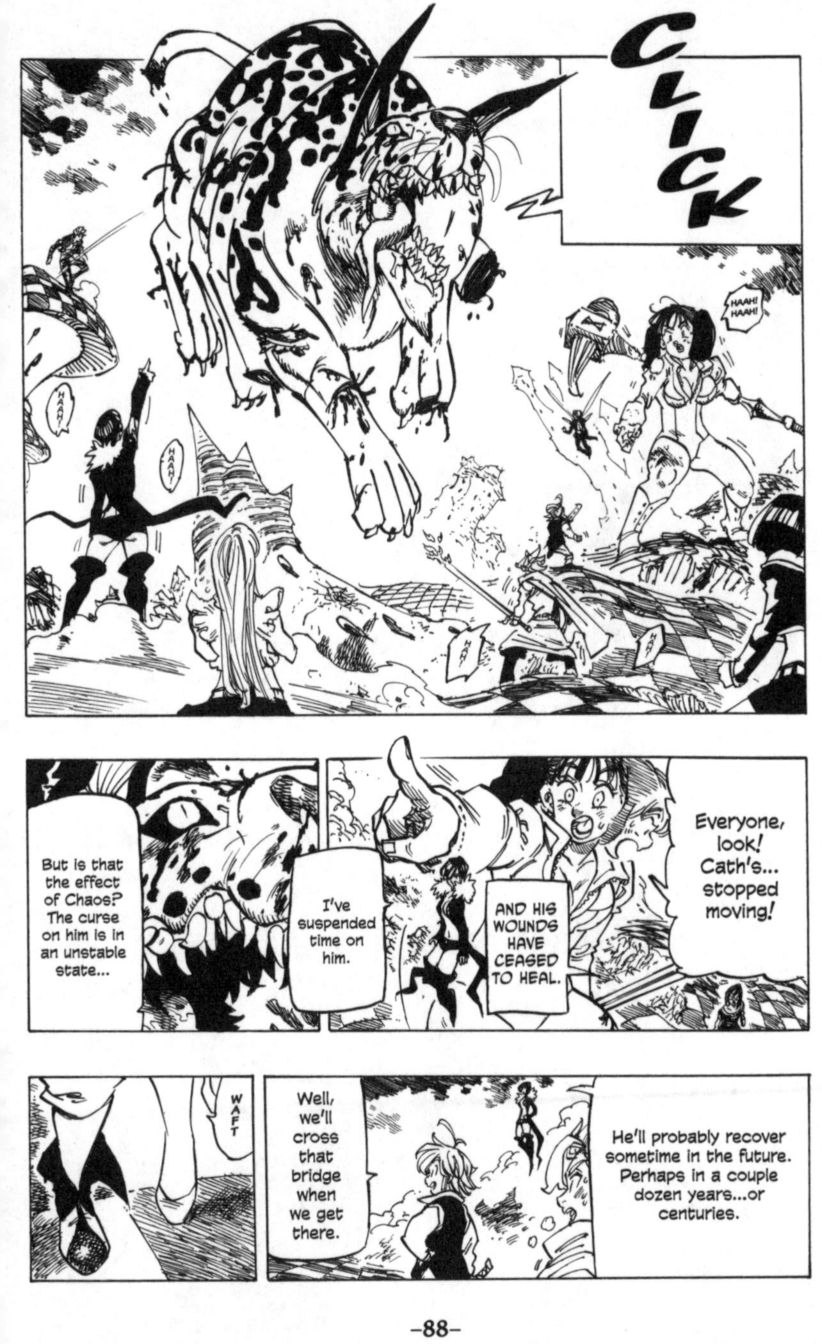
CLICK
HAAH! HAAH!
HAAH!
HAAH!
HAAH!
HAAH!
Everyone, look! Cath's... stopped moving!
AND HIS WOUNDS HAVE CEASED TO HEAL.
I've suspended time on him.
But is that the effect of Chaos? The curse on him is in an unstable state...
He'll probably recover sometime in the future. Perhaps in a couple dozen years...or centuries.
Well, we'll cross that bridge when we get there.
WAFT

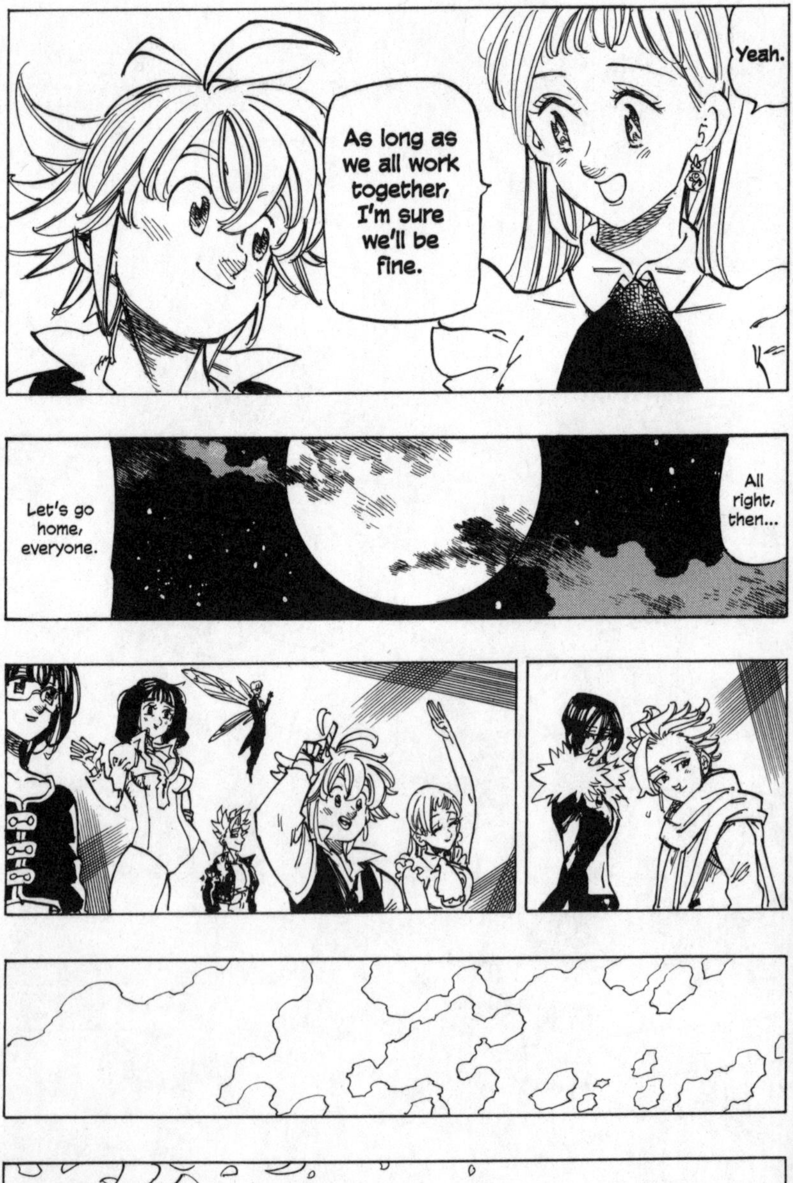
Yeah.
As long as we all work together, I'm sure we'll be fine.
All right, then...
Let's go home, everyone.

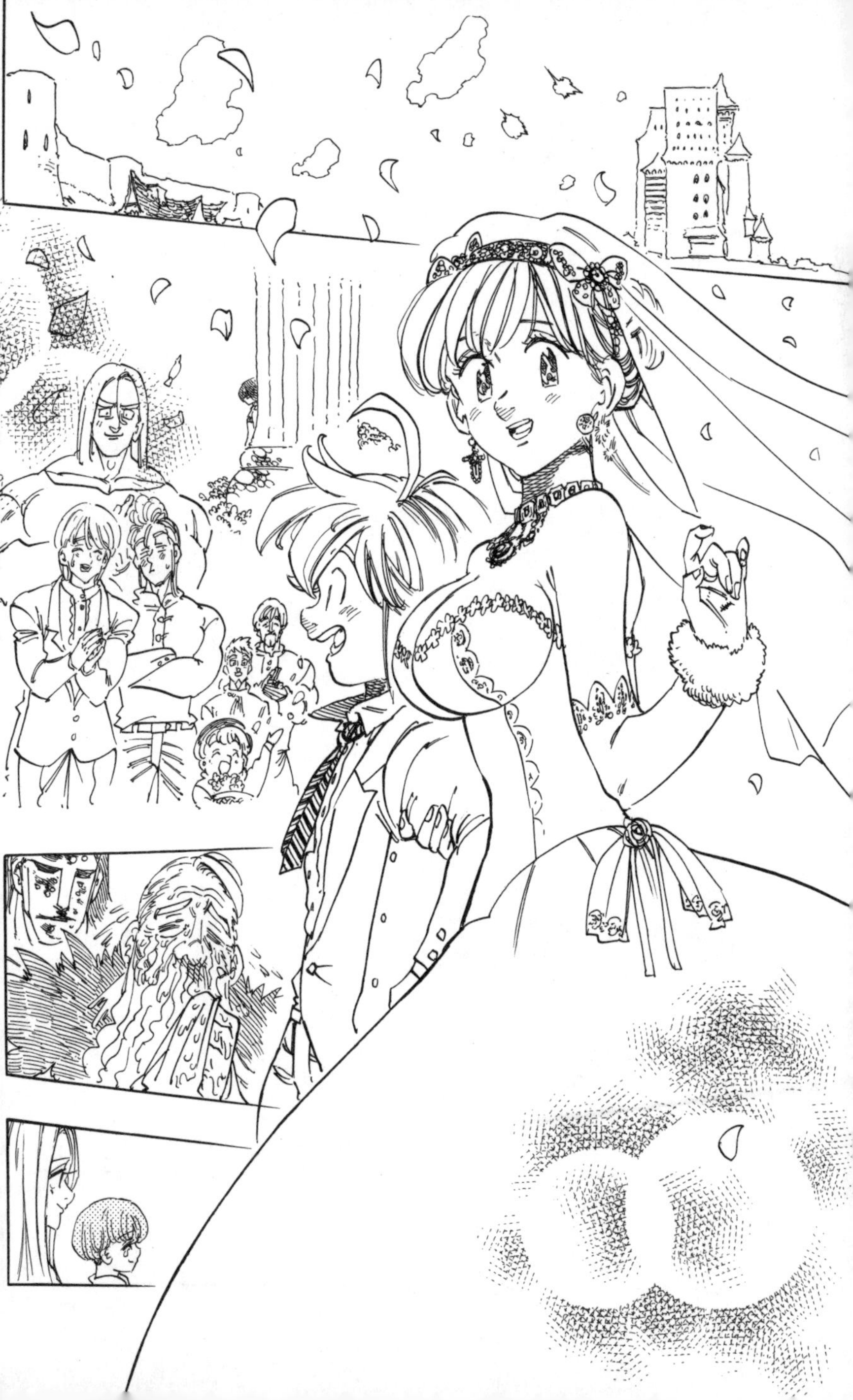

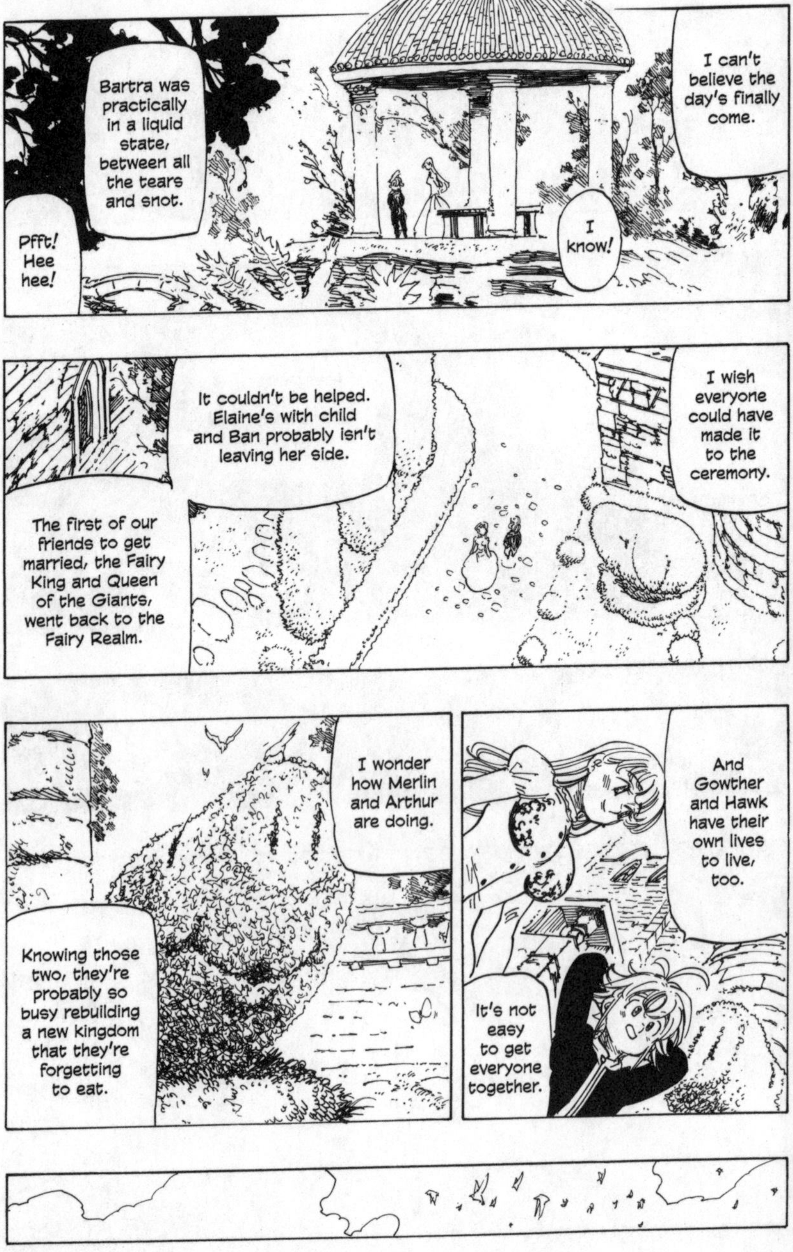
I can't believe the day's finally come.
I know!
Bartra was practically in a liquid state, between all the tears and snot.
Pfft! Hee hee!
I wish everyone could have made it to the ceremony.
It couldn't be helped. Elaine's with child and Ban probably isn't leaving her side.
The first of our friends to get married, the Fairy King and Queen of the Giants, went back to the Fairy Realm.
And Gowther and Hawk have their own lives to live, too.
It's not easy to get everyone together.
I wonder how Merlin and Arthur are doing.
Knowing those two, they're probably so busy rebuilding a new kingdom that they're forgetting to eat.

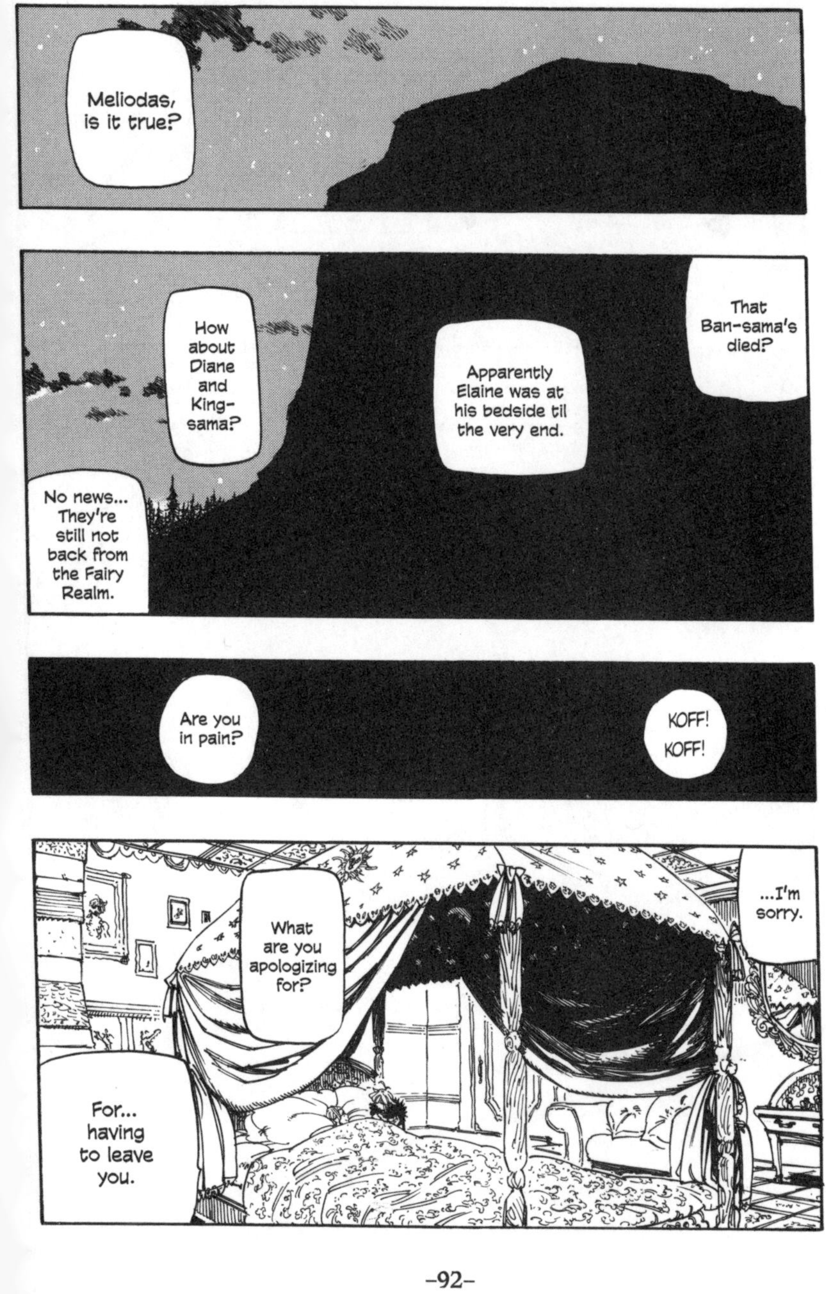
Meliodas, is it true?
That Ban-sama's died?
Apparently Elaine was at his bedside til the very end.
How about Diane and King-sama?
No news... They're still not back from the Fairy Realm.
KOFF! KOFF!
Are you in pain?
...I'm sorry.
What are you apologizing for?
For... having to leave you.

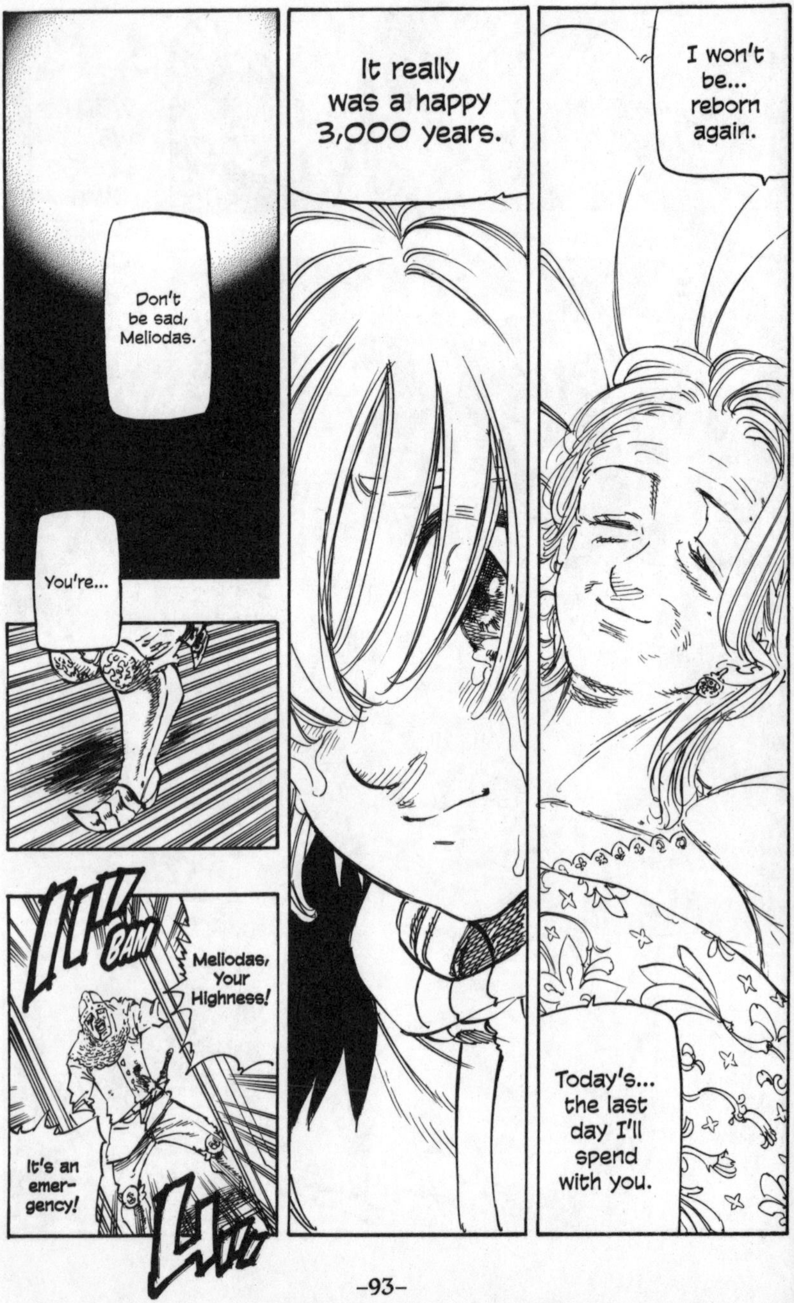
I won't be... reborn again.
Today's... the last day I'll spend with you.
It really was a happy 3,000 years.
Don't be sad, Meliodas.
You're...
BAM
Meliodas, Your Highness!
It's an emergency!

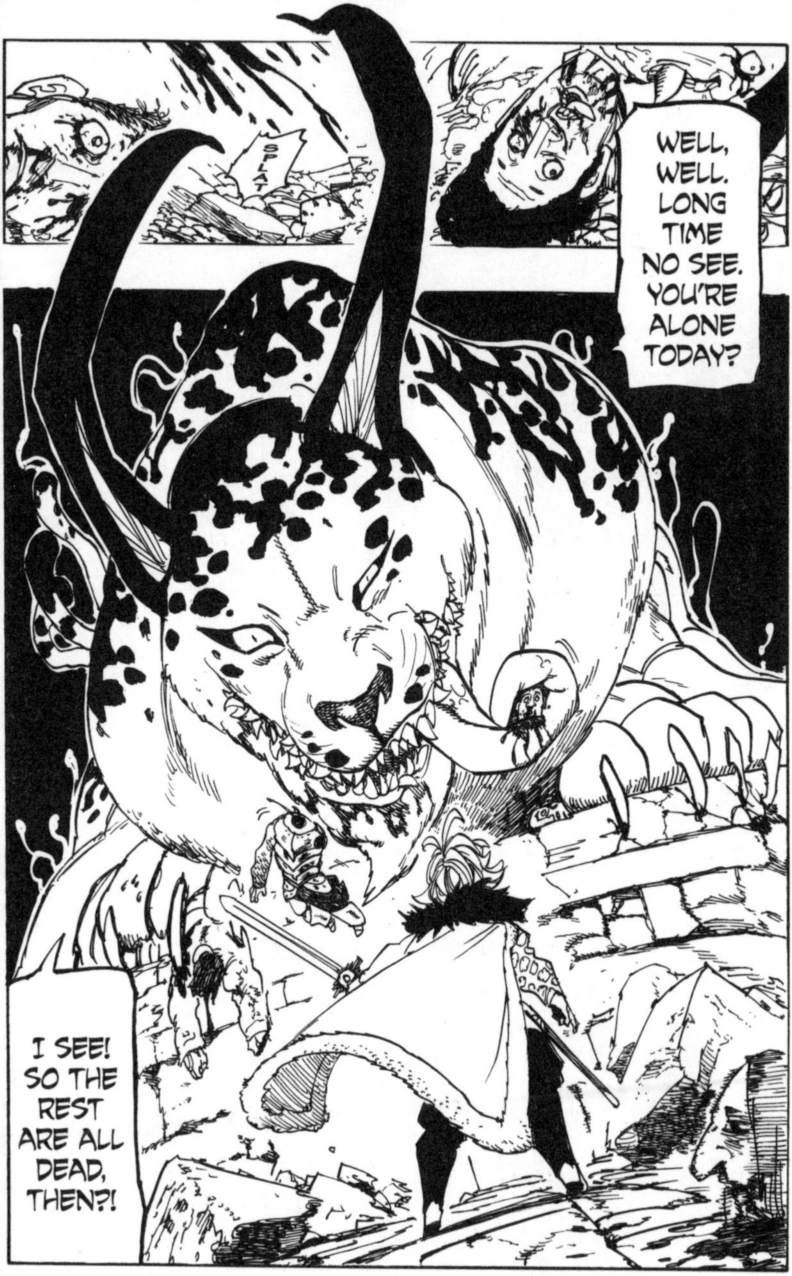
SPLAT
WELL, WELL. LONG TIME NO SEE. YOU'RE ALONE TODAY?
I SEE! SO THE REST ARE ALL DEAD, THEN?!

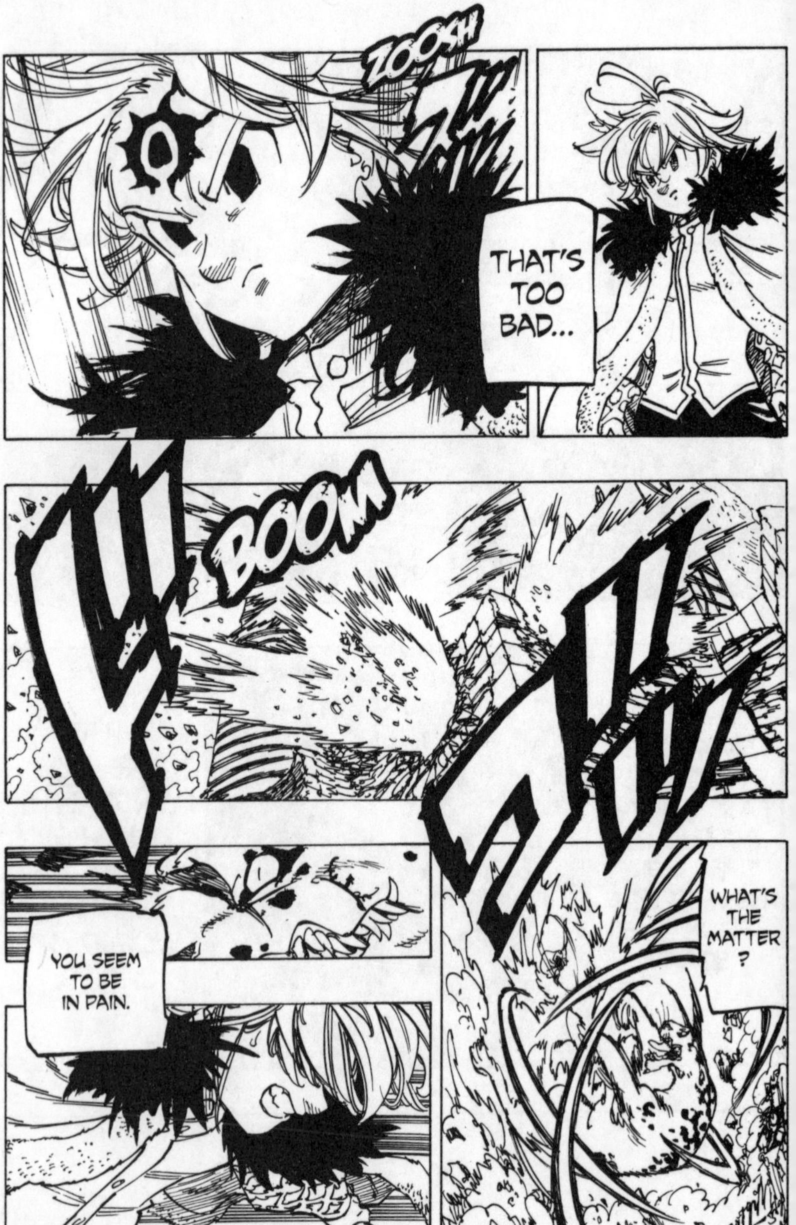
THAT'S TOO BAD...
ZOOSH
BOOM
WHAT'S THE MATTER ?
YOU SEEM TO BE IN PAIN.

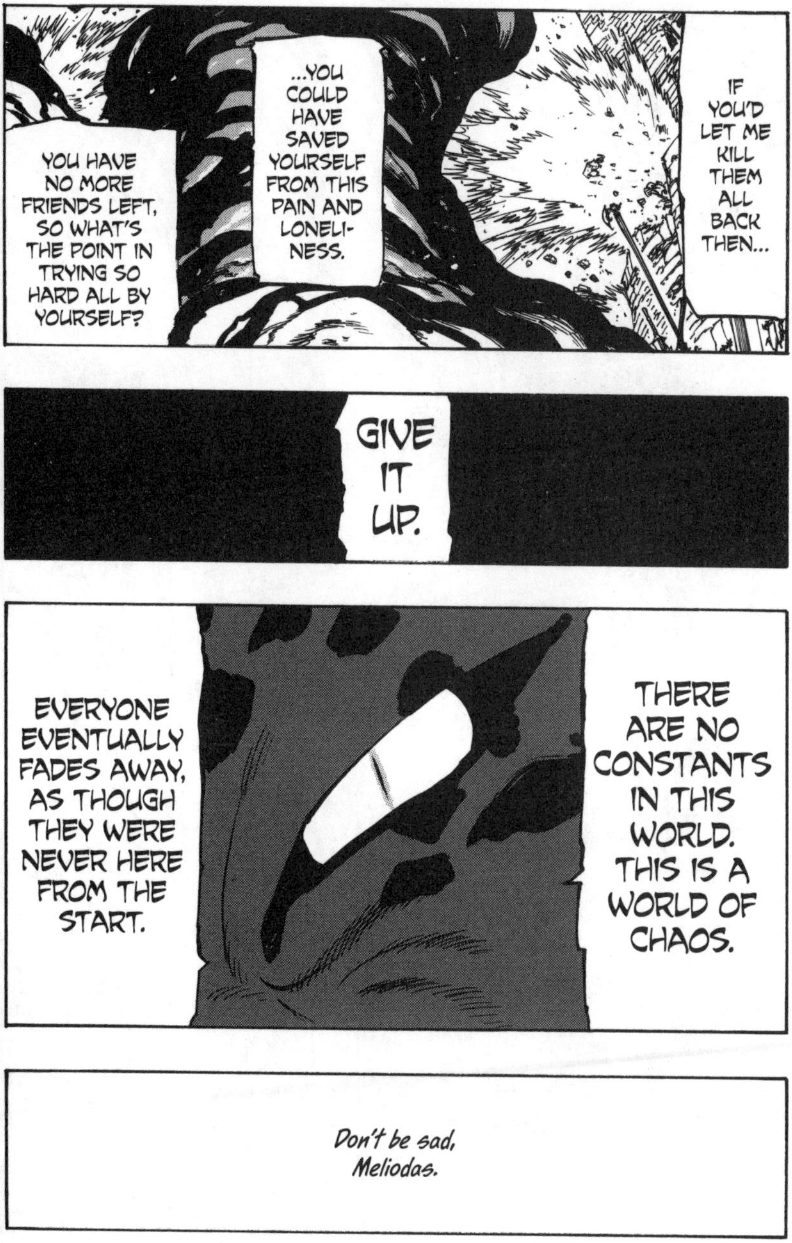
IF YOU'D LET ME KILL THEM ALL BACK THEN...
...YOU COULD HAVE SAVED YOURSELF FROM THIS PAIN AND LONELI-NESS.
YOU HAVE NO MORE FRIENDS LEFT, SO WHAT'S THE POINT IN TRYING SO HARD ALL BY YOURSELF?
GIVE IT UP.
THERE ARE NO CONSTANTS IN THIS WORLD. THIS IS A WORLD OF CHAOS.
EVERYONE EVENTUALLY FADES AWAY, AS THOUGH THEY WERE NEVER HERE FROM THE START.
Don't be sad, Meliodas.

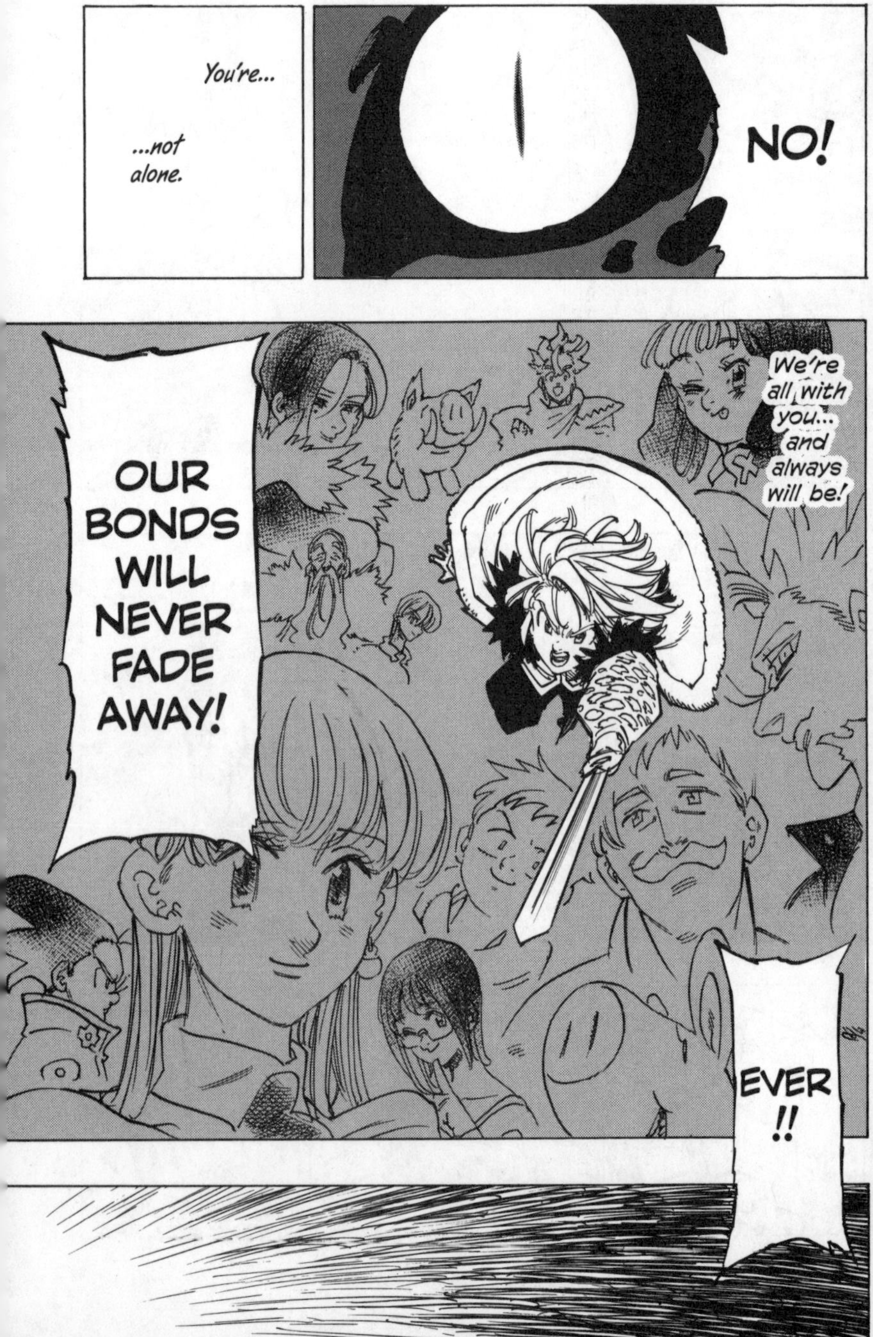
NO!
You're...
...not alone.
We're all with you... and always will be!
OUR BONDS WILL NEVER FADE AWAY!
EVER!!

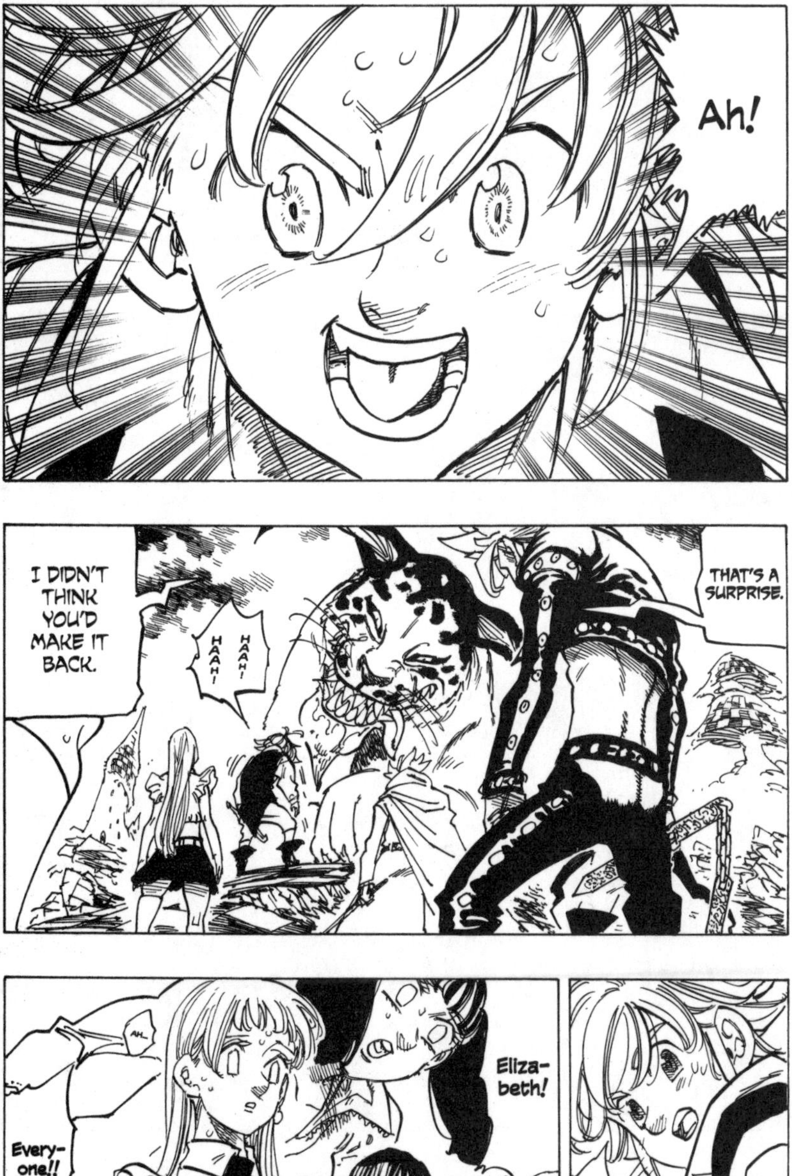
Ah!
THAT'S A SURPRISE.
HAAH! HAAH!
I DIDN'T THINK YOU'D MAKE IT BACK.
AH!
Eliza-beth!
AH...
Every-one!!

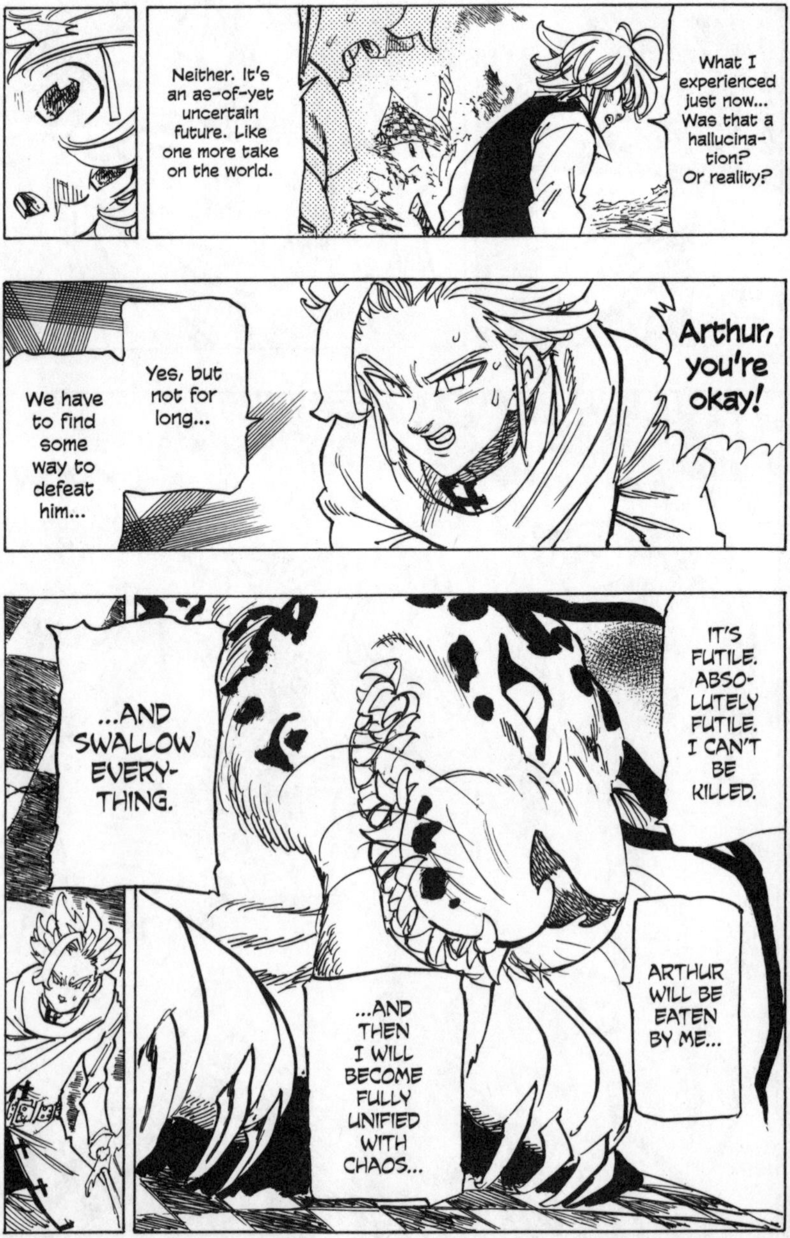
What I experienced just now... Was that a hallucination? Or reality?
Neither. It's an as-of-yet uncertain future. Like one more take on the world.
Arthur, you're okay!
Yes, but not for long...
We have to find some way to defeat him...
IT'S FUTILE. ABSOLUTELY FUTILE. I CAN'T BE KILLED.
ARTHUR WILL BE EATEN BY ME...
...AND THEN I WILL BECOME FULLY UNIFIED WITH CHAOS...
...AND SWALLOW EVERYTHING.

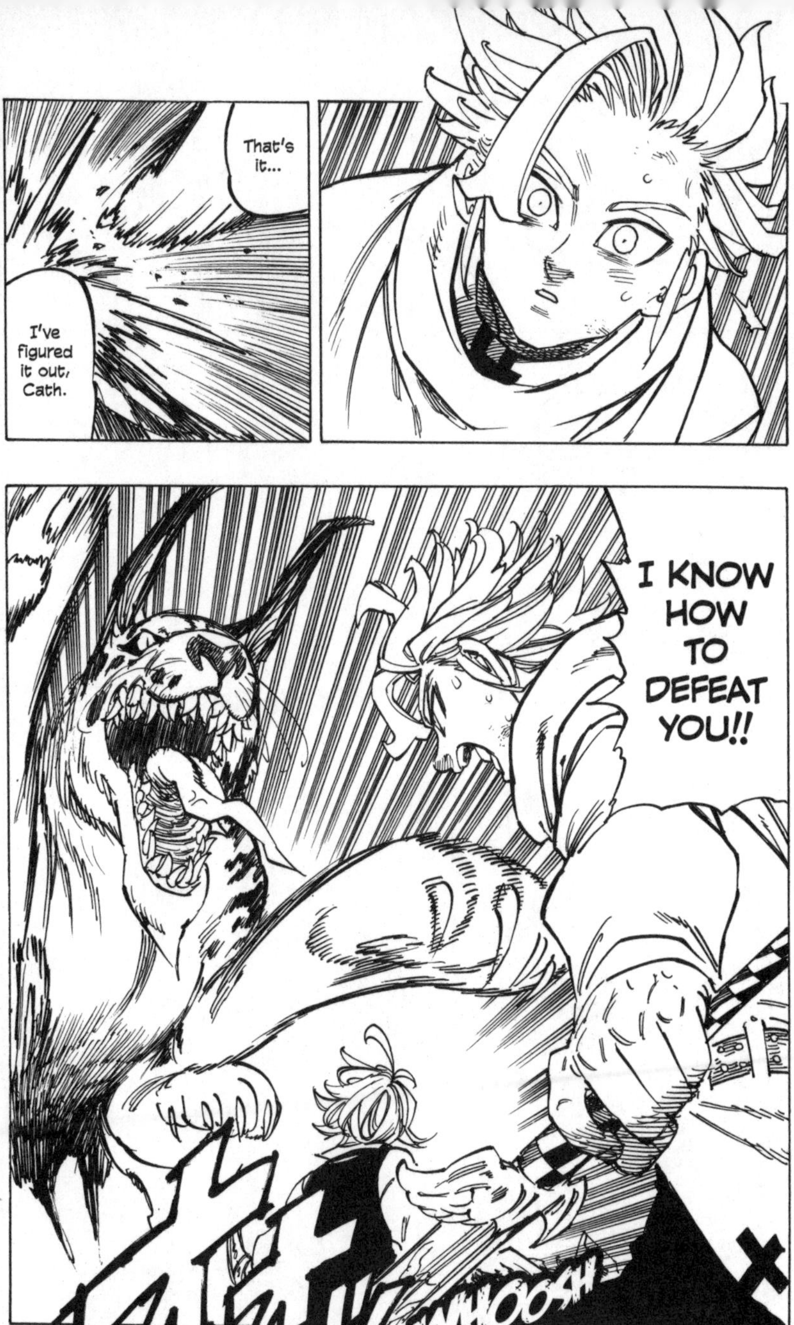
That's it...
I've figured it out, Cath.
I KNOW HOW TO DEFEAT YOU!!
WHOOSH

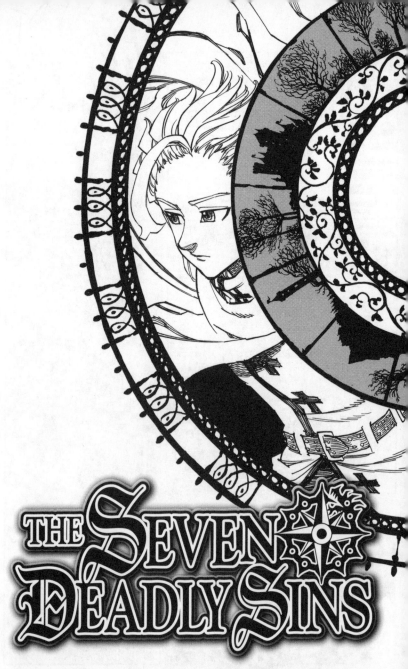

THE SEVEN DEADLY SINS

Chapter 343 - An Everlasting Kingdom

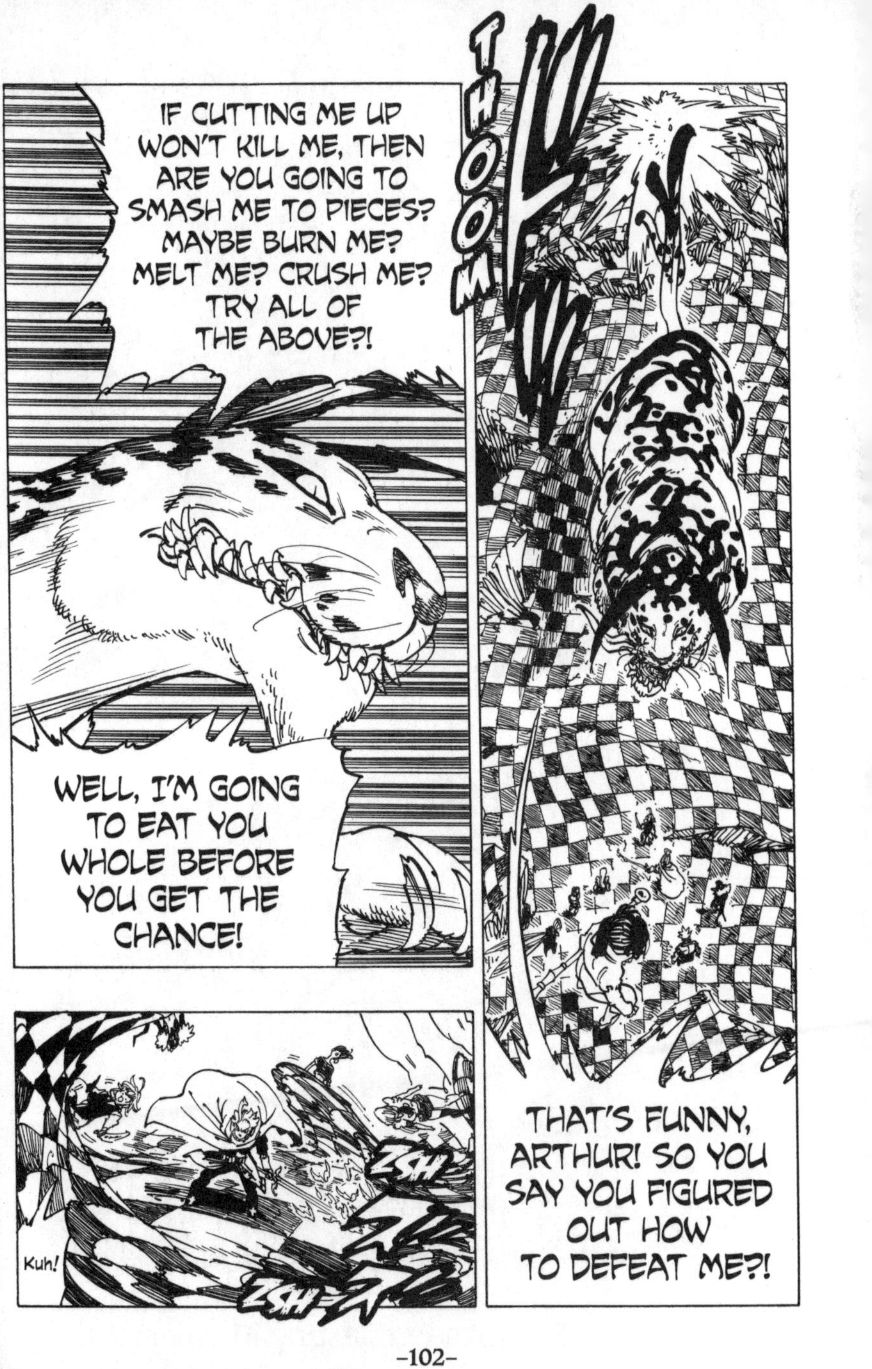
THOOM
THAT'S FUNNY, ARTHUR! SO YOU SAY YOU FIGURED OUT HOW TO DEFEAT ME?!
IF CUTTING ME UP WON'T KILL ME, THEN ARE YOU GOING TO SMASH ME TO PIECES? MAYBE BURN ME? MELT ME? CRUSH ME? TRY ALL OF THE ABOVE?!
WELL, I'M GOING TO EAT YOU WHOLE BEFORE YOU GET THE CHANCE!
ZSH
ZSH
Kuh!

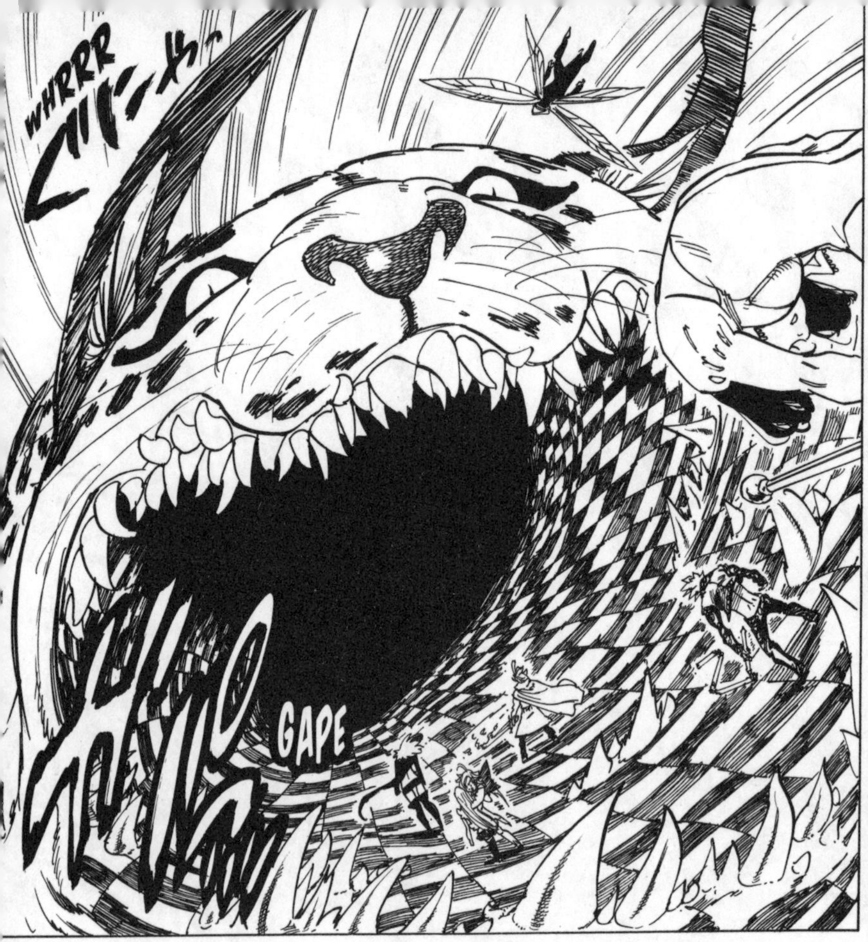
WHRRR
GAPE

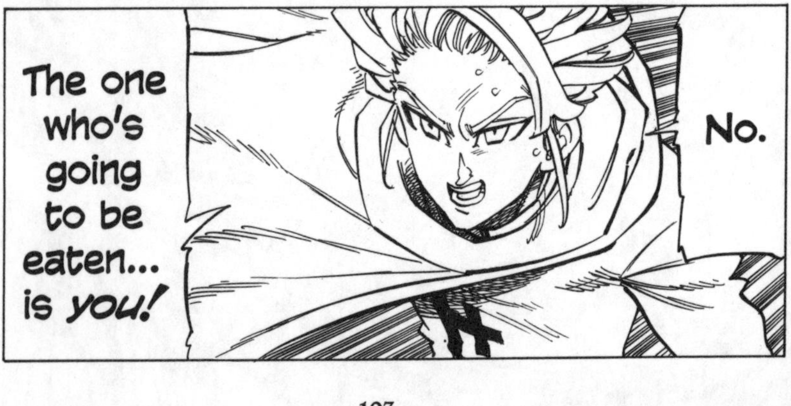
No.
The one who's going to be eaten... is *you!*

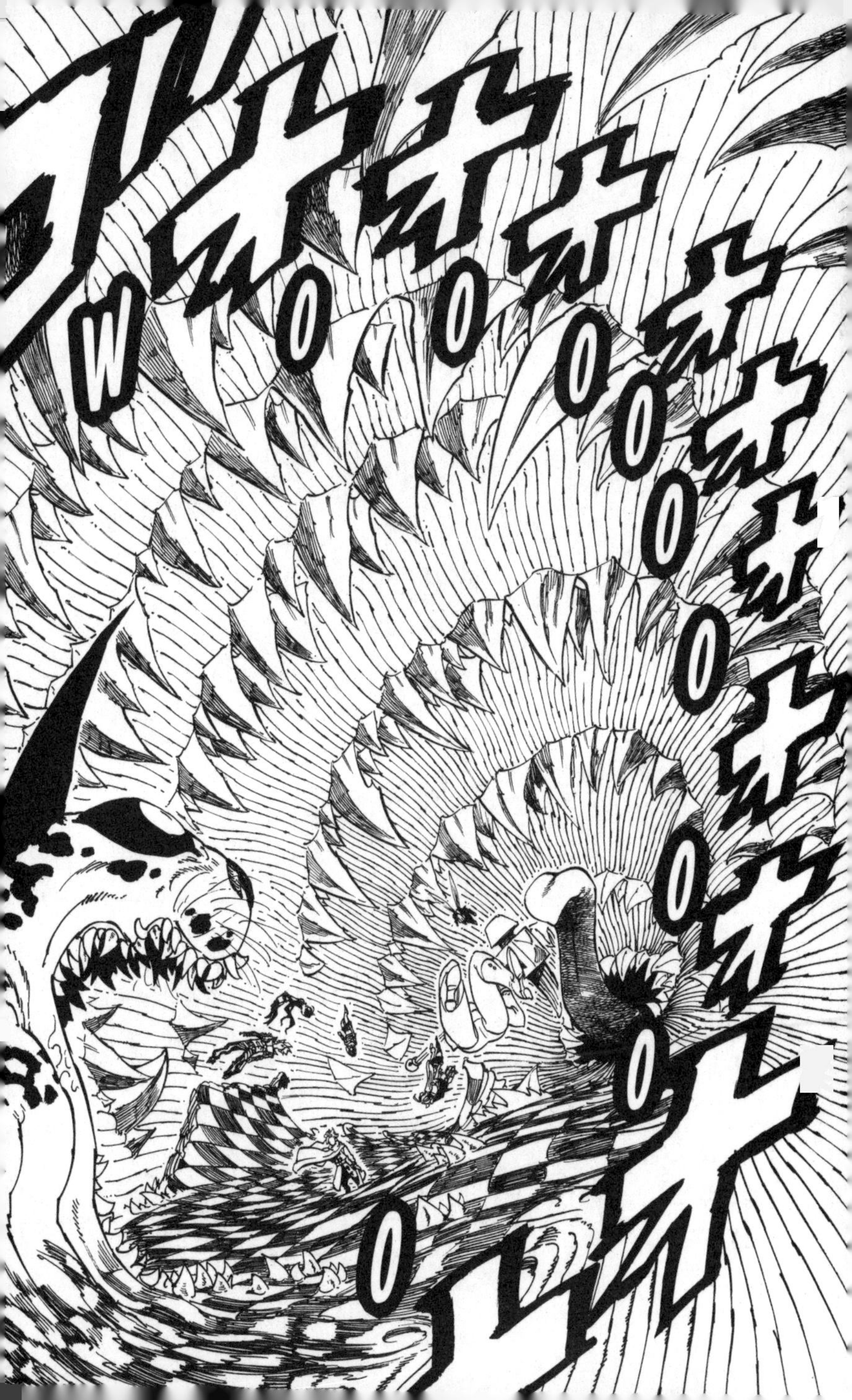
WOOOOOOOOO

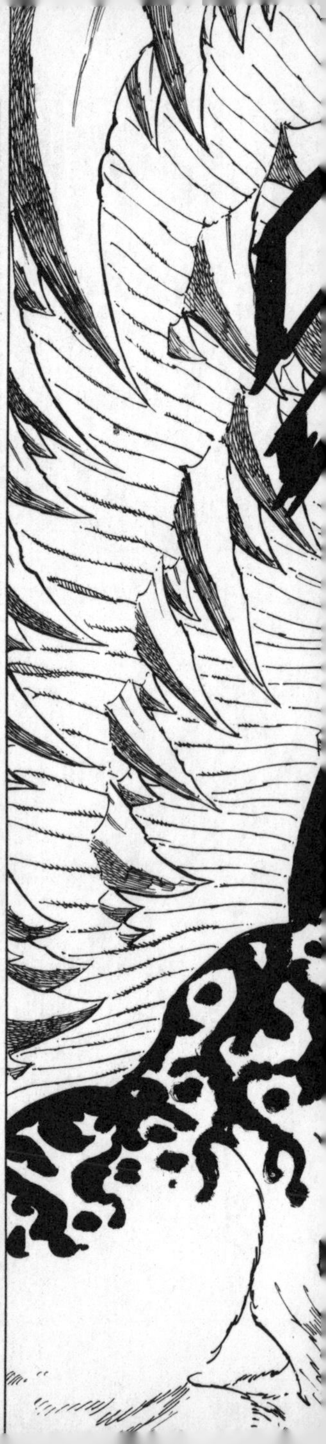

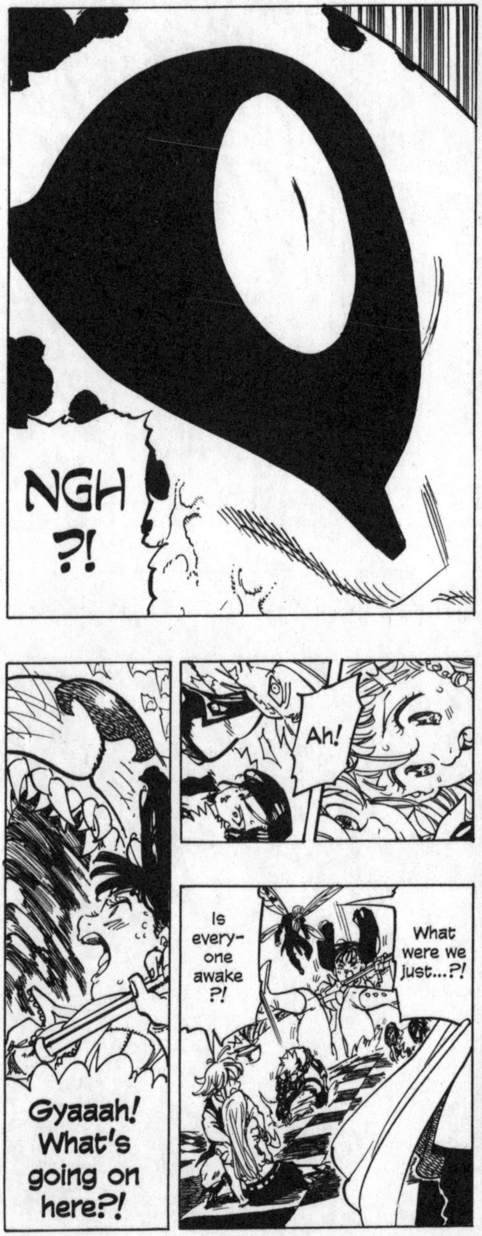
NGH ?!
Ah!
What were we just...?!
Is every-one awake ?!
Gyaaah! What's going on here?!

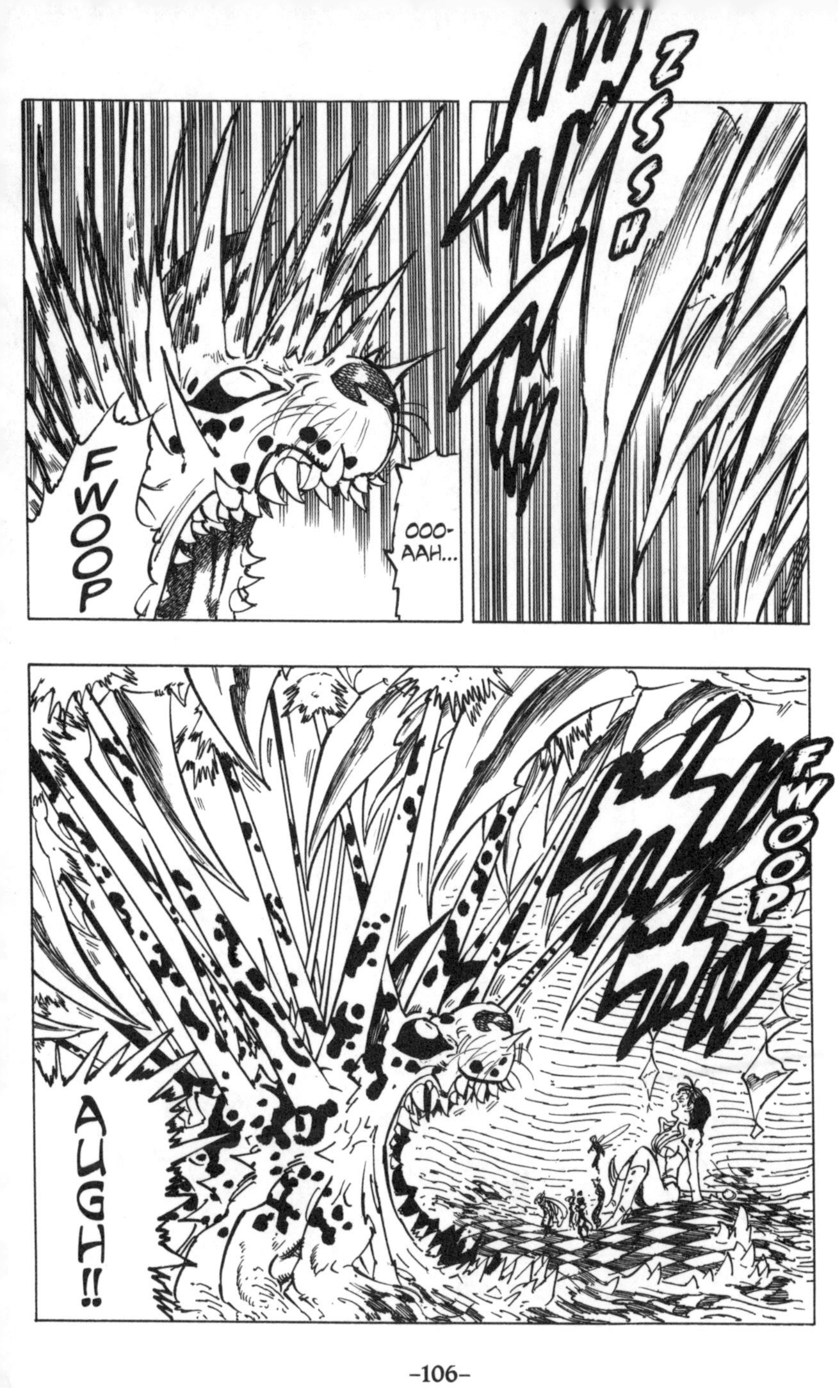
ZSSSH
FWOOP
OOO-
AAH...
FWOOP
AUGH!!

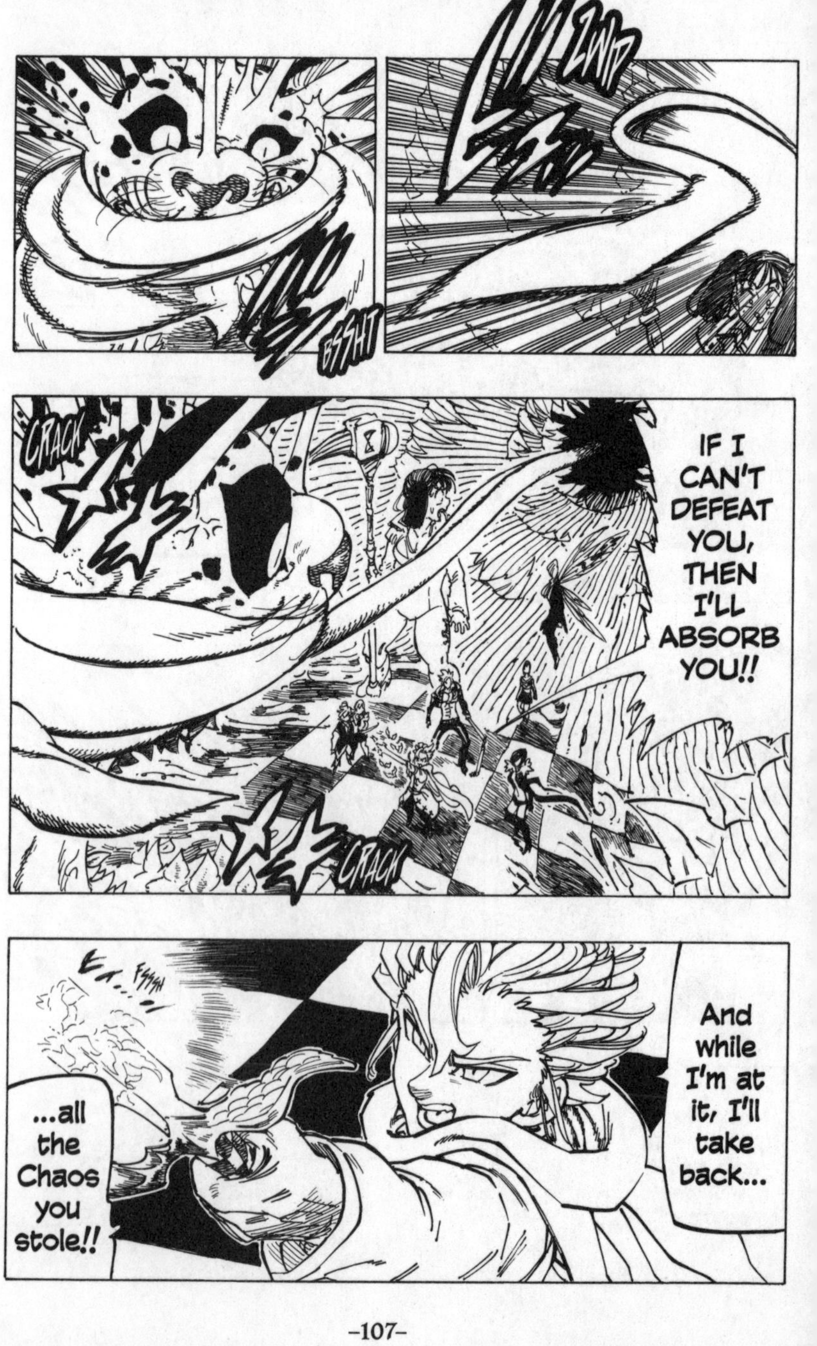
BSSHT
CRACK
IF I CAN'T DEFEAT YOU, THEN I'LL ABSORB YOU!!
CRACK
And while I'm at it, I'll take back...
...all the Chaos you stole!!
FSSSH

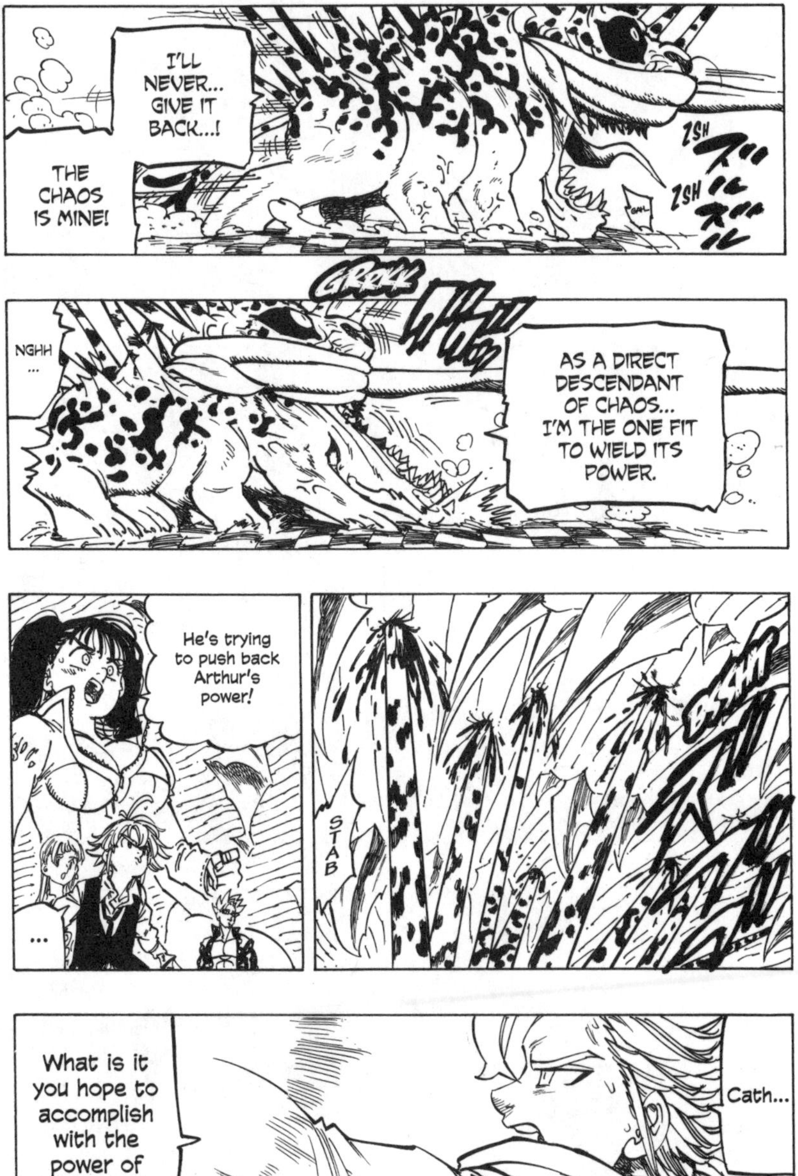
ZSH
ZSH
GAH
I'LL NEVER... GIVE IT BACK...!
THE CHAOS IS MINE!
GRRKK
AS A DIRECT DESCENDANT OF CHAOS... I'M THE ONE FIT TO WIELD ITS POWER.
NGHH...
STAB
He's trying to push back Arthur's power!
...
Cath...
What is it you hope to accomplish with the power of Chaos?!

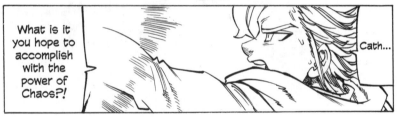

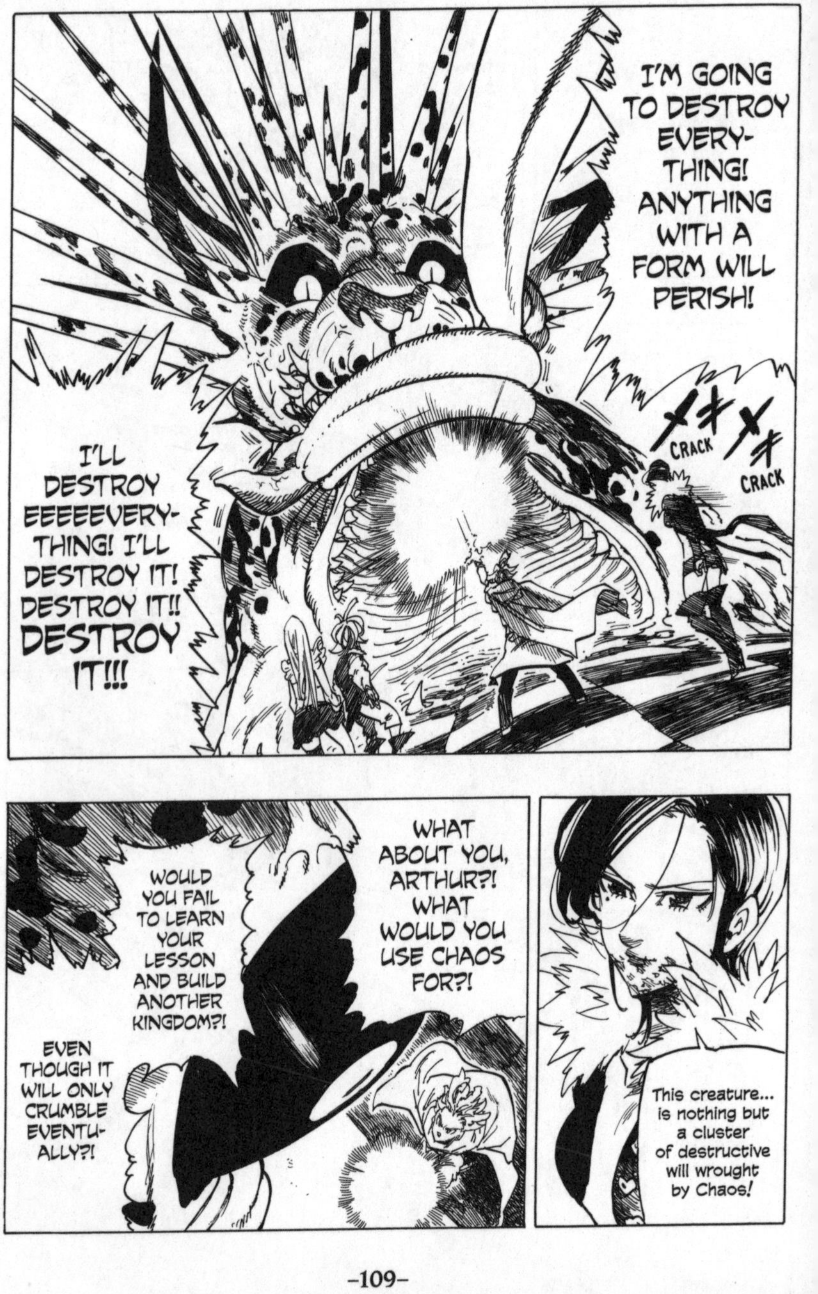
I'M GOING TO DESTROY EVERYTHING! ANYTHING WITH A FORM WILL PERISH!
CRACK
CRACK
I'LL DESTROY EEEEEEVERYTHING! I'LL DESTROY IT! DESTROY IT!! DESTROY IT!!!
This creature... is nothing but a cluster of destructive will wrought by Chaos!
WHAT ABOUT YOU, ARTHUR?! WHAT WOULD YOU USE CHAOS FOR?!
WOULD YOU FAIL TO LEARN YOUR LESSON AND BUILD ANOTHER KINGDOM?!
EVEN THOUGH IT WILL ONLY CRUMBLE EVENTUALLY?!

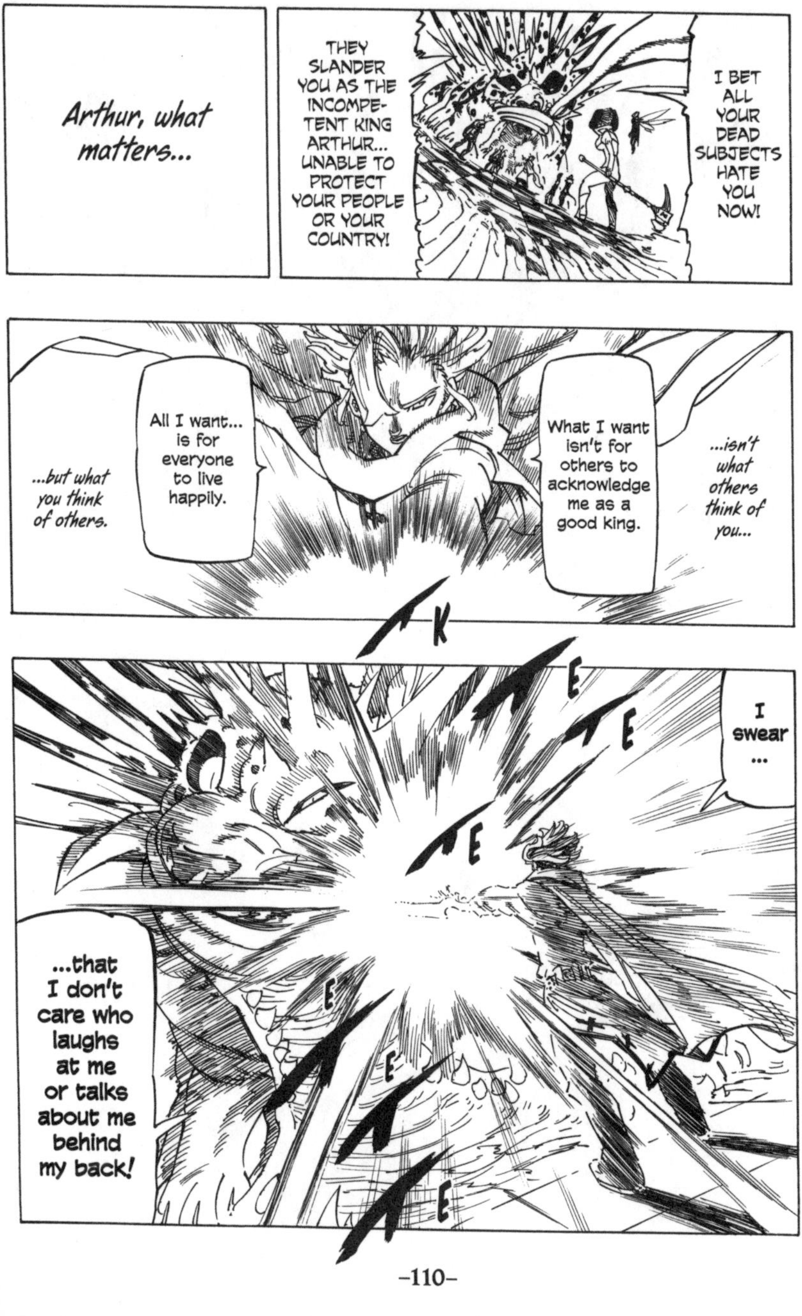
THEY SLANDER YOU AS THE INCOMPETENT KING ARTHUR... UNABLE TO PROTECT YOUR PEOPLE OR YOUR COUNTRY!
I BET ALL YOUR DEAD SUBJECTS HATE YOU NOW!
Arthur, what matters...
...isn't what others think of you...
What I want isn't for others to acknowledge me as a good king.
All I want... is for everyone to live happily.
...but what you think of others.
KEEEEEEE
I swear...
...that I don't care who laughs at me or talks about me behind my back!

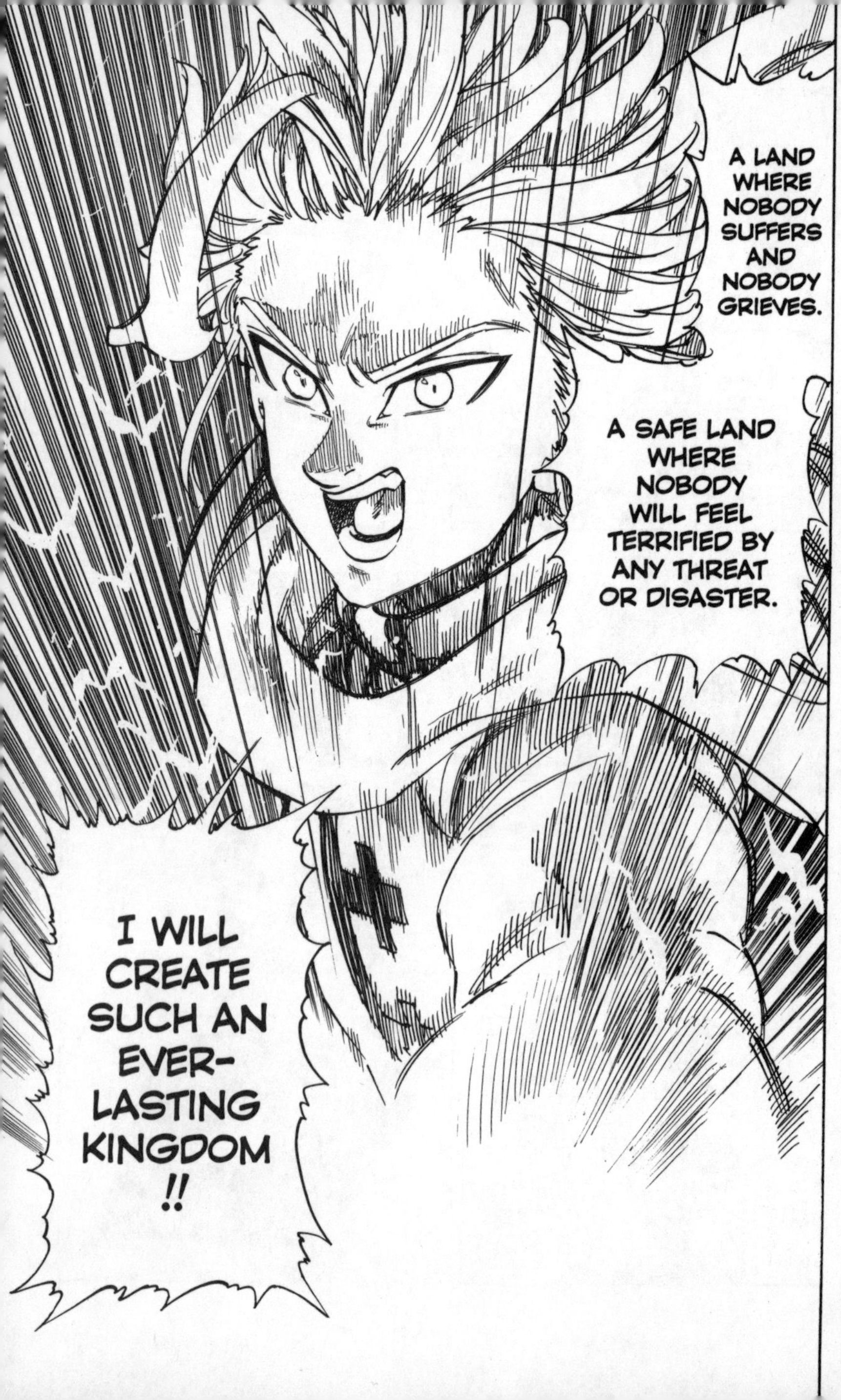
A LAND WHERE NOBODY SUFFERS AND NOBODY GRIEVES.
A SAFE LAND WHERE NOBODY WILL FEEL TERRIFIED BY ANY THREAT OR DISASTER.
I WILL CREATE SUCH AN EVER-LASTING KINGDOM !!

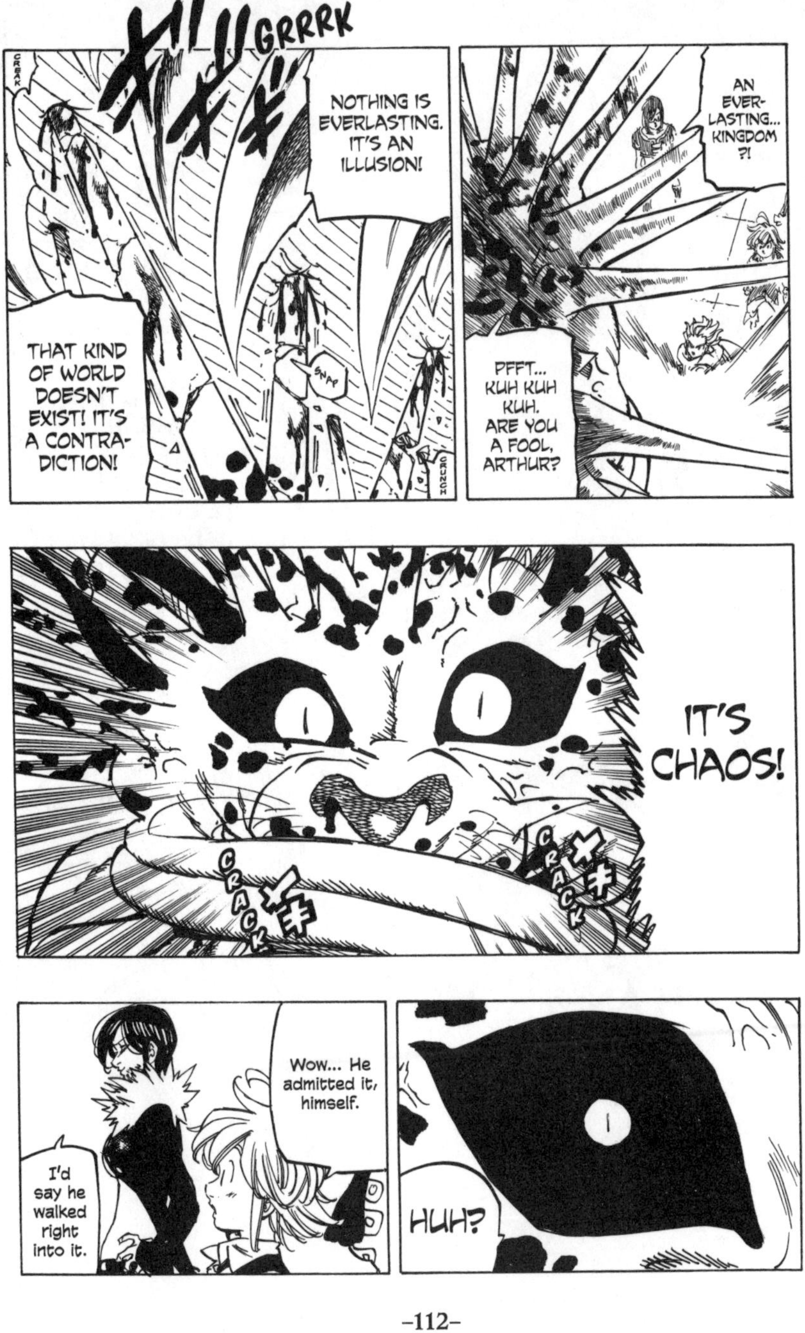
AN EVER-LASTING... KINGDOM ?!
PFFT... KUH KUH KUH. ARE YOU A FOOL, ARTHUR?
GRRRK
CREAK
NOTHING IS EVERLASTING. IT'S AN ILLUSION!
THAT KIND OF WORLD DOESN'T EXIST! IT'S A CONTRA-DICTION!
SNAP
CRUNCH
IT'S CHAOS!
CRACK
CRACK
HUH?
Wow... He admitted it, himself.
I'd say he walked right into it.

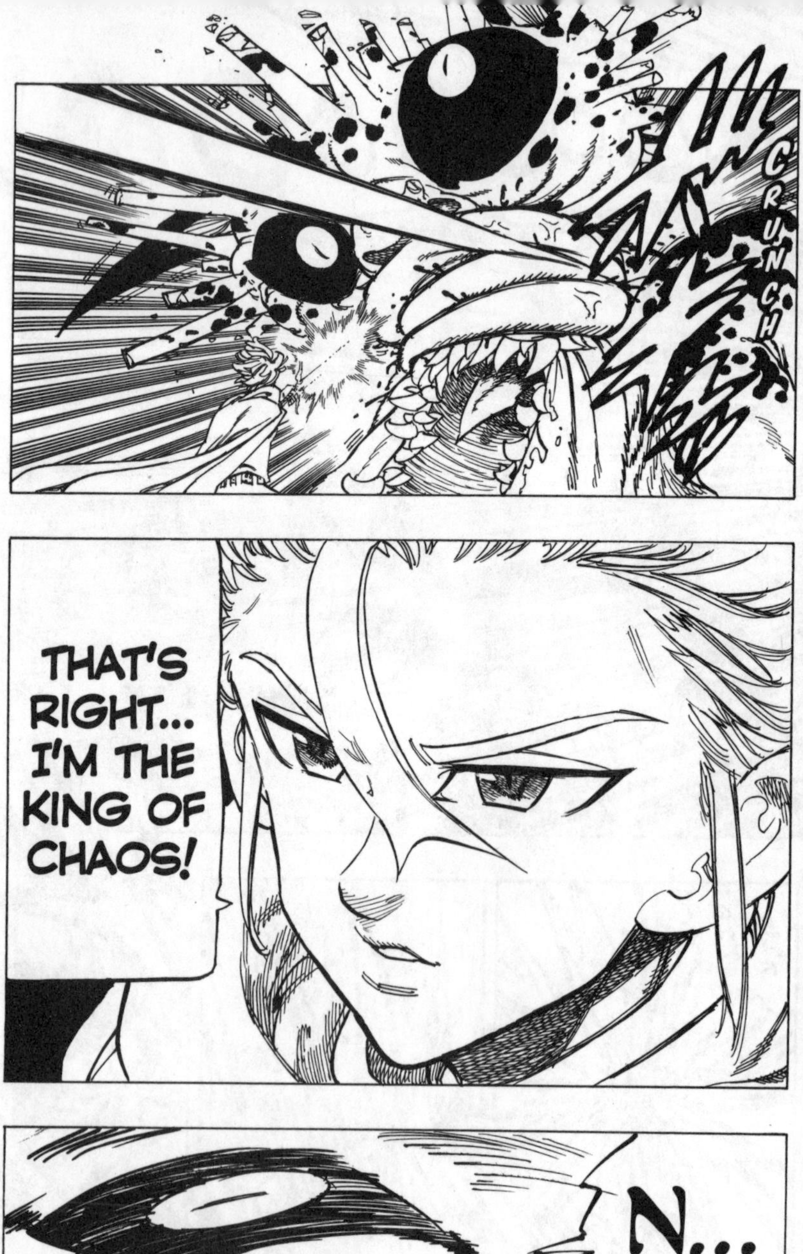
CRUNCH
THAT'S RIGHT... I'M THE KING OF CHAOS!
N...

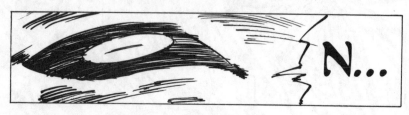

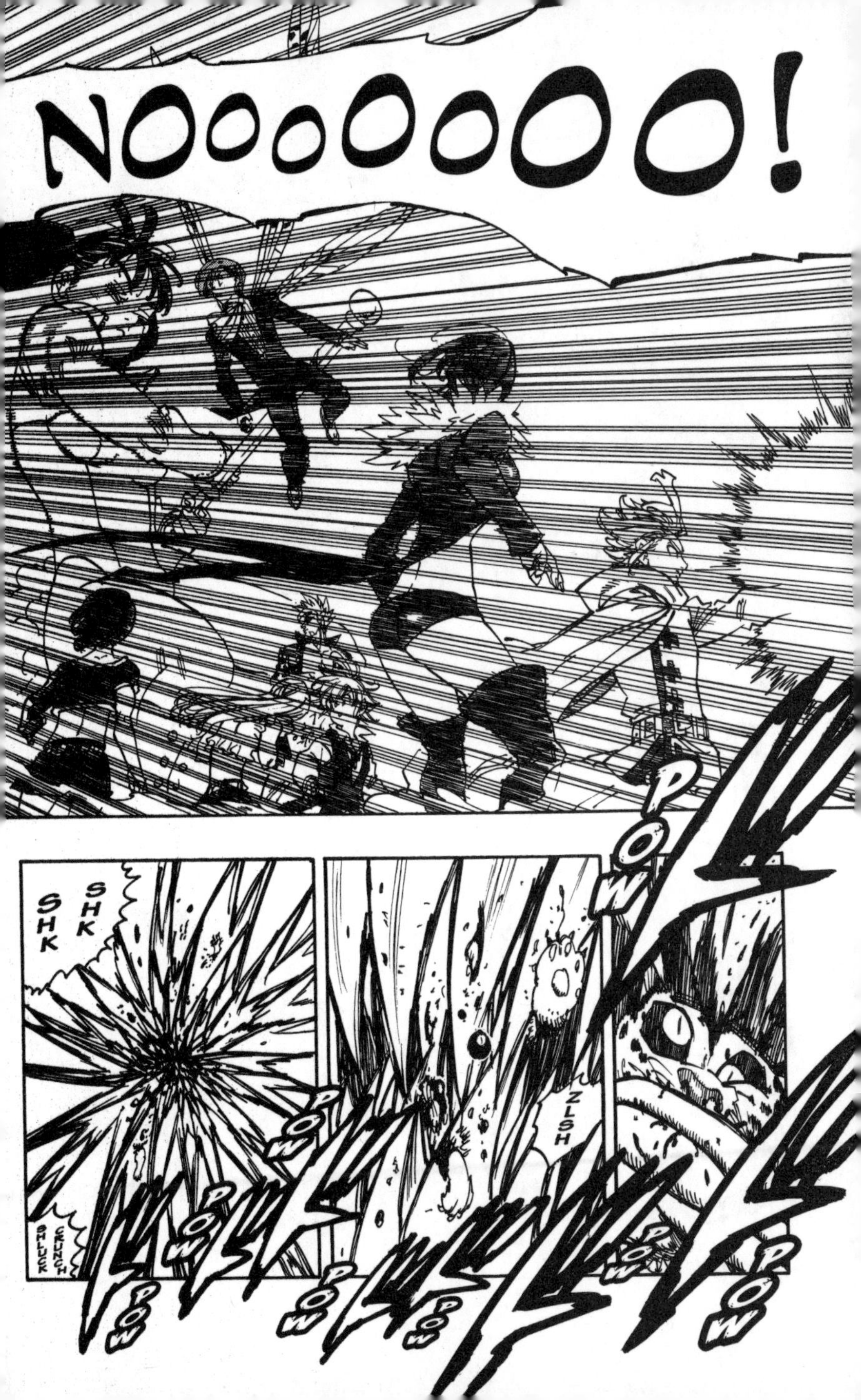
NOOOOOOO!
POW
POW
POW
ZLSH
POW
POW
SHK
SHK
POW
POW
POW
SHLUCK
CRUNCH

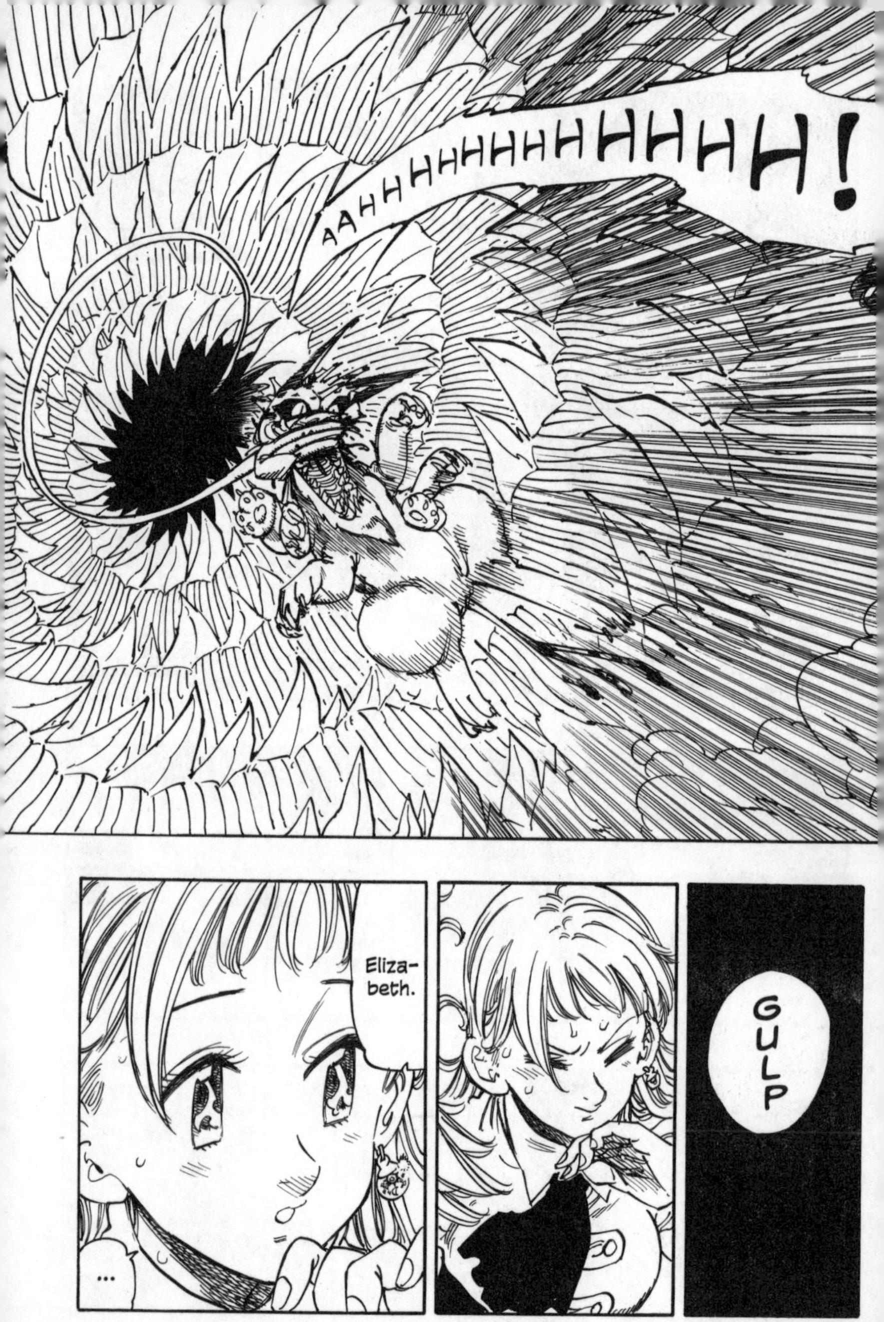
AAHHHHHHHHHHHHHHH!
GULP
Eliza-beth.
...

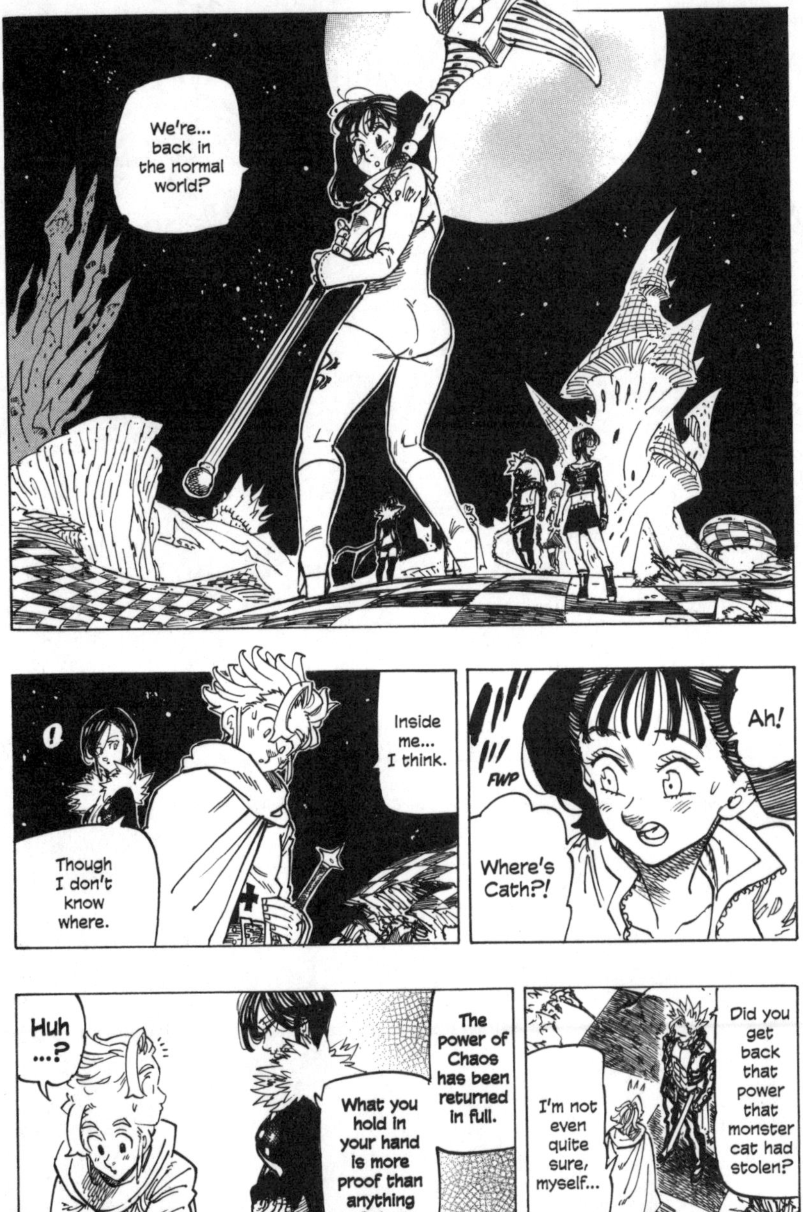
We're... back in the normal world?
Ah!
FWP
Where's Cath?!
Inside me... I think.
Though I don't know where.
Did you get back that power that monster cat had stolen?
I'm not even quite sure, myself...
The power of Chaos has been returned in full.
What you hold in your hand is more proof than anything of that.
Huh ...?

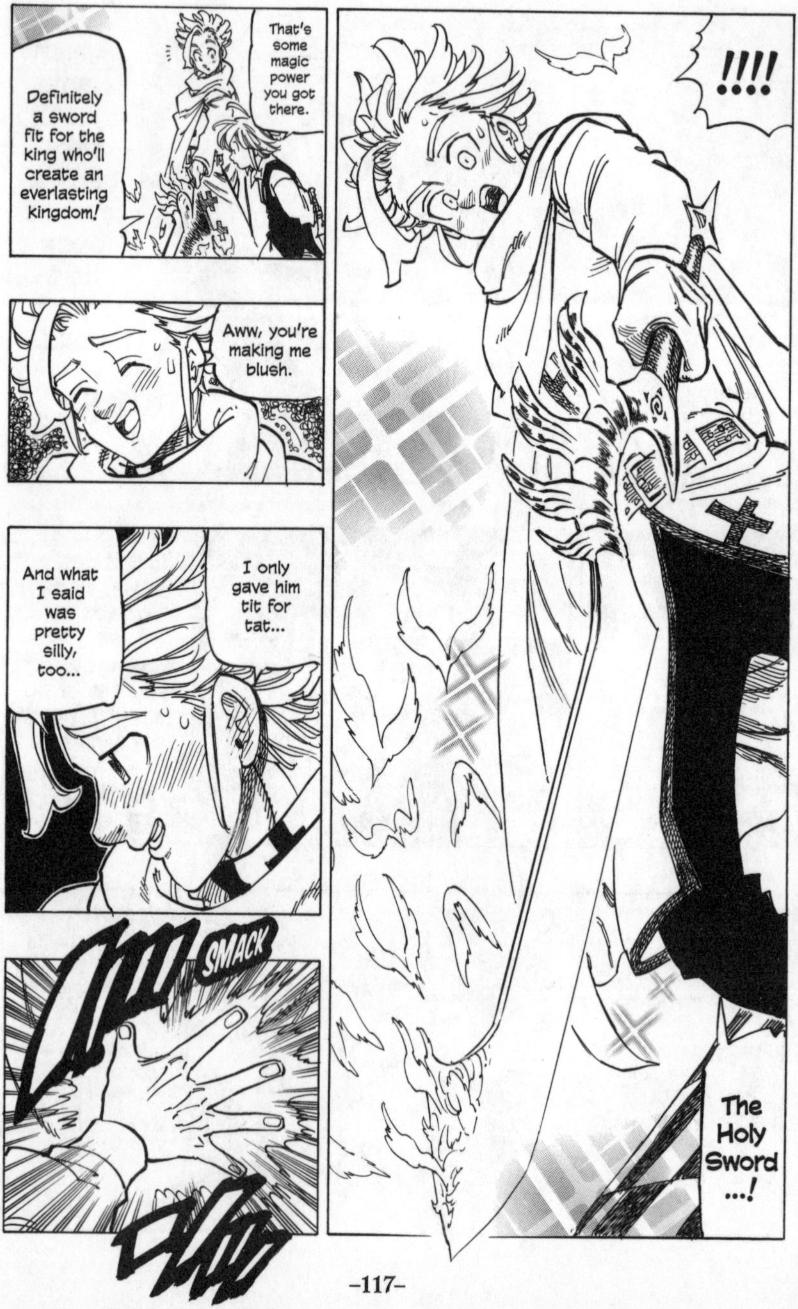
!!!!
The Holy Sword...!
That's some magic power you got there.
Definitely a sword fit for the king who'll create an everlasting kingdom!
Aww, you're making me blush.
I only gave him tit for tat...
And what I said was pretty silly, too...
SMACK

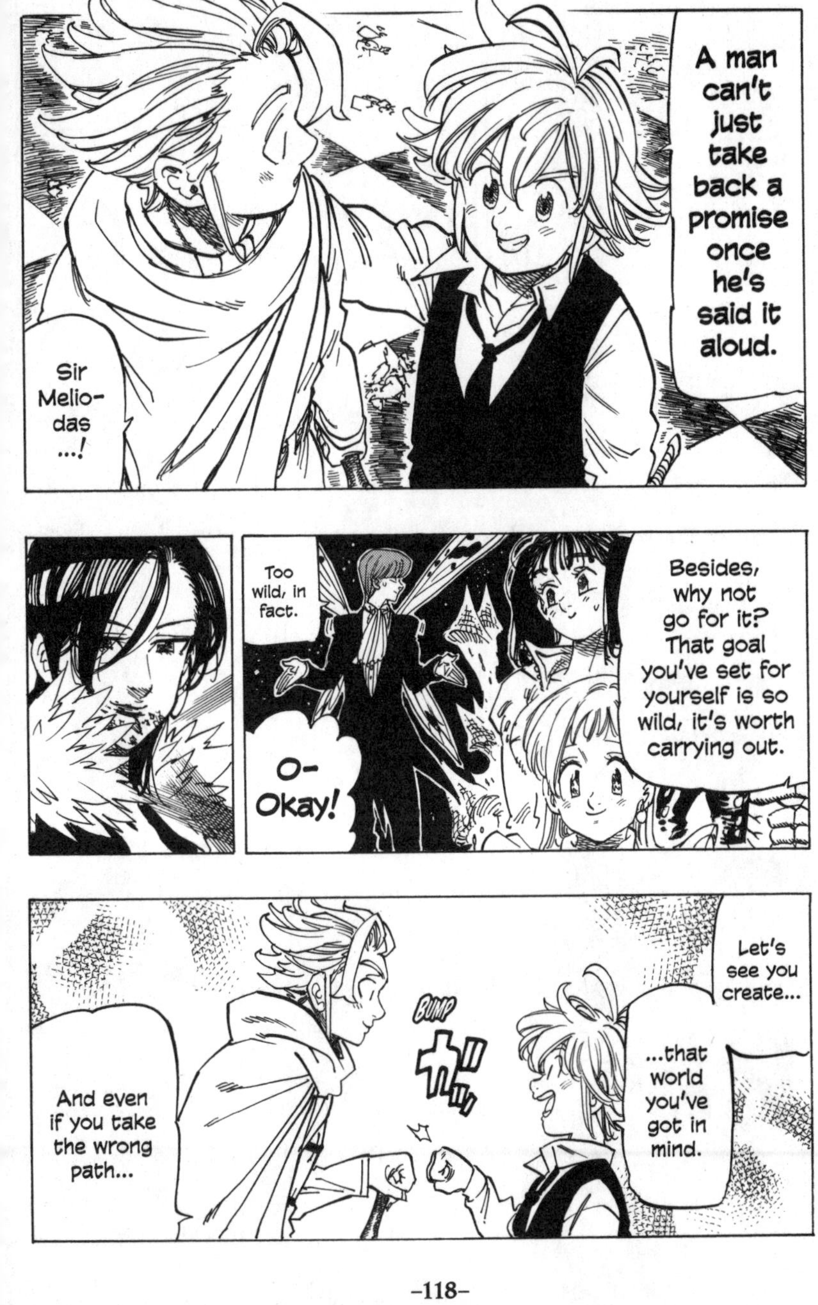
A man can't just take back a promise once he's said it aloud.
Sir Melio-das ...!
Besides, why not go for it? That goal you've set for yourself is so wild, it's worth carrying out.
Too wild, in fact.
O- Okay!
Let's see you create...
...that world you've got in mind.
BUMP
And even if you take the wrong path...

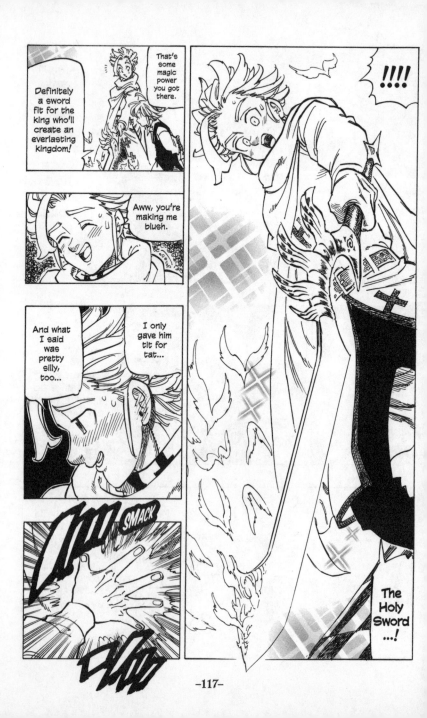

Definitely a sword fit for the king who'll create an everlasting kingdom!

That's some magic power you got there.

Aww, you're making me blush.

And what I said was pretty silly, too...

I only gave him tit for tat...

SMACK

!!!!

The Holy Sword ...!

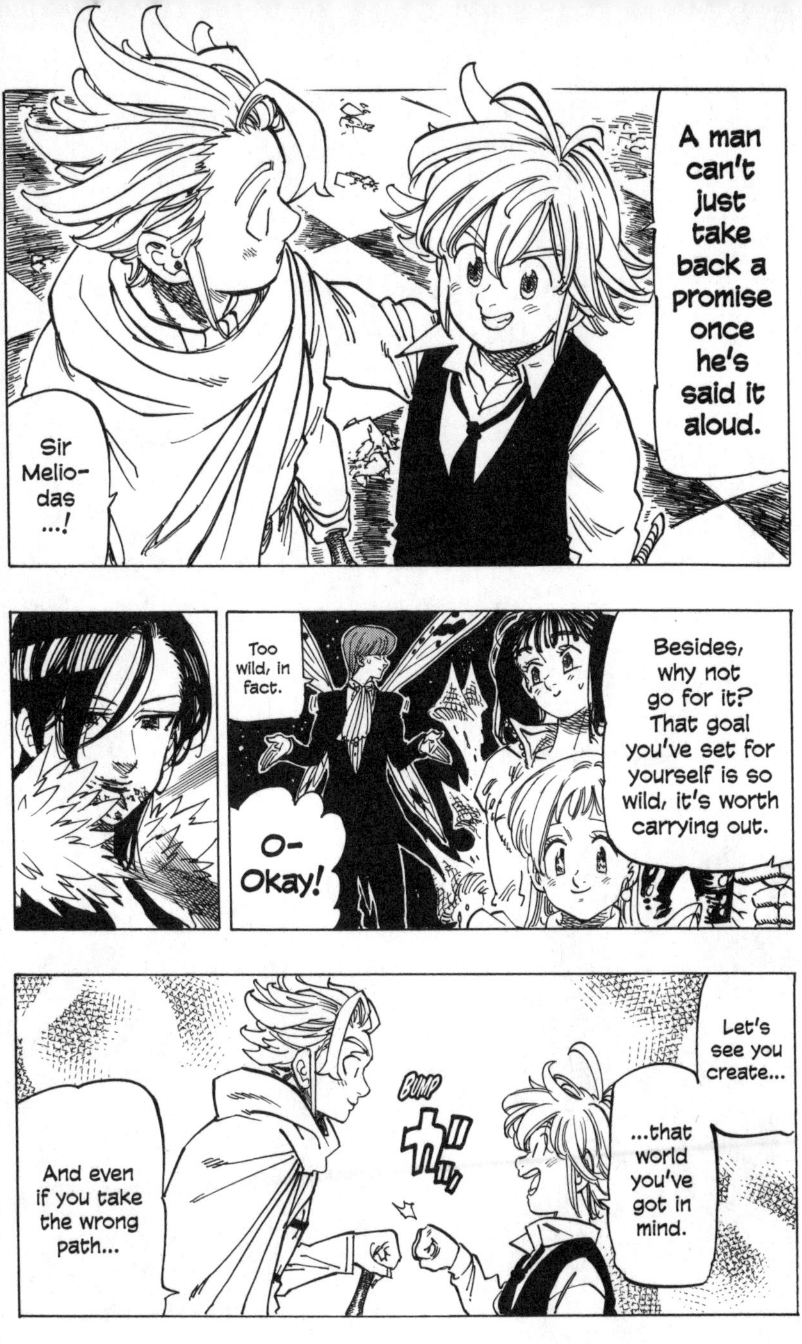
A man can't just take back a promise once he's said it aloud.
Sir Melio-das ...!
Besides, why not go for it? That goal you've set for yourself is so wild, it's worth carrying out.
Too wild, in fact.
O-Okay!
Let's see you create...
...that world you've got in mind.
BUMP
And even if you take the wrong path...

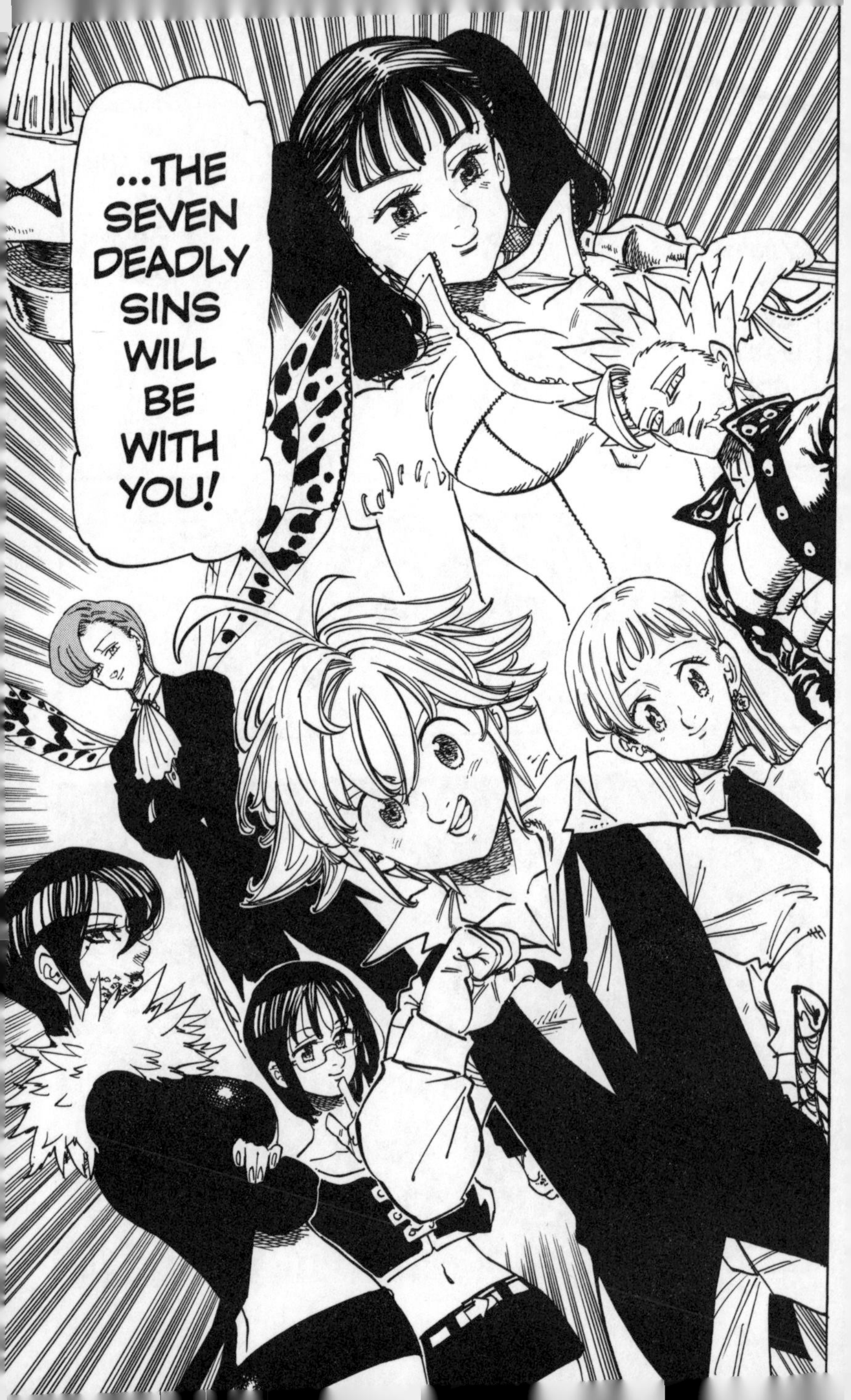
...THE SEVEN DEADLY SINS WILL BE WITH YOU!

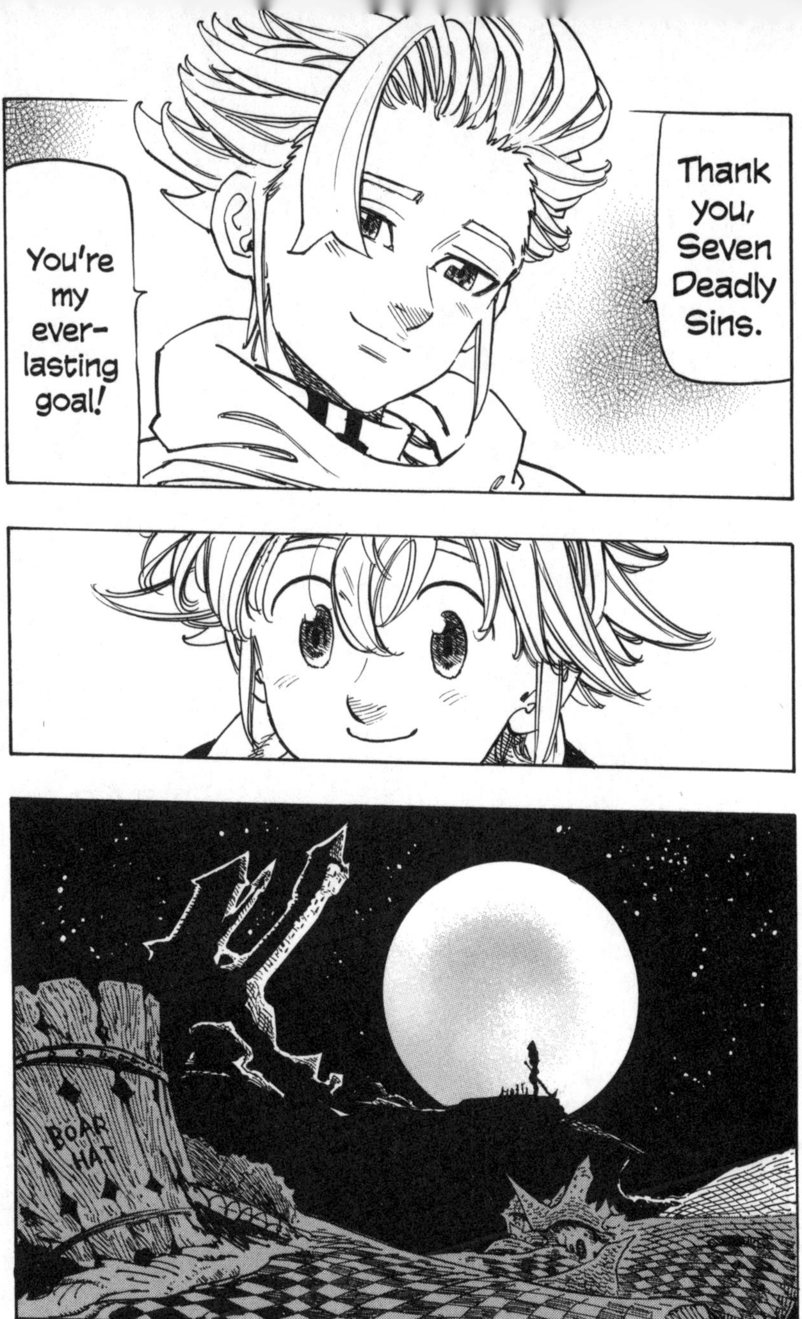
Thank you, Seven Deadly Sins.
You're my ever-lasting goal!
BOAR HAT

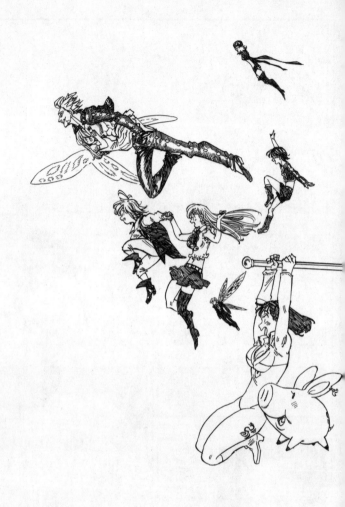

Chapter 344 - Towards The Future

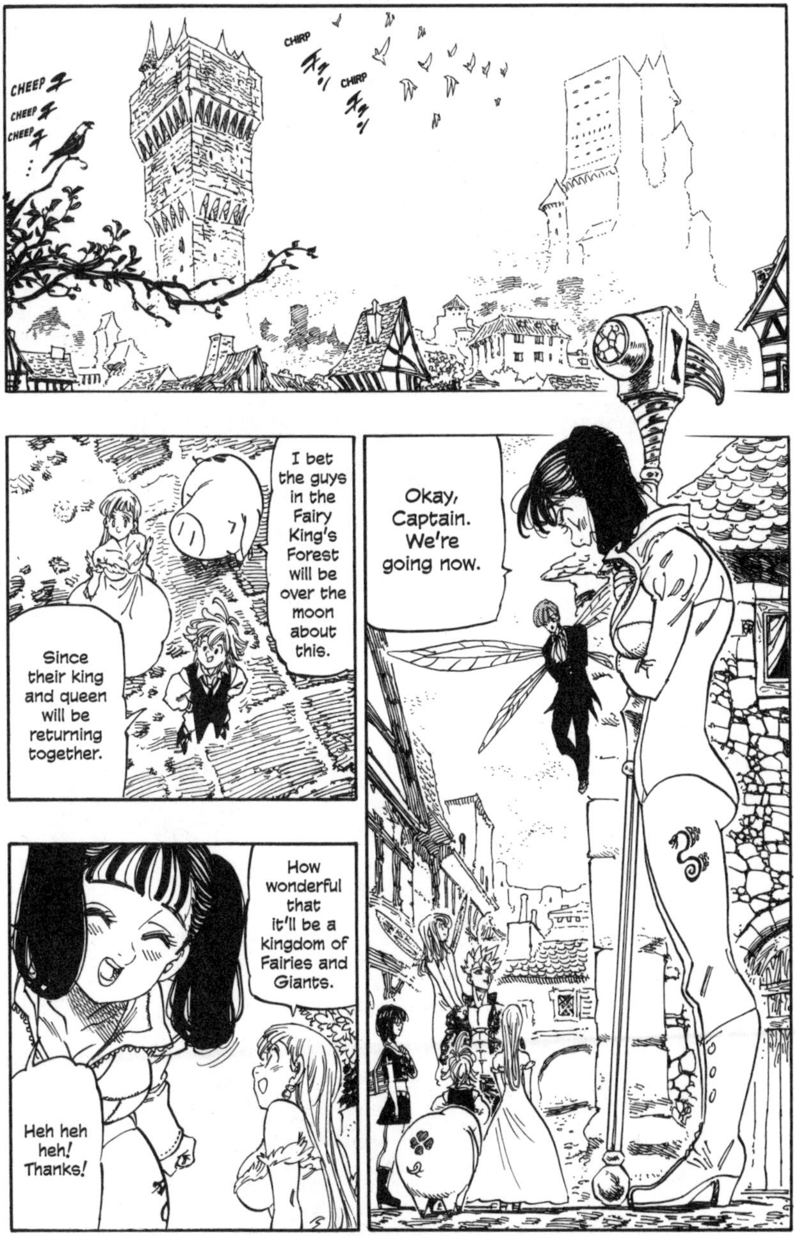
CHIRP
CHIRP
CHEEP
CHEEP
CHEEP
Okay, Captain. We're going now.
I bet the guys in the Fairy King's Forest will be over the moon about this.
Since their king and queen will be returning together.
How wonderful that it'll be a kingdom of Fairies and Giants.
Heh heh heh! Thanks!

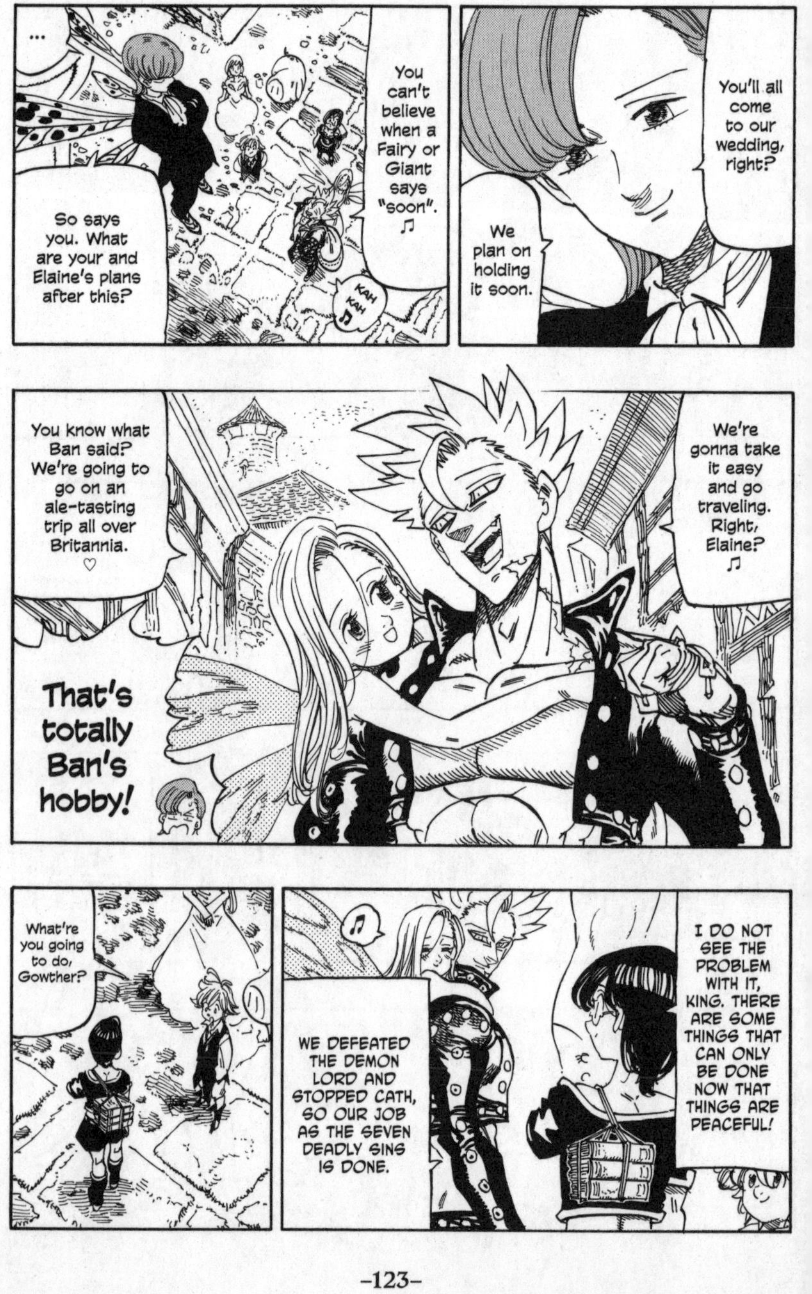
You'll all come to our wedding, right?
We plan on holding it soon.
You can't believe when a Fairy or Giant says "soon". ♫
...
KAH KAH ♫
So says you. What are your and Elaine's plans after this?
We're gonna take it easy and go traveling. Right, Elaine? ♫
You know what Ban said? We're going to go on an ale-tasting trip all over Britannia. ♡
That's totally Ban's hobby!
I DO NOT SEE THE PROBLEM WITH IT, KING. THERE ARE SOME THINGS THAT CAN ONLY BE DONE NOW THAT THINGS ARE PEACEFUL!
♪
WE DEFEATED THE DEMON LORD AND STOPPED CATH, SO OUR JOB AS THE SEVEN DEADLY SINS IS DONE.
What're you going to do, Gowther?

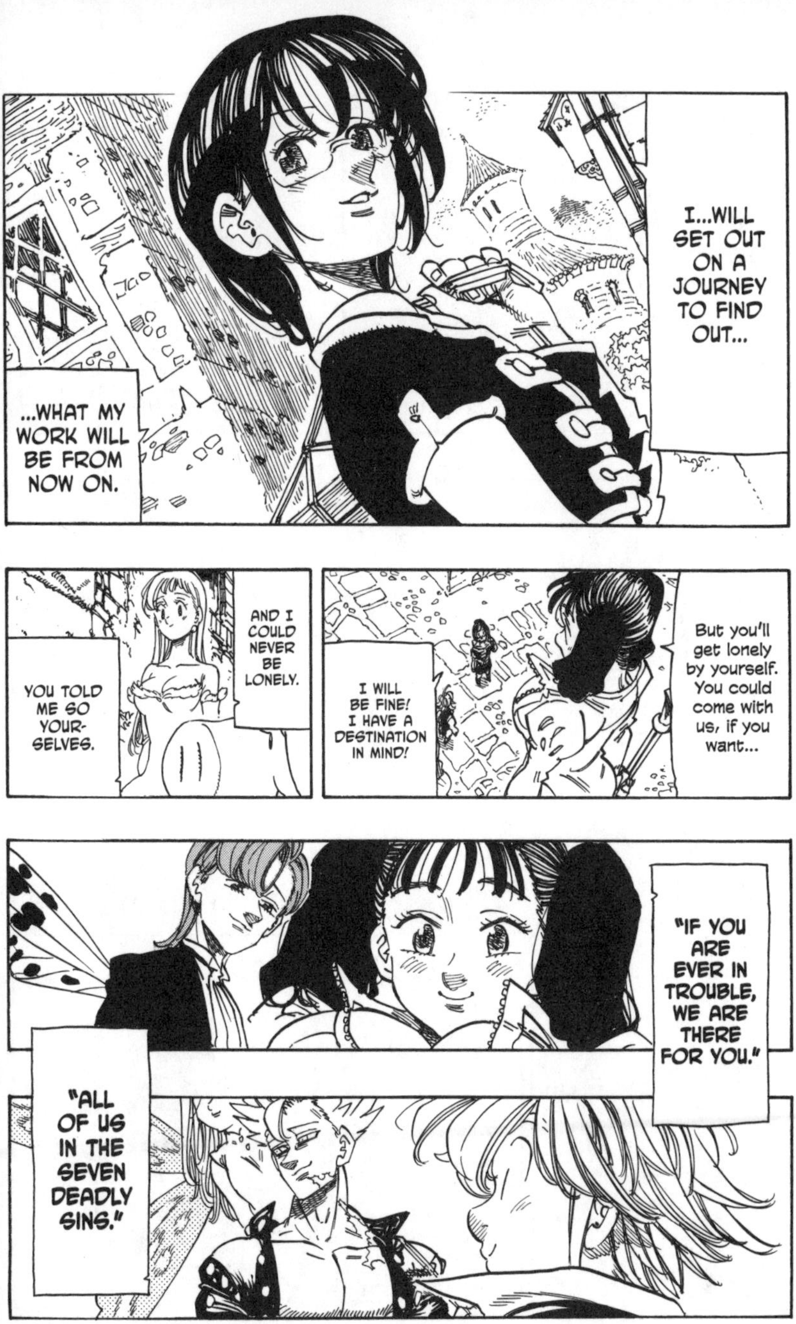
I...WILL SET OUT ON A JOURNEY TO FIND OUT...
...WHAT MY WORK WILL BE FROM NOW ON.
But you'll get lonely by yourself. You could come with us, if you want...
I WILL BE FINE! I HAVE A DESTINATION IN MIND!
AND I COULD NEVER BE LONELY.
YOU TOLD ME SO YOUR-SELVES.
"IF YOU ARE EVER IN TROUBLE, WE ARE THERE FOR YOU."
"ALL OF US IN THE SEVEN DEADLY SINS."

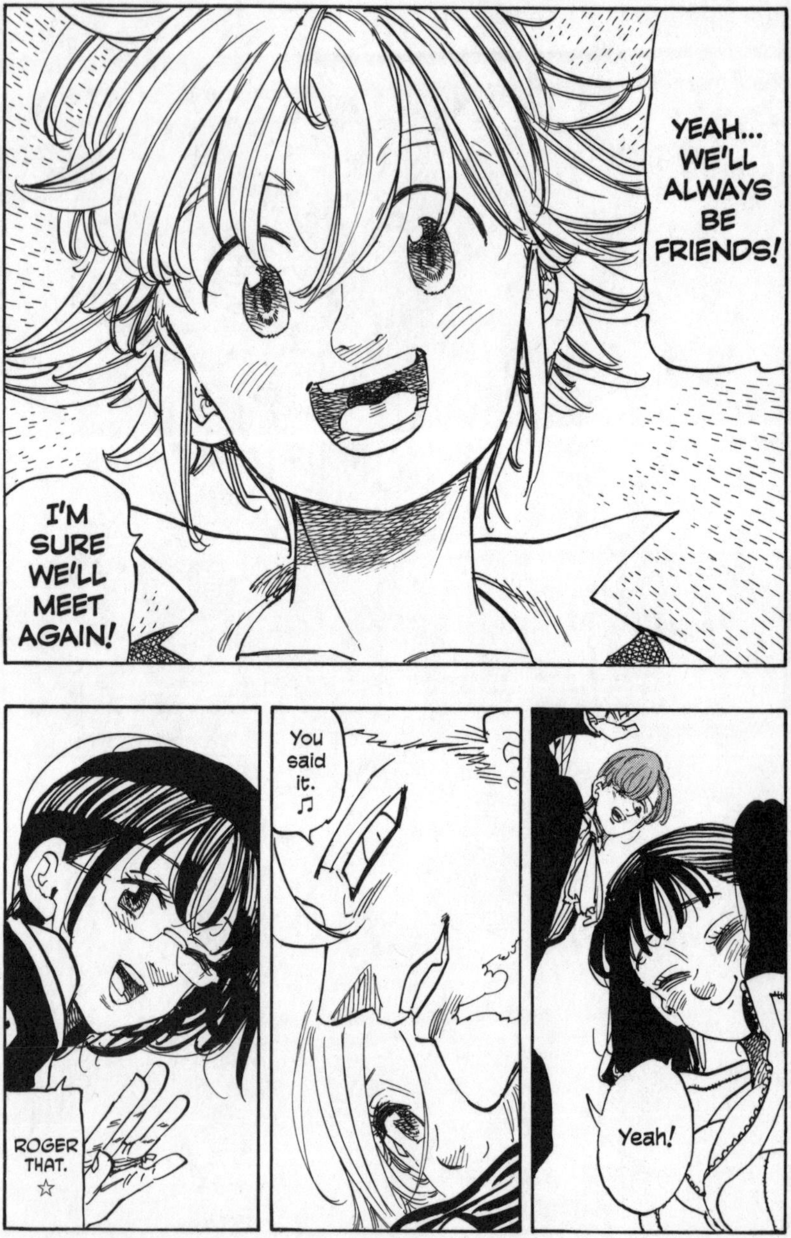
YEAH... WE'LL ALWAYS BE FRIENDS!
I'M SURE WE'LL MEET AGAIN!
Yeah!
You said it. ♫
ROGER THAT. ☆

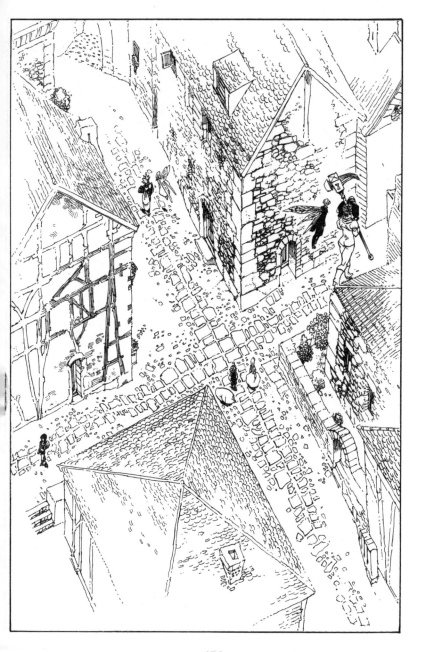

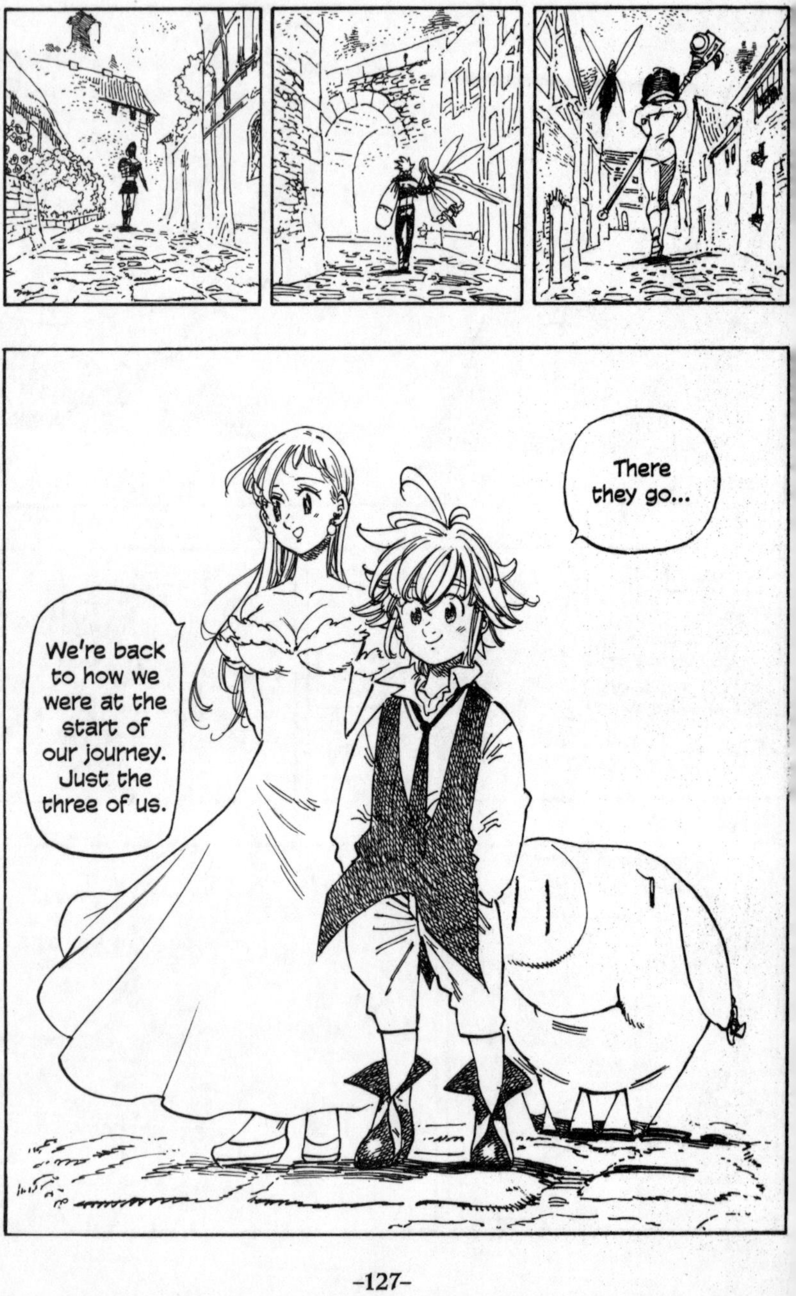
There they go...
We're back to how we were at the start of our journey. Just the three of us.

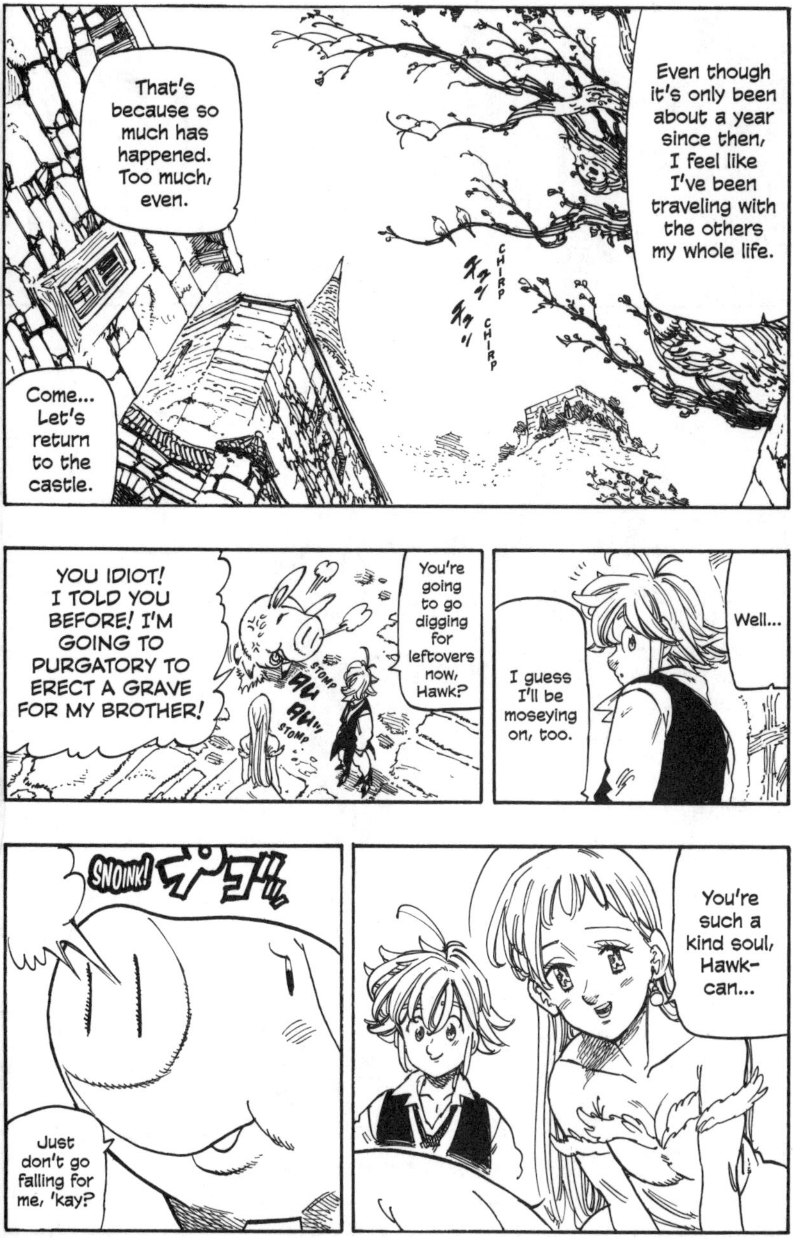
Even though it's only been about a year since then, I feel like I've been traveling with the others my whole life.
That's because so much has happened. Too much, even.
CHIRP
CHIRP
Come... Let's return to the castle.
Well...
I guess I'll be moseying on, too.
You're going to go digging for leftovers now, Hawk?
YOU IDIOT! I TOLD YOU BEFORE! I'M GOING TO PURGATORY TO ERECT A GRAVE FOR MY BROTHER!
STOMP
STOMP
You're such a kind soul, Hawk-can...
SNOINK!
Just don't go falling for me, 'kay?

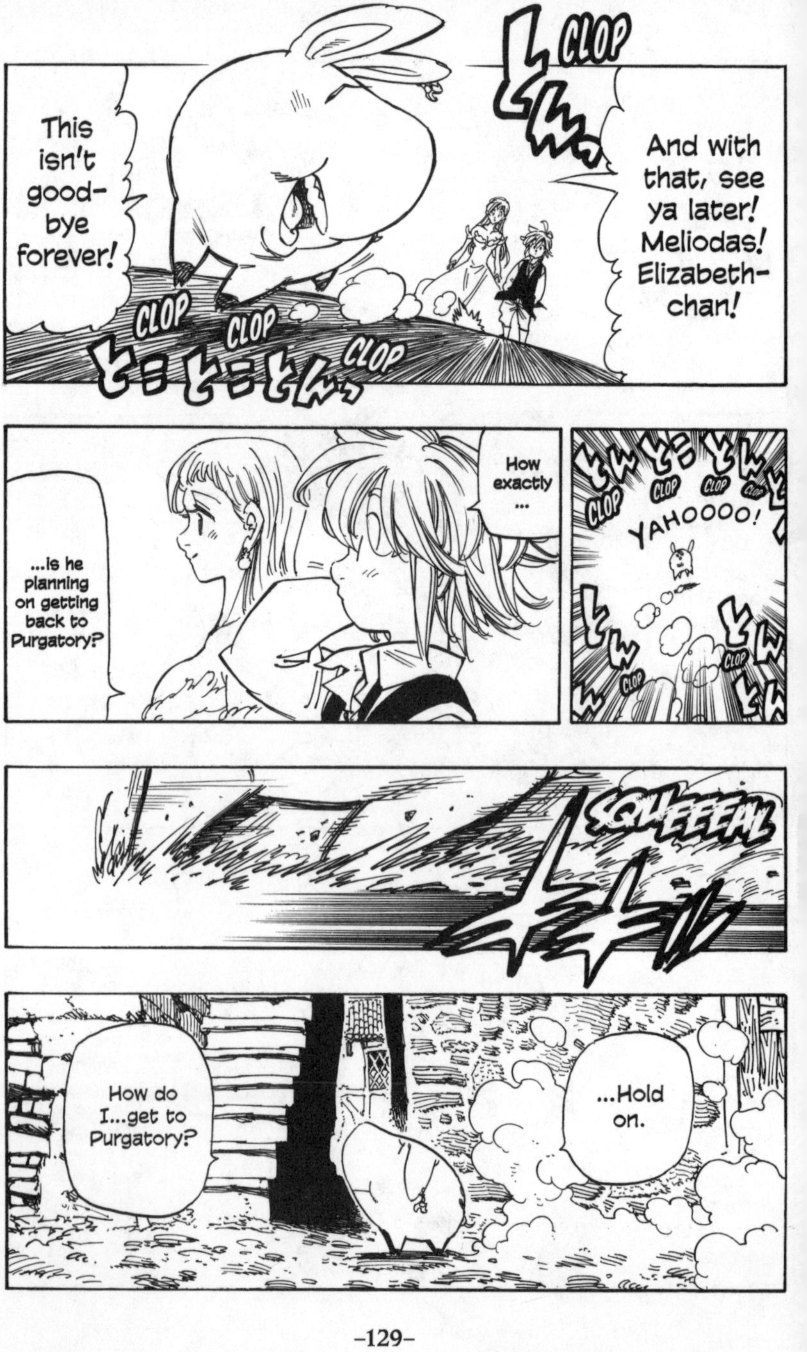
CLOP
And with that, see ya later! Meliodas! Elizabeth-chan!
This isn't good-bye forever!
CLOP
CLOP
CLOP
CLOP
CLOP
CLOP
CLOP
YAHOOOO!
CLOP
CLOP
How exactly...
...is he planning on getting back to Purgatory?
SQUEEEAL
...Hold on.
How do I...get to Purgatory?

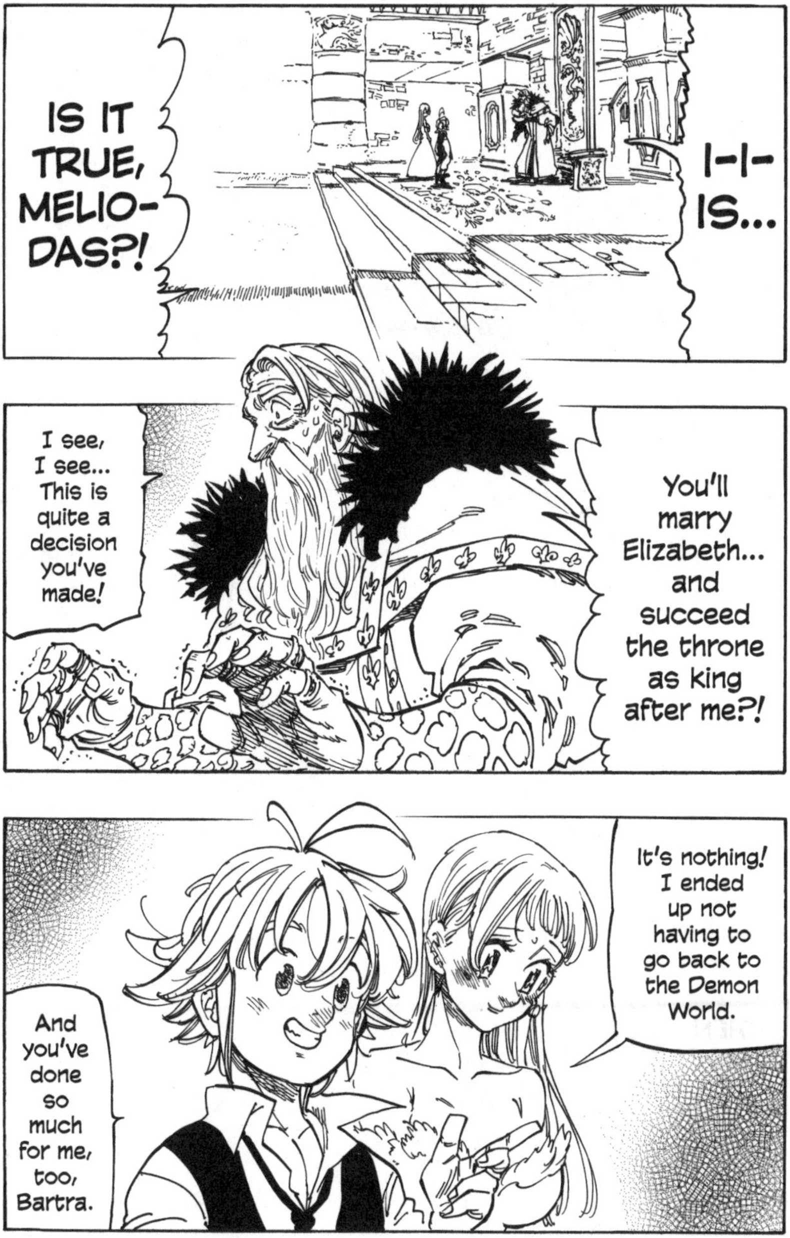
I-I-IS...
IS IT TRUE, MELIODAS?!
You'll marry Elizabeth... and succeed the throne as king after me?!
I see, I see... This is quite a decision you've made!
It's nothing! I ended up not having to go back to the Demon World.
And you've done so much for me, too, Bartra.

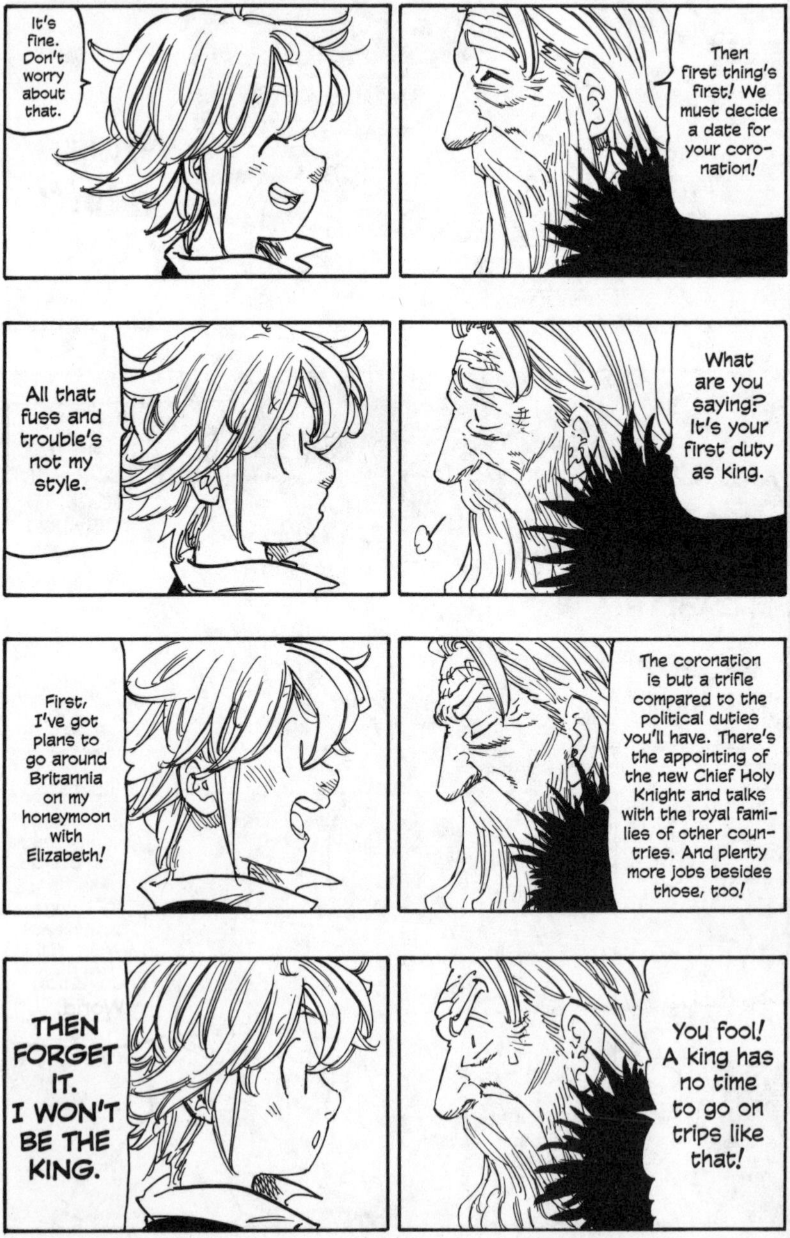
Then first thing's first! We must decide a date for your coronation!
It's fine. Don't worry about that.
What are you saying? It's your first duty as king.
All that fuss and trouble's not my style.
The coronation is but a trifle compared to the political duties you'll have. There's the appointing of the new Chief Holy Knight and talks with the royal families of other countries. And plenty more jobs besides those, too!
First, I've got plans to go around Britannia on my honeymoon with Elizabeth!
You fool! A king has no time to go on trips like that!
THEN FORGET IT. I WON'T BE THE KING.

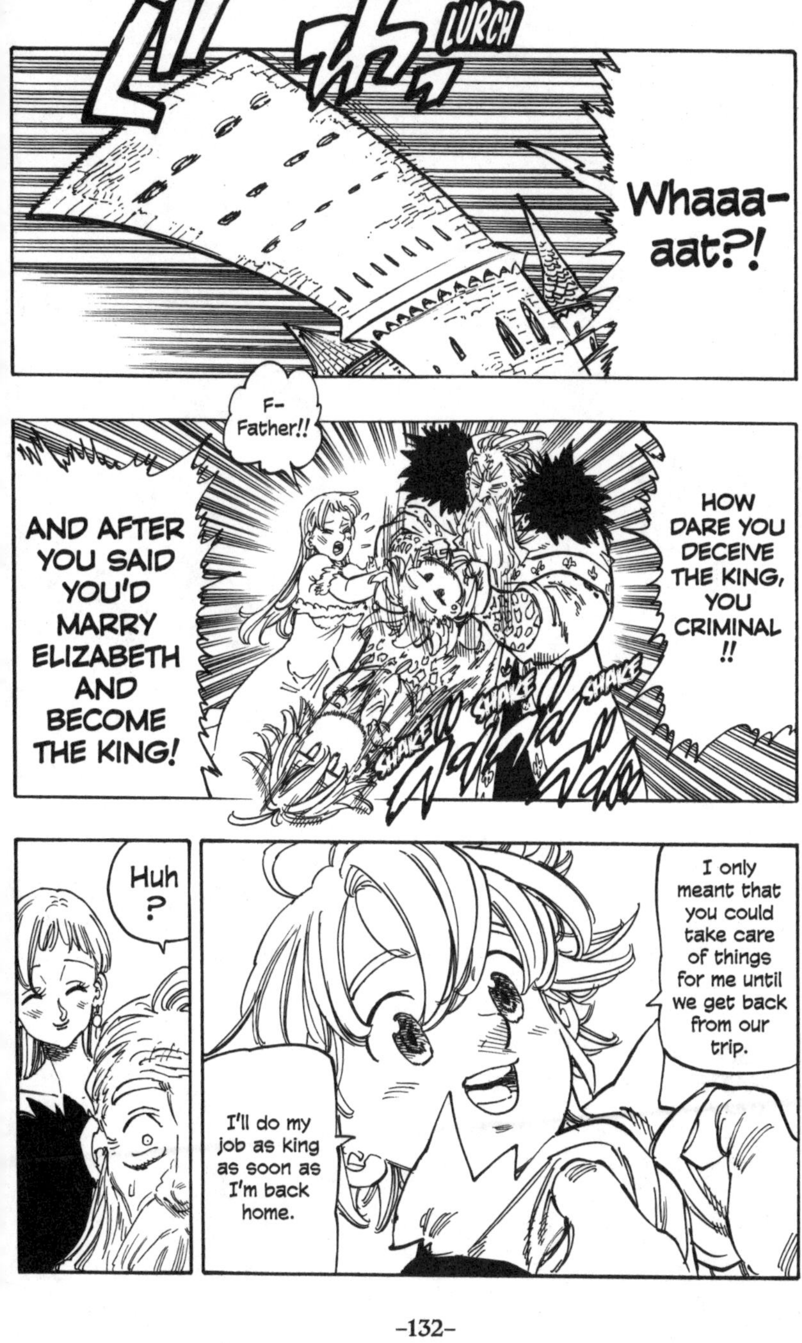
LURCH
Whaaaa-aat?!
HOW DARE YOU DECEIVE THE KING, YOU CRIMINAL!!
F-Father!!
SHAKE
SHAKE
SHAKE
AND AFTER YOU SAID YOU'D MARRY ELIZABETH AND BECOME THE KING!
I only meant that you could take care of things for me until we get back from our trip.
I'll do my job as king as soon as I'm back home.
Huh?

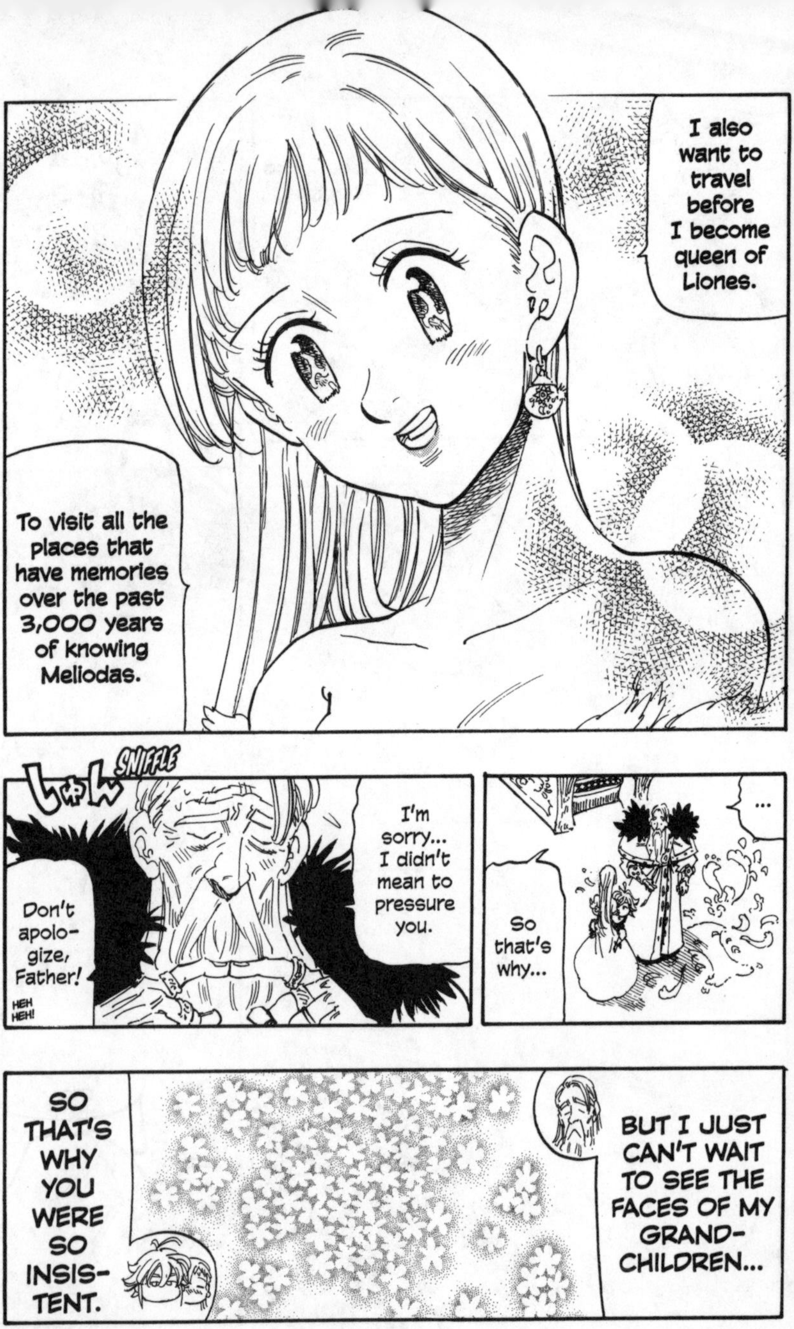
I also want to travel before I become queen of Liones.
To visit all the places that have memories over the past 3,000 years of knowing Meliodas.
...
So that's why...
しゅん SNIFFLE
I'm sorry... I didn't mean to pressure you.
Don't apolo-gize, Father!
HEH HEH!
BUT I JUST CAN'T WAIT TO SEE THE FACES OF MY GRAND-CHILDREN...
SO THAT'S WHY YOU WERE SO INSIS-TENT.

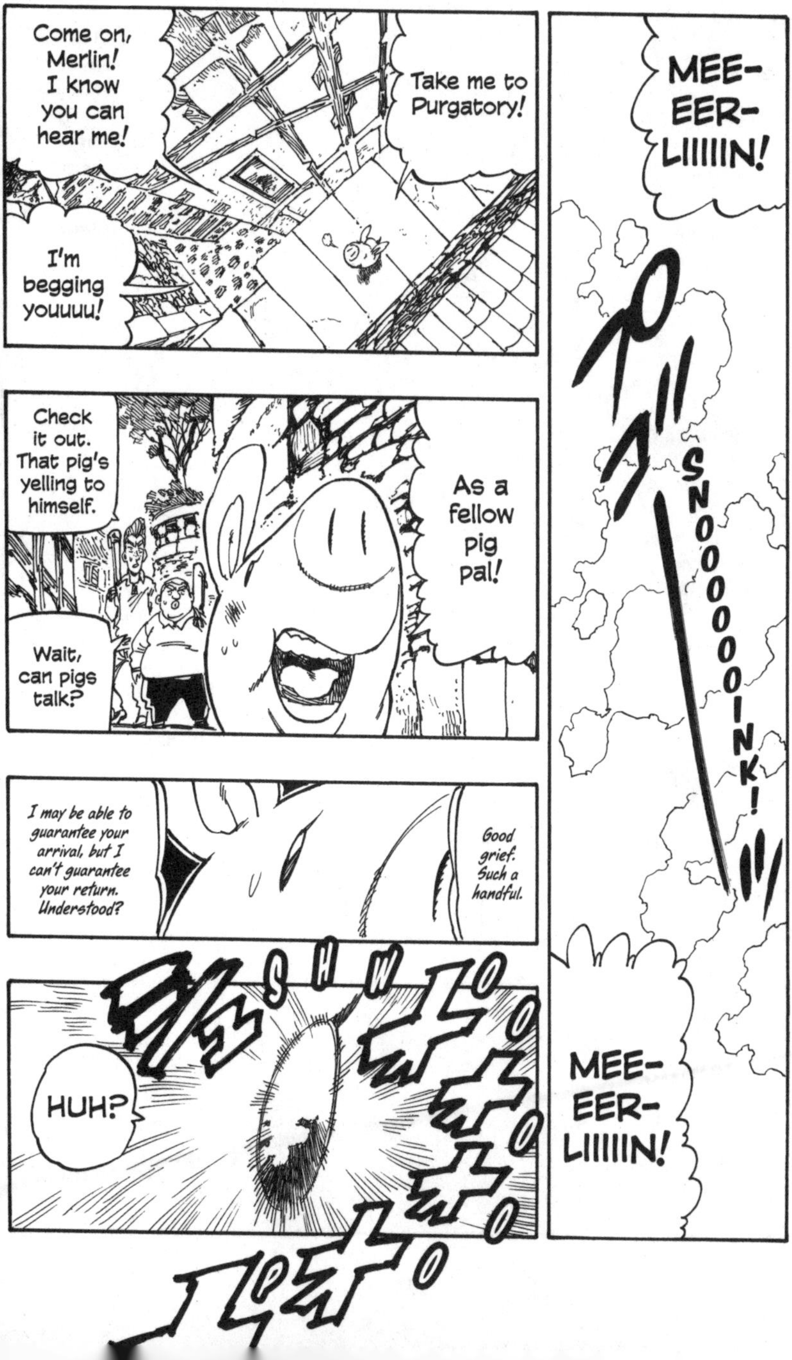
MEE-EER-LIIIIIN!
SNOOOOOOINK!
MEE-EER-LIIIIIN!
Take me to Purgatory!
Come on, Merlin! I know you can hear me!
I'm begging youuuu!
As a fellow pig pal!
Check it out. That pig's yelling to himself.
Wait, can pigs talk?
Good grief. Such a handful.
I may be able to guarantee your arrival, but I can't guarantee your return. Understood?
SHWOOOOOOO
HUH?

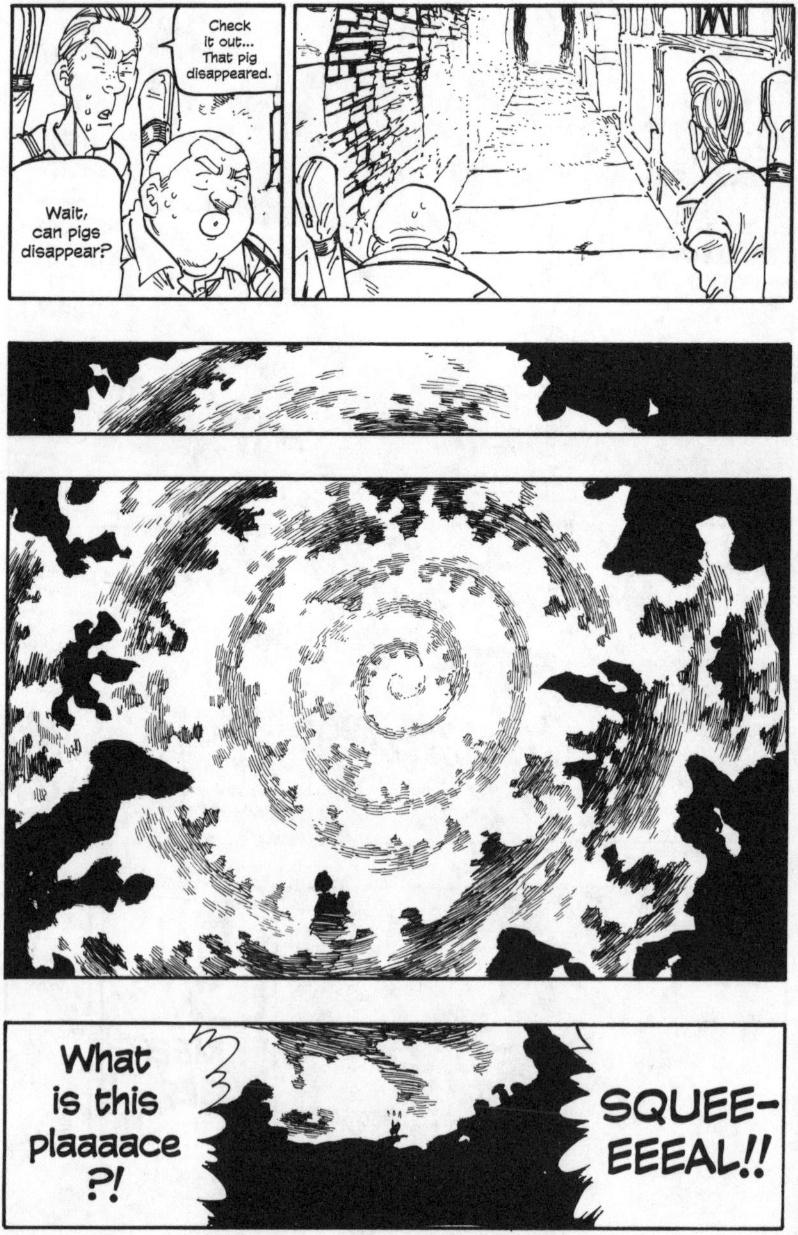
Check it out... That pig disappeared.
Wait, can pigs disappear?
SQUEEE-EEEAL!!
What is this plaaaace ?!

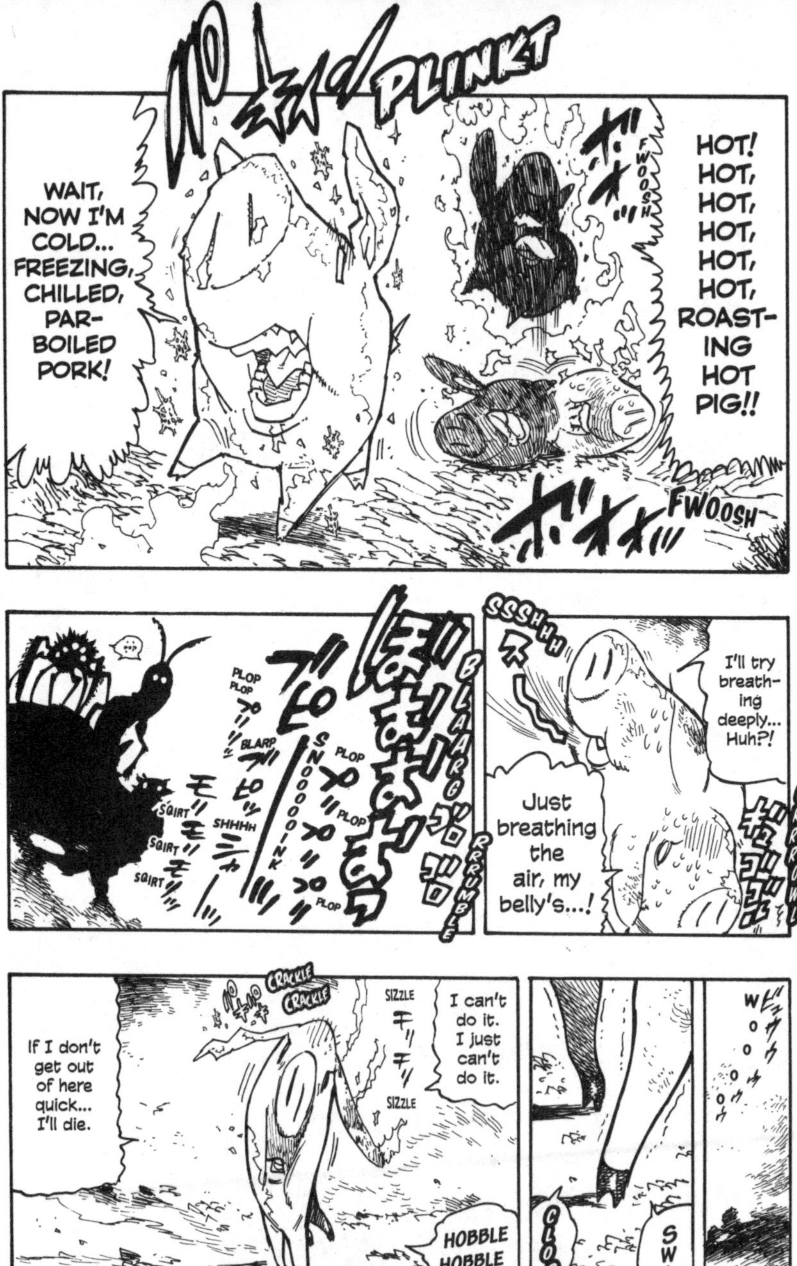
PLINKT
FWOOSH
HOT! HOT, HOT, HOT, HOT, HOT, ROASTING HOT PIG!!
WAIT, NOW I'M COLD... FREEZING, CHILLED, PAR-BOILED PORK!
FWOOSH
SSSHHH
I'll try breathing deeply... Huh?!
GRRROWL
Just breathing the air, my belly's...!
BLAAARG
RRRUMBLE
SNOOOOOOINK
PLOP PLOP
BLARP
PLOP
PLOP
PLOP
SHHHH
SQIRT
SQIRT
SQIRT
WOOOO
SWAY
CLOP
I can't do it. I just can't do it.
CRACKLE CRACKLE
SIZZLE
SIZZLE
HOBBLE HOBBLE HOBBLE
If I don't get out of here quick... I'll die.

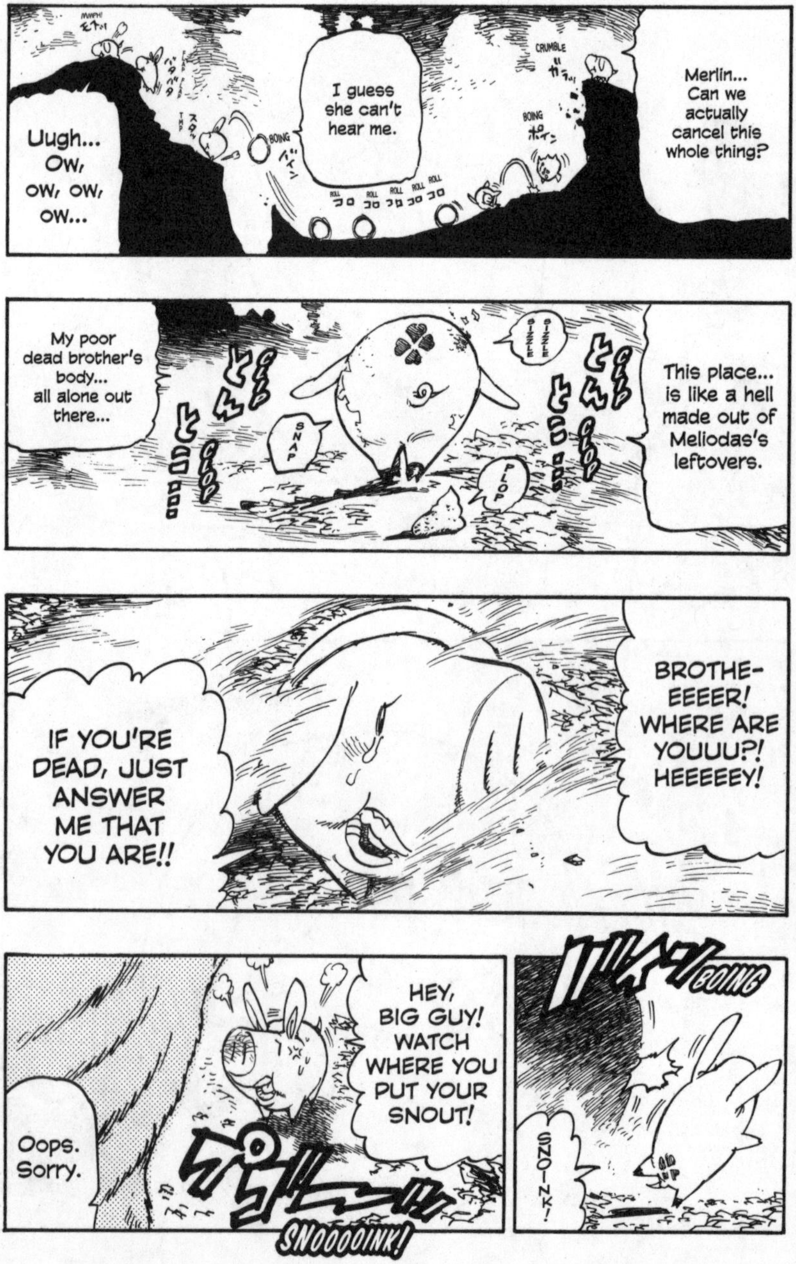
Merlin... Can we actually cancel this whole thing?
CRUMBLE
BOING
I guess she can't hear me.
ROLL ROLL ROLL ROLL ROLL
BOING
MMPH!
Uugh... Ow, ow, ow, ow...
This place... is like a hell made out of Meliodas's leftovers.
CLOP
SIZZLE SIZZLE
PLOP
SNAP
CLOP
My poor dead brother's body... all alone out there...
BROTHE-EEEER! WHERE ARE YOUUU?! HEEEEEY!
IF YOU'RE DEAD, JUST ANSWER ME THAT YOU ARE!!
BOING
SNOINK!
HEY, BIG GUY! WATCH WHERE YOU PUT YOUR SNOUT!
SNOOOOINK!
Oops. Sorry.

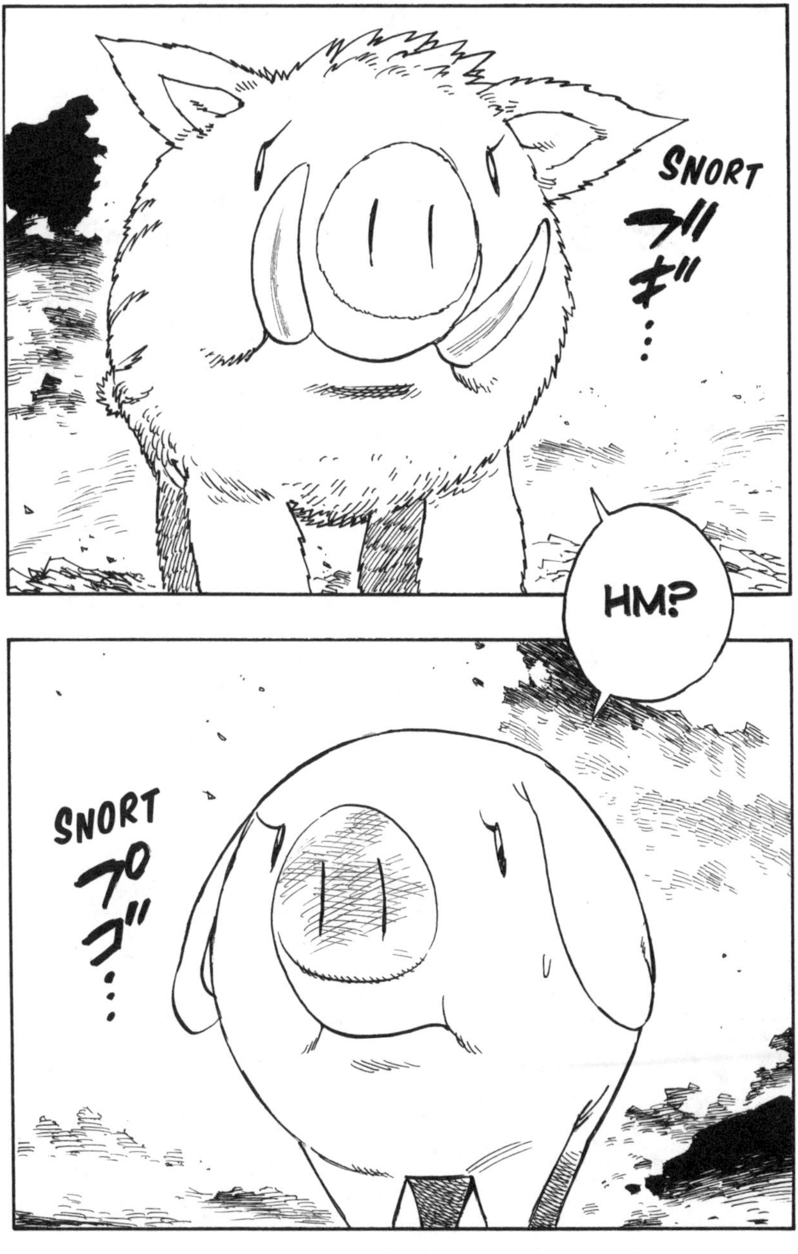
SNORT
ブギ…
HM?
SNORT
プゴ…

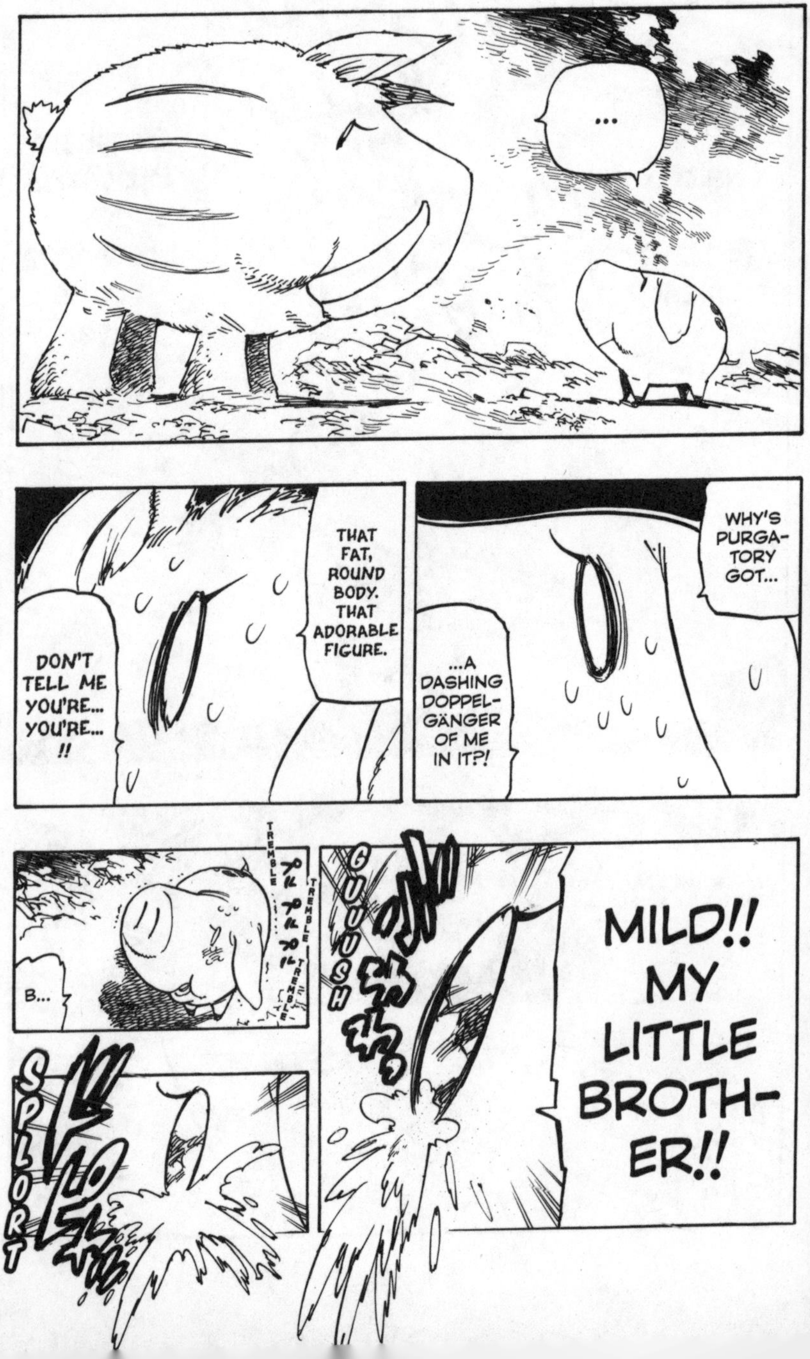
...
WHY'S PURGATORY GOT...
...A DASHING DOPPELGÄNGER OF ME IN IT?!
THAT FAT, ROUND BODY. THAT ADORABLE FIGURE.
DON'T TELL ME YOU'RE... YOU'RE... !!
MILD!! MY LITTLE BROTHER!!
GUUUSH
TREMBLE TREMBLE TREMBLE
B...
SPLORT

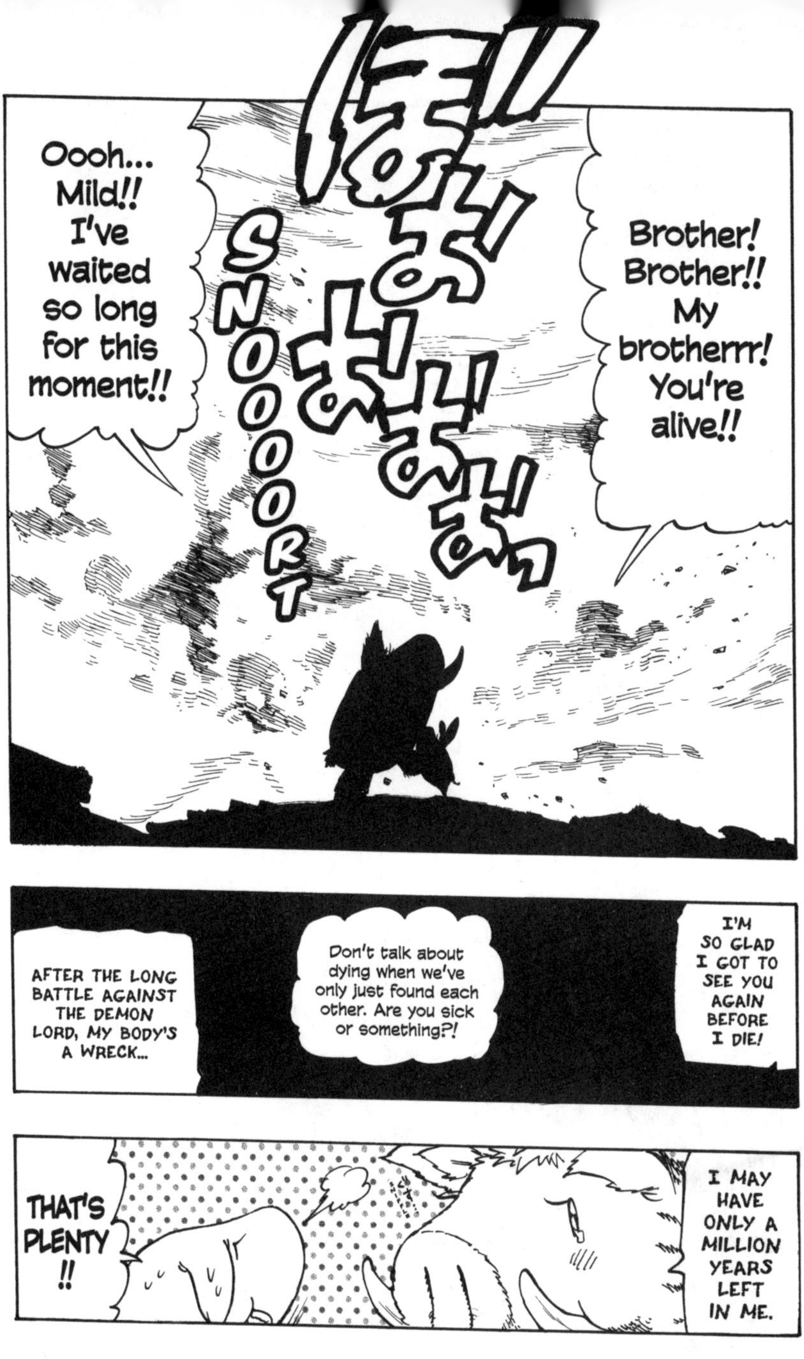
Brother! Brother!! My brotherrr! You're alive!!
SNOOOOORT
Oooh... Mild!! I've waited so long for this moment!!
I'M SO GLAD I GOT TO SEE YOU AGAIN BEFORE I DIE!
Don't talk about dying when we've only just found each other. Are you sick or something?!
AFTER THE LONG BATTLE AGAINST THE DEMON LORD, MY BODY'S A WRECK...
I MAY HAVE ONLY A MILLION YEARS LEFT IN ME.
THAT'S PLENTY!!

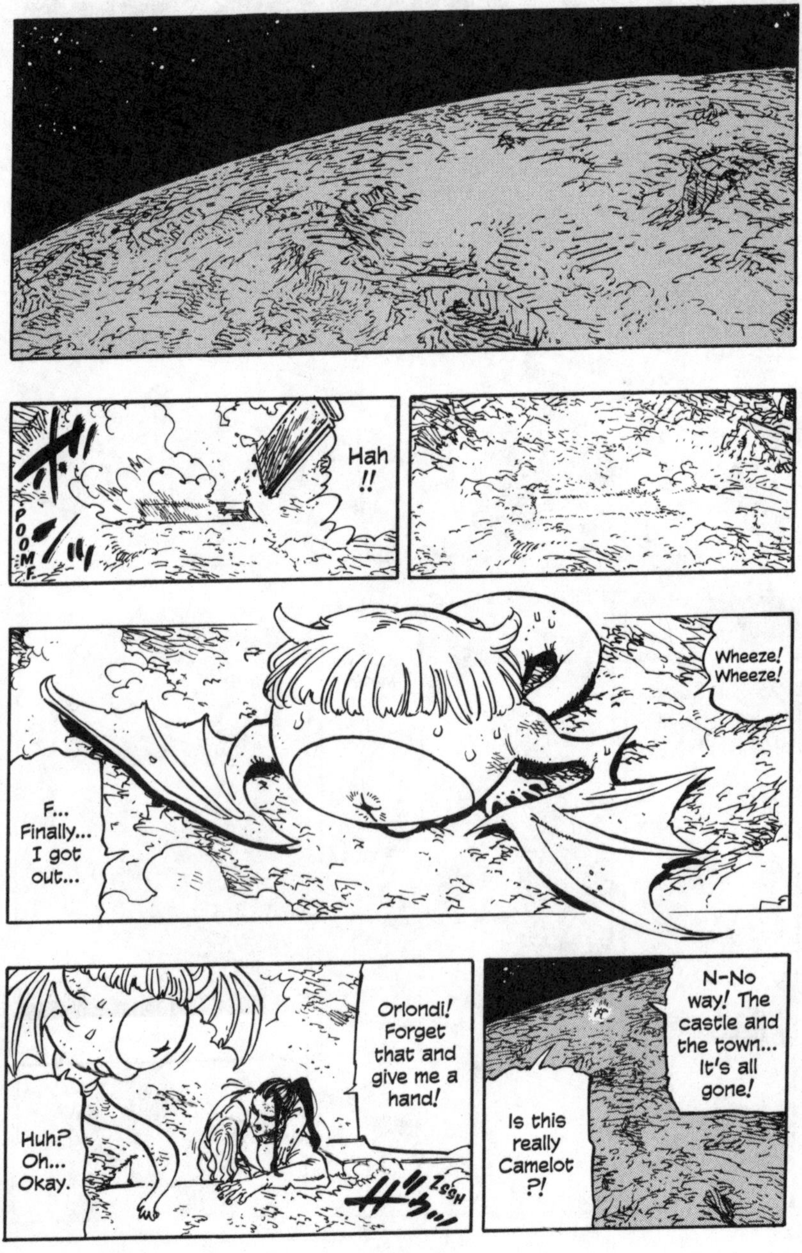
Hah!!
POOMF
Wheeze! Wheeze!
F... Finally... I got out...
N-No way! The castle and the town... It's all gone!
Is this really Camelot?!
Orlondi! Forget that and give me a hand!
HSSZ
Huh? Oh... Okay.

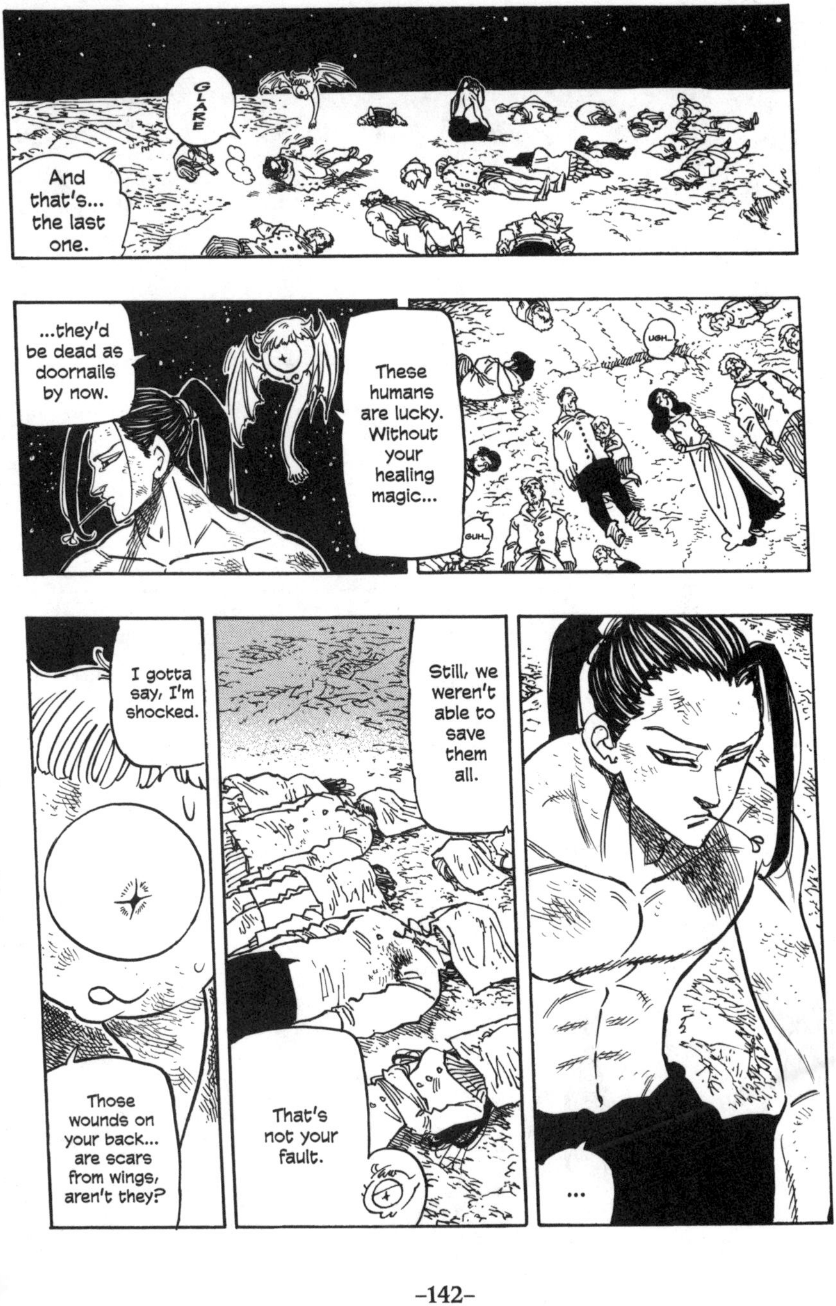
GLARE
And that's... the last one.
UGH...
GUH...
These humans are lucky. Without your healing magic...
...they'd be dead as doornails by now.
...
Still, we weren't able to save them all.
That's not your fault.
I gotta say, I'm shocked.
Those wounds on your back... are scars from wings, aren't they?

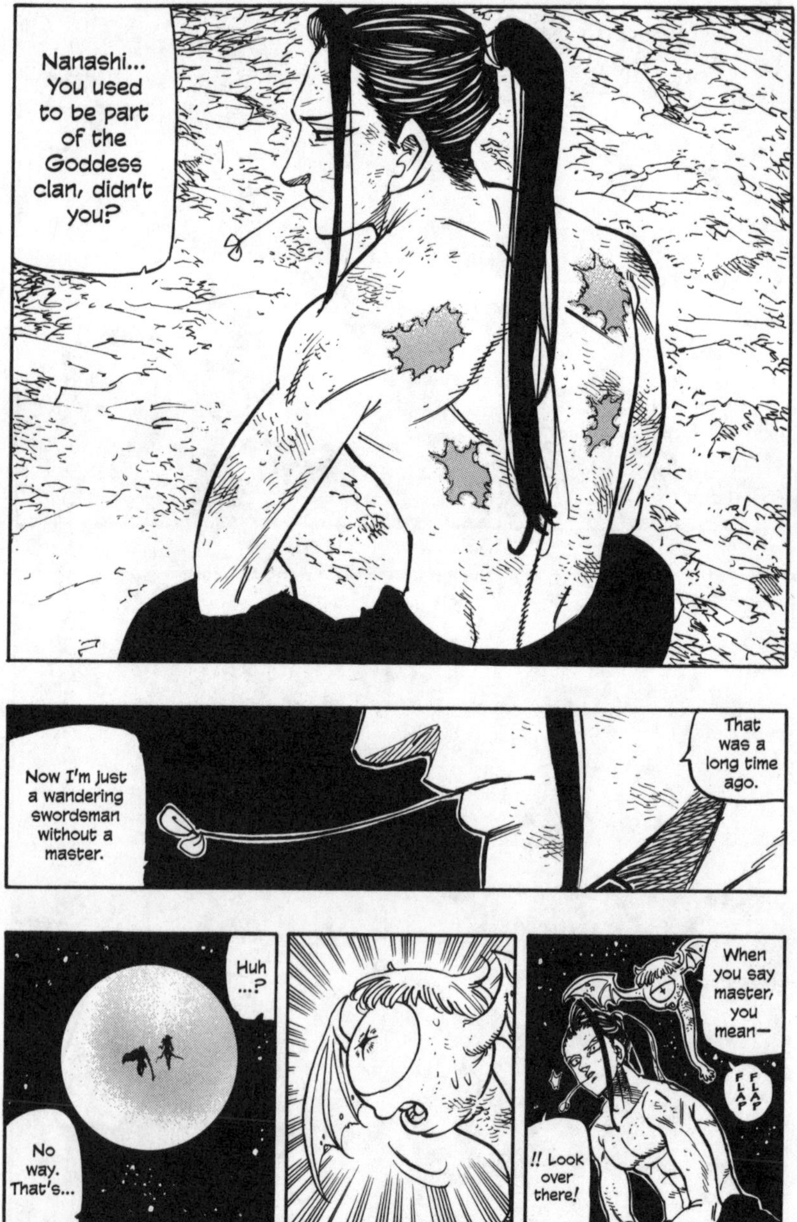
Nanashi... You used to be part of the Goddess clan, didn't you?
That was a long time ago.
Now I'm just a wandering swordsman without a master.
When you say master, you mean—
FLAP FLAP
!! Look over there!
Huh ...?
No way. That's...

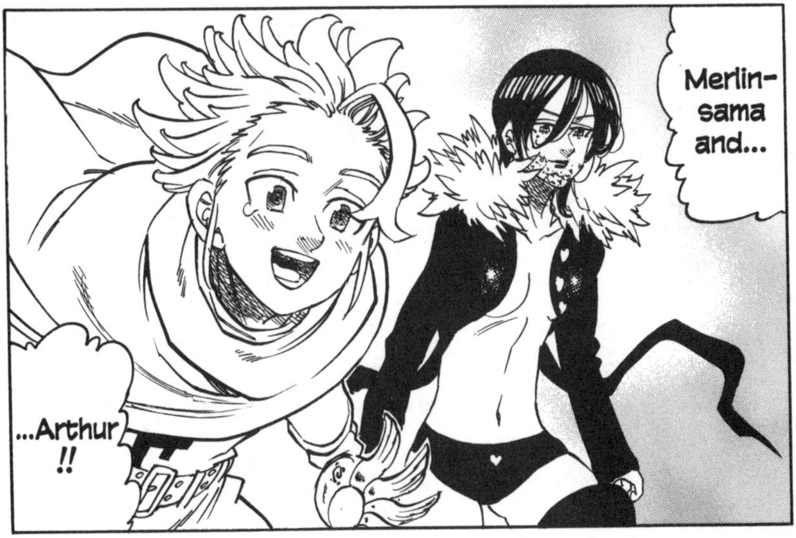
Merlin-sama and...
...Arthur!!
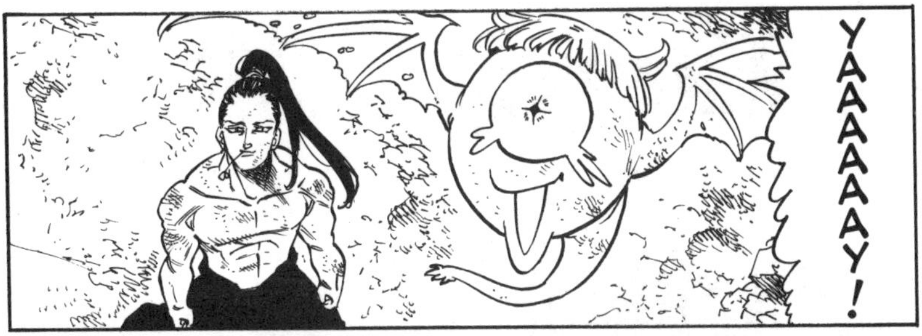
YAAAAAAY!
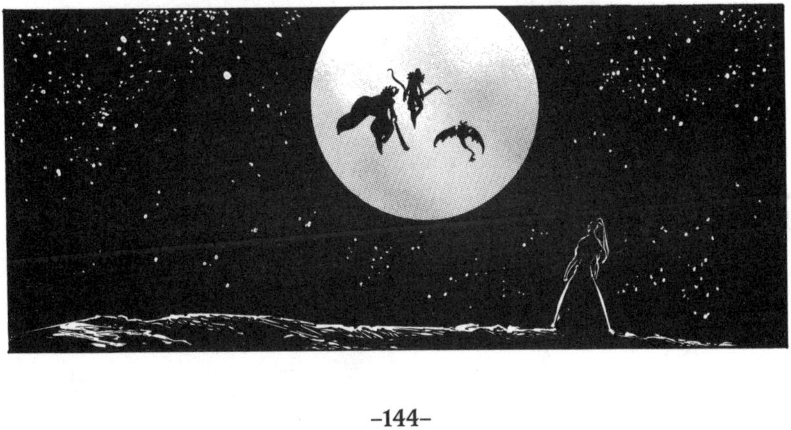

Chapter 345 - Heirs

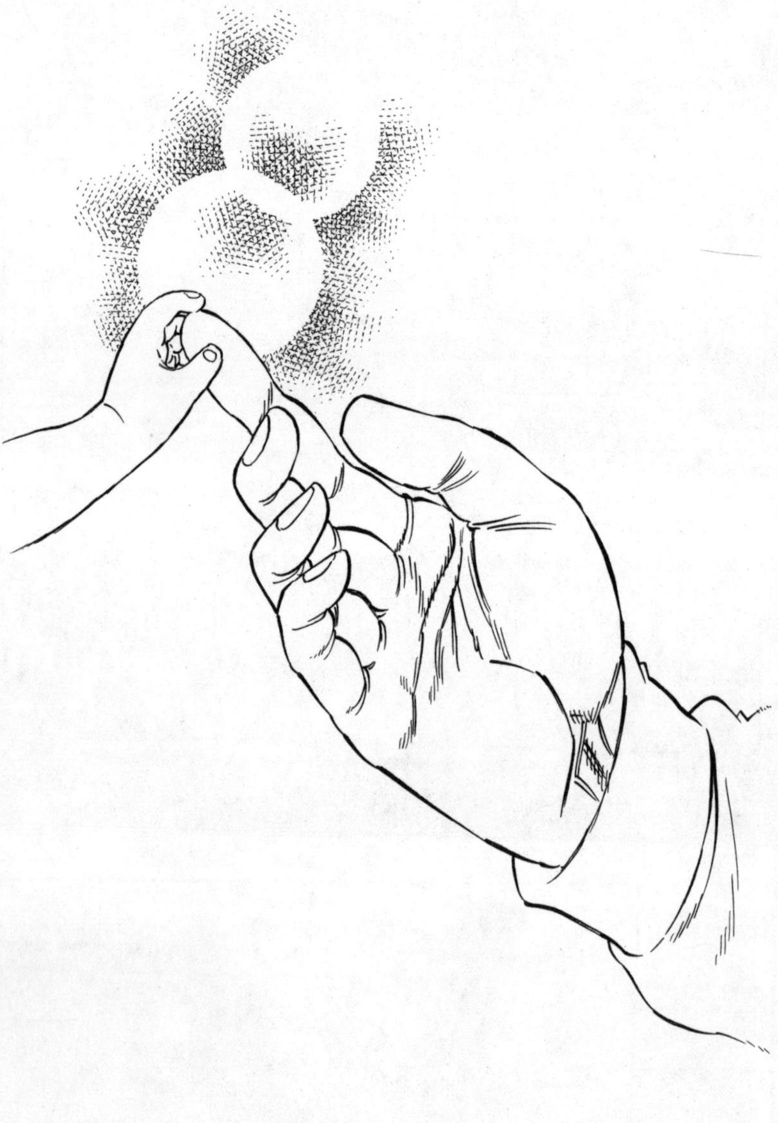

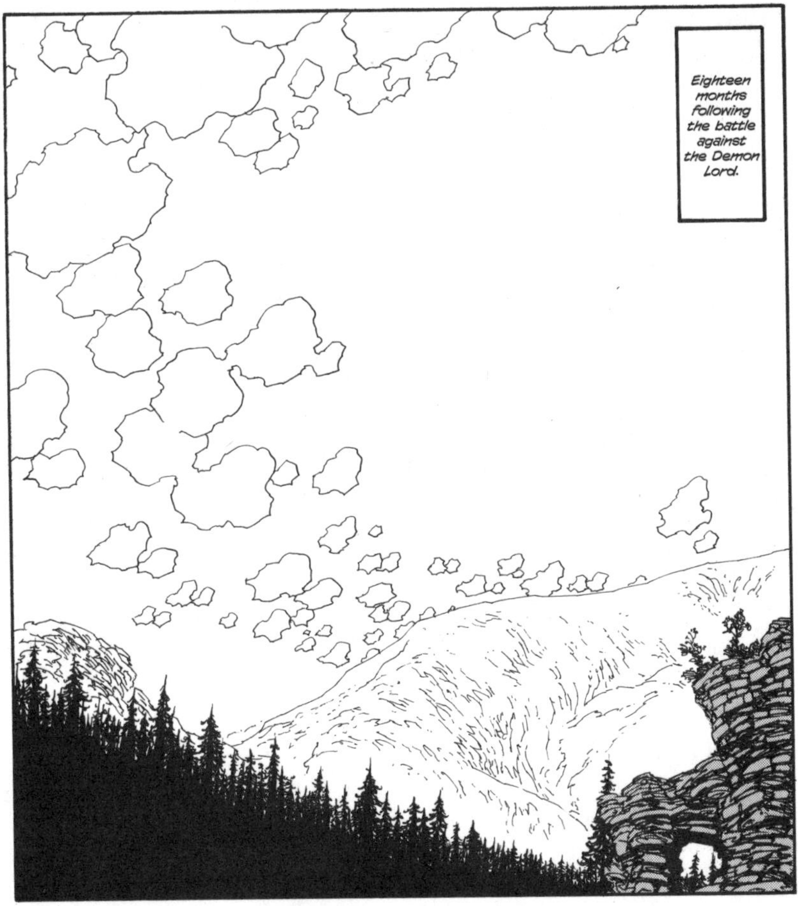
Eighteen months following the battle against the Demon Lord.

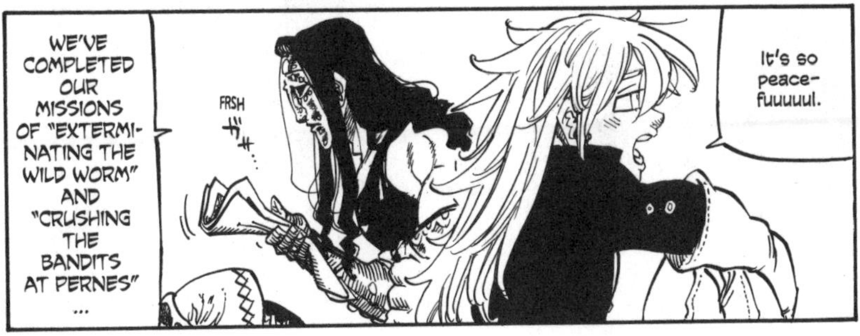
It's so peace-fuuuuul.
FRSH
WE'VE COMPLETED OUR MISSIONS OF "EXTERMINATING THE WILD WORM" AND "CRUSHING THE BANDITS AT PERNES"...

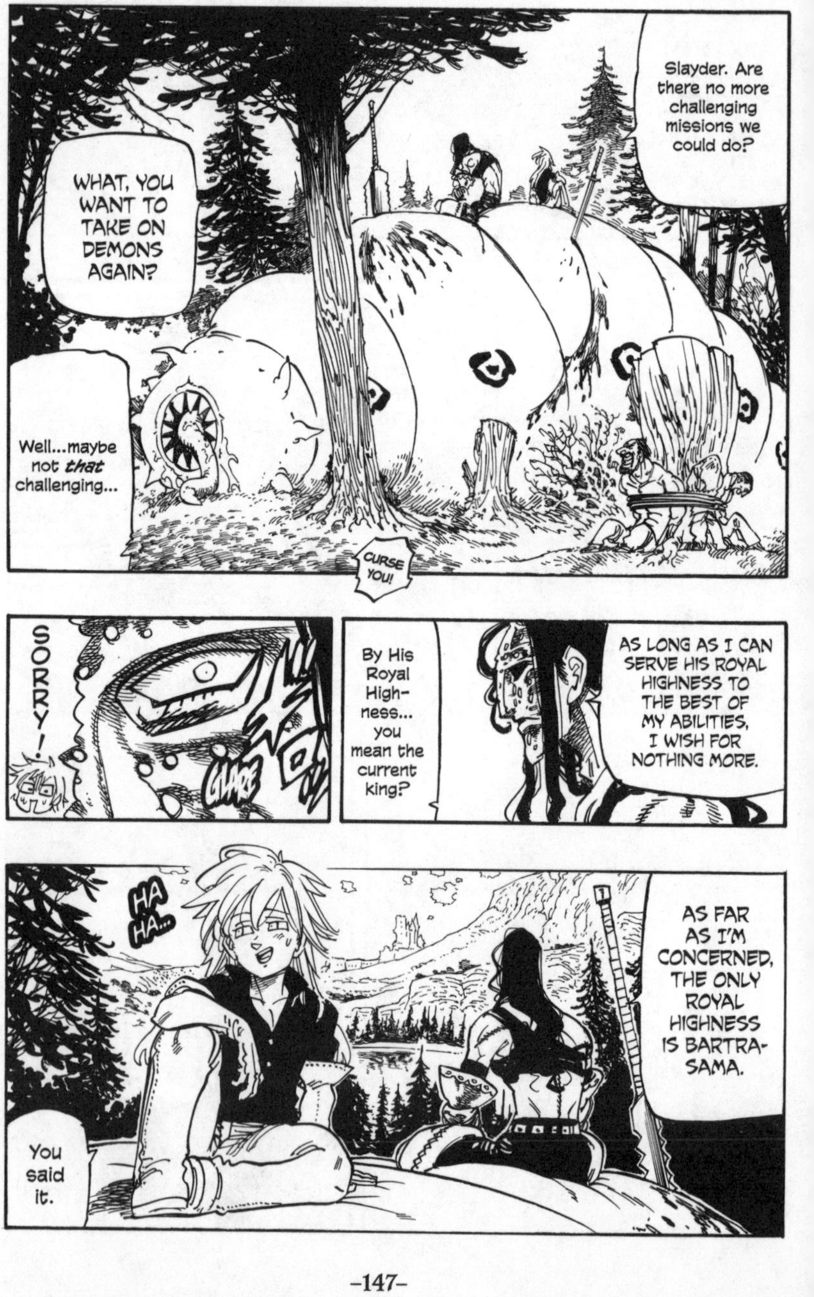
Slayder. Are there no more challenging missions we could do?
WHAT, YOU WANT TO TAKE ON DEMONS AGAIN?
Well...maybe not *that* challenging...
CURSE YOU!
AS LONG AS I CAN SERVE HIS ROYAL HIGHNESS TO THE BEST OF MY ABILITIES, I WISH FOR NOTHING MORE.
By His Royal High-ness... you mean the current king?
GLARE
SORRY!
AS FAR AS I'M CONCERNED, THE ONLY ROYAL HIGHNESS IS BARTRA-SAMA.
HA HA...
You said it.

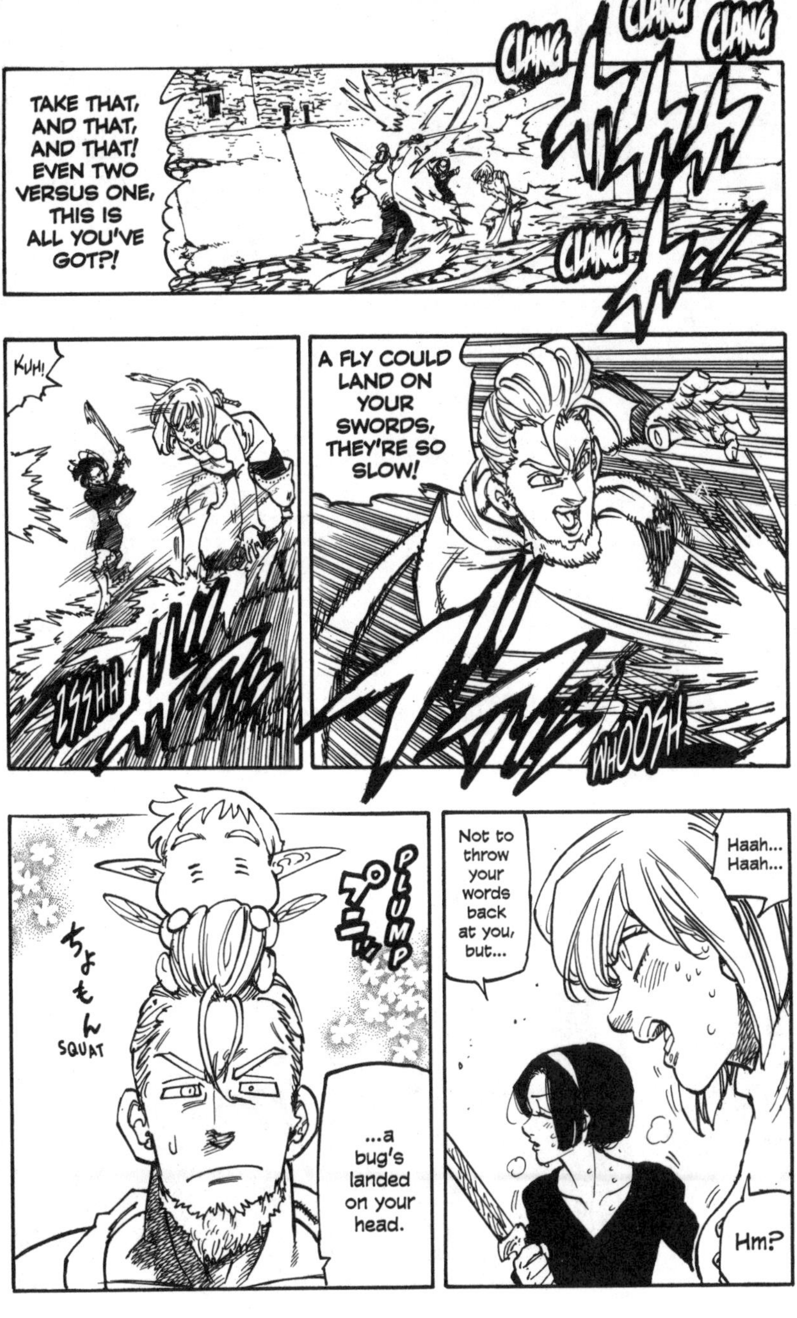
TAKE THAT, AND THAT, AND THAT! EVEN TWO VERSUS ONE, THIS IS ALL YOU'VE GOT?!
CLANG
CLANG
CLANG
CLANG
A FLY COULD LAND ON YOUR SWORDS, THEY'RE SO SLOW!
WHOOSH
KUH!
ZSSHH
Haah... Haah...
Not to throw your words back at you, but...
Hm?
PLUMP
ちょもん
SQUAT
...a bug's landed on your head.

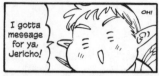

IT'S HUGE!
SWOOSH
SWOOSH
I ain't no bug!
PUORA?!
OH!
I gotta message for ya, Jericho!
?
PSST PSST
BOB BOB BOB
BBB
S... SERI-OUSLY?!
BAN AND ELAINE ARE...?!
Chief Holy Knight! I've got something to take care of at the Fairy King's Forest, so if you'll excuse me!
Wait... Huh? Something to take care of...?
Let's go, Puora!
SEE YA!
DASH
Woot!
What the heck...? She certainly doesn't treat me like a Chief Holy Knight, now does she...?
I think that's what makes you so wonderful.
That's not a compli-ment.

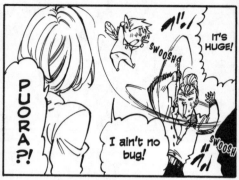

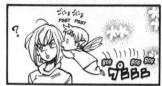

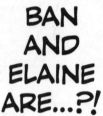

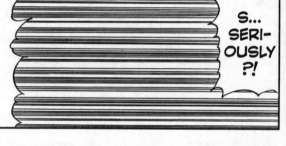

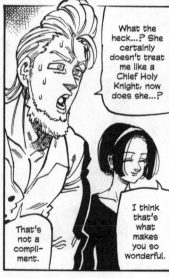

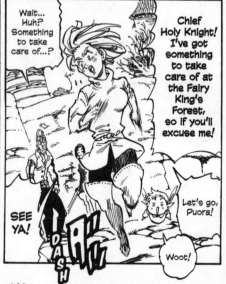

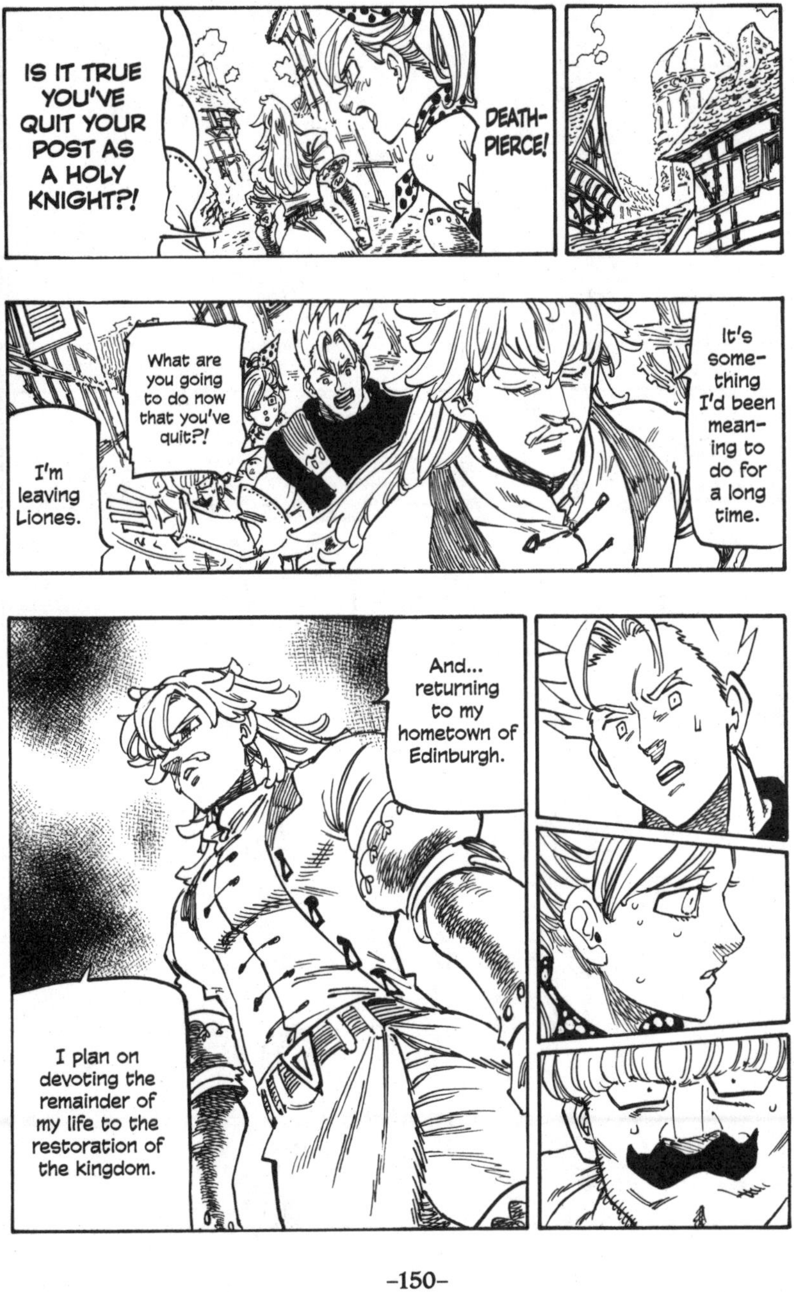
DEATH-PIERCE!
IS IT TRUE YOU'VE QUIT YOUR POST AS A HOLY KNIGHT?!
It's something I'd been meaning to do for a long time.
What are you going to do now that you've quit?!
I'm leaving Liones.
And... returning to my hometown of Edinburgh.
I plan on devoting the remainder of my life to the restoration of the kingdom.

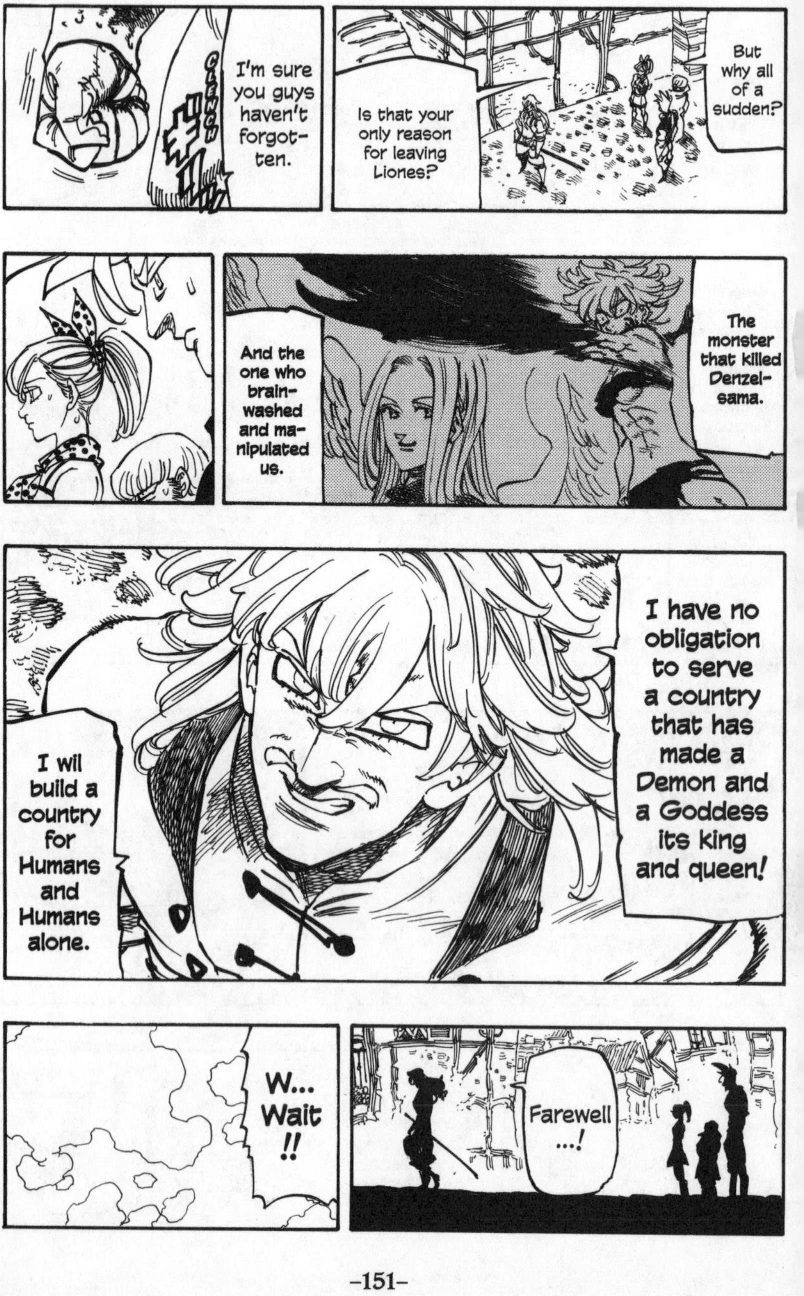
But why all of a sudden?
Is that your only reason for leaving Liones?
I'm sure you guys haven't forgot-ten.
CLENCH
The monster that killed Denzel-sama.
And the one who brain-washed and ma-nipulated us.
I have no obligation to serve a country that has made a Demon and a Goddess its king and queen!
I wil build a country for Humans and Humans alone.
Farewell ...!
W... Wait !!

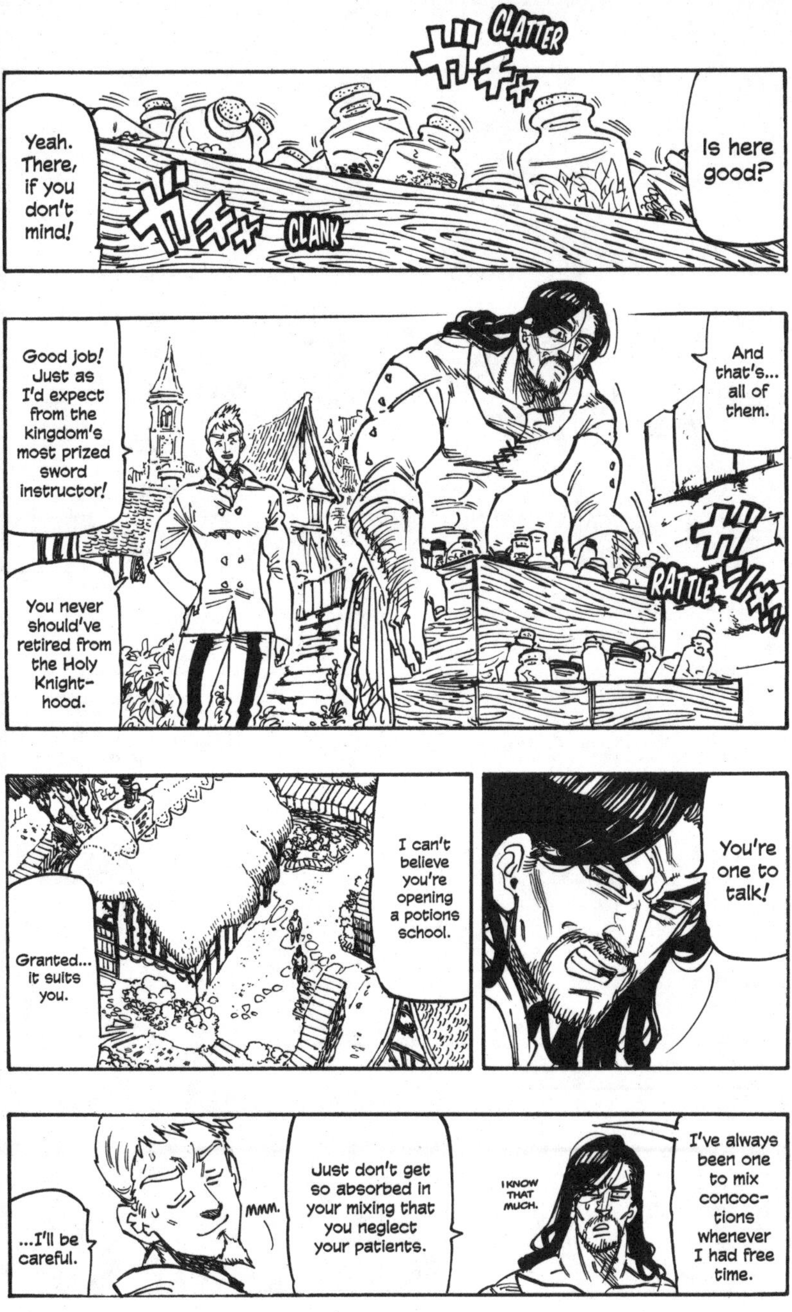
ガチャ
CLATTER
Is here good?
Yeah. There, if you don't mind!
ガチャ
CLANK
And that's... all of them.
RATTLE
Good job! Just as I'd expect from the kingdom's most prized sword instructor!
You never should've retired from the Holy Knight-hood.
You're one to talk!
I can't believe you're opening a potions school.
Granted... it suits you.
I've always been one to mix concoc-tions whenever I had free time.
I KNOW THAT MUCH.
Just don't get so absorbed in your mixing that you neglect your patients.
MMM.
...I'll be careful.

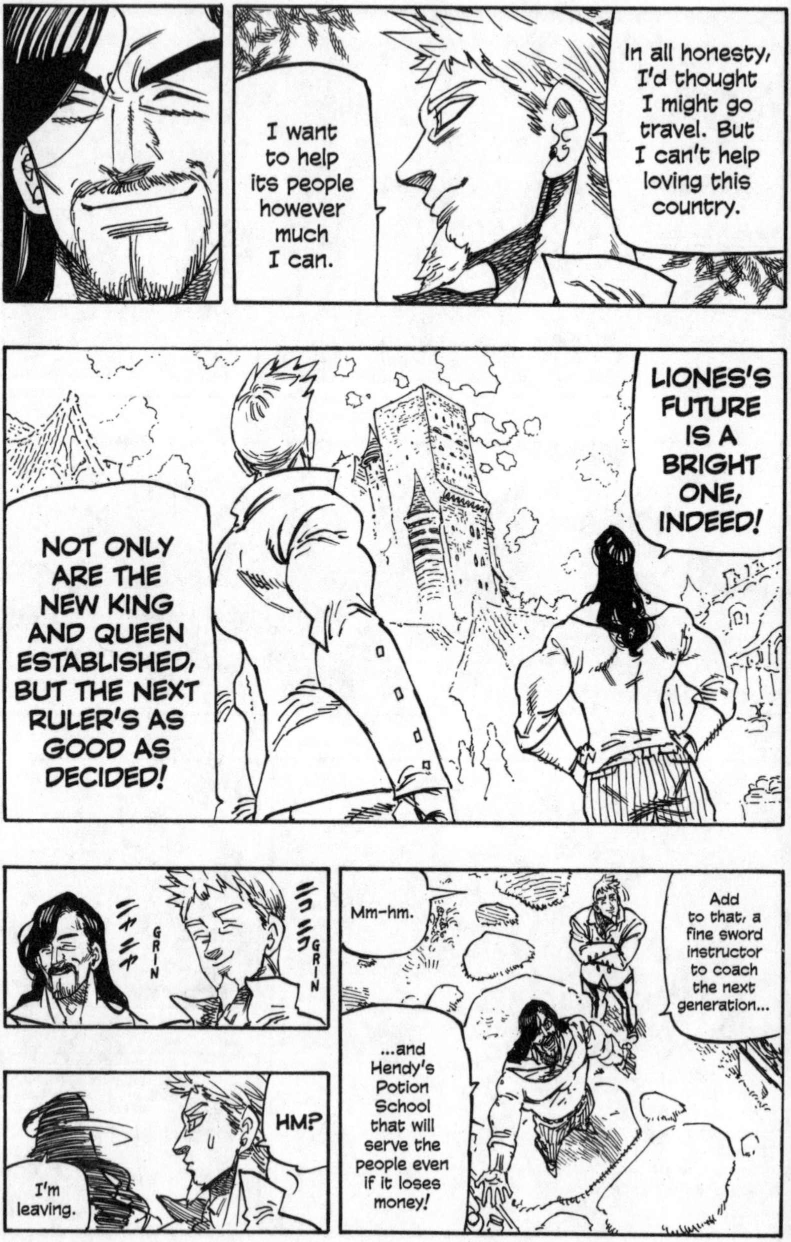
In all honesty, I'd thought I might go travel. But I can't help loving this country.
I want to help its people however much I can.
LIONES'S FUTURE IS A BRIGHT ONE, INDEED!
NOT ONLY ARE THE NEW KING AND QUEEN ESTABLISHED, BUT THE NEXT RULER'S AS GOOD AS DECIDED!
Add to that, a fine sword instructor to coach the next generation...
Mm-hm.
...and Hendy's Potion School that will serve the people even if it loses money!
GRIN
GRIN
HM?
I'm leaving.

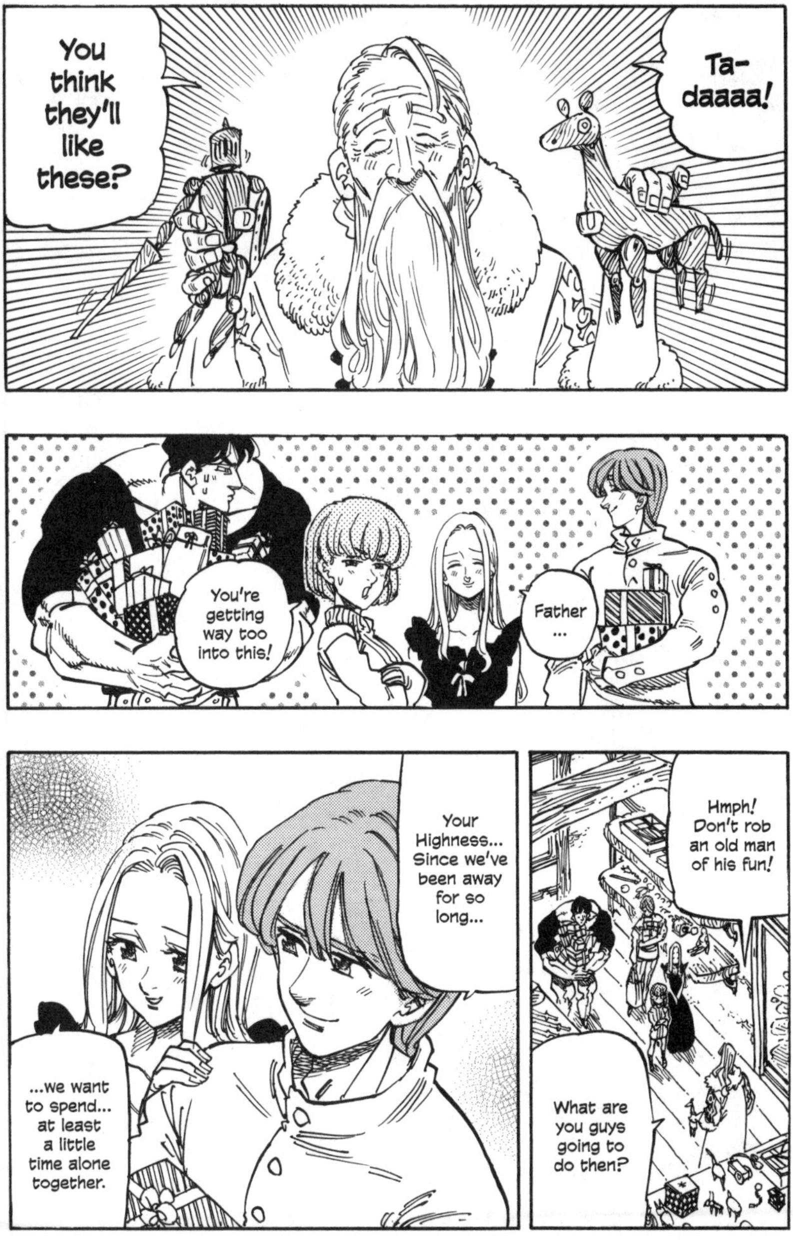

Ta-daaaa!
You think they'll like these?
Father ...
You're getting way too into this!
Hmph! Don't rob an old man of his fun!
What are you guys going to do then?
Your Highness... Since we've been away for so long...
...we want to spend... at least a little time alone together.

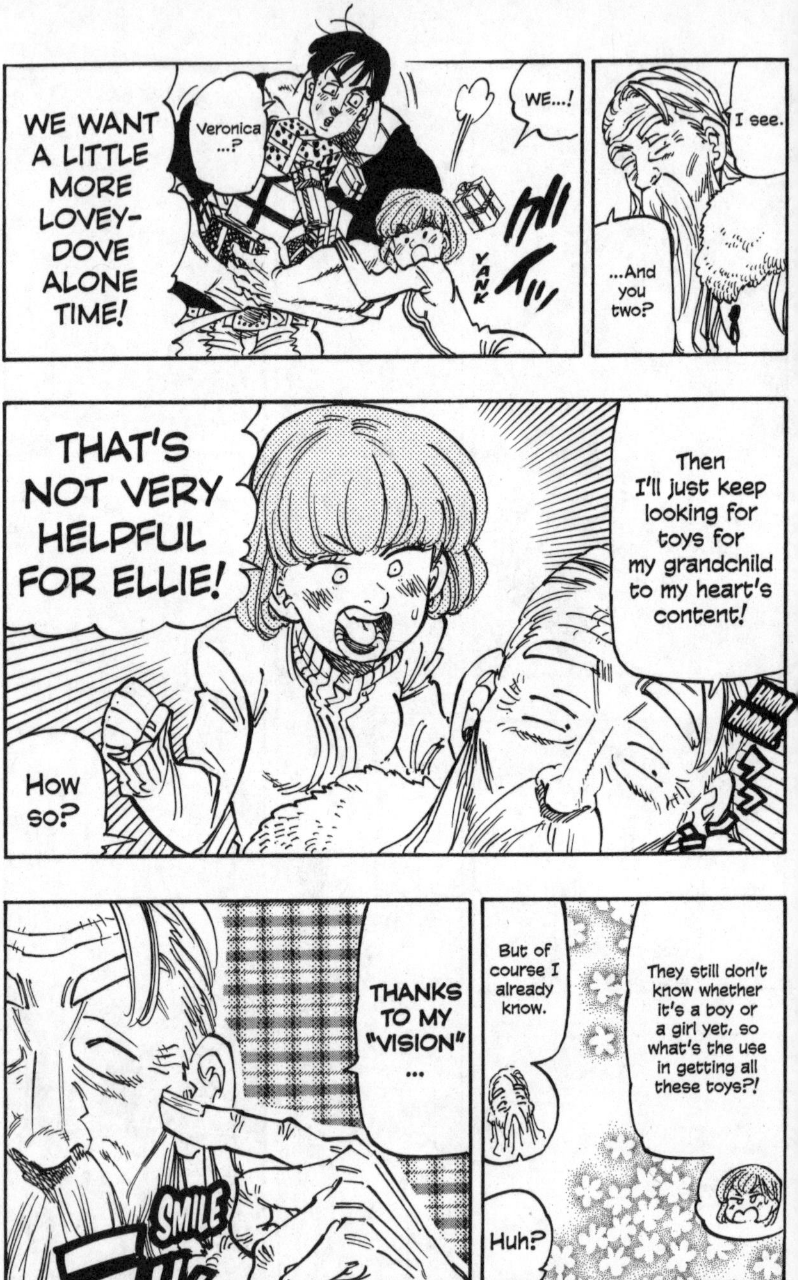
I see.
...And you two?
WE...!
YANK
Veronica ...?
WE WANT A LITTLE MORE LOVEY-DOVE ALONE TIME!
Then I'll just keep looking for toys for my grandchild to my heart's content!
HMM HMM
THAT'S NOT VERY HELPFUL FOR ELLIE!
How so?
They still don't know whether it's a boy or a girl yet, so what's the use in getting all these toys?!
But of course I already know.
Huh?
THANKS TO MY "VISION" ...
SMILE

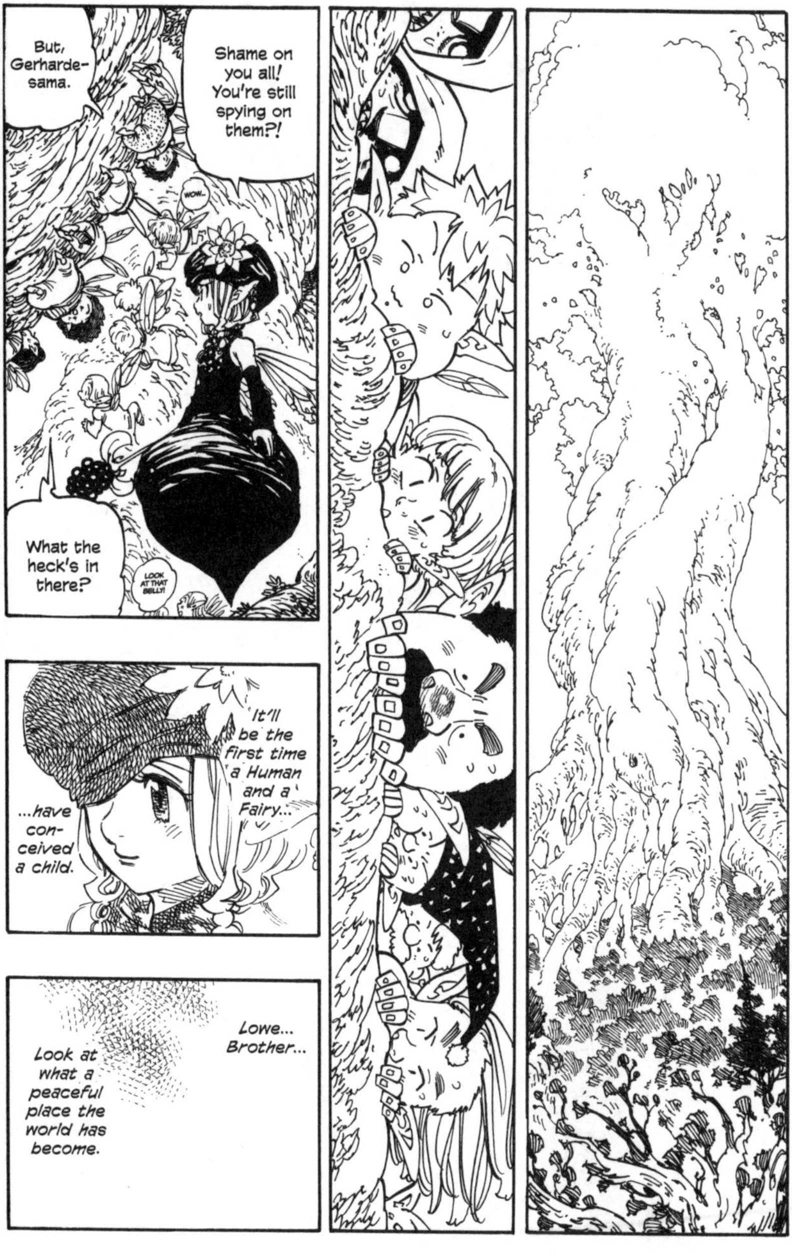
Shame on you all! You're still spying on them?!
But, Gerharde-sama.
WOW...
LOOK AT THAT BELLY!
What the heck's in there?
It'll be the first time a Human and a Fairy...
...have conceived a child.
Lowe... Brother...
Look at what a peaceful place the world has become.

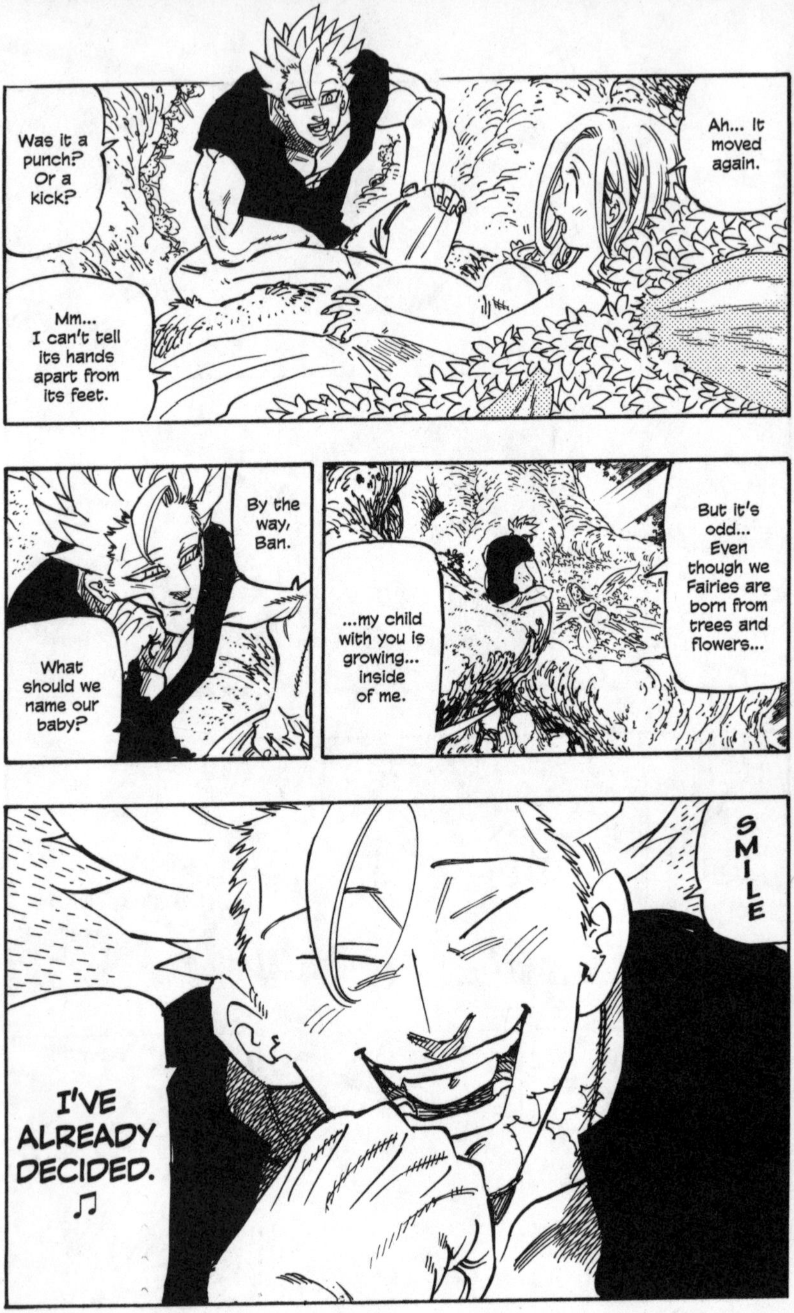
Ah... It moved again.
Was it a punch? Or a kick?
Mm... I can't tell its hands apart from its feet.
But it's odd... Even though we Fairies are born from trees and flowers...
...my child with you is growing... inside of me.
By the way, Ban.
What should we name our baby?
SMILE
I'VE ALREADY DECIDED. ♫

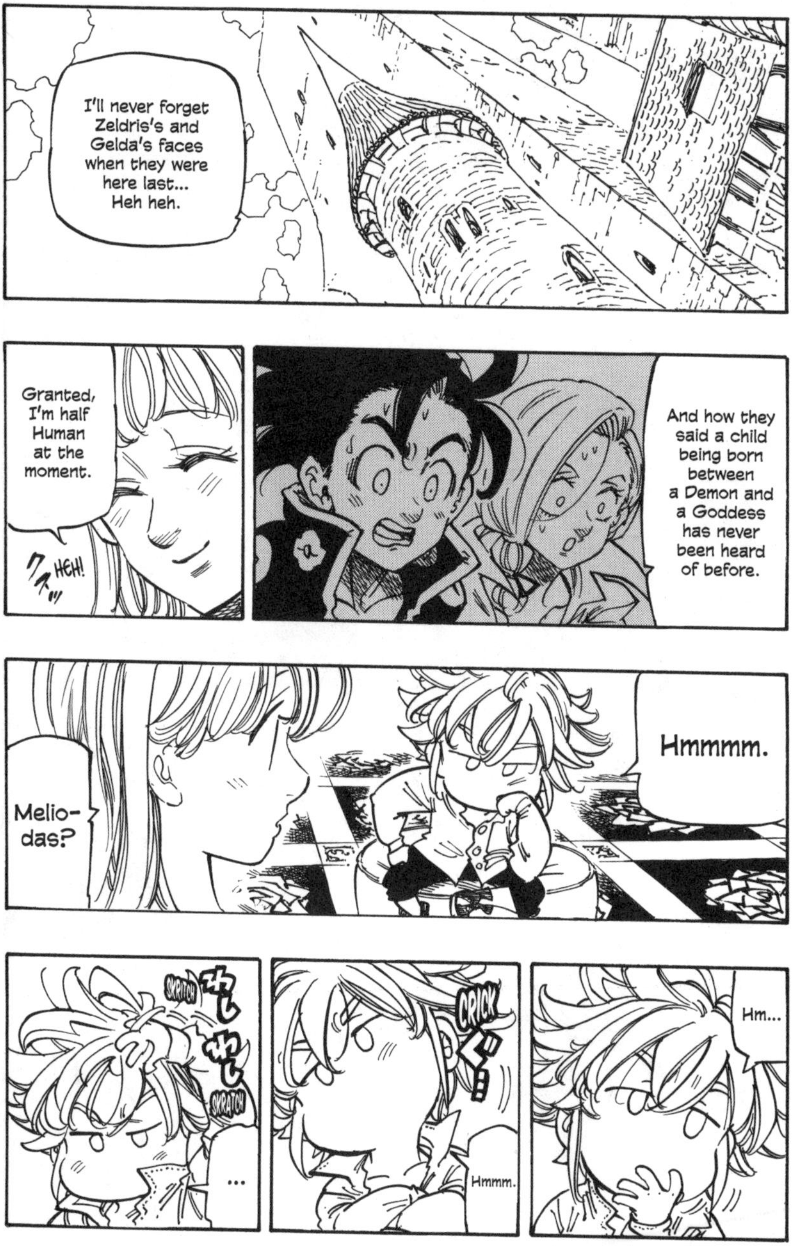
I'll never forget Zeldris's and Gelda's faces when they were here last... Heh heh.
And how they said a child being born between a Demon and a Goddess has never been heard of before.
Granted, I'm half Human at the moment.
HEH!
Hmmmm.
Melio- das?
Hm...
CRICK
Hmmm.
SKRITCH
SKRATCH
...

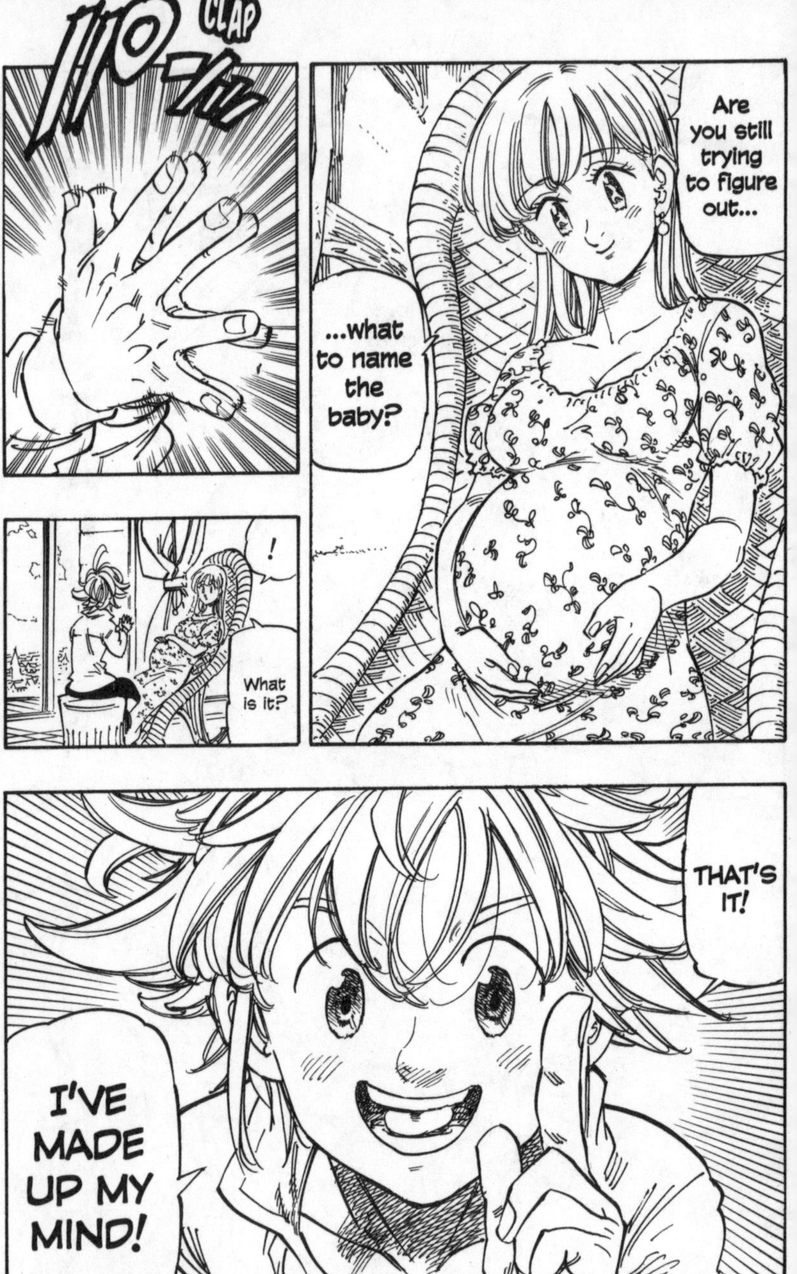
Are you still trying to figure out...
...what to name the baby?
CLAP
!
What is it?
THAT'S IT!
I'VE MADE UP MY MIND!

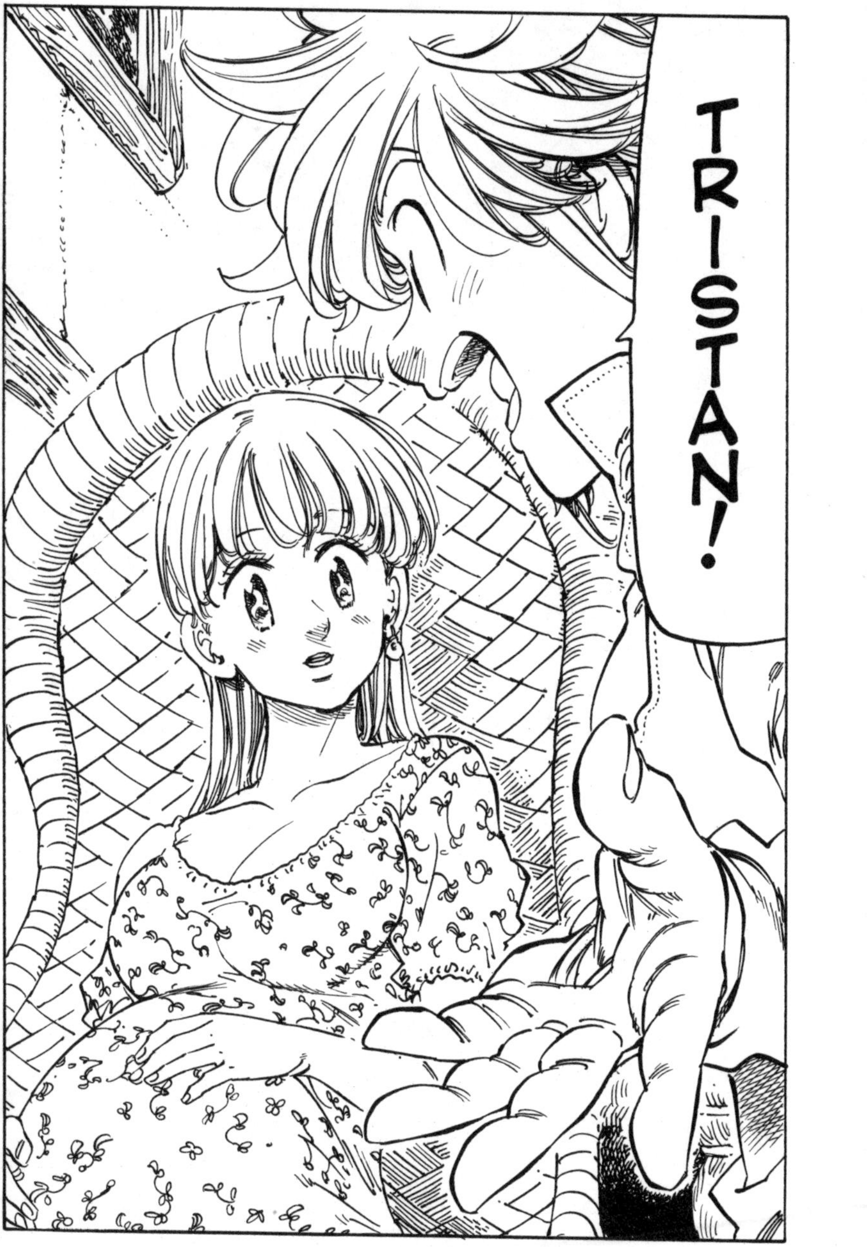
TRISTAN!

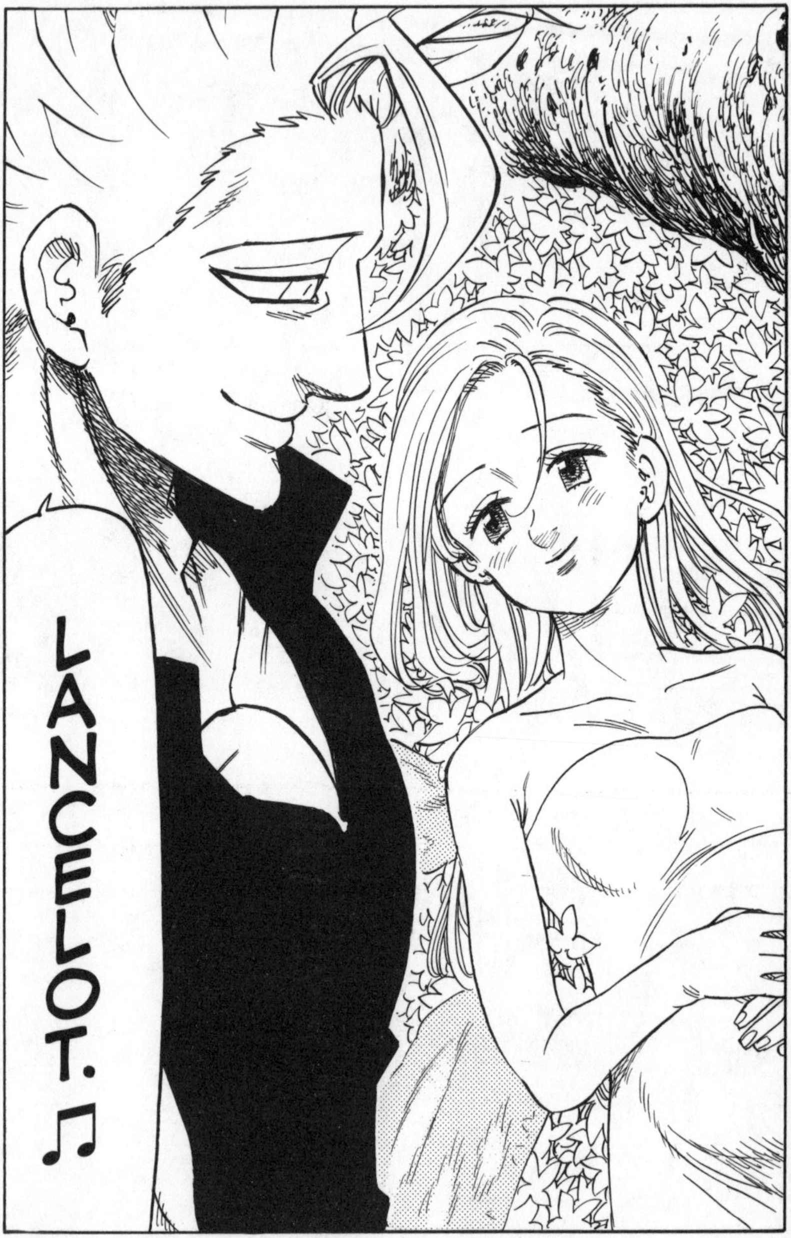
LANCELOT. ♫

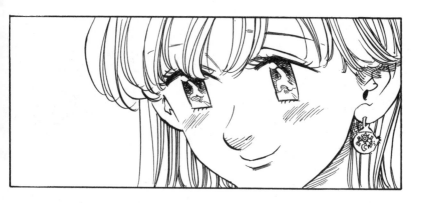

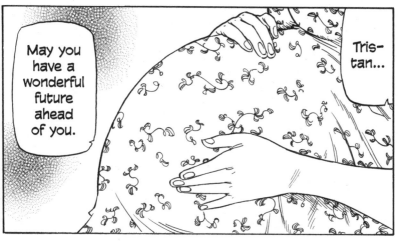

May you
have a
wonderful
future
ahead
of you.

Tris-
tan...

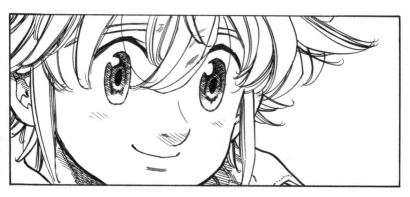

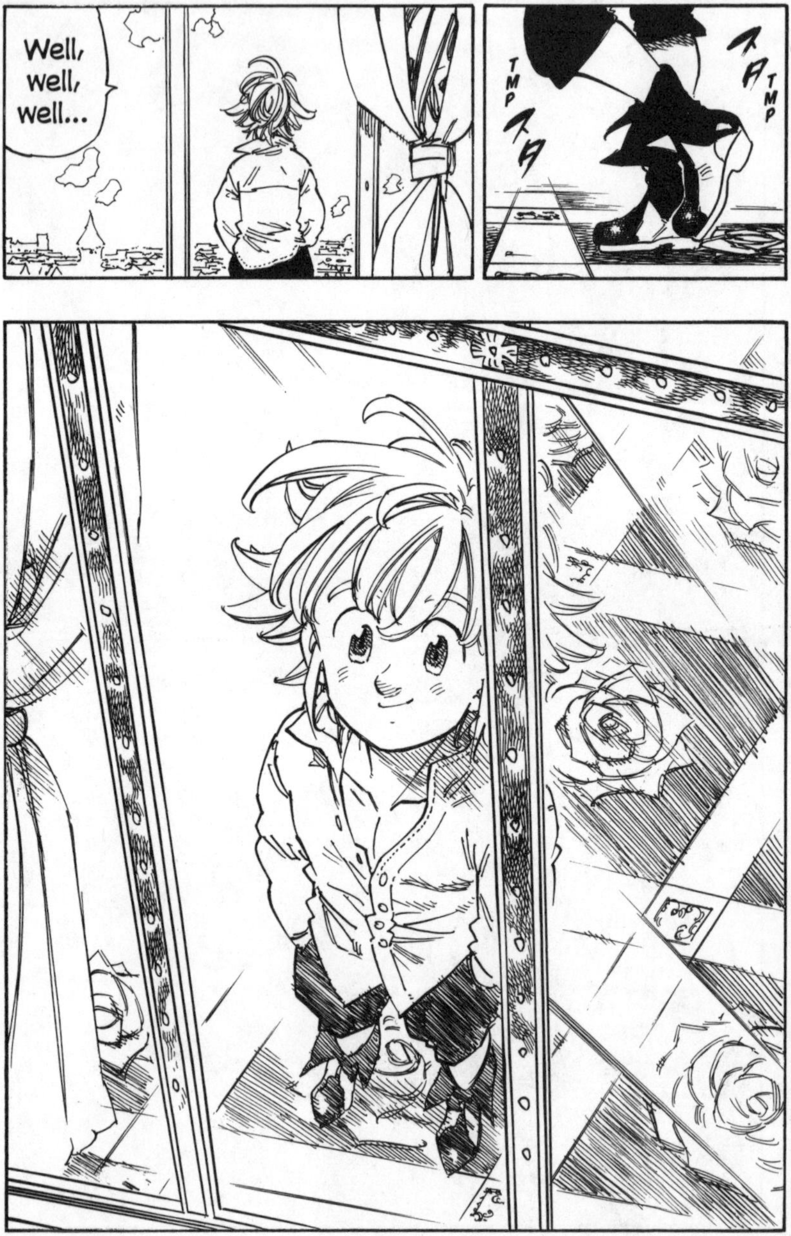
スタ TMP
TMP スタ
Well, well, well...

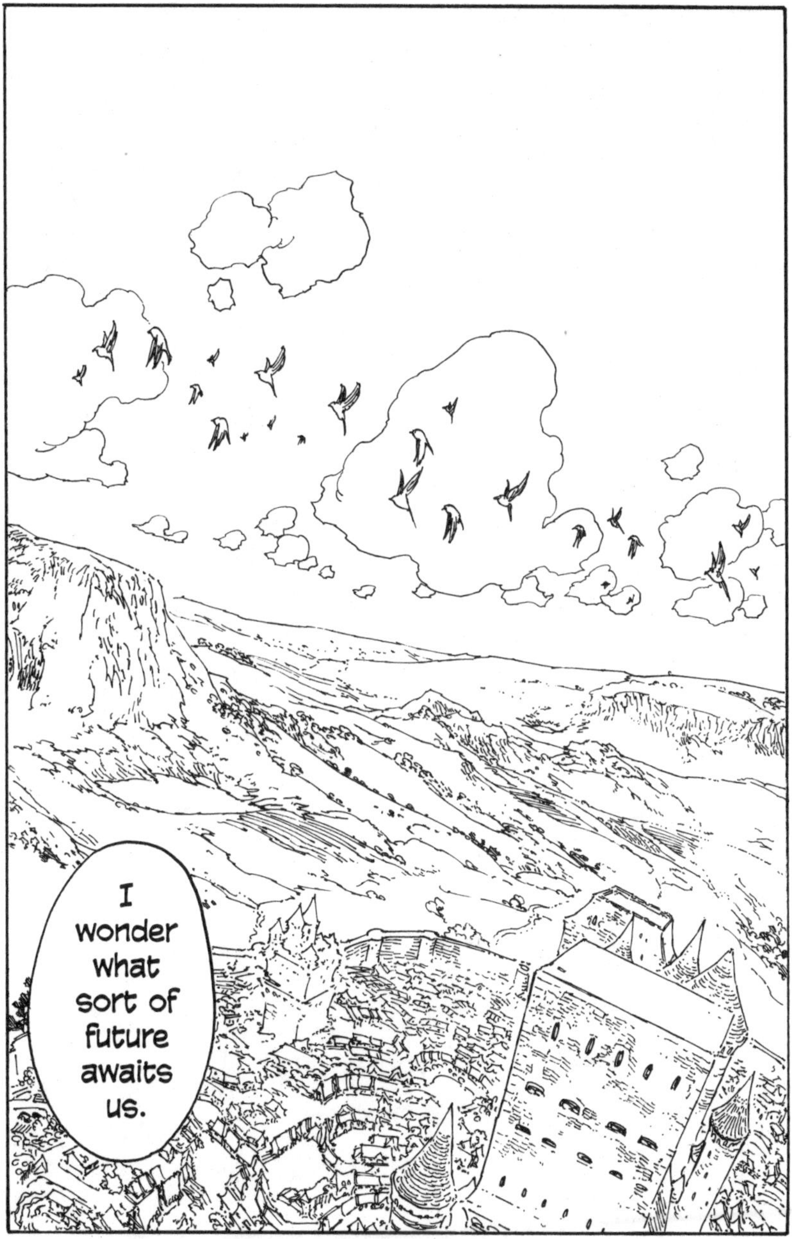
I wonder what sort of future awaits us.

THE SEVEN DEADLY SINS

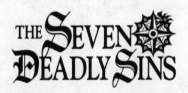

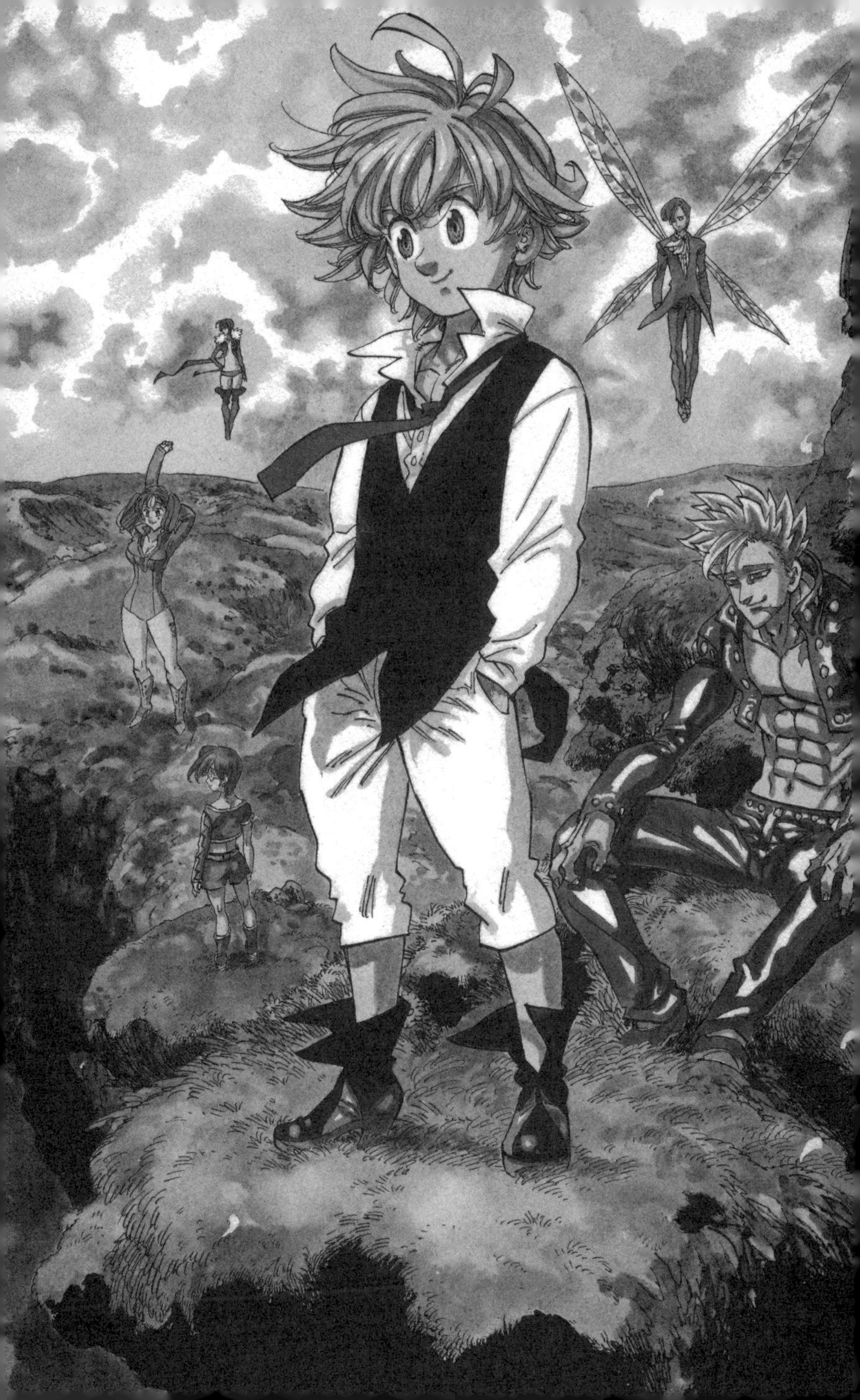

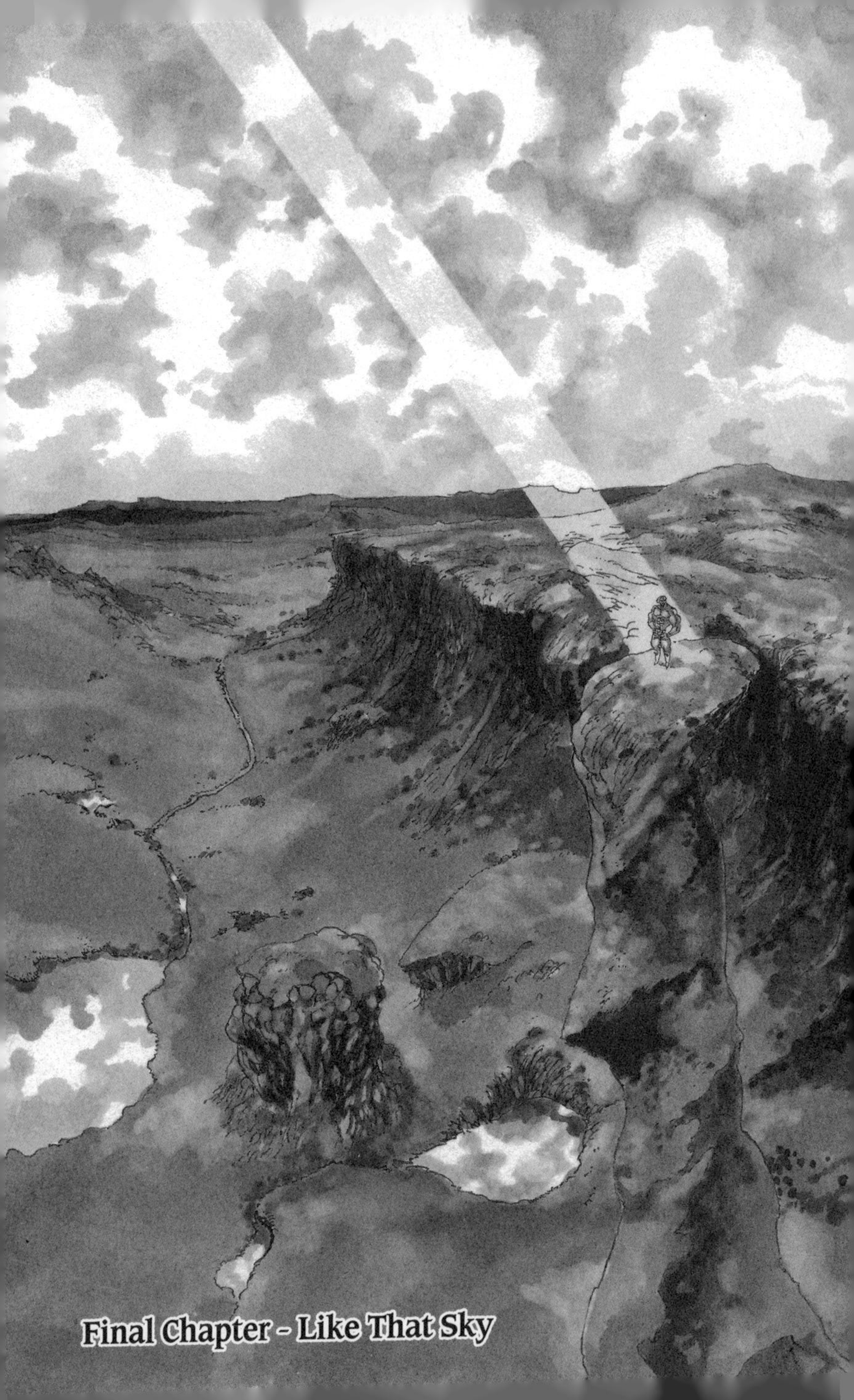

Final Chapter - Like That Sky

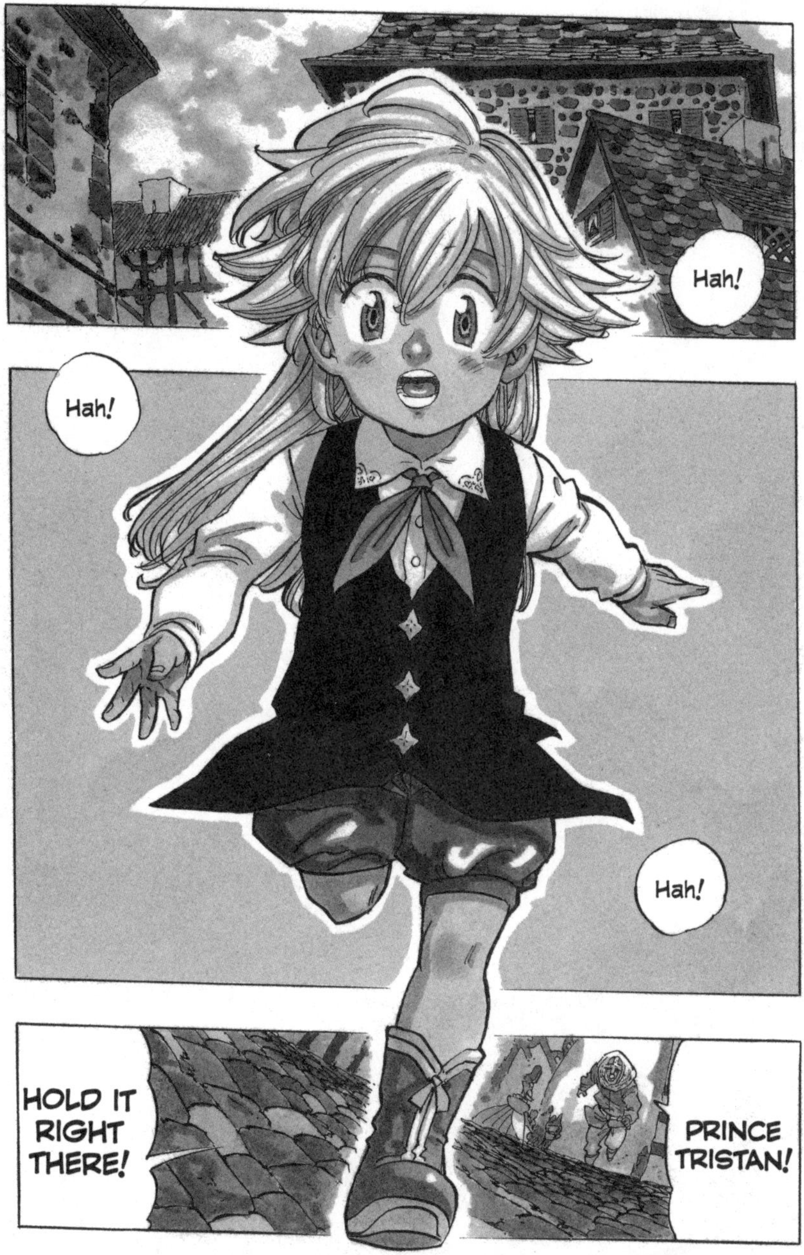

Hah!
Hah!
Hah!
PRINCE TRISTAN!
HOLD IT RIGHT THERE!

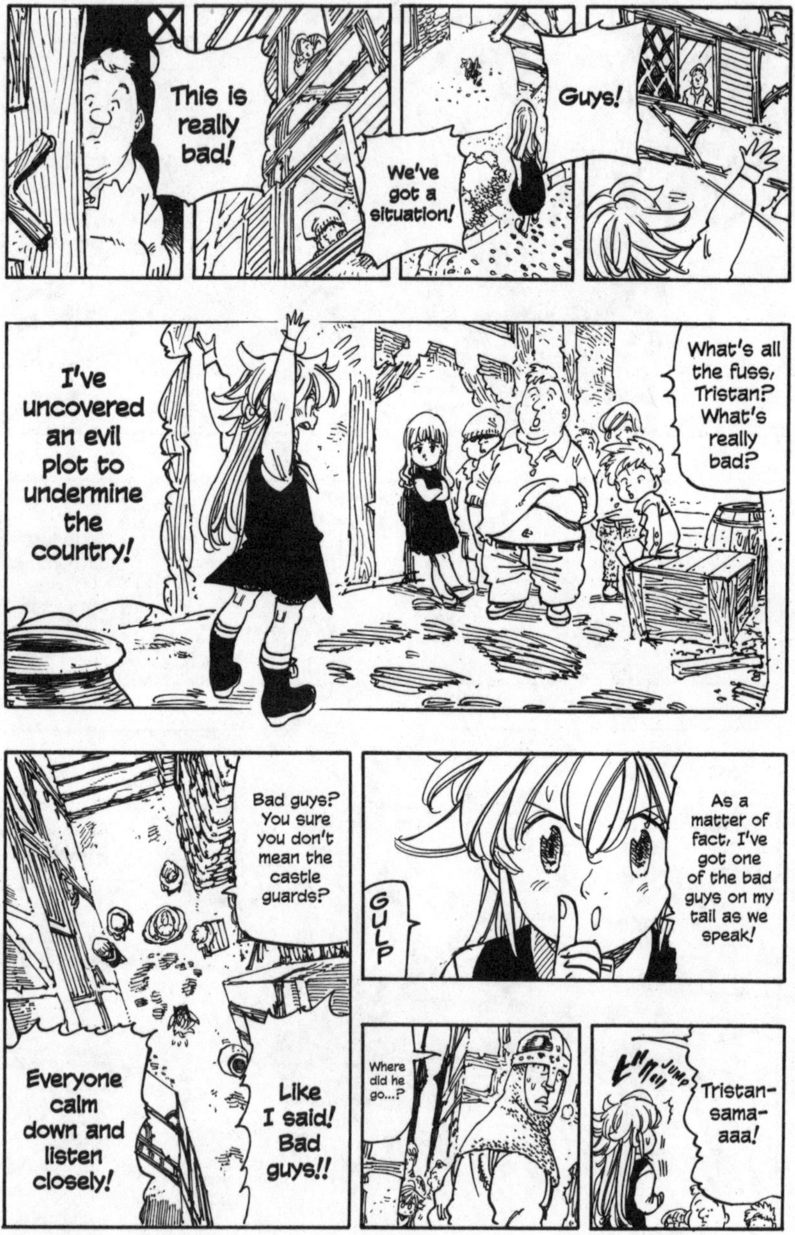
Guys!
We've got a situation!
This is really bad!
What's all the fuss, Tristan? What's really bad?
I've uncovered an evil plot to undermine the country!
As a matter of fact, I've got one of the bad guys on my tail as we speak!
GULP
Tristan-sama-aaa!
JUMP
Where did he go...?
Bad guys? You sure you don't mean the castle guards?
Like I said! Bad guys!!
Everyone calm down and listen closely!

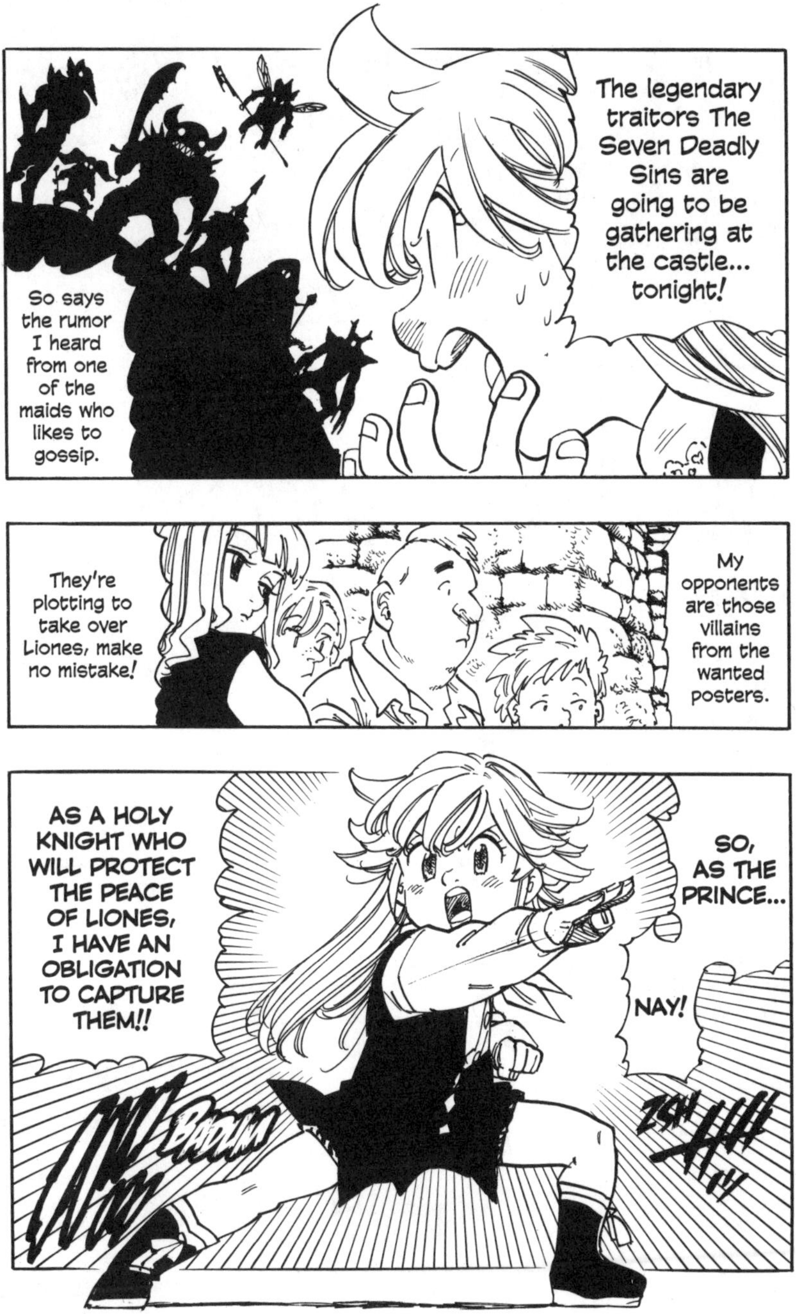
The legendary traitors The Seven Deadly Sins are going to be gathering at the castle... tonight!
So says the rumor I heard from one of the maids who likes to gossip.
My opponents are those villains from the wanted posters.
They're plotting to take over Liones, make no mistake!
SO, AS THE PRINCE...
NAY!
AS A HOLY KNIGHT WHO WILL PROTECT THE PEACE OF LIONES, I HAVE AN OBLIGATION TO CAPTURE THEM!!
ZSH
BADUM

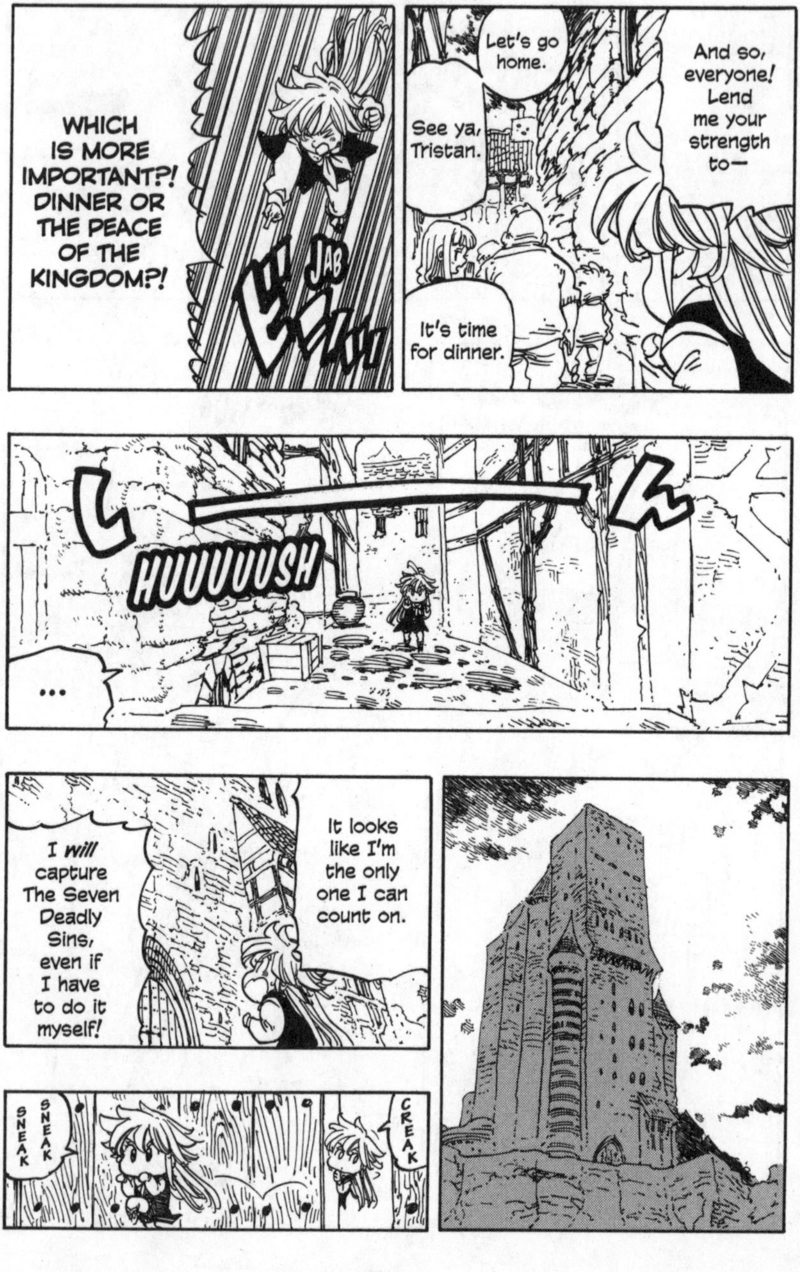
And so, everyone! Lend me your strength to—
Let's go home.
See ya, Tristan.
It's time for dinner.
WHICH IS MORE IMPORTANT?! DINNER OR THE PEACE OF THE KINGDOM?!
JAB
HUUUUUUSH
...
It looks like I'm the only one I can count on.
I *will* capture The Seven Deadly Sins, even if I have to do it myself!
CREAK
SNEAK
SNEAK

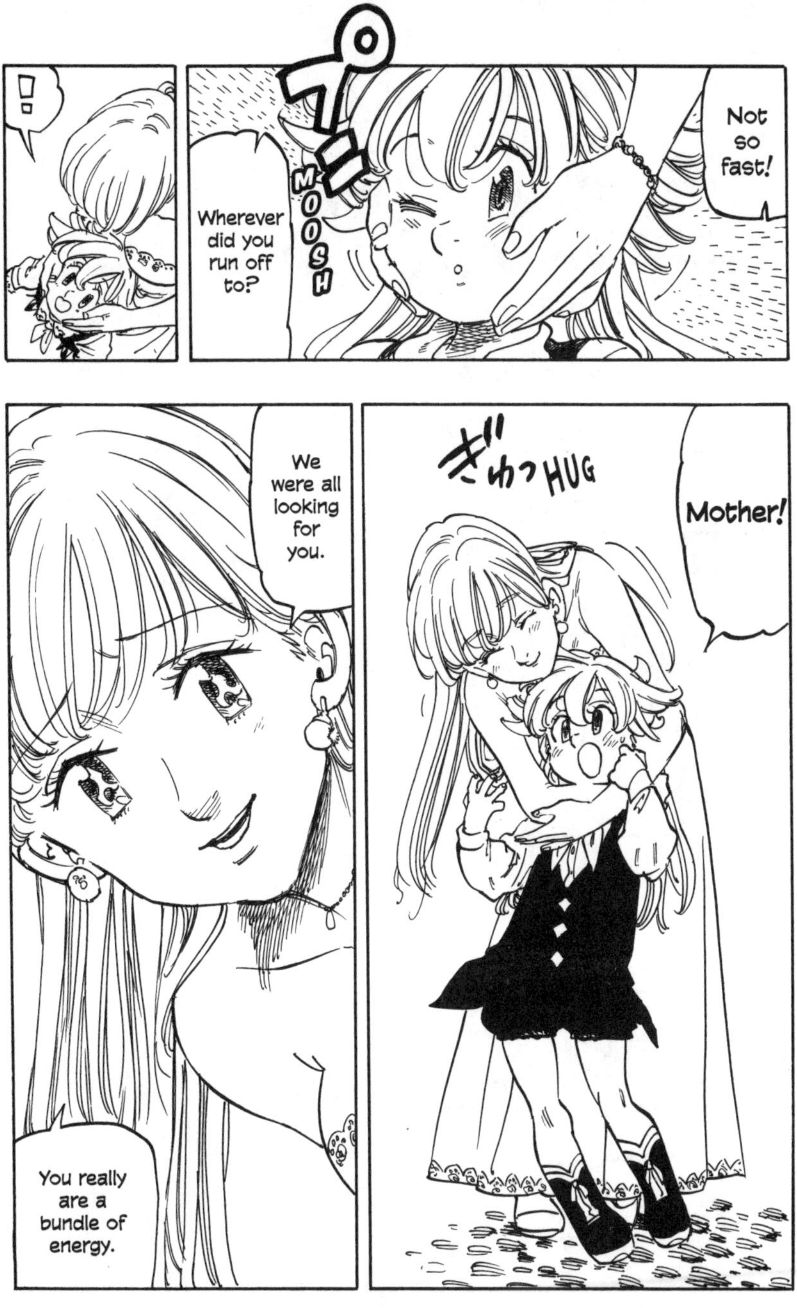
Not so fast!
MOOSH
Wherever did you run off to?
!?
ぎゅっ HUG
Mother!
We were all looking for you.
You really are a bundle of energy.

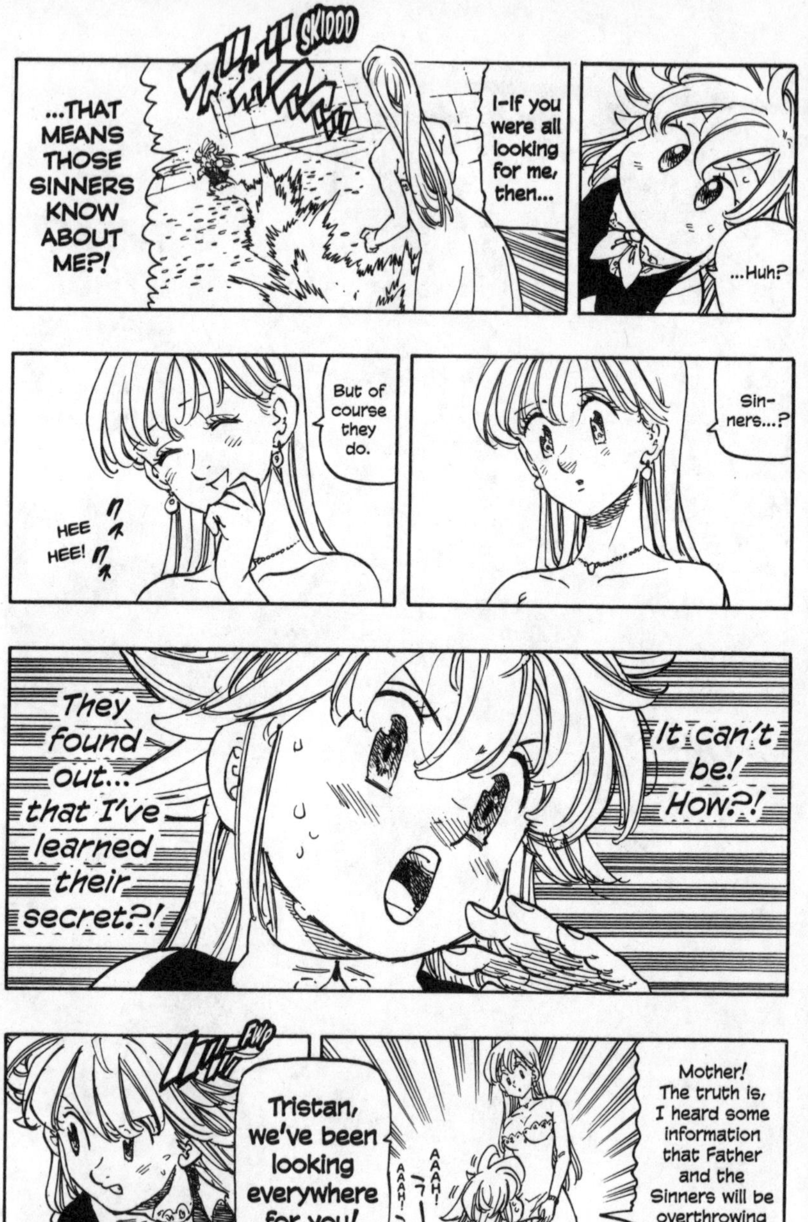
...Huh?
I-If you were all looking for me, then...
SKIDOOO
...THAT MEANS THOSE SINNERS KNOW ABOUT ME?!
Sin-ners...?
But of course they do.
HEE HEE!
It can't be! How?!
They found out... that I've learned their secret?!
Mother! The truth is, I heard some information that Father and the Sinners will be overthrowing the kingdom tonight!
AAAH!
AAAH!
Tristan, we've been looking everywhere for you!
FWP

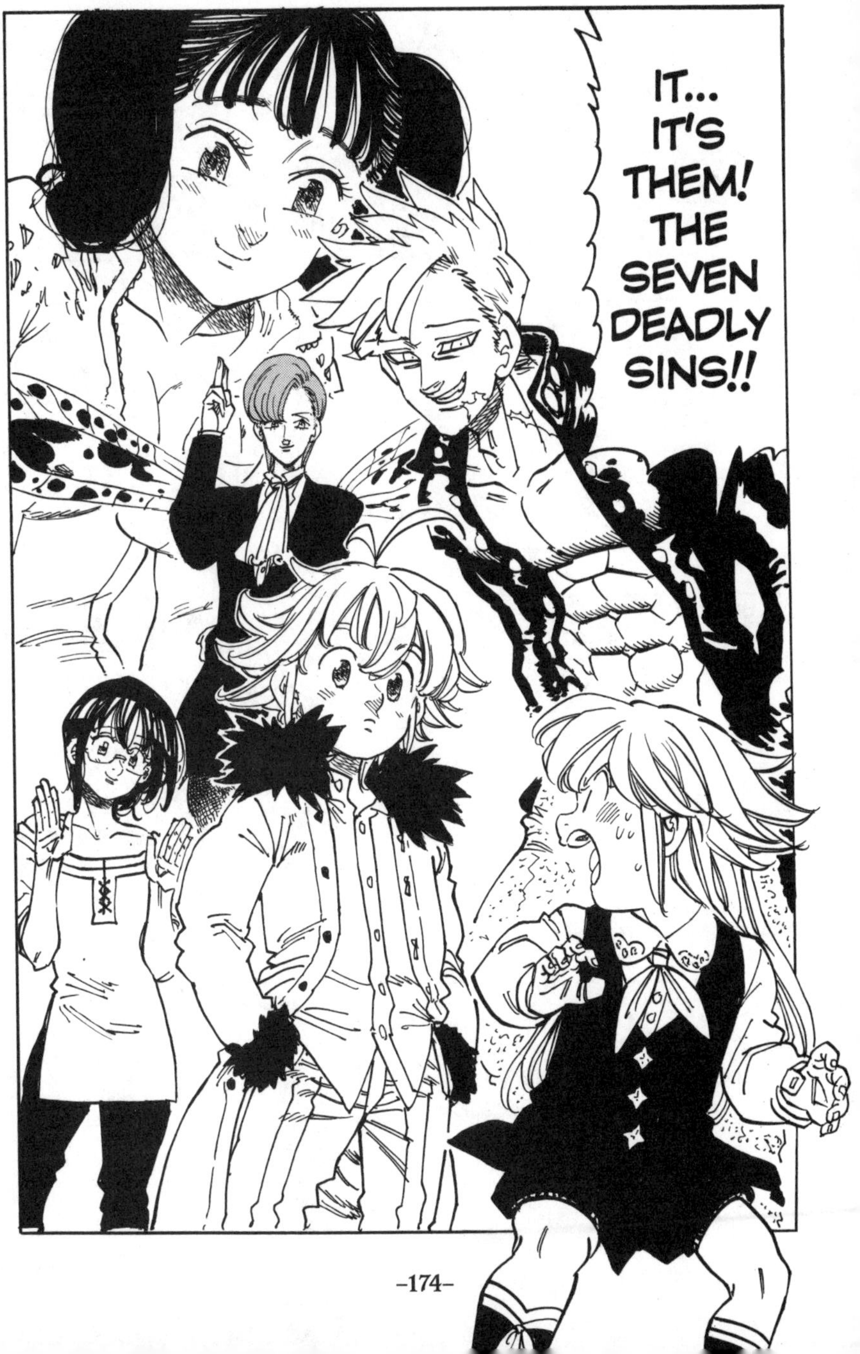
IT... IT'S THEM! THE SEVEN DEADLY SINS!!

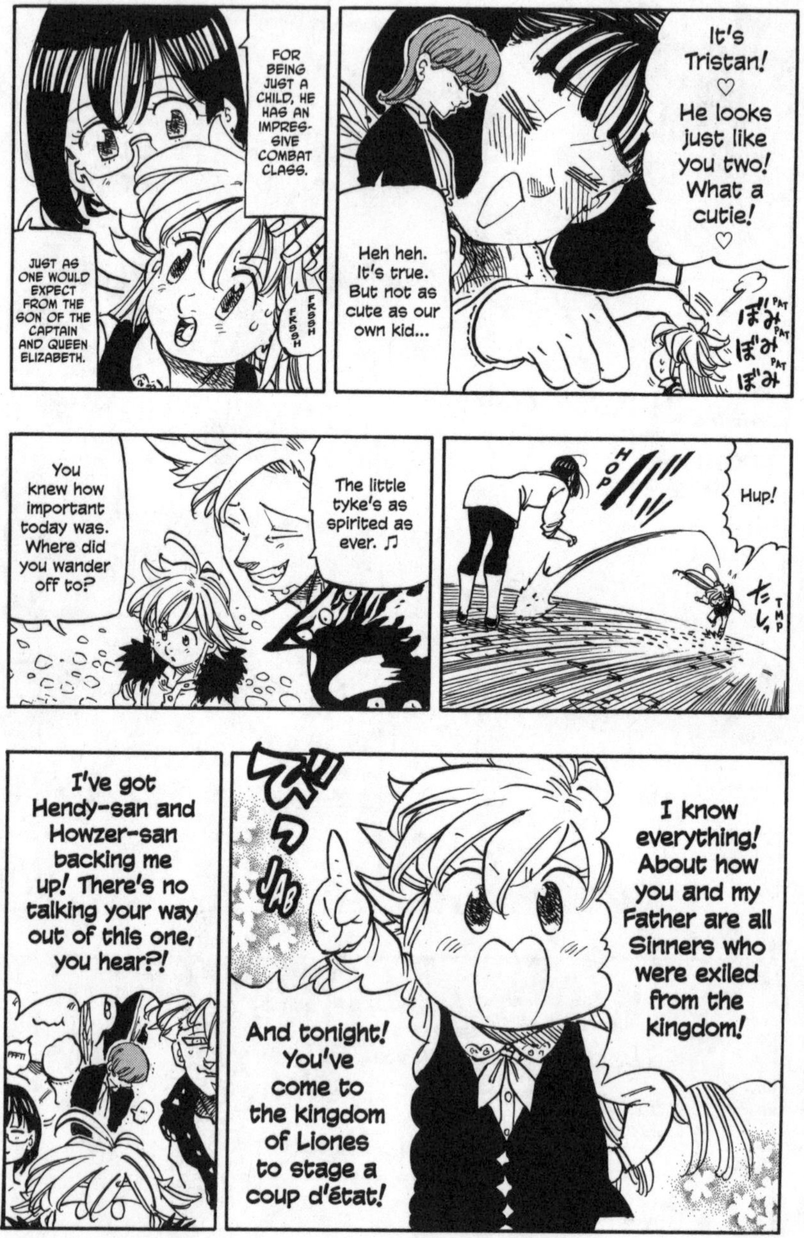

It's Tristan! ♡ He looks just like you two! What a cutie! ♡
ぽみ PAT ぽみ PAT ぽみ PAT
Heh heh. It's true. But not as cute as our own kid...
FOR BEING JUST A CHILD, HE HAS AN IMPRESSIVE COMBAT CLASS.
FRSSH FRSSH
JUST AS ONE WOULD EXPECT FROM THE SON OF THE CAPTAIN AND QUEEN ELIZABETH.
Hup!
HOP
TMP
The little tyke's as spirited as ever. ♫
You knew how important today was. Where did you wander off to?
JAB
I know everything! About how you and my Father are all Sinners who were exiled from the kingdom!
And tonight! You've come to the kingdom of Liones to stage a coup d'état!
I've got Hendy-san and Howzer-san backing me up! There's no talking your way out of this one, you hear?!

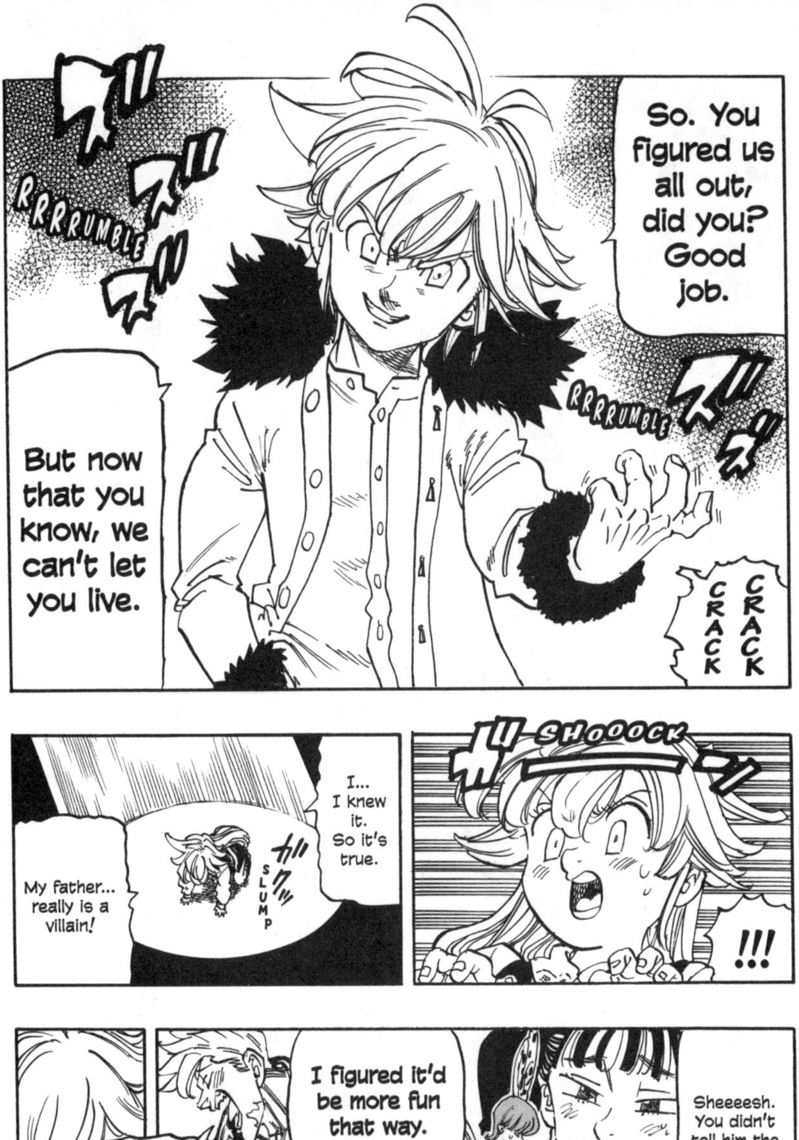
So. You figured us all out, did you? Good job.
RRRRUMBLE
RRRRUMBLE
CRACK CRACK
But now that you know, we can't let you live.
SHOOOCK
!!!
I... I knew it. So it's true.
SLUMP
My father... really is a villain!
Sheeeesh. You didn't tell him the truth, did you?
I figured it'd be more fun that way.
Aaaaw, man. I should've done that, too. ♫

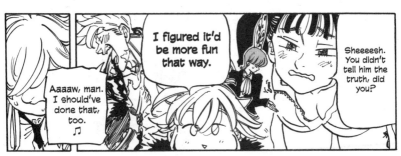

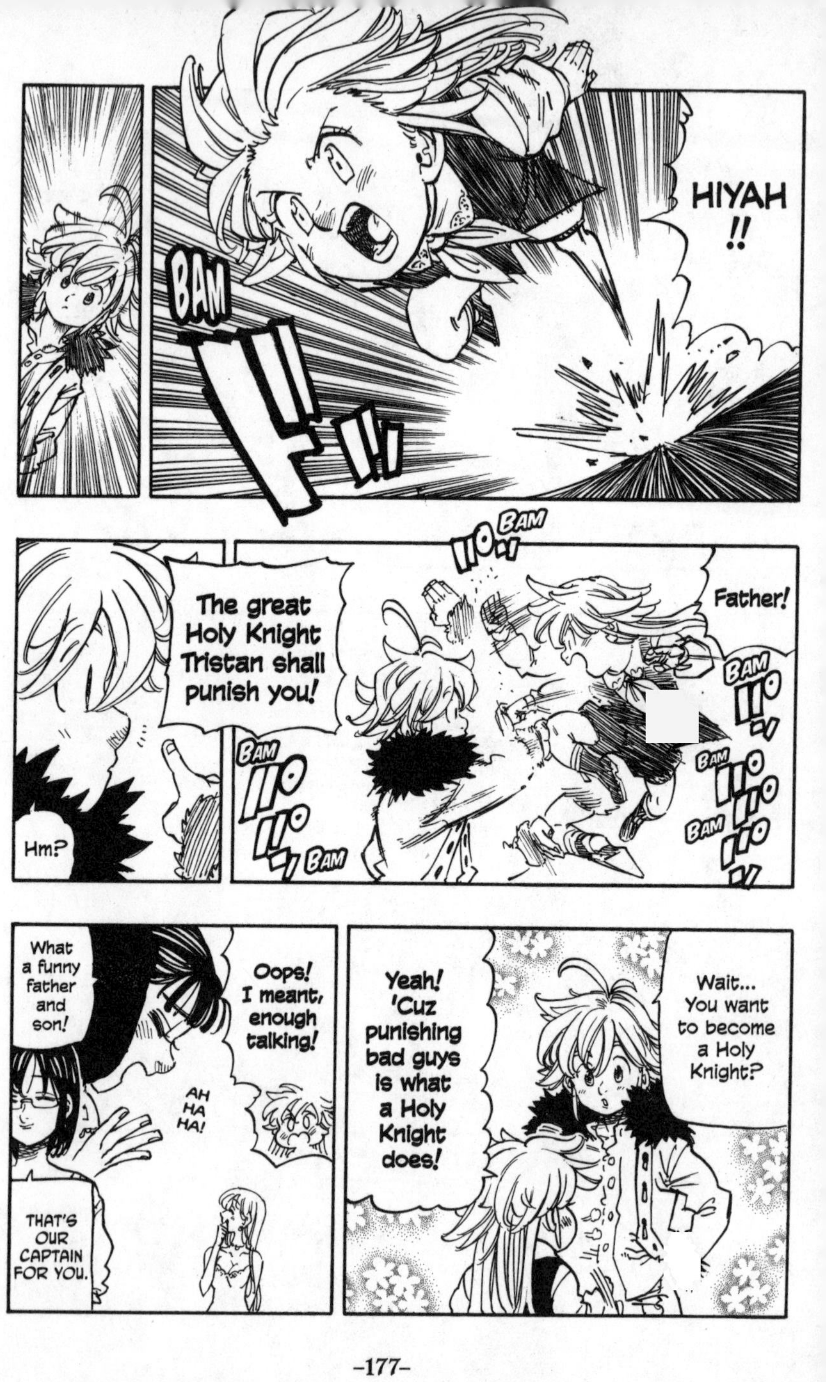
HIYAH!!
BAM
BAM
Father!
BAM
BAM
BAM
BAM
The great Holy Knight Tristan shall punish you!
Hm?
Wait... You want to become a Holy Knight?
Yeah! 'Cuz punishing bad guys is what a Holy Knight does!
Oops! I meant, enough talking!
AH HA HA!
What a funny father and son!
THAT'S OUR CAPTAIN FOR YOU.

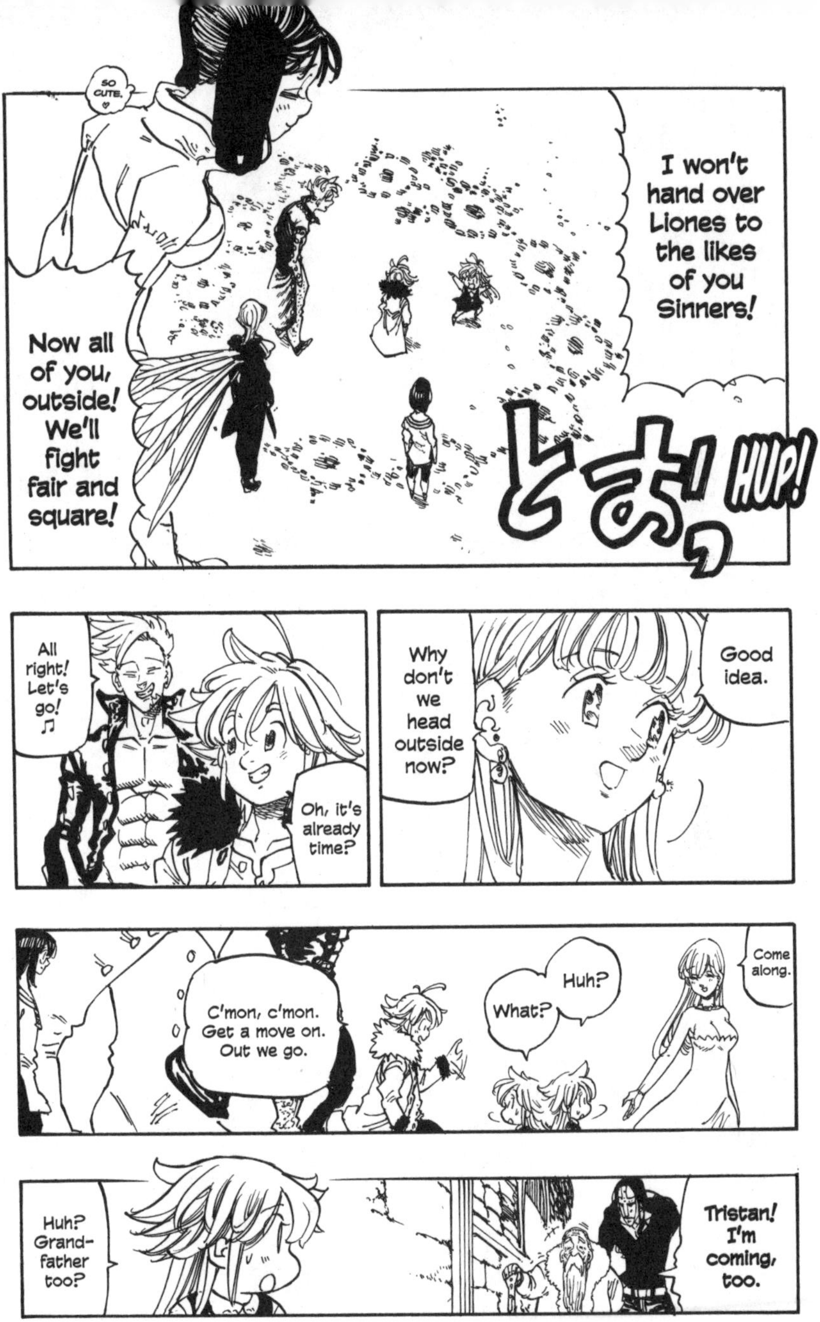
I won't hand over Liones to the likes of you Sinners!
SO CUTE. ♥
Now all of you, outside! We'll fight fair and square!
とお, HUP!
Good idea.
Why don't we head outside now?
All right! Let's go! ♫
Oh, it's already time?
Come along.
Huh?
What?
C'mon, c'mon. Get a move on. Out we go.
Tristan! I'm coming, too.
Huh? Grand-father too?

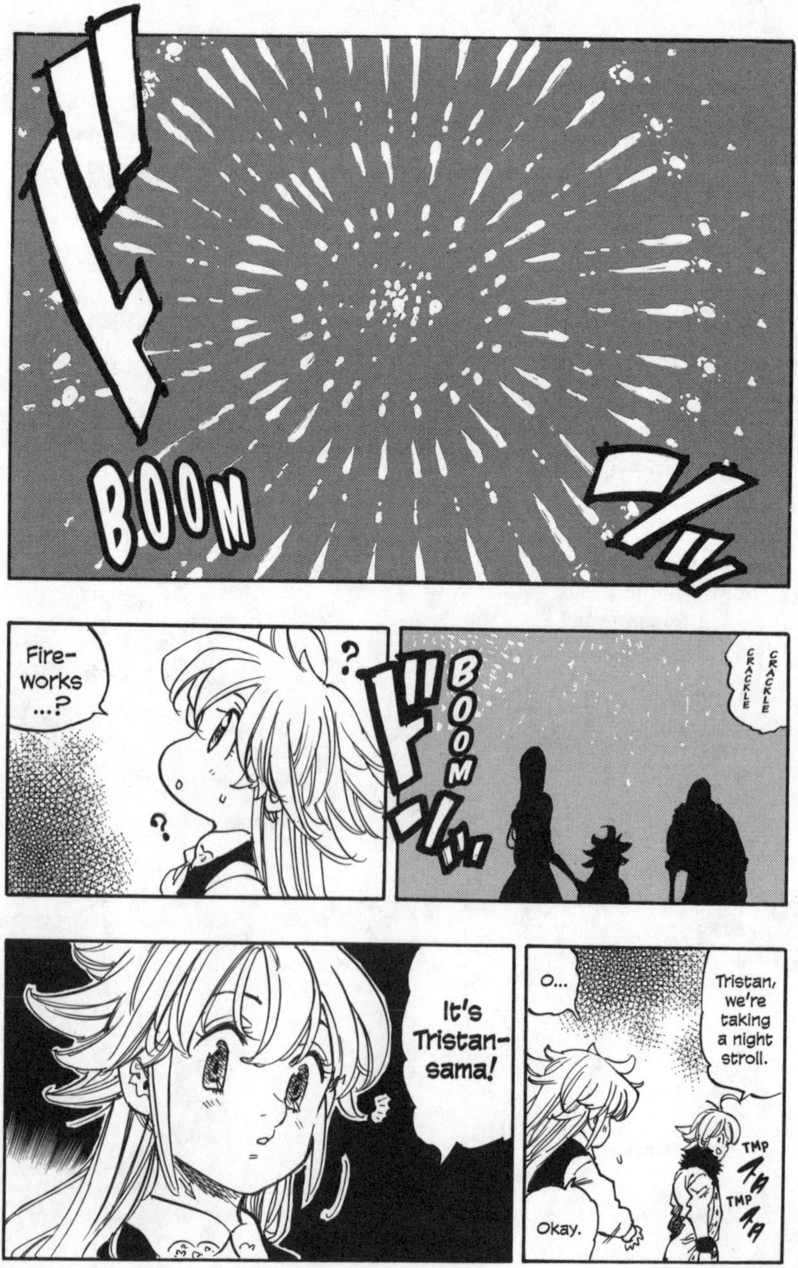
BOOM
BOOM
CRACKLE
CRACKLE
Fire-works...?
Tristan, we're taking a night stroll.
O...
Okay.
TMP
TMP
It's Tristan-sama!

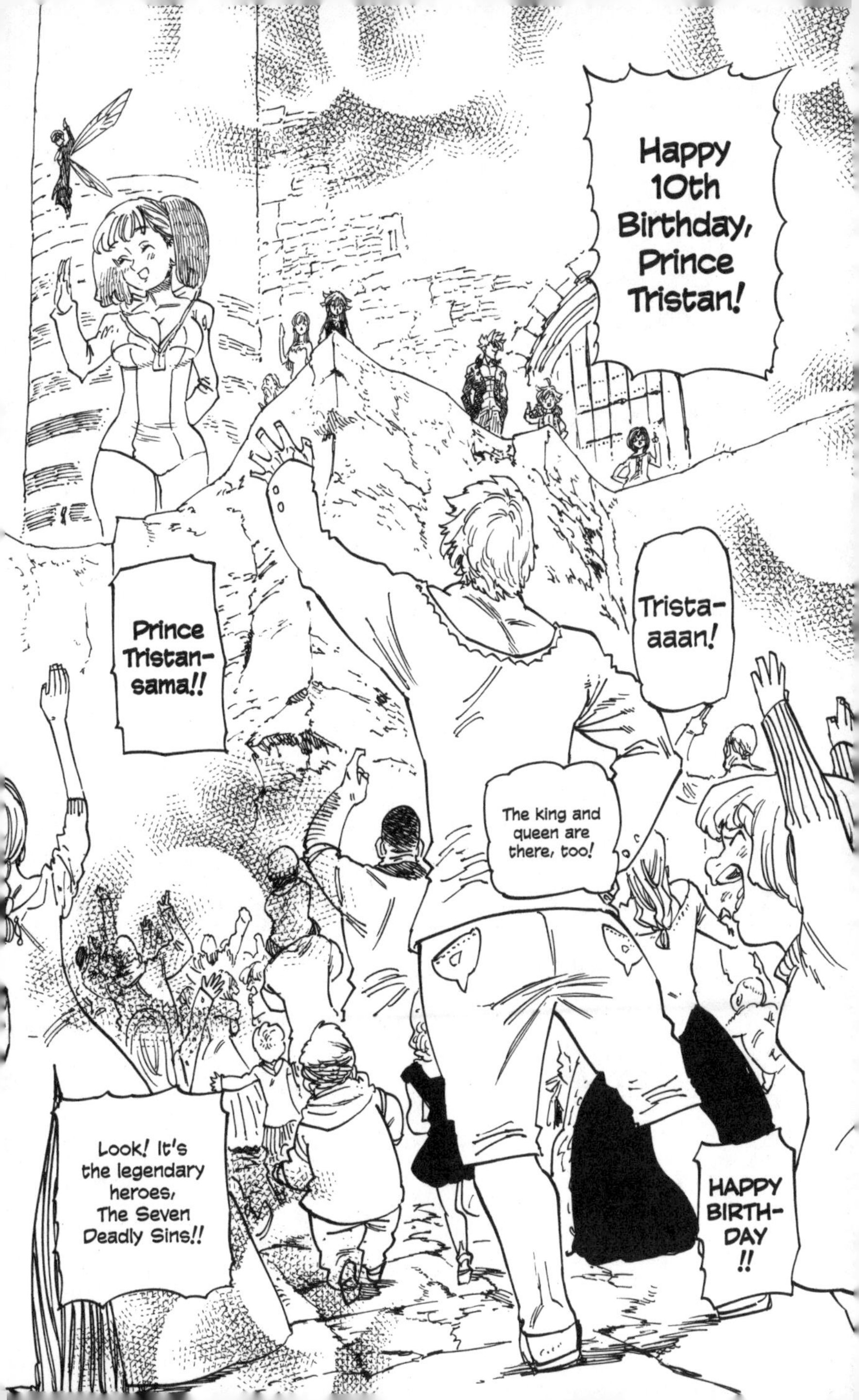
Happy 10th Birthday, Prince Tristan!
Trista-aaan!
Prince Tristan-sama!!
The king and queen are there, too!
HAPPY BIRTH-DAY!!
Look! It's the legendary heroes, The Seven Deadly Sins!!

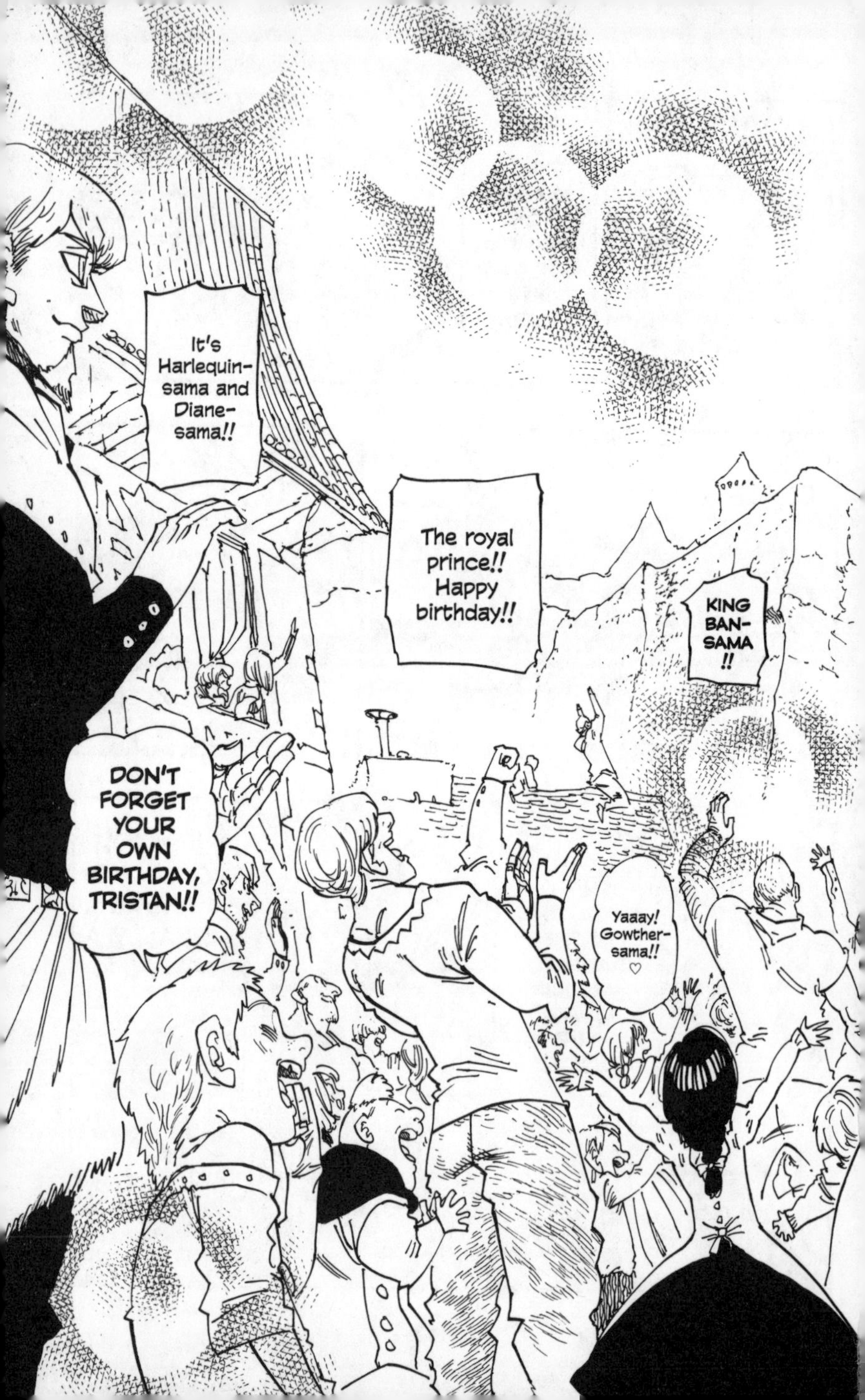
It's Harlequin-sama and Diane-sama!!
The royal prince!! Happy birthday!!
KING BAN-SAMA!!
Yaaay! Gowther-sama!! ♡
DON'T FORGET YOUR OWN BIRTHDAY, TRISTAN!!

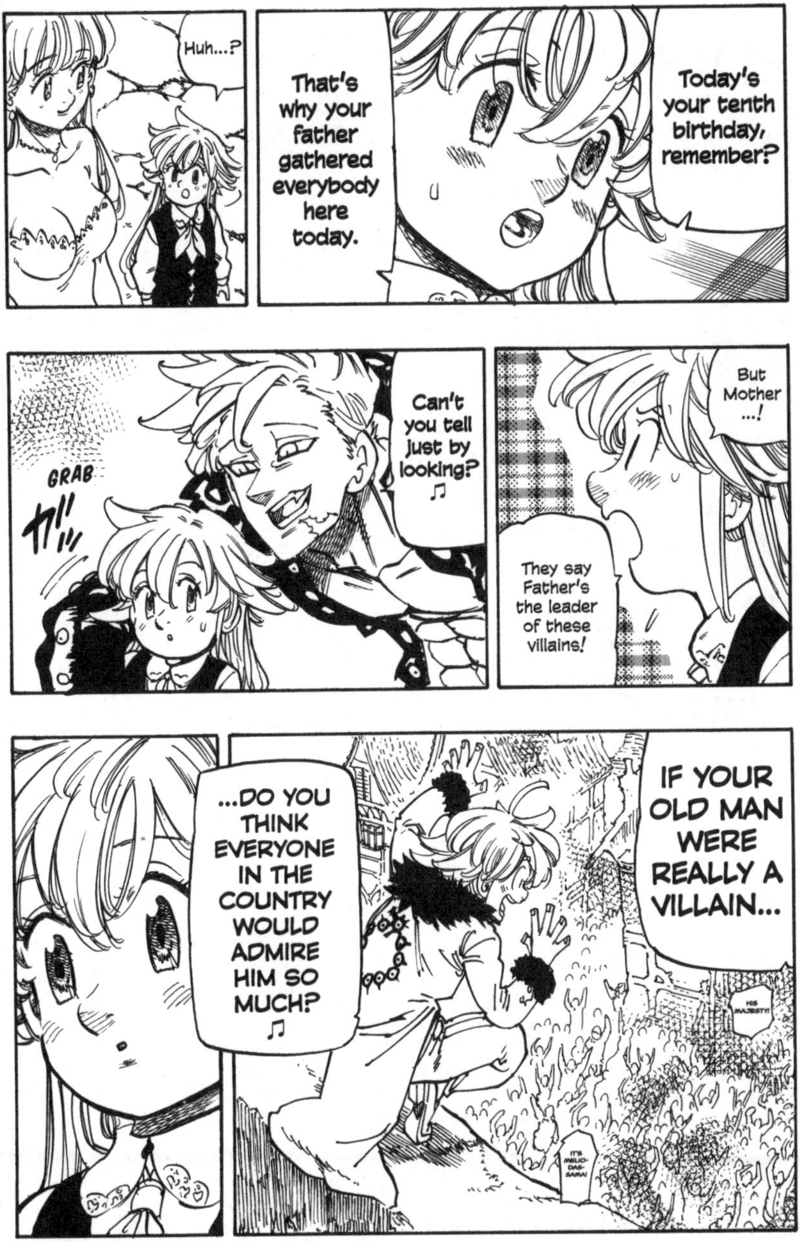
Today's your tenth birthday, remember?
That's why your father gathered everybody here today.
Huh...?
But Mother...!
They say Father's the leader of these villains!
Can't you tell just by looking? ♫
GRAB
IF YOUR OLD MAN WERE REALLY A VILLAIN...
HIS MAJESTY!
IT'S MELIODAS-SAMA!
...DO YOU THINK EVERYONE IN THE COUNTRY WOULD ADMIRE HIM SO MUCH? ♫

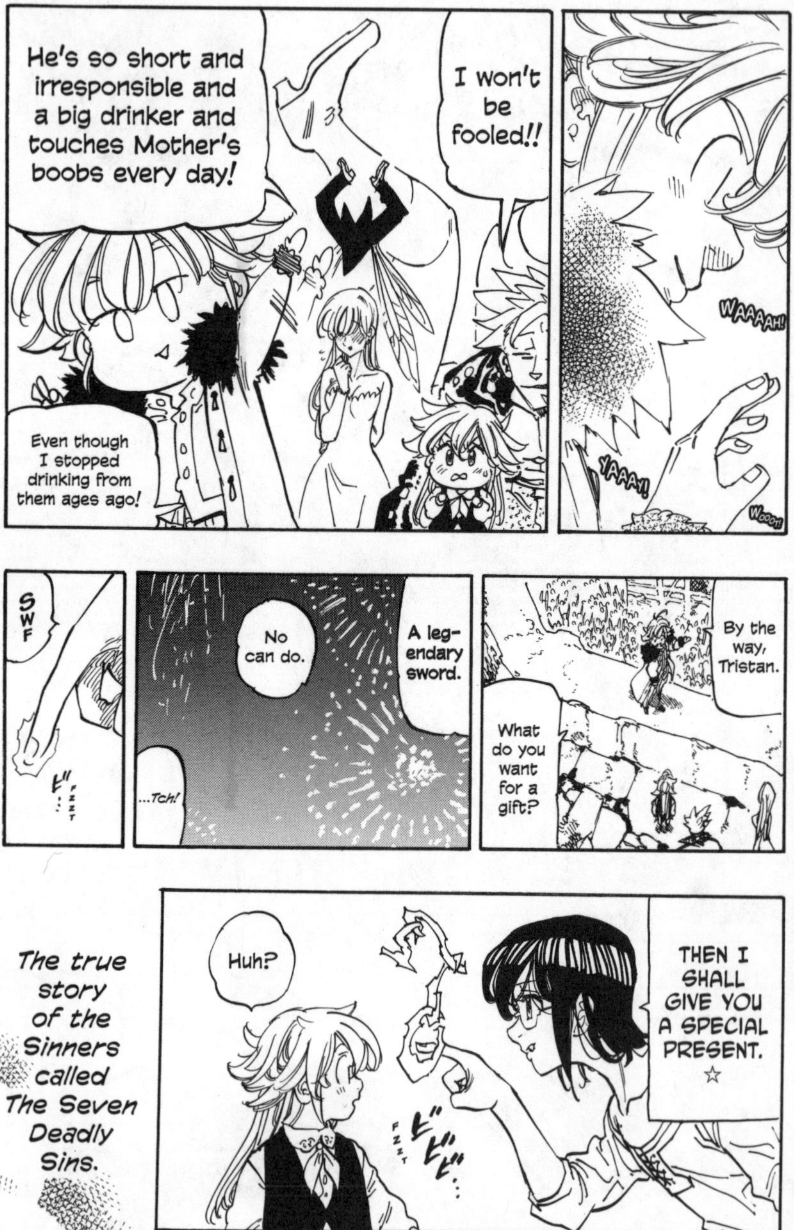
WAAAAH!
YAAAY!
WOOOH!
I won't be fooled!!
He's so short and irresponsible and a big drinker and touches Mother's boobs every day!
Even though I stopped drinking from them ages ago!
By the way, Tristan.
What do you want for a gift?
A legendary sword.
No can do.
...Tch!
SWF
FZZT
THEN I SHALL GIVE YOU A SPECIAL PRESENT. ☆
FZZT
Huh?
The true story of the Sinners called The Seven Deadly Sins.

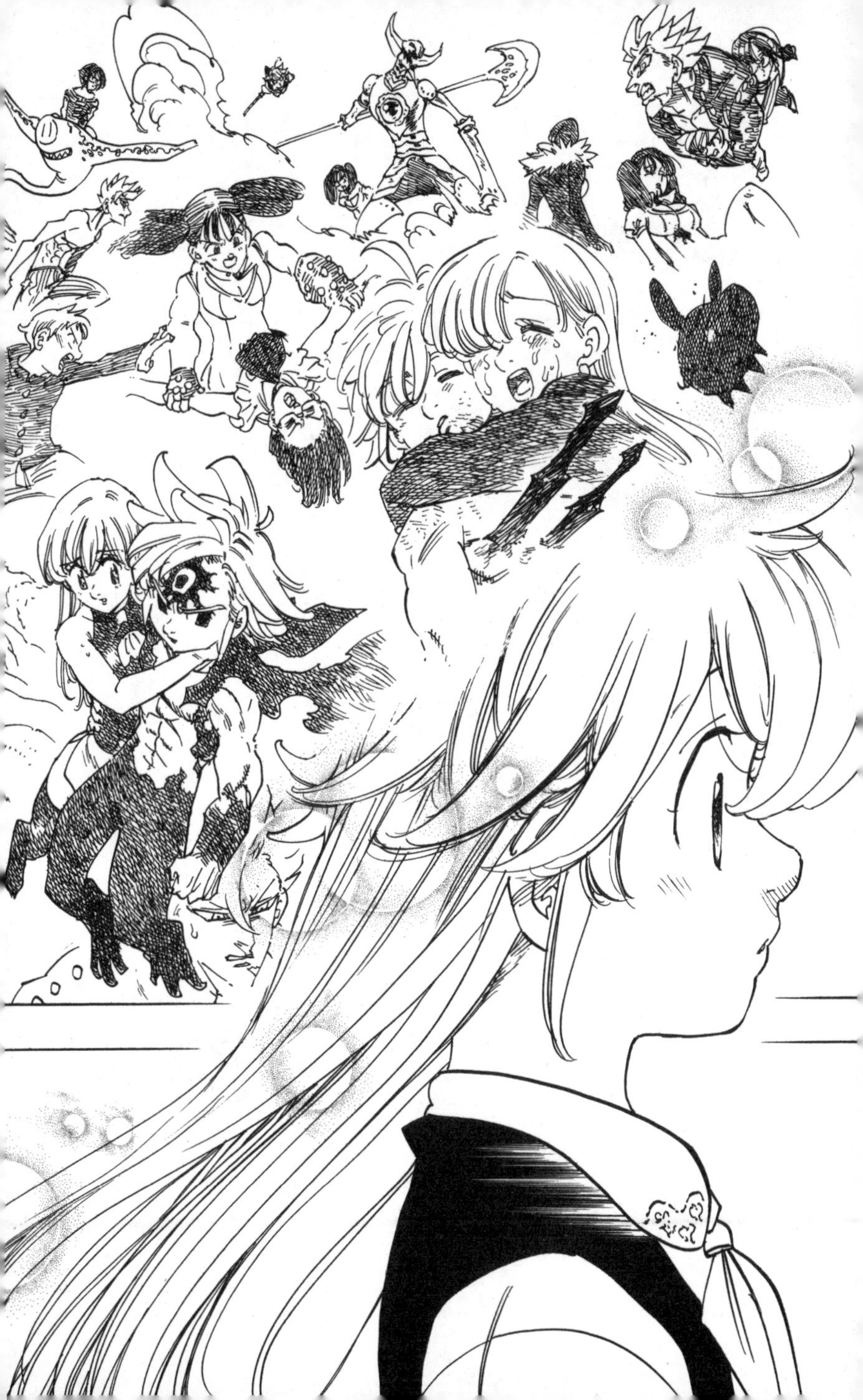

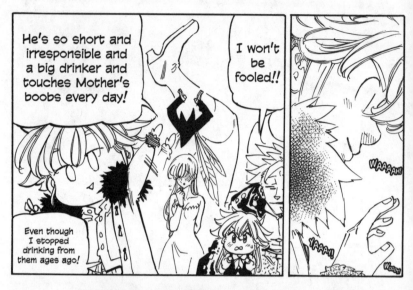

He's so short and irresponsible and a big drinker and touches Mother's boobs every day!

Even though I stopped drinking from them ages ago!

I won't be fooled!!

WAAAAH!

YAAA!

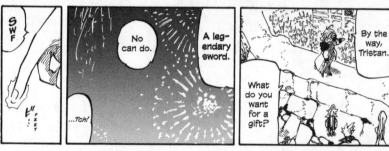

S W F

FZZT

No can do.

...Tch!

A legendary sword.

By the way, Tristan.

What do you want for a gift?

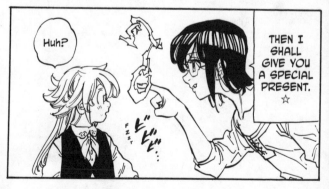

The true story of the Sinners called The Seven Deadly Sins.

Huh?

THEN I SHALL GIVE YOU A SPECIAL PRESENT. ☆

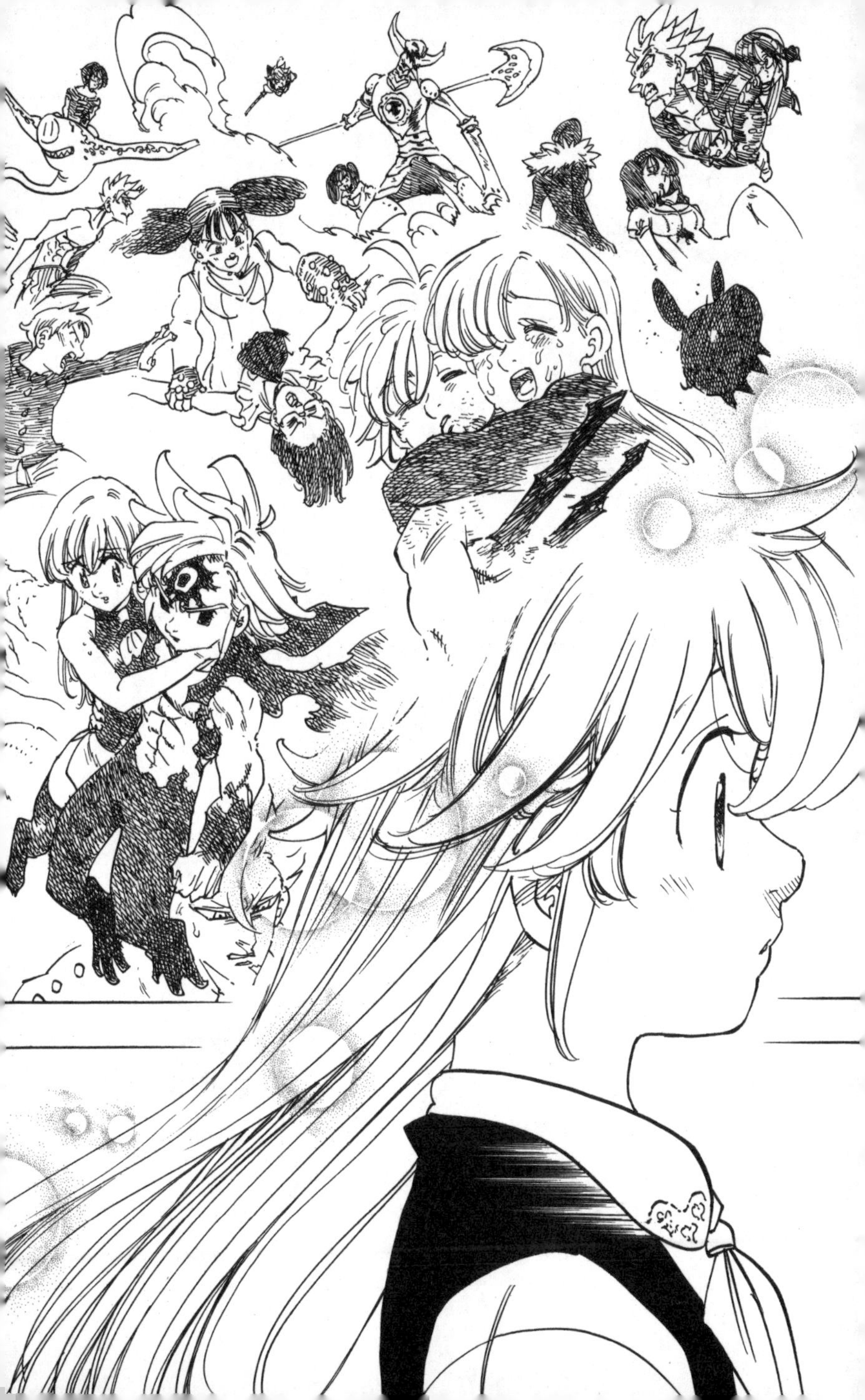

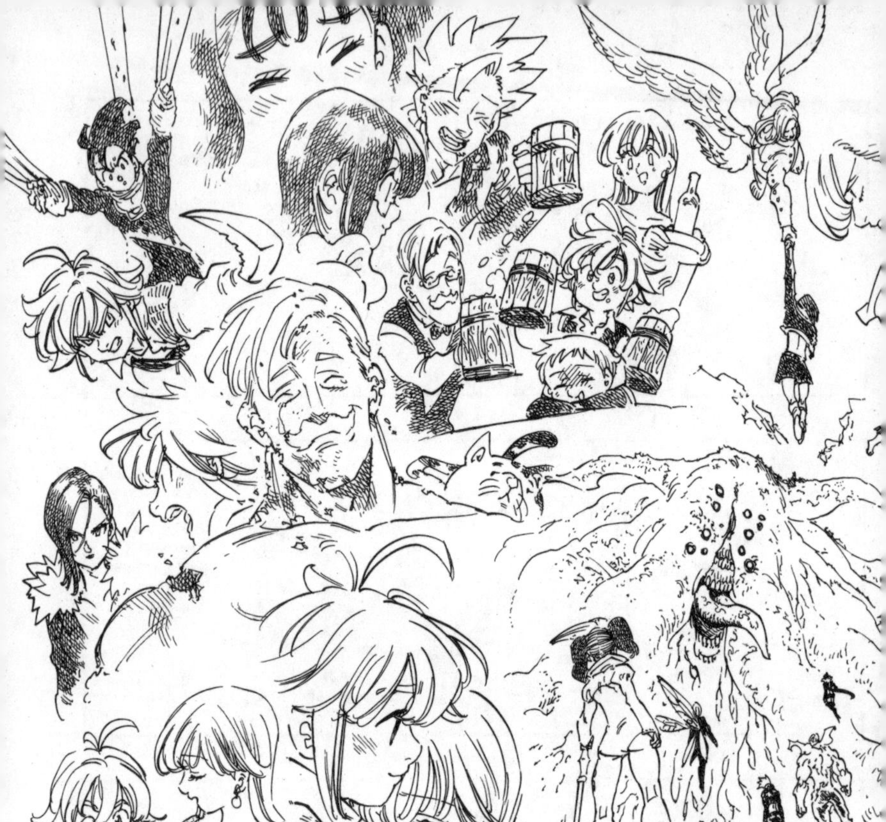
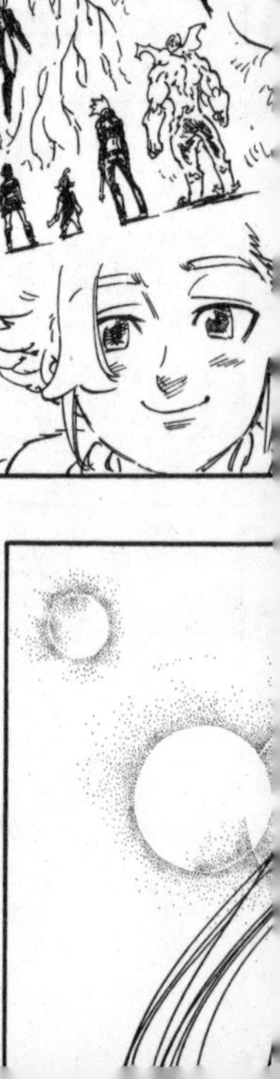
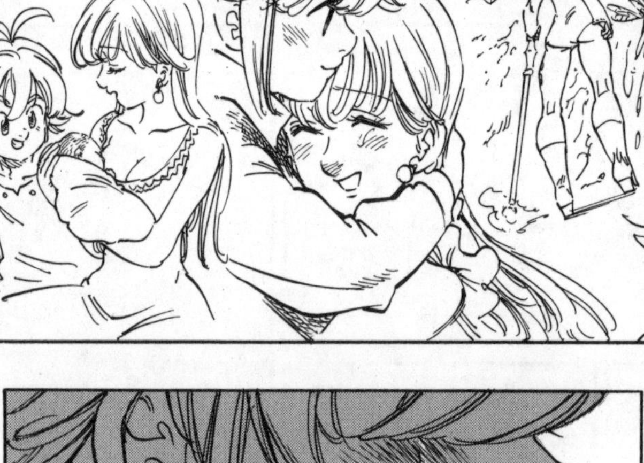

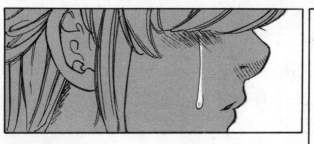

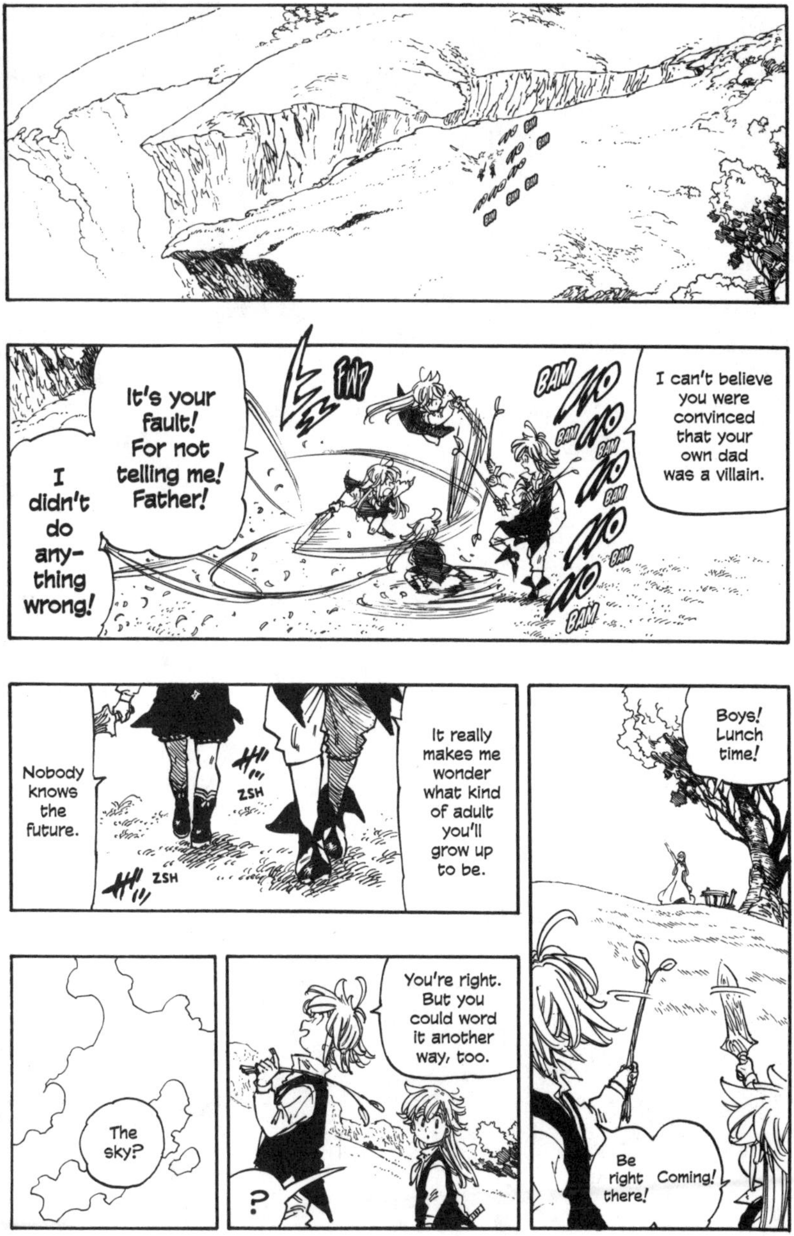
BAM
I can't believe you were convinced that your own dad was a villain.
BAM
FWP
It's your fault! For not telling me! Father!
I didn't do any-thing wrong!
Boys! Lunch time!
Coming!
Be right there!
It really makes me wonder what kind of adult you'll grow up to be.
ZSH
Nobody knows the future.
ZSH
You're right. But you could word it another way, too.
?
The sky?

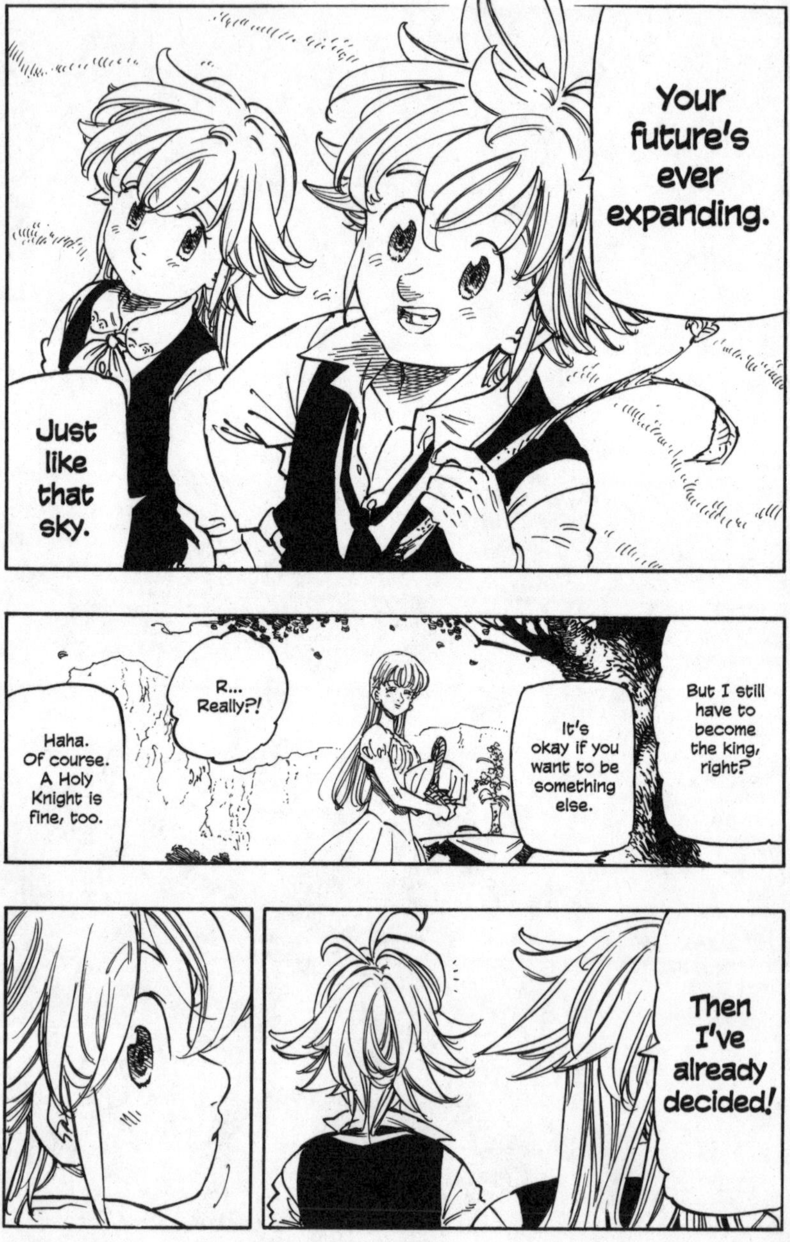
Your future's ever expanding.
Just like that sky.
But I still have to become the king, right?
It's okay if you want to be something else.
R... Really?!
Haha. Of course. A Holy Knight is fine, too.
Then I've already decided!

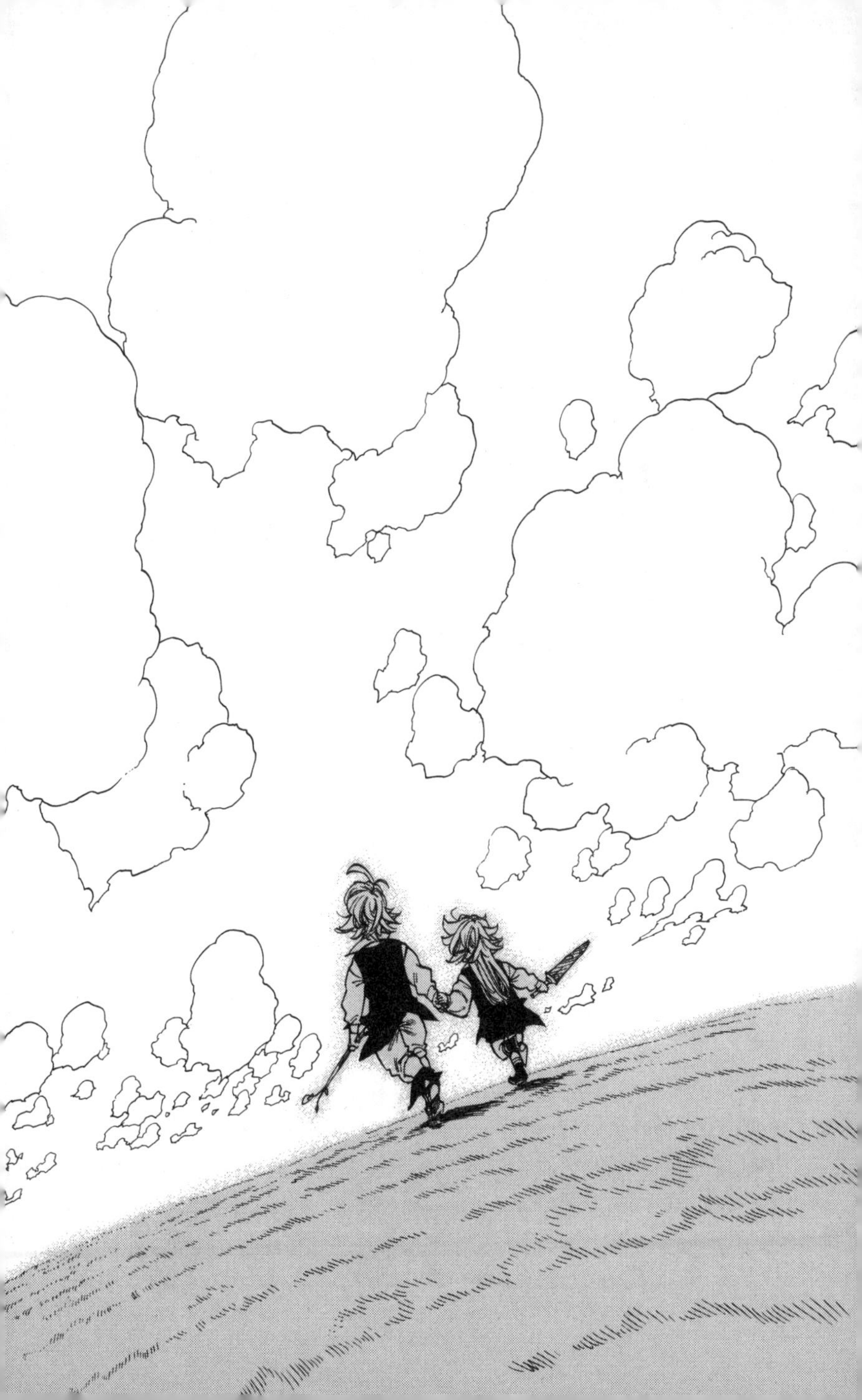

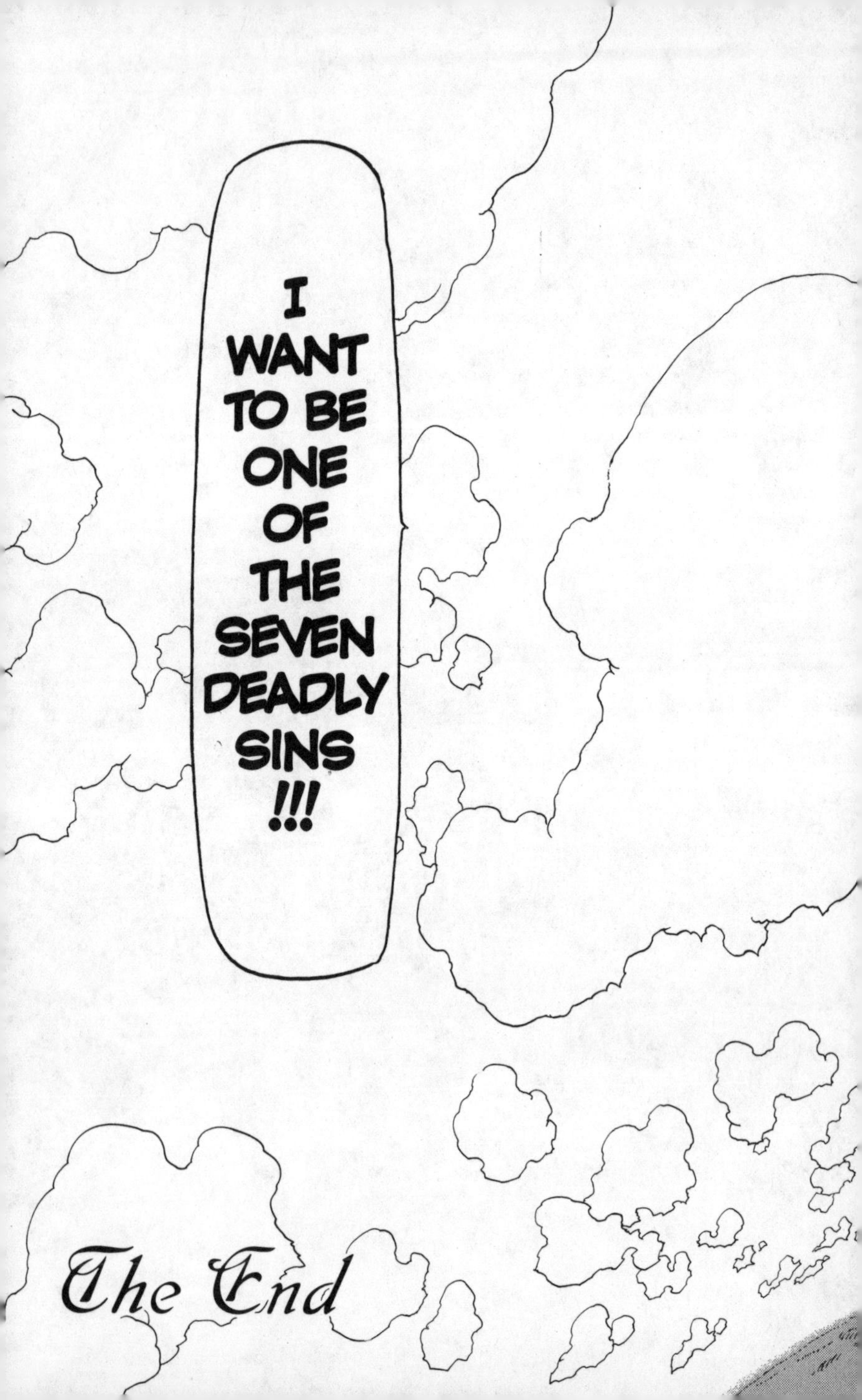
I WANT TO BE ONE OF THE SEVEN DEADLY SINS!!!
The End

THE LEGEND CONTINUES WITH THE NEXT GENERATION.

…EADLY SINS” …SET FOR …CTION!!

THE FOUR HORSEMEN OF THE APOCALYPSE (TITLE PENDING)

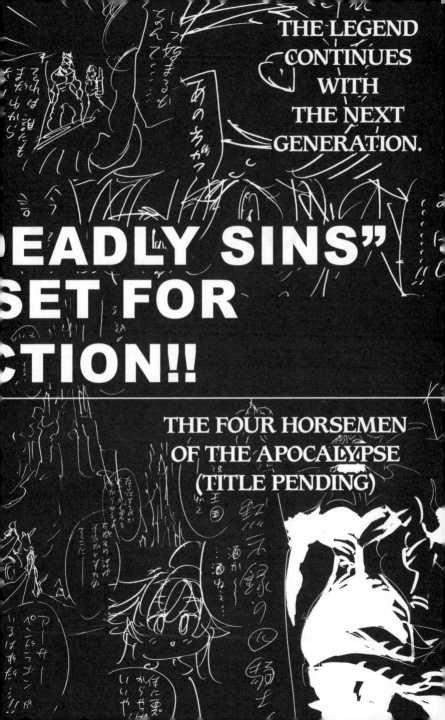

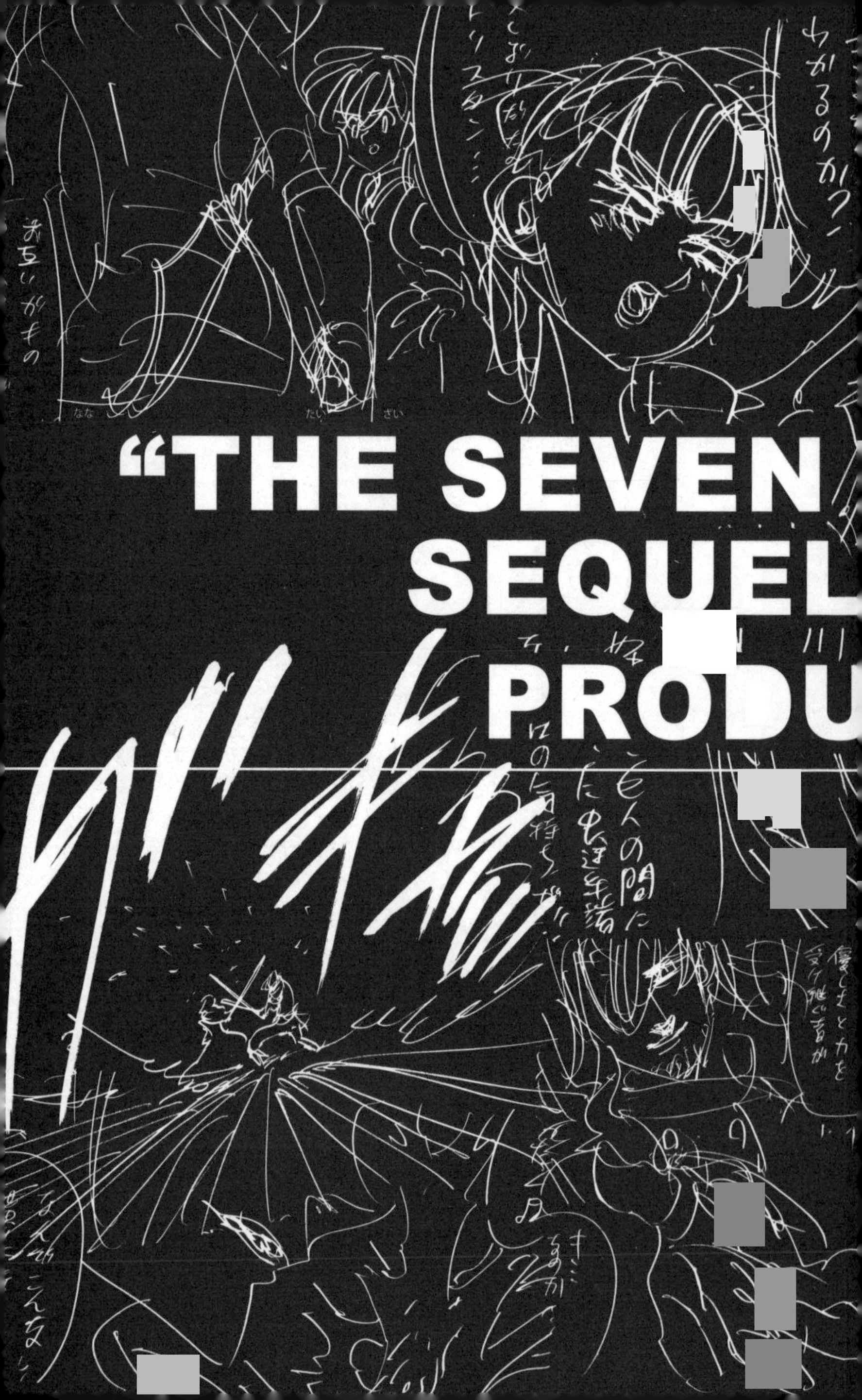
わかるのか？！
なな たい さい
“THE SEVEN
SEQUEL
PRODU
二人の間に
優しさと力を
受け継ぐ者が

The Seven Deadly Sins 41 is a work of fi
places, and incidents are the products o
or are used fictitiously. Any resemblance to actual events, locales, or persons, living or dead, is entirely coincidental.

A Kodansha Comics Trade Paperback Original

Published in the United States by Kodansha Comics, an imprint of Kodansha USA Publishing, LLC, New York.

Publication rights for this English edition arranged through Kodansha Ltd., Tokyo.

First published in Japan in 2020 by Kodansha Ltd., Tokyo as *Nanatsu no taizai*, volume 41.

ISBN 978-1-64651-066-5

Original cover design by Ayumi Kaneko (hive & co., Ltd.)

Printed in the United States of America.

www.kodanshacomics.com

9 8 7 6 5 4 3
Translation: Christine Dashiell
Lettering: James Dashiell
Editing: Tiff Ferentini
Kodansha Comics edition cover design by Phil Balsman

KODANSHA COMICS

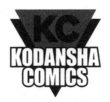

Publisher: Kiichiro Sugawara

Director of publishing services: Ben Applegate
Associate director of operations: Stephen Pakula
Publishing services managing editor: Noelle Webster
Assistant production manager: Emi Lotto, Angela Zurlo